Security Dilemmas in Russia and Eurasia

Security Dilemmas in Russia and Eurasia

Edited by Roy Allison and Christoph Bluth

THE ROYAL INSTITUTE OF INTERNATIONAL AFFAIRS

Russia and Eurasia Programme

First published in Great Britain in 1998 by
Royal Institute of International Affairs, 10 St James's Square, London SW1Y 4LE
(Charity Registration No. 208 223)

Distributed worldwide by
The Brookings Institution, 1775 Massachusetts Avenue NW,
Washington DC 20036-2188, USA

British Library Cataloguing in Publication Data
A CIP catalogue record for this book is available from the British Library.

Hardback: ISBN 1 86203 026 X
Paperback: ISBN 1 86203 016 2

Typeset in Times by Koinonia Ltd
Printed and bound in Great Britain by Selwood Printing
Cover design by Ian Youngs

Contents

Contributors

Hannes Adomeit – Senior Research Associate, Stiftung Wissenschaft und Politik, Ebenhausen.

Roy Allison – Head, Russia and Eurasia Programme, Royal Institute of International Affairs, London.

Jonathan Aves – Research and Analysis Department, Foreign and Commonwealth Office, London.

Pavel Baev – Senior Researcher, International Peace Research Institute, Oslo, Norway.

Christoph Bluth – Director, Graduate School of European and International Studies, University of Reading.

Julian Cooper – Director, Centre for Russian and East European Studies, University of Birmingham.

Alexander Goncharenko – Department of National and International Security, Institute for World Economy and International Relations, Kiev.

Oumirserik Kasenov – Kainar University, Almaty and former Director, Kazakstan Institute for Strategic Studies under the President of the Republic of Kazakstan.

Taras Kuzio – Research Fellow, Centre for Russian and East European Studies, University of Birmingham.

Vyachaslau Paznyak – Director, International Institute for Policy Studies, Minsk.

Hans-Henning Schröder – Bundesinstitut für ostwissenschaftliche und internationale Studien, Cologne.

Sergei Solodovnik – Senior Research Fellow, Centre for International Studies, Moscow State Institute of International Relations, Moscow.

Andrei Zagorski – Vice Rector, Moscow State Institute of International Relations, Moscow.

Preface

The dissolution of the Soviet Union in December 1991 was itself the culmination of a long process which transformed the international security environment in Europe. The consequences of the break-up of the soviet Union in turn were multi-faceted and difficult to predict. Nevertheless, by the mid-1990s it was apparent that a project directed at analysing the overall impact on international security of the dissolution of the Soviet Union and the creation of the new security policy identities of the post-Soviet states would be valuable and timely. Sufficient time had elapsed to take stock of the momentous events under way among the new states of Eurasia and their implications for the broader international security environment.

A joint research project was initiated by Christoph Bluth and Hans-Henning Schröder between the Russia and Eurasia Programme of the Royal Institute of International Affairs (Chatham House) in London and the Bundesinstitut für Internationale und Ostwissenschaftliche Studien (BIOst) in Cologne. This collaborative project, 'The Post-Soviet States and European Security', was generously funded by the Volkswagen Foundation and was conducted under the direction of Heinrich Vogel, director of BIOst, and Roy Allison, Head of the Russia and Eurasia Programme at Chatham House. The initial programme of research was conducted during 1994–96. A six-month extension of the research project permitted additional research on the states of Central Asia and the Caucasus as well as on the Chechenia conflict.

The research programme was distinguished by the active involvement of scholars from various post-Soviet CIS states. Project workshop were convened in Moscow, Cologne and London, involving academic specialists from Russia, Ukraine, Belarus, Kazakstan and Uzbekistan. Andrei Zagorski, the Vice-Rector of the Moscow State Institute of International Relations (MGIMO), provided liaison for the project in Moscow. A wide range of working papers was commissioned from scholars from the new Eurasian states, to address key aspects of the security dilemmas of the region. A second specific feature was the compilation at BIOst of the remarkable and extensive database GUSTEL, which is composed of primary and secondary printed sources available in western Europe and the former Soviet Union. This was and remains a unique resource for scholarly research.

The book forms the principal publication of the project and contains its main findings. When the project was first conceived its subject matter was in a rapid state of flux and as a consequence the structure and focus of research subsequently had to be adapted and revised. Since the start of the project some more definite patterns of relations in security policy have emerged among the new post-Soviet Eurasian states and in their interaction with the broader international security environment. These can be analysed and the key emerging trends can be projected forward. The chapters in this volume were initially presented and discussed as papers at a project conference held at Chatham House in September 1995, but have been comprehensively revised, updated and in some cases virtually rewritten to take account of developments up to summer 1997. The book represents the current state of research, therefore, at the time of publication.

The drafting and re-drafting of the chapters of this volume depended on the painstaking administrative support of staff in the Russia and Eurasia Programme, specifically Ann Cropper, Julie Martin and Caroline Gentry, as well as the RIIA Publications Department. Barbara Wells at the Graduate School for European and International Studies at the University of Reading provided research support for Christoph Bluth and assisted with the editorial work for two of the chapters. Dr Anna Matveeva participated in discussion meetings and interviews in Moscow. The initial and supplementary research for the chapters could not have been undertaken without the flexibility and commitment of the Volkswagen Foundation in their provision of financial support for the overall viability of the project. Another project at Chatham House, 'Keeping the Peace in the CIS', supported by the Ford Foundation, provided additional funding at the final stage of research on the Chechenia conflict and the overall pattern of Russian and Eurasian security policy.

November 1997   Roy Allison
                                                                      Christoph Bluth

Abbreviations

ABD	airborne division
ABM	anti-ballistic missile
ACV	armoured combat vehicle
ANM	Armenian National Movement
AO	joint-stock company (Russia)
APF	Azerbaijani Popular Front
ASW	anti-submarine warfare
BIOst	Bundesinstitut für ostwissenschaftliche und internationale Studien, Cologne
C^3I	Command, Control, Communications and Intelligence
CCCMA	Conference on Cooperation and Confidence-building Measures in Asia
CCGAF	coalition command of a group of armed forces
CD	Conference on Disarmament
CDM	CIS Council of Defence Ministers
CFE	Conventional Forces in Europe
CHS	CIS Council of Heads of States
CIS	Commonwealth of Independent States
CMEA	Council for Mutual Economic Assistance (Comecon)
CPSU	Communist Part of the Soviet Union
CSC	CIS Collective Security Council
CSCE	Conference on Security and Cooperation in Europe
CTBT	Comprehensive Test Ban Treaty
CWC	Chemical Weapons Convention
EBRD	European Bank for Reconstruction and Development
EU	European Union
FIG	financial-industrial group
FNPT	federal research and production centre (Russia)
FSU	former Soviet Union
GATT	General Agreement on Tariffs and Trade
GHJAF	General Headquarters of Joint Armed Forces of the CIS
GNT	state research centre (Russia)
GRU	Main Intelligence Directorate
HEU	highly enriched uranium
IAEA	International Atomic Energy Agency
ICBM	intercontinental ballistic missile

Abbreviations

IMF	International Monetary Fund
INF	intermediate nuclear forces
IPA	Inter-Parliamentary Assembly (of the CIS)
JAF	joint armed forces
KSO	coalition defence forces (*koalitsionnye sily oborony*)
LWR	light water reactor
MD	military district
MIC	military-industrial complex
MIRV	multiple independently targetable re-entry vehicle
MOX	mixed oxide
MPC&A	materials protection, control and accounting
MRD	motor rifle division
MRL	multiple rocket launcher
NACC	North Atlantic Cooperation Council
NIS	newly independent states
NPT	Non-Proliferation Treaty
NSC	(US) National Security Council
OSCE	Organization for Security and Cooperation in Europe
PfP	Partnership for Peace
PJC	Permanent Joint Council
PTBT	Partial Test Ban Treaty
RSFSR	Russian Soviet Federal Socialist Republic
SAM	sea-to-air missile
SCMC	Staff for Coordination of Military Cooperation of CIS states
SLBM	sea-launched ballistic missile
SNDV	strategic nuclear delivery vehicles
SON	common purpose forces (*sily obshchego naznacheniya*)
SSD	safe and secure dismantling (of nuclear weapons)
SSBN	strategic nuclear ballistic missile submarine
START	Strategic Arms Reduction Talks
TLE	treaty-limited equipment
VDV	(Russian) airborne forces
WEU	Western European Union

Introduction
Roy Allison

The Eurasian security policy arena in transition

The differences among the security policy objectives and options of the new Eurasian states which arose from the collapse of the Soviet Union are clearly greater than their common features.* The member states of the Commonwealth of Independent States (CIS), which replaced the USSR in December 1991, had divergent goals from the outset. Russia was intent on preserving the ties that bind the new states, while Ukraine, for example, viewed the CIS as an instrument to facilitate a civilized divorce from the former metropolitan control of Moscow. The CIS has acquired new member states since December 1991, but it has failed to create and implement the mechanisms and legal instruments to integrate the post-Soviet Eurasian states into a supranational political entity or an agency for a coordinated security policy. Only lesser forms of coordination have been achieved.

This limited development reflects the growing geopolitical and geo-economic pluralism of interests among these states, which limits integration processes within the Eurasian region that do not correspond to such interests, despite the continued vocal Russian promotion of 'CIS integration'. In fact the Eurasian states have responded pragmatically to new opportunities for developing relations in the regions west, southwest and south of Russian borders to confirm and consolidate their independence.

Despite the new geopolitical environment, Russia still remains the most important partner state for the majority of CIS member states. All the non-

---

* In this book the Eurasian states comprise the states which have entered the Commonwealth of Independent States (CIS states), and the latter term is used frequently. These include all the post-Soviet states except for the Baltic states. The title of the book has been chosen to emphasize the Russian influence in Eurasia; Russia is itself a key Eurasian state. This restricted definition should be kept in mind since 'Eurasia' and the 'Eurasian region' have also been used to denote an area covering many more states of the Euro-Asian land mass. These terms have also appeared in a historical and contemporary debate about national identity, particularly in Russia, but this has not influenced the definition chosen for this book. Clearly some of these states are more European in their orientation, culture and characteristics (and may have a strong official orientation towards Europe), some are more Asian, but they share a Soviet legacy and their future orientations will vary according to their location, political impulses and cultural heritage.

Russian CIS states are positioned around Russian borders or have their communications still largely orientated towards the former metropolitan centre of the Soviet/Russian state. In this sense Russia could set out to identify common interests and approaches in its policy towards the other former Union republics which still form a geographical buffer between Russia and states further afield – hence the Russian term for the post-Soviet states, 'the near abroad' (which, at least in the initial Russian debate during 1991–4, included the Baltic states). One aspect of this approach has been Moscow's effort to maintain the borders of the former USSR effectively as the Russian strategic border. The desire to establish some kind of CIS buffer region for Russia was reflected in Yeltsin's proposal in June 1994 for a CIS military structure 'similar to NATO' and his decree of the same month, 'On Approving the Russian Federation's Strategic Course in Relations with CIS Member States', which called for a defence union based on common interests and military–political goals. Moscow also presented this objective as a necessary countermeasure to NATO enlargement.

However, although Russia may identify common interests in its policy towards the other Eurasian CIS states, these states themselves have in common only their proximity to Russia and their Soviet legacy. The wide variations in both the geographical locations and the resources of the other CIS states have meant that the Russian-driven effort to pool their interests as well as important elements of their sovereign decision-making has met growing resistance, except in the case of those states which still depend heavily economically or militarily on Russian support.

This creates a central dilemma for Russian security policy between its overweening ambitions and its declining capabilities for involvement beyond its frontiers in the erstwhile Soviet republics. Moscow simply lacks the resources to support an ambitious multilateral security and foreign policy in the region. Weakness and overcommitment fuel unpredictability in Russian foreign and security policy and a suspicion of Western intentions; they 'confuse this policy in the short term and complicate the reconstitution of Russian power over the long term'. It could even be argued that in the CIS region 'only in Russia's foreign policy community [to which we could add the Belarusian presidential office] are the forces of integration and reassertion stronger than those of disintegration and withdrawal.'[1]

The dilemma of matching ends with means and the reluctance to acknowledge the limits of power or to qualify the nature of Russia's 'great-power' status were apparent in a frustrated outburst by President Yeltsin at the March 1997 CIS summit. 'We have no interest in seeing the former [Soviet] Union's territory dominated by anyone, particularly in the political-military sphere, or in seeing any country playing a role of buffer against Russia,' he asserted. He urged that more attention be paid 'to ensuring security and developing military cooperation in view of unceasing attempts to establish power-centres in the post-Soviet space' and declared that 'the consolidation of anti-integration and anti-Russian tendencies is absolutely unacceptable.'[2] This inclination to draw a simple parallel between anti-integration currents and anti-Russian tendencies shows the unwillingness of the Russian leadership, more than five years after the collapse of the Soviet Union, to accept or judge the real impulses for political and military integration among the post-Soviet states or to view countervailing influences (such as Ukrainian security policy initiatives with other CIS and non-CIS states) in other than zero-sum terms.

Despite such Russian assumptions, the non-Russian CIS states have continued to pursue their national interests and seize new opportunities as they have arisen. Their political, economic, trade and security policy ties among themselves, with non-CIS neighbours and with states further afield have become increasingly diverse. At the same time they have acknowledged that Russia has certain significant and legitimate interests in the CIS region. In the field of security policy these interests, for example, would include conflict prevention and border security, although such interests neither demand nor justify hegemonic Russian policies.

Such diversification of the ties of the new Eurasian states involves a partial reorientation (or, for states like Ukraine and Azerbaijan, a major reorientation) of the pattern of their external relations towards Western states and European institutions as well as towards other regional neighbours (see Chapter 1, 'The network of new security policy relations in Eurasia'). There clearly remain areas of interstate relations among the CIS states where bilateral integration with Russia based on an equal partnership, or multilateral integration through CIS structures, benefits all parties concerned. Yet the dynamic of integration/differentiation between Russia and other CIS states in security policy – an underlying theme of this volume – has been fluid and often reflected in political struggles between Russian and non-Russian CIS state leaders in the 1990s.

For this study it has been helpful to analyse the evolution of the security policies of all these states on four levels: ambitions; capabilities; process; and impact on European security.

Ambitions

The security policy ambitions of the Eurasian states have been influenced by security concepts and priorities promoted by influential non-governmental political elites, by the views of officials and by the concerns of senior military officers. Russia itself inherited a metropolitan outlook, and the prevailing assumption in Moscow was that Russian and CIS-wide security interests should be fused together. However, the scope of the interests of the new Russian state and the definition of that state itself became the object of heated debate. The new Russian military doctrine proclaimed in 1993 was equally controversial, and its relevance to the real threats and military needs of Russia itself was open to serious doubt from its inception. In particular, Russian military thinking failed to take into account the defence demands of local wars and insurgencies. Ambitions for a forward defence in the CIS region far outstripped the capabilities to support such a traditional buffer defence concept.

In contrast, the security debate in several other CIS states, driven by the need to assert their national interests at the expense of the metropolitan centre, often included an explicit or implicit assumption that Russia itself was a potential threat. While the formal military doctrines of these states tended to avoid such references to Russia and to adopt a concept of defence *tous azimuts* (with the assumption that potential attack may originate from any direction), an uncertain basis for defence planning and a lack of funds made it difficult to use military doctrines or national security concepts to plan the development of new force structures or deployments. Moreover, it was soon clear that the main threats to the national security of most of these states stemmed from internal economic failure, lack of political consensus and (in the Caucasus until 1995) the existence of unofficial militias, although ethnic Russian minorities have been viewed as a potential fourth column in several CIS states which Moscow could exploit.

The ambitions of most CIS states have included the goals of becoming engaged in a multilateral security policy framework with Western states, the OSCE and other international organizations, as well as in a new network of bilateral relations with CIS neighbour states and regional states outside the CIS orbit. These ambitions are not viewed as necessarily inconsistent with their CIS membership and commitments. This search for a diversified security policy, which reflects the reality of greater geopolitical pluralism, and the Russian response to it, form a key expression of the dynamic of integration/ differentiation in the CIS region.

Capabilities

The security policy ambitions of all the new Eurasian states have been severely constrained by their resources and capabilities, although the military inheritance gained by Ukraine and Belarus from the USSR force structure was impressive for countries of their size. Other smaller states of the Caucasus and Central Asia inherited little from former Soviet military deployments. The Russian military forces themselves suffered severely in the protracted and disorganized process of withdrawals, retrenchment and contraction that followed the division of the former Soviet armed forces and their infrastructure. This legacy has continued to impede the creation of new and restructured armed forces for the Russian state (see Chapter 4).

Most of the new armed forces of the CIS states have lacked trained officers, and even in the case of Russia have found it difficult to conscript or contract the personnel required to flesh out their military units. Problems of morale, discipline and corruption have been pervasive. For Russia, the Chechenia conflict greatly exacerbated such difficulties, which were reflected in military effectiveness on the ground.

The defence industrial legacy of the Soviet Union was also unevenly distributed among the CIS states; this aspect of their economies has been important to provide at least some rudimentary national self-sufficiency in military production, as well as a source of earnings. Russia inherited most of the former Soviet defence industrial base and this was forced to contract and undergo reform in the five years after the collapse of the USSR. Russian military production and procurement slumped drastically, and only in 1996–7 did the first signs of a new Russian defence industry begin to emerge which might be able to supply the Russian army of the future with modern weapons (see Chapter 5).

The radical reduction of defence budgets for the new national armies has been a principal constraint on the military and security policy ambitions of the Eurasian states. This financial shortfall has meant that a significant proportion of the forces inherited from the Soviet Union has been allowed to deteriorate beyond repair (the case of Ukraine is examined in Chapter 7). It has also prevented the new states from restructuring and redeploying forces to correspond to their new national security concepts and military doctrines or to suit new multilateral security policy commitments, whether within or outside the CIS framework.

The shortfall in military funding has been a potent limitation on Russian efforts to construct a forward security zone in neighbouring CIS states (as emphasized later in this chapter) or to support large peacekeeping forces outside its borders (as analysed in Chapter 11), and it helps explain the non-implementation or failure of those bilateral and multilateral military/security treaties signed by CIS states which Russia had offered to underwrite. It also confirmed the Russian failure to prevail in the bitter military campaign in Chechenia (as emphasized in Chapter 13) and it poses broader dilemmas for Russia over how to respond to regional conflicts, to the enlargement of NATO or to growing Chinese capabilities.

Process

The third level of analysis which may be applied to the unfolding security policy of the Eurasian states is that of process: that is, the nature of security policy decision-making. The extensive academic literature on Soviet military and security policy decision-making is of limited value for understanding the role of key institutions and personalities in formulating policy since the USSR was dissolved. The existence of competing sources of decision-making authority can account for policy outputs which are not explicable simply in terms of the debate over national priorities and defence concepts, or in terms of the practical constraints on military capabilities.

One uncertain area has been the fluctuating role of the Russian military as an institution in framing or influencing central policy in Moscow (see Chapter 3). Many of the disputed issues in Russian 'near abroad' policy since December 1991 have been military-related or have been seen to require a military involvement. In this sense the Russian military has been an indispensable instrument for Russian designs for the CIS region. However, political control over this vital instrument has been exercised only imperfectly. Russian civil–military relations have been uneasy and at times resulted in policy disarray. The Chechenia campaign led to fragmentation in the Russian military elite and confusion over which security policy institutions should define Russian policy on conflict within the Russian Federation itself.

In the non-Russian CIS states the civil–military relationship has been less controversial, other than in the Caucasus states which faced specific challenges from militias during 1991–5. But security policy has clearly been influenced by the changing role of political institutions, particularly the role of the president. The case of Belarusian security policy illustrates how a maverick president can change national security priorities significantly. The policy of Belarusian President Lukashenka also shows that the integration dynamic in the CIS region has not been promoted only by Russian leaders.

Impact on European security

A fourth level of analysis applied in this volume is that of the impact of security policy developments in the Eurasian region on relations with Western states, and specifically on European security. As the legacy of the USSR recedes it becomes easier to consider a continuum to exist in security policy issues in Eurasia between Europe outside the CIS region, the European part of the CIS region and the Central Asian states, especially if the Caucasus countries are defined as being in eastern Europe – a definition which has been adopted by the European Union. In fact, the involvement of the CIS states in multilateral institutions (such as the OSCE), frameworks (such as the Partnership for Peace) and treaties (such as the CFE Treaty for most of the CIS states), as well as their keen interest in the NATO enlargement controversy, demonstrate that European and Eurasian security are interwoven in many important respects.

The impact of Russian security policy on Europe beyond the CIS region occurs directly through various bilateral and multilateral relations with such European states, through participation in joint treaties on disarmament, arms control and proliferation (see Chapter 15), through developments in the Russian nuclear weapons infrastructure, or through the spread of 'soft security' threats arising from the weak Russian state. There may also be more indirect influences on non-CIS Europe resulting from Russian policy towards its neighbours, particularly Ukraine, and its efforts to develop an integrated 'security space' with key CIS neighbours. For these reasons, and because of the strong Russian reaction to the prospect of NATO enlargement, the NATO–Russia Council was created in spring 1997, providing important new channels through which to address joint Russian and NATO security policy concerns in Europe and Eurasia (see Chapter 16).

Many of the non-Russian CIS states hope to be an integral part of the European security debate rather than an external influence on it. Furthermore, they do not wish their security policy *vis-à-vis* NATO states and central Europe to be mediated through Russian or CIS institutional channels. Yet among the non-Russian CIS states it is only in Ukraine that security policy developments have the potential to influence seriously the security of the larger European region.[3] Among other CIS states the issues are secondary, although they may still be taken quite seriously by European statesmen. Such issues could include Belarusian inclinations to integrate with Russia, Caucasian regional conflicts and the controversy over the security of energy supply routes and Central Asian fears of radical Islamic movements or drug trafficking. Failures in economic reform efforts in all these states could also provoke serious social and political unrest which in turn could foster a range of soft security problems for more stable European states, from illegal migration to crime syndicates.

These four levels of analysis offer a general framework for this book within which attempts are made to understand current security policy dynamics and the evolution of the security policy environment for Russia and other Eurasian states in the second half of the 1990s. Chapter 1 by Roy Allison sets the scene by analysing the overall network of security and military policy agreements and ties achieved by the Eurasian states by summer 1997. It appears that the CIS-level and bilateral treaties Russia has signed have progressively been displaced or qualified by the diversification of security policy ties in Eurasia and by the proliferation of new agreements without Russian participation between CIS states and non-CIS states or international bodies.

The first part of this book examines Russian national security thinking, the role of the Russian army in politics, Russian military planning and structural weaknesses, and the future role of the Russian defence industry. Part II extends the analysis of national security concepts, military planning, military capabilities and new treaty arrangements to Ukraine, Belarus, the Caucasus states and Central Asia. Part III focuses on major conflicts, peacekeeping efforts and Russian-led efforts to create CIS collective security structures. The final part of the volume examines aspects of the broader multilateral security policy framework with Western states – such as arms control and proliferation and NATO enlargement – and assesses security policy risks ahead.

In Chapter 2 Hannes Adomeit evaluates the key Russian debates on the Russian identity and national interests in the period since 1991. He charts the shift in Russian foreign and security policy thinking towards a new assertiveness and the struggles to codify Russian interests along these lines. He pays particular attention to the Russian self-proclaimed responsibilities and rights in its 'near abroad' and to the domestic roots of the Russian return to geopolitical thinking. Adomeit calls for more Russian 'security realism' reflecting economic realities, in place of efforts to promote unrealizable political and security integration processes on CIS territory.

Chapter 3 moves from Russian ambitions to the controversial issue of the engagement of the Russian armed forces in politics. The power represented by the Russian army, Hans-Henning Schröder argues, is derived from its ability to use direct force and its existence as an electorate that can be mobilized through military issues. One question is whether the army perceives itself as an independent political actor or an instrument of the political leadership. Schröder finds that despite their shared institutional interests and conservative patriotic views, the officer corps and military leaders during 1991–6 were split into factions and had conflicting opinions which made any concerted political action impossible.

In Chapter 4 Christoph Bluth highlights the problems of applying doctrinal statements to the practical requirements of restructuring and reforming Russian nuclear and conventional forces, and emphasizes the growing role of nuclear forces in Russian military thinking. He examines the military reorganization forced on Russian leaders after the collapse of the Soviet integrated force structure and pays particular attention to the severe financial and budgetary constraints which restrict current Russian force development. He also analyses sceptically the various plans during 1995–7 for radical reduction and reform of the Russian military organization.

In Chapter 5 Julian Cooper addresses a basic issue in any evaluation of Russian military capabilities: the future role of the Russian defence industry. Although no coherent strategy for the contraction and reform of the defence-industrial base could be implemented, Cooper argues that a new Russian defence industry is beginning to emerge. This may not compare in scale to its Soviet precursor and it is no longer a privileged sector of the economy, but it should retain the capability to supply the Russian armed forces with modern weapons and to remain competitive in the world arms market.

Ukraine's quest to identify its national interests between the CIS framework and the West is assessed in Chapter 6 by Alexander Goncharenko. He shows how it took almost four years for Ukraine to begin to form a united system of national interests and a consistent national strategy. Part of this is a 'strategic partnership' with Russia, but Goncharenko emphasizes that Ukraine could not accept a CIS structure used as a proxy instrument by Russia. Options for Ukrainian security policy are compared and the author advocates that of Ukrainian 'active' neutrality, which would include 'special relations' with NATO. He anticipates Ukraine's progressive integration into European political, economic and security structures.

Ukrainian security policy and military plans depend, however, on the capabilities of the state to underwrite them and are subject to significant socio-economic and political constraints. These are scrutinized in detail by Taras Kuzio in Chapter 7. Initially, attention is paid to budgetary problems, the morale of the armed forces and corruption within the military services. Kuzio then proceeds to analyse prospects for Ukrainian military reform and the implications of the new military doctrine agreed at the end of 1996. Against this background he draws conclusions for Ukrainian security policy.

The case of post-Soviet Belarus, the subject of Chapter 8, represents a clear contrast to that of Ukraine. Vyachaslau Paznyak provides a detailed analysis of the shift of the security policy orientation of Belarus during 1991–7, especially under President Lukashenka. Paznyak argues that Belarusian national interests have been neither consistently perceived nor formulated as a concept and that security concepts have been hostage to domestic politics. Belarusian 'security policy revisionism' is expressed in revising the goal of neutrality and efforts towards merging the state with that of Russia. The author then appraises Belarusian military forces, the growing interaction of Belarusian and Russian security policies, and Belarus's difficult relations with NATO.

Jonathan Aves argues in Chapter 9 that national security in the three Caucasian CIS states has been dominated by their relationships with Russia. It has depended on whether they have viewed Moscow as a threat or a partner. Through the prism of this key relationship Aves examines the development of the national security policies of Georgia, Armenia and Azerbaijan during 1991–5 in three stages: first, the phase of the struggle for independence; secondly, a phase when nationalist movements struggled against internal militias but also faced a Russia which identified vital national interests in the Caucasus; and, thirdly, a phase of growing differentiation in their security policy orientations.

The five Central Asian CIS states are analysed within a broad framework in Chapter 10 by Oumirserik Kasenov. In appraising potential threats Kasenov pays more attention to the potential of China and the situation on the Tajik–Afghan border than to scenarios involving Russia, but points out that any fracturing of the Central Asian states holds dangers for Russia. However, in a separate section on Russian national interests and military doctrine Kasenov notes the paradox that Russia is both the guarantor of Kazakstan's security and a threat to it. He evaluates the armed forces of Kazakstan, Kyrgyzstan and Uzbekistan and explains steps towards military integration among these three states. Finally, he explores the idea of a Euro-Central Asian security space and the rapid development of links between NATO and the new Central Asian states.

The key topic of peacekeeping and conflict management in the CIS region is tackled in Chapter 11 by Pavel Baev. The chapter does not describe in detail the various peacekeeping or peace-enforcement operations which have been undertaken, since these have been analysed by other scholars. Its purpose is rather to assess the efficiency of these peacekeeping activities in resolving conflicts and the extent to which they have been instrumental in promoting Russian national interests. Baev compares the evolution of Russian political and military goals in conflict management and assesses the military pattern of peacekeeping. He concludes by estimating the sustainability of Russian involvement in such operations.

The conflict outside Russian borders which has attracted the greatest Russian involvement since the end of the USSR, that in Tajikistan, is analysed by Sergei Solodovnik in a regional context in Chapter 12. He assesses the limits of Russian military control in the conflict and critically considers the rationale for Russian intervention. Solodovnik also appraises possible conflict scenarios and outcomes for Tajikistan and the role of Uzbekistan. In conclusion, he maintains that the Russian intervention in Tajikistan has for the most part had a negative effect on the future of multilateral CIS conflict management.

The greatest military trauma and failure of the Russian armed forces since the end of the Soviet Union, the war in Chechenia, is in turn the subject of Chapter 13. Roy Allison uses this campaign partly as a case study to reinforce significant themes raised in other chapters in this volume. He also examines the overall military and security policy consequences of the war. Problems of Russian national security decision-making, military command and control, and military operational weaknesses are assessed. The author also offers a systematic analysis of the effect of the war on the Caucasian region, the Russian Federation, the CIS states and Western states. Finally, he considers the issue of conflict resolution and Russian options for future relations with the republic of Chechenia.

Chapter 14 is devoted to the debate over, and institutional development of, CIS regional security policy structures during 1991–5. Andrei Zagorski does not address the entire set of security-related issues linked to CIS structures (more recent developments concerning some of these issues during 1995–7 are examined below in the second part of this introduction). Instead, he seeks first to locate the CIS 'collective security' framework among other security-related instruments of the CIS and to identify the kind of security cooperation that exists at the CIS level. He then examines the evolution of the collective security discourse in the CIS, including efforts to develop CIS security cooperation as a means of projecting the Russian military posture beyond Russia's national borders.

In Chapter 15 Christoph Bluth broadens the agenda by addressing the entire nexus of arms control and proliferation concerns between the post-Soviet states and their treaty partners in the West and in east/central Europe. The main issues covered are nuclear arms reduction, safety and control; the CFE Treaty and conventional arms proliferation and export; and broader proliferation concerns. He assesses the main challenges in these areas and their likely impact on Russian and broader European security as well as on the course of Russian–American relations.

The final chapter, also written by Christoph Bluth, addresses Russia's relations with Europe, with a particular focus on the implications for the European security environment, and the interaction of this relationship with the dynamics of integration and disintegration in the CIS region. The author considers initially why the concept of a Russian partnership with the West has come into question since 1993. He appraises Russian policy objectives towards Europe and Russian priorities in the developing European security architecture. Special attention is given to Russian proposals for the OSCE, the causes of Russian opposition to NATO enlargement, and the new emerging framework of Russian relations with NATO. In conclusion, he emphasizes the fundamental importance for the nations of Europe of constructing an effective system of collective security.

Notes

1. Sherman Garnett, 'Russia's Illusory Ambitions', *Foreign Affairs*, vol. 76, no. 2, March–April 1997, p. 69.
2. Boris Yeltsin, Statement at Council of CIS Heads of State meeting, 28 March 1997, in *Prism*, The Jamestown Foundation, vol. 3, no. 4, pt. 1, 4 April 1997.
3. For the internal developments in Ukraine which could have such security policy implications, see Tor Bukvoll, *Ukraine and European Security* (London: Royal Institute of International Affairs, 1997).

1 The network of new security policy relations in Eurasia

Roy Allison

The changing security policy arena in Eurasia is expressed in a network of bilateral and multilateral treaties, agreements and links between CIS member states, their neighbours and international organizations. Although Russia occupies a central place in this new emerging structure of relations and is the driving force behind integration efforts on a CIS basis and many important bilateral treaties, it is no longer the hub of the overall network. It considers itself challenged by many new agreements which exclude it and which represent the gradual but inexorable diversification of the security policy relations of most of the other new Eurasian states. To understand this complex of new security and defence policy relations and the processes they reflect it is important to consider the full range of new ties, to separate rhetoric from policy and to focus on agreements which are implemented rather than those which lack the political will or physical means to be realized.

Multilateral CIS-wide security policy interactions among the new Eurasian states have steadily been displaced by bilateral relations since the dissolution of the USSR at the end of 1991. It has become progressively clearer even to Russian politicians that these states have no common strategic goal (indeed, some define themselves as neutral states), that different kinds of functional cooperation between CIS states, mediated by CIS structures, tend to involve different groupings of states and that the security policy coordination that has arisen has its own dynamics. Russian leaders have sought to control these dynamics and steer a process of growing CIS military-security integration. But the Russian capacity to be proactive in this way has been more limited than most Russian political leaders or defence officials have been ready to accept.[1]

Moreover, regional security ties, whether multilateral or bilateral, have carried the risk for Russia of rendering it hostage to unpredictable and uncontrollable developments far from its real frontiers, just as the Soviet Union could have been a hostage to crises in the Warsaw Pact region, regardless of whether such entanglements were in the considered national interest of the USSR. This is the counterpart to the danger for smaller CIS states, especially in Central Asia, that military-security links to Russia to bolster regime or frontier security can make the weaker party a hostage to the vicissitudes of politics and civil–military relations in Moscow or to the reliability of the Russian chain of military command and control. For most CIS states these risks have reduced the attraction of promoting Russia as some kind of 'security manager' for the CIS region, regardless of whether this is attempted through multilateral or bilateral structures.

CIS multilateral military–security relations
Efforts towards collective security

Russian-led efforts during 1991–5 to develop multilateral collective security mechanisms at the CIS level are analysed in detail by Andrei Zagorski in Chapter 14 of this volume. But it is important to recognize here that the CIS collective security agreement, signed in Tashkent in May 1992, has basic limitations. First, it applies to threats originating from outside the former Soviet borders and therefore could not be used to mitigate conflicts within the CIS region, or indeed between CIS states. There are few likely scenarios of such external threats to the CIS states in the medium term that could be used to invoke the collective security machinery. It is true that the signatory states of the Tashkent agreement met in May 1997 to discuss developments in Afghanistan and specifically the danger of Taliban fighters reaching and seeking to cross the Tajik–Afghan border, but the CIS states represented decided only to consult and monitor the situation.[2]

Secondly, only nine countries have signed the treaty (six CIS states originally signed it in 1992). In refusing to sign it Ukraine, Moldova and Turkmenistan have referred to the constitutionally confirmed neutrality of their states. In June 1994 Yeltsin proposed a CIS military structure 'similar to NATO' and issued a decree 'On Approving the Russian Federation's Strategic Course in Relations with CIS Member States', which called for a defence union based on common interests and military-political goals. More recently, this was presented also as a necessary counterstep to NATO enlargement.

The CIS collective security agreement has been followed by only limited military coordination among its signatories. The CIS Joint Staff for Coordinating Military Cooperation has been a toothless structure. The idea aired at times by Russian military leaders of creating regular international troops of the CIS, including coalition forces, has not been realized. The favoured goal of officials representing CIS defence structures – a CIS military–political alliance with permanent coordination and control structures, coordinated operational plans and combat training programmes, as well as separate regional commands of coalition forces – has remained an unrealizable blueprint.[3] In spring 1997 a sub-group of CIS states approved proposals to create a system of control by CIS coalition forces in so-called 'collective security regions'. But these proposals were only in the form of recommendations to the CIS armies' general staffs and are likely to remain unimplemented.[4] More limited and recent ideas have been related to the real defence demands of peacekeeping. One proposal is the creation of permanent military formations in the armed forces of the CIS states for participation in peacekeeping operations. Such formations could serve as the basis for a coalition (regional) group of forces.[5] But this proposal similarly is far from implementation.

Prospects for a Russian forward security zone

The Russian effort to establish the basic infrastructure for a forward security zone in the CIS region is less ambitious in its requirements than the goal of CIS coalition forces and it is consistent with a declaration of intent by Yeltsin in spring 1994 to set up some thirty Russian bases in CIS states. The creation of such a forward security zone would require progress in a number of interrelated aspects of CIS multilateral military coordination, specifically border protection, air defence and peacekeeping.[6] However, in each area the constraints on CIS military coordination have become evident. Russia has lacked the personnel to occupy the bases it covets and lacks the financial means effectively to enact these and other joint military tasks.

The idea of joint CIS border defences reflected a political compulsion in Moscow to view the borders of the former Soviet Union as Russian strategic borders. But it was also intended to release Russia from the need to try to establish real Russian borders, which has been financially impracticable in the short term. However, the principles of the Russian border protection policy and perceived cross-border threats have begun to apply also to former USSR administrative borders between the Russian Federation and CIS states.[7] In particular, the war in Chechenia has confused the Russian border protection requirement. Whereas previously Russia had been trying to prevent conflicts spilling over into Russia from unstable CIS regions, since the onset of the Chechenia campaign Moscow feared that conflict within the Russian Federation (i.e. in Chechenia) could extend into other areas of the North Caucasus or possibly into a CIS hinterland outside Russia. Russian defence priorities had to adjust to this new reality. This development and the difficulties in actually ensuring an effective forward security zone have compelled Moscow to consider establishing more effective border protection along the more transparent Russian Federation frontiers with CIS states, such as the Russian–Kazak border.

At the CIS summit of May 1995 an agreement on the protection of the outer CIS borders (with non-CIS states) failed to receive the signatures of five CIS states: Ukraine, Moldova, Azerbaijan, Uzbekistan and Turkmenistan. The productive work of the CIS Council of Border Troop Commanders has been limited to matters related to bilateral contacts or arrangements at a regional level (particularly towards the situation in Tajikistan) rather than CIS-wide multilateral cooperation.

In fact, Russia has placed emphasis on securing bilateral border protection agreements with those CIS states which are willing. These can subsequently be presented in a multilateral guise and given a CIS imprimatur. Such treaties correspond to Russian national interests and fit in with the goal of seeking to maintain a forward security perimeter or an extended Russian security zone, but they may also offer a service to smaller CIS states which lack the resources to defend adequately their outer, non-CIS state borders. Even so, border troops under Russian jurisdiction are often recruited from local ethnic groups. Russia has confirmed such bilateral agreements with all CIS states except Ukraine, Moldova, Azerbaijan and Uzbekistan. These states resist the creation of a Russian-led CIS border regime (whether based effectively on bilateral agreements or not) and the Ukrainian president has argued openly that 'there are no external borders in the CIS, there are only external and internal borders of each specific state.'

The functioning of a supposed unified CIS air defence system (a goal approved at a CIS summit in February 1995) has come to depend similarly on bilateral agreements. Such agreements exist between Russia and Kazakstan, Armenia, Uzbekistan, Kyrgyzstan and Georgia. By early summer 1996 Russia was undertaking joint air patrols with Kazakstan, Georgia and Belarus on outer CIS borders and had reportedly merged its air defence efforts with Armenia.[8] However, despite the existence of a CIS Air Defence Coordination Committee, a unified command has not yet been created, Moldova, Azerbaijan and Turkmenistan remain outside the agreement on a CIS air defence and Ukraine has accepted it only with reservations. It seems that the expense of maintaining any future unified air defence system would need to be incurred by Russia, and this system excludes an early warning system for missiles.

The third strand of the Russian attempted strategy of forward defence has been the provision of Russian forces for peacekeeping efforts in CIS conflicts. In some cases the peacekeeping operations established have acquired a CIS imprimatur; however, the CIS collective aspect of such peacekeeping operations has remained controversial (as analysed by Pavel Baev and Andrei Zagorski in Chapters 11 and 14, respectively, of this volume).

Options for a more established structural CIS role for the disparate peacekeeping operations which exist in the CIS region are still aired among Russian defence specialists – for example the creation of a centre to control peacekeeping activities in the CIS; the granting of powers to the CIS Staff for Military Cooperation; or the creation of permanent military formations in the armed forces of CIS states to take part in peacekeeping operations.[9] But it appears unlikely that these proposals will be accepted by those CIS states which are sensitive to Russian military preponderance. It is true that the March 1997 CIS summit decided to establish a CIS Committee on Conflict

Situations, and Russian officials have suggested that this should be a military structure to which the CIS peacekeeping forces would be subordinated. But it seems more likely that this will remain a fact-finding and advisory body with no military functions.[10]

Essentially, after a period during 1992–5 when Russia adopted an ambitious agenda for peacekeeping and peace enforcement in CIS conflicts, Russian leaders have been searching for ways to reduce Russian commitments in these conflicts as the military resources available for such operations, partly as a result of the Chechenia campaign, have shrunk. But Moscow has failed to convince other CIS states that they should provide a contingent of peace-keeping forces to reduce the burden on the Russian peacekeeping troops deployed along the border between Abkhazia and the rest of Georgia. It is true that the CIS mandate for the so-called collective CIS peacekeeping forces for Tajikistan has been periodically extended, but the commitments of other CIS states to this essentially Russian operation have continued to decline and Uzbekistan has been developing its own regional security policy agenda towards Tajikistan (see Chapter 12). In fact, this peacekeeping operation has been implemented on the basis of bilateral agreements with Russia and multilateral, regionally based agreements involving Russia, Uzbekistan, Kyrgyzstan and Kazakstan.

The final area of CIS military coordination efforts to be considered is that of military production. In this field, despite the existence of a CIS Military-Industrial Committee, coordination between CIS state defence industries and the attempt to unify armaments in the service of the armies of CIS states have been limited by a growing competition between certain CIS states, especially between Russia and Ukraine, for access to international arms markets. Ukraine is also emerging as a competitor to Russia over military transfers and military-technical maintenance for other CIS states such as Georgia and Turkmenistan. In these circumstances Russian agreements on military production with CIS states (including Ukraine itself) have operated mostly on a bilateral basis. Any revived network of ties between CIS states for the development of weapon systems and components could anyway develop only slowly since their defence budgets have contracted so much, and such ties would not require any high-level CIS stamp of approval or inflexible code of conduct.

International security policy coordination

The CIS framework has failed to generate unified stands by the CIS states in an East–West context on important international security issues, such as NATO enlargement, arms control and arms reduction treaties. Such international security policy coordination may be more possible among sub-groups of CIS states. One option stems from the quadripartite agreement signed by Russia, Belarus, Kazakstan and Kyrgyzstan in March 1996. An agreement on regional security signed at the same time by these four states has been left open to other CIS states and even potentially to non-CIS states such as Bulgaria. But its vagueness suggests that it will have little effect and its compatibility with separate regional security schemes such as the 'Eurasian Union' promoted by Kazak President Nazarbayev remains uncertain.

Russian bilateral security/military policy relations with CIS states

The Russian failure to develop effective or extensive multilateral CIS security policy coordination has been accompanied by considerable success in constructing bilateral military-security links within the CIS region. This is where the real substance of regional security integration lies, to the extent that it exists, even if many of the bilateral treaties signed have remained unratified or unimplemented because they have lacked the necessary financial support.

Russian military spokesmen themselves admitted by early 1997 that Russian military relations with the other Eurasian states existed on three levels, according to the extent of military integration with Russia. First, a group of states remain prepared for close military, even alliance, relations with Russia: Belarus, Armenia, Kyrgyzstan, Tajikistan and probably Kazakstan. Secondly, certain states maintain normal friendly relations with Russia: Turkmenistan, Georgia and Azerbaijan (despite some military frictions between Moscow and the latter two). Thirdly, Ukraine is distinct in distancing itself from military cooperation with Russia and seeking closer security coordination with NATO and Western states.[11] Uzbekistan might be placed between the last two categories.

Taking these differences into account in strategic planning, Russian leaders appear to have developed an ad hoc strategy of prioritizing Russian security policy ties along three basic axes in a form first prominently proposed by the Council on Foreign and Defence Policy lobby in September 1992: to the west with Belarus, to the southwest with Georgia (to which Armenia may be added), and to the south with Kazakstan.[12] The substance of these military axes has varied, but the basic strategic orientations have been confirmed since 1992.[13]

The western axis

The Russian western strategic axis with Belarus developed by default, since the preferred but increasingly unlikely strategic partnership for Russian leaders on Russia's western flanks would be one with Ukraine. Ukraine under President Kuchma has been ready for closer links between the Russian and Ukrainian defence industries for mutual benefit and could pool information on air defence with Russia and other CIS states, but is not prepared for deeper defence cooperation with Moscow.

In contrast, Belarusian–Russian bilateral military cooperation has steadily deepened and has been given political impetus by a treaty of union between the two states (see Chapter 8 in this volume). With the establishment of an operational group of border troops on the western Belarusian border, Russian border interests have shifted 615 kilometres to the west of Russian administrative borders, to the borders of Lithuania, Latvia and Poland. By spring 1997 Belarus had also agreed to lease military sites on its territory to Russia, to develop common air defence and missile defence systems, and even to unify the two countries' chain of military command, coordinate combat training and engage in joint military research.[14]

Russian leaders have claimed that these developments are unrelated to the controversy over NATO enlargement and do not represent military counter-measures to the enlargement process. It is quite possible, however, that the Russian general staff have considered the possibility of trying to recreate a proper western strategic axis in military planning terms, involving a military–political alliance with Belarus and perhaps a revived role for the Kaliningrad region, with all this implies for European security and the nature of the East–West partnership.[15] But Russia would not have the resources available for such an effort and the idea has anyway been undercut by the conclusion of the Founding Act on Mutual Relations, Cooperation and Security between Russia and NATO, which excludes Belarus.

The southwest axis

The southwest strategic axis reflects a traditional Russian and Soviet military preoccupation with the Caucasian region. The strategic interrelationship between the north and south Caucasian sub-regions has become pronounced in Russian military thinking. The region is specific in the dangers it poses for the stability of the Russian Federation itself. However, it is not clear how far Russian resources and local political conditions will permit continued Russian military engagement in the key state of Georgia. The Russian force in the Transcaucasus (covering forces in Georgia and Armenia) is being subordinated to the command of the North Caucasus military district, which reinforces the military interaction between the two Caucasian sub-regions.[16]

Before the Chechenia military campaign commenced in December 1994, Russia had reached agreements with Tbilisi on the maintenance of four military bases in Georgia for a 25-year period and on Russian patrols on the Georgian–Turkish border.[17] A far-reaching friendship and cooperation treaty was signed between the two states. However, the Georgian parliament has refused to ratify the agreement on the bases or the February 1994 treaty on border defence, and indeed has threatened to reject them. Russian peacekeeping units in Abkhazia have offered Moscow further leverage on Georgia, but by 1996 were used more as a source of pressure on the Abkhazian leadership. Two Russian mechanized infantry divisions (one in Batumi and the other in Akhalkalaki) and one regiment (in Vaziani) are scheduled to remain on Georgian territory,[18] but some Russian politicians have proposed further reductions in these forces.

By 1995 the value for Russia of these ties with Georgia had clearly changed. They were valued less to seal the southwest marches of Russia against Turkey – a traditional goal – and more to help contain the spread of North Caucasian instabilities from the south with the help of the efforts of the North Caucasian military district from the north. The Chechenia conflict challenged the Russian Federation from within its borders and forced a basic reappraisal in Russian security policy thinking. The 58th Russian Army in the North Caucasian military district has acquired a new importance as Moscow tries to limit the spill-over of future crises in the North Caucasus republics into the Stavropol district and neighbouring southern regions of Russia.

Armenia has also emerged as a strategic partner for Russia, a relationship which was prefigured by a mutual defence pact signed in 1992. This could even develop into a three-way relationship with Iran, since Tehran has increasingly been described in Moscow as a strategic partner for Russia. Russia has obtained a military base in northwest Armenia at Gyumri for the 127th Motorized Rifle Division and been permitted to locate a command group and motorized rifle regiment in Yerevan for 25 years (the treaty on Russian basing rights was ratified in April 1997).[19] In August 1997 a bilateral treaty of friendship, cooperation and mutual assistance was signed. Russian forces have also carried out joint military exercises with Armenia to defend its southern borders and more controversially clandestinely transferred to Armenia large quantities of arms during 1994–6, which reinforced Armenian dependency on Russia to maintain military superiority over Azerbaijan.[20]

In contrast, Azerbaijan has resisted the Russian goal of a joint Caucasian air defence system and system of external CIS border defence. However, a Russian–Azerbaijani border agreement was signed in May 1997, which envisages joint border guard teams for at least their common 'internal' border. Moldova, for its part, is not clearly integrated in this southwestern strategic axis. The Russian military contingent and Russian peacekeeping forces (which form part of a trilateral arrangement) in the Transdniester region are a beleaguered outpost rather than a real military asset for Moscow. Although Yeltsin has agreed to withdraw the remnants of the Russian 14th Army from Moldova eventually, this offer has been undermined by his repeated efforts to gain Moldovan agreement to the transformation of these forces into a Russian military base.

The southern axis

Russian–Kazak military relations are the key component of Moscow's southern strategic axis, although Moscow has tried to develop an outer security belt through military and border force agreements with the other CIS Central Asian states, and has locked itself into commitments to shore up the crumbling internal and external defences of the Tajik state under the government of President Rakhmonov. The latter effort made Russian security policy hostage to events beyond its effective control and this approach was revised during 1996–7.

A Russian–Kazak military treaty signed in May 1992 has been reinforced by various specific agreements on bilateral military cooperation.[21] The two countries also concluded a treaty on outer CIS border defences at the end of 1994 and agreed that Baikonur will remain Russia's main space launch facility for the next twelve to fifteen years, on a lease arrangement. Russia and Kazakstan decided to create a common defensive space and in early 1995 agreed upon the organization of a joint group of Russian and Kazak troops, which would operate 'on the principles of joint planning for the training and use of troops'.[22] The latter agreement legalized the Russian military presence on Kazak territory. Yet the status of these plans is uncertain, since little has been done to put them into practice, other than the creation of joint air defence patrols.

Kazakstan remains a core buffer state for Russia, but Russia is seeking ways to reduce the transparency of the Russian–Kazak border since it cannot fully rely on the southern CIS border regime. The use of unarmed Siberian Cossack forces to guard this border is one option, although the Kazak leadership is critical of this plan.[23]

Treaties signed in Shanghai in April 1996 between Russia, Kazakstan, Kyrgyzstan and China on confidence-building and border delimitation have reduced traditional Russian concerns about Chinese pressures on the southern frontier of the former USSR. However, continued conflict in Afghanistan reinforces the Russian interest in shoring up the southern strategic axis. One element of this process, a package of military agreements signed by Russia and Turkmen-istan in July 1992, has now unravelled. In spring 1995 Yeltsin decided not to ratify the 1992 treaty on the grounds that its agreements had become useless after Turkmenistan had created its own army and there were no longer any Russian troops on active duty on Turkmen territory.[24] This reflected Turkmenis-tan's stand on 'positive neutrality'. Nevertheless a Russian agreement on the protection of Turkmenistan's southern border remains in force (as does a similar agreement with Kyrgyzstan). In June 1997 the commander of Russian border troops emphasized in Ashgabat that 'we are interested in having our national security problems taken care of as far from our borders as possible.'[25]

Uzbekistan has distanced itself further still from Russian strategic planning. It signed a treaty with Moscow in 1994 which anticipated close military cooperation, but this has now been rejected by Tashkent in favour of a more balanced security policy orientation and an independent regional policy. President Karimov's description of Russia as Uzbekistan's 'strategic partner' assumes Russian recognition of an 'equal' partnership. Tashkent expresses its own interests in the settlement of the conflict in Tajikistan and has refused to permit Russian border guards on its border with Afghanistan.

The Tajik government, in contrast, has locked itself into military dependency on Moscow for its own survival. But the presence of Russian border guards on the Tajik–Afghan border (some 20,000 in 1997) has been only a stop-gap measure, since Russia has lacked the trained troops available for any large increase in response to armed Afghan cross-border infiltration. In this sense this border cannot simply be viewed as a 'Russian border' as Yeltsin once described it. Moreover, the Russian 201st Division (which has about 6,000 soldiers) is unable to enforce peace through military means in Tajikistan and may well be withdrawn.[26] If the peace agreement between the parties to the internal Tajik conflict, signed in Moscow in June 1997, does not endure then the Russian southern strategic axis may depend still more on the core Russian–Kazak security policy relationship.

Security policy diversification among the CIS states

It is argued above that the CIS states have become increasingly differentiated in their security policy interests and requirements. They are influenced significantly by regional security policy dynamics and non-CIS neighbours which provide alternative gravitational fields to the traditional ones centred on Moscow during the Soviet period. Strong regional security complexes engaging CIS and non-CIS neighbour states outside the former USSR (such as Turkey, Iran and China) are only beginning to develop, but it is illusory for Russian leaders to believe that they can seal off other CIS states from external security policy influences and ties. For Moscow to regard such ties in simple zero-sum terms, to view them as evidence of other states trespassing in a region of dominant Russian security interests, as Russian official statements frequently suggest, reflects an unrealistic commitment to a former geostrategic reality which can no longer be restored.[27]

Bilateral agreements

Bilateral military cooperation and security policy coordination between CIS states without Russian participation is developing. Ukraine offers several smaller CIS states an alternative to Russia for such cooperation in certain areas. As early as February 1993 a Ukrainian–Moldovan defence pact indicated that Moldova would rely largely on Kiev in developing its national forces.[28] More recent Ukrainian military assistance to Georgia suggests that Ukraine could develop into a strategic ally for Georgia, and Kiev has offered to send a peacekeeping contingent to the Georgian–Abkhazian conflict zone under UN auspices. In October 1996 Ukraine and Turkmenistan signed agreements on the technical maintenance of Turkmenistan's military equipment and the training of Turkmen cadets and officers.[29] The previous month Georgia and Uzbekistan signed a package of bilateral agreements on various aspects of military and military-technical cooperation.[30] There has been speculation, too, about the emergence of a new strategic axis of Ukraine–Georgia–Uzbekistan, perhaps including Azerbaijan, but effective structures for joint security policy coordination between this sub-group of CIS states are unlikely to emerge.

CIS states have been steadily developing bilateral military links with non-CIS countries. Ukraine again has been at the forefront of this process, initially through its conclusion of a variety of agreements on defence and military-technical coordination with east/central European states, which were viewed in Kiev as the basis for possible new multilateral frameworks (see below).[31]

Ukraine has also been one of several CIS states prepared to explore military contacts with Turkey and Iran. Ukrainian–Turkish military discussions could offer Ukraine a potential strategic axis to the south if tensions with Russia in the Black Sea were to increase. Azerbaijan, Turkmenistan and Kazakstan have also initiated military contacts with Turkey on training and technical assistance.[32] In contrast, Armenia has concluded military cooperation agreements with Greece and Bulgaria, states which share Yerevan's distrust of Turkey, although this is unlikely to reduce Armenia's military dependence on Russia. Ukrainian arms deliveries to Iran have become significant, although Iran's main CIS military partner and arms supplier remains Russia. Turkmenistan for its part has agreed on future joint manoeuvres and exchanging experience on developing armed forces with Iran.[33]

China has also been cultivating a military relationship with Kiev, mainly based on arms purchases. The April 1996 Shanghai agreements between Beijing, Kazakstan and Kyrgyzstan (as well as Russia) offer the basis for future direct bilateral Chinese security policy interaction with these neighbouring states and were followed by Chinese bilateral accords with Uzbekistan, Kyrgyzstan and Kazakstan in July 1996.

Multilateral agreements and proposals

The only significant effort to establish multilateral security policy coordination among CIS states (and confined to those states) excluding Russian participation has been between Kazakstan, Kyrgyzstan and Uzbekistan. In December 1995 the Interstate Council of these three states decided to establish a joint Council of Defence Ministers which is tasked with considering issues of regional security and defence coordination, including coordination of military exercises, air defence and defence supplies.[34] Resource constraints, rivalries and policy differences among these states mean that this goal appears to be premature. But a decision by these states in spring 1996 to create a joint Kazak–Kyrgyz–Uzbek Central Asian peacekeeping battalion for use under UN auspices is being implemented. This battalion has attracted technical assistance from the UN and European Union.

In contrast, despite some idealistic proposals for a 'common Caucasian home', there have been no prospects for a regional union or defence coordination between the three Caucasian CIS states on account of the bitter division formed by the Nagorno-Karabakh conflict. At the sub-state level there have been efforts to create an organization to promote the interests of the non-Russian peoples of the North Caucasus through a Confederation of Peoples of the Caucasus (KNK), which would stretch from the Black Sea to the Caspian Sea. But the vision of a confederation based on a tradition of struggle with Moscow and a collective Islamic heritage has not offered a prospect for cooperation among the non-Russian peoples of the North Caucasus or for regional integration.[35] The transformation of KNK militias into joint regional military forces (excluding Russian troops) has remained unrealizable, as has the separate idea of forming a union of certain North Caucasian republics and a Caucasian CIS state such as Georgia,[36] because of the disparate interests of the various parties and the hostility of the central Russian authorities to such initiatives.

Kazakstan's effort to promote the concept of a Eurasian Union represents an alternative and broader security framework to CIS-style integration formulae. This idea, which was first floated by President Nazarbayev in March 1994, may be viewed as an attempt to shift the initiative and terms of integration from Moscow to Almaty (and to enlarge its scope to cover non-CIS Asian states). Although Russia would be included in such a Eurasian Union, the Kazak notion emphasizes parity in voting procedures. The Union remains a blueprint, partly since Moscow and Tashkent have discouraged its development. Uzbekistan has offered alternative proposals for regional security which highlight Uzbek involvement.

Another initiative by Nazarbayev, the Conference on Cooperation and

Confidence-building Measures in Asia (CCCMA), modelled on the OSCE, was promoted by a meeting in Almaty in February 1996 at deputy foreign minister level, which attracted representatives of fifteen member countries and ten observers. Although a resolution on peace, stability and cooperation in Asia was adopted, this group appears too amorphous and represents too many conflicting interests to develop as a functional organization on Eurasian security.

Other possible groupings of CIS states with their neighbours to the west of Moscow were aired during 1991–3. Ukrainian leaders mooted the option of an eventual military–political coalition with Poland, the Czech Republic and Hungary, and in 1992 some politicians proposed a broader alliance of Ukraine with all east European and Balkan countries. In May 1993 the idea of an east-central European collective security system or consultative security zone which would exclude Russia, a kind of 'NATO-2', was discussed by the Ukrainian and Polish presidents.[37] Polish interest in entering NATO later led to this idea being dropped, and the Ukrainian hope that Poland would become a political and security ally has been dashed.[38]

The former Belarusian leader Stanislav Shushkevich proposed that Belarus, together with other east European states and perhaps the Baltic states and Ukraine, could form 'a belt of neutral states'. Another idea was represented by a meeting in June 1993 of the most influential opposition movements of Ukraine, Moldova, Belarus, Lithuania and Poland, which committed themselves to a Baltic–Black Sea Union as a counterbalance to Russia. However, this objective was never adopted as official policy by these states.

Agreements with NATO (NACC, PfP)

These schemes by Ukraine and Belarus for developing multilateral security policy frameworks to forge links with central European states have been displaced by Ukraine's emphasis on a security policy orientation towards Western institutions and the Belarusian commitment to integration in defence policy with Russia.

Despite its efforts, Ukraine has not obtained any direct NATO or US security guarantees, though it has received assurances, as a non-nuclear weapon state party to the Non-Proliferation Treaty, by all five nuclear weapon states which are parties to the treaty. Ukraine concluded a memorandum on cooperation in the sphere of defence with the United States in July 1993,[39] and this was followed by similar memoranda later that year with Germany and Britain. Kiev entered the North Atlantic Cooperation Council (NACC) in 1992 and has been an early and active participant in the Partnership for Peace (PfP) programme with NATO since joining it in 1994.

Under the PfP Ukraine has engaged in a variety of military and peacekeeping exercises with NATO military forces and has hosted several PfP exercises on its own territory. These links were crowned by the signing of a Charter on a Distinctive Partnership between NATO and Ukraine at the Madrid NATO summit in July 1997, which gives Ukraine the right to call for 'consultations' with NATO if it feels threatened. Among its clauses the charter specifies a wide range of issues for consultation and/or cooperation between the parties. In broad terms these include the security of Ukraine, conflict prevention, crisis management, peace support and conflict resolution. More specifically they cover defence planning, budgeting, policy, strategy and national security concepts, as well as military training and NATO support for a Polish–Ukrainian peacekeeping battalion.[40] A new forum known as the NATO–Ukraine commission has been set up to enable the North Atlantic Council to meet with Ukrainian representatives to discuss implementation of the Charter and ways to further develop cooperation.

Belarus, which under President Lukashenka has followed a maverick and critical policy towards NATO, has not been offered a charter like Ukraine's and was the last CIS state to join the PfP programme. It can only hope that Belarusian interests are taken into account by Russia in the Permanent Joint Council (PJC) which has been created to serve as a mechanism for consultations and coordination and possible decisions between Russia and NATO.

Despite the poor relations between NATO and Belarus at the time the PJC was formed in 1997, the enlargement of NATO to include states of central Europe is likely to extend the range of NATO security concerns and links eastwards. In particular, Poland's inclusion in NATO 'would create Western interests in and increased interaction with the bordering Baltic states, Belarus and Ukraine'. Increased Western activity in and security policy ties with these states need not conflict with Russian interests; but they would constitute a further illustration of how currents from outside former Soviet frontiers are influencing countries that Russia has traditionally sought to keep as its exclusive domain.[41]

The Central Asian and Caucasian states have all joined the NATO affiliates, the NACC and the PfP (apart from Tajikistan which remains outside the PfP). The NACC and PfP have played a role in conventional disarmament issues and offered a mechanism for individually tailored programmes of military cooperation with these states, including officer training and joint exercises. In Central Asia Uzbekistan (which joined the PfP in October 1995) hosted joint exercises with US army units in September 1996 and the next year became the venue for a larger exercise with contingents from other Central Asian states and NATO. Kyrgyzstan has also emerged as an active PfP participant and Turkmenistan, which joined the programme in May 1994, has sent officers to American military schools for training.[42]

Azerbaijan and Georgia have developed as eager PfP programme participants among the Caucasus states. In its presentation document setting out proposals for its participation in the programme, Azerbaijan described CIS collective security arrangements as 'purely declarative' and placed 'special hopes on NATO to help restore Azerbaijan's territorial integrity' (in relation to Nagorno-Karabakh). It even anticipated the deployment of NATO units for peacekeeping operations in Karabakh after the conclusion of a political agreement on the principles for settling that conflict.[43] However, reliance on this level of NATO engagement in the Caucasian region is misplaced. No other CIS state has expected such an engagement in its proximity. NATO security guarantees do not follow participation in the NACC or PfP. Russian declarations that the Caucasus cannot be within NATO's zone of activity and that NATO involvement will not help resolve the conflicts in the region express both a reluctance to acknowledge the relatively modest PfP programme activities already under way in the Caucasus and an exaggerated concern about the scale of potential NATO involvement here.[44]

The UN and OSCE presence

The Russian attempt to limit diversification in the security policies of the new Eurasian states has been expressed in the only grudging acceptance by many Russian officials of the legitimacy of even a limited UN or OSCE presence in CIS regions and in suspicions about the intentions of these international organizations (to which Russia, of course, belongs). OSCE missions have been in Georgia (focused on South Ossetia) since December 1992 and in Tajikistan since February 1994; another contributed to the ceasefire agreement between Russia and Chechenia in August 1996. An OSCE peacekeeping force has been earmarked for Nagorno-Karabakh on the basis of an OSCE summit decision in December 1994. It remained a key element of proposals in spring 1997 to secure a corridor between Armenia and Nagorno-Karabakh. A small UN observer mission (UNOMIG) was established in Georgia in August 1993 and one was deployed in Tajikistan in December 1994.

These UN and OSCE missions have played only a secondary role in the regulation of the conflicts concerned. But they have ensured that regional security issues related to the conflicts have been aired in key international fora, not just in those of CIS organs, and they have created greater transparency around Russian or Russian-led CIS military activities. The independent member-ship of the new Eurasian states in the UN and the OSCE has naturally also enlarged their security policy horizons, areas of responsibility and engagement.

This analysis of the network of new security policy relations in Eurasia is necessarily incomplete. It pays little attention to sub-state security policy interactions, which are important in the development of any 'security community' (whether one of a limited Russian–Belarusian kind, one on a broader CIS basis, or one based on OSCE principles or on a familiarization with Western practices through the PfP programme). In the case of Eurasia, such sub-state interactions would reflect, for example, ties between former Soviet military officers and defence enterprises, but also new links with and opportunities to visit non-CIS states. The orientation of what may be termed the 'security policy culture' of the CIS states is important; the legacy of the Soviet past is certainly a potent influence, but opportunities through the PfP programme are already diluting this legacy in countries such as Ukraine.

There is a range of non-military security policy concerns which create regional linkages in Eurasia between the states most concerned on functional lines, on an economic or environmental basis or in relation to a variety of societal or internal security threats. These are not the main concern of this volume, although they are issues which increasingly preoccupy the security agencies of all the new Eurasian countries. Despite this, new agreements concerning economic security or trade may prefigure the development of military-security ties where benefits can be identified for the states involved, or where the goal of diversification of external relations is part of a broader political strategy. For this reason it is important to keep in focus the overall scope and direction of the emerging relations in the new states of Eurasia.[45]

Notes

1. See, e.g., the lament over the Russian loss of influence in the CIS countries and call for measures to reinforce 'integration processes' by the Duma Defence Committee Chairman, Lev Rokhlin, *Nezavisimaya gazeta*, 4 March 1997.
2. This followed a meeting between Russia and the Central Asian CIS states in October 1996, which decided that military units would not be moved within the CIS in the near future in response to events in Afghanistan, but that the CIS Collective Security Council should create an operational group for observing events in the southern border regions of the CIS. See *Krasnaya zvezda*, 8 October 1996. On reports that Russian defence minister Rodionov asked the Central Asian CIS states to offer proposals for more substantial military responses, see A. Gorodnov in *Segodnya*, 27 February 1997.
3. In spring 1997 the CIS Collective Security Council secretary, Vladimir Zemsky, still spoke of calling for establishing 'coalition (allied) army groups designed to repel aggression coming from any direction', but admitted that 'the task of achieving a full-fledged military–political integration stretches far beyond the near future'. *Krasnaya zvezda*, 15 May 1997.
4. Proposals at the session of the CIS Defence Ministerial Council on 26 March 1997, *Krasnaya zvezda*, 28 March 1997.
5. Report on meetings of the CIS Council of Defence Ministers; I. Korotchenko, *Nezavisimaya gazeta*, 14 February 1997.
6. See, e.g., the analysis by Alexander Sergounin, *On the Way to Integration: Military–Technical Cooperation between the CIS Member States* (Nizhny Novgorod: University of Nizhny Novgorod Press, 1996).

7. Yeltsin approved a document on the Russian border protection policy in October 1996; see *Krasnaya zvezda*, 10 October 1996.
8. See interview of Commander of Russian Air Defence Forces and Chairman of the CIS Air Defence Coordinating Committee, General Viktor Prudnikov, *Krasnaya zvezda*, 12 April 1997.
9. See I. Korotchenko, *Nezavisimaya gazeta*, 14 February 1997.
10. *Prism*, 4 April 1997.
11. Interview with Leonid Ivashov, chief of the Main Department for International Military Cooperation of the Russian Ministry of Defence, in *Nezavisimoe voennoe obozrenie*, no. 4, January 1997, pp. 1, 3.
12. 'Strategiya dlya Rossii', *Nezavisimaya gazeta*, 19 August 1992.
13. For details of developments along these axes to autumn 1995 see Gudrun Persson, 'Military–political Trends within the CIS During the Chechen Campaign. Part II: Bilateral Approaches', *Aktuelle Analysen*, no. 65, 1995, BIOst, Cologne, pp. 1–6. For a detailed unofficial Russian military assessment of the various strategic directions for Russia and the opportunities and threats they offer, see Major-General Valentin Larionov, 'The Problem with NATO Expansion and CIS Regional Security', *FSU 15 Nations: Policy and Security*, May 1997, pp. 6–10.
14. Interview with Belarusian defence minister Colonel-General Alexander Chumakov, *Krasnaya zvezda*, 23 April 1997.
15. This was proposed by the Russian general staff according to a high-ranking officer in its Main Operations Department; as reported by I. Korotchenko and M. Karpov, *Nezavisimaya gazeta*, 7 October 1995.
16. See report by Georgian defence minister Vardiko Nadibaidze, *Nezavisimaya gazeta*, 22 March 1997.
17. For details on these bases see I. Kakheli, *Obshchaya gazeta*, 2–11 November 1995. For the preparation of the bases agreement see *Nezavisimaya gazeta* and *Krasnaya zvezda*, 23 March 1995.
18. These forces are planned to remain after the Russian force in the Transcaucasus is reorganized into two operational forces, 'Georgia' and 'Armenia'; report of Georgian defence minister, *Nezavisimaya gazeta*, 22 March 1997.
19. See 'Rossiyskaya voennaya baza v Armenii', *Nezavisimaya gazeta*, 18 March 1995.
20. On these illicit arms transfers see *Nezavisimaya gazeta*, 27 June 1997.
21. The two countries signed a treaty of friendship, cooperation and mutual assistance on 25 May 1992. This was developed in a bilateral treaty on military cooperation signed on 28 March 1994; for the text of this second treaty, published in *Sovety Kazakhstana*, 19 October 1994, see *Summary of World Broadcasts. Former Soviet Union* (henceforth BBC, *SWB*, SU) 2139 G/1.
22. Joint declaration on deepening Russian–Kazak cooperation signed on 20 January 1995, reported in *Segodnya* and *Kazakhstanskaya pravda*, 21 January 1995.
23. A treaty on the Siberian Cossack forces guarding the Russian–Kazak border was signed in Omsk on 5 June 1997; see S. Gavrilov and I. Spiridonov, *Kommersant-Daily*, 5 June 1997.
24. Decree reported by Interfax, 14 April 1995, in BBC, *SWB* SU 2280 S1/4–5.
25. Army General Andrei Nikolaev, in A. Zhilin, *Moscow News*, 8–15 June 1997, p. 9.
26. This scenario is developed by e.g. A. Baranov in *Pravda*, 19 June 1997.
27. An excellent summary of such security policy diversification among the CIS states is found in Mark Webber, *CIS Integration Trends: Russia and the Former Soviet South*, Former Soviet South Project Paper (London: Royal Institute of International Affairs, 1997), pp. 44–7. The following section relies partly on this analysis.
28. Itar-Tass World Service, 19 February 1993, in BBC, *SWB*, SU/1619 C2/3.
29. Agreements signed on 29 October 1996; in *Monitor*, Jamestown Foundation, October 1996, vol. 2, 31 October 1996.
30. Agreements signed on 10 September 1996; in *OMRI Daily Digest I*, no, 176, 11 September 1996.
31. See e.g. the details of the February 1993 Ukrainian–Polish agreement, ITAR-TASS, Moscow, 3 February 1993, in BBC, *SWB*, SU/1605 C2/2; the March 1992 Ukrainian–Hungarian agreement, *Izvestiya*, 4 March 1992.
32. For example, Azerbaijan and Turkey signed an agreement on military cooperation on 11 June 1996; BBC, *SWB*, SU/2637 F/1, 13 June 1996. Turkey signed a military cooperation agreement with Kazakstan on 8 August 1994; RFE/RL, *Daily Report*, 9 August 1994.
33. R. Kangas, 'With an Eye on Russia, Central Asian Militaries Practise Cooperation', *Transition*, vol. 2, no. 16, 9 August 1996, p. 19.
34. The five Central Asian CIS states held several summits on regional cooperation before this but failed to develop any effective defence coordination. Uzbekistan, Kazakstan and Kyrgyzstan developed a trilateral grouping in February 1994, on the basis of bilateral Kazak–Uzbek treaties and coordination

efforts dating back to 1992, which was principally concerned with economic cooperation as well as cooperation over transport and communications, energy and water management.

35. See the analysis by Fiona Hill, *'Russia's Tinderbox': Conflict in the North Caucasus and its Implications for the Future of the Russian Federation'*, Harvard University, Strengthening Democratic Institutions Project, September 1995, pp. 24–9. Proponents of the confederation failed to win the support of the republican governments of the North Caucasus, except those of Abkhazia and Chechenia.

36. For speculation about such a regional union involving Georgia, Chechenia and Ingushetia see T. Muzayev, *Novoe vremya*, no. 13, 1997, p. 22.

37. R. Allison, 'Ukraine: External Relations', 'Post-Soviet Periphery', *JIIA Paper* no. 8, Japan Institute of International Affairs, Tokyo, 1994, pp. 13–15.

38. See Bukvoll, *Ukraine and European Security*, pp. 75–7.

39. ITAR-TASS and UNIAN news agencies, Moscow and Kiev, 2 August 1993; in BBC, *SWB*, SU/1759 C2/2.

40. Charter signed in Madrid on 9 July 1997; the text is available at http://www.nato.int/docu/basictxt/ukrchrt.htm

41. Garnett, 'Russia's Illusory Ambitions', p. 73.

42. Kangas, 'With an Eye on Russia', p. 19; Webber, *CIS Integration Trends,* p. 45; for Kyrgyzstan's activities under the PfP see I. Shestakov, *Segodnya*, 19 February 1997.

43. Interfax, 25 April 1996; in Jamestown Foundation, *Monitor*, 26 April 1996.

44. For an official Russian response to NATO Secretary-General Javier Solana's visit to Moldova, Georgia, Armenia and Azerbaijan in February 1997, see President Yeltsin's press secretary, *Kommersant-Daily*, 14 February 1997.

45. Webber, *CIS Integration Trends*, provides the most comprehensive and up-to-date assessment of these relations for the Caucasian and Central Asian CIS states.

Part I

Russia

2 Russian national security interests

Hannes Adomeit

'National interests' (*natsional'nye interesy*) and policies commensurate with the status of a 'great power' (*velikaya derzhava*) have become central themes in the Russian foreign policy debate.[1] This was clearly apparent in Yevgeny Primakov's first press conference as foreign minister. He saw his appointment as having been prompted by 'the need to strengthen the foreign ministry's efforts to protect Russia's national interests' and he confidently asserted that 'we are a great power and our policy must reflect our status'.[2] The implication of these statements was obvious. The Russian foreign ministry under Andrei Kozyrev had allegedly neglected or even violated Russia's national interests and failed to conduct policies befitting a great power.

Russia needs to redefine its identity. This has been made necessary by the Soviet Union's disintegration, the collapse of its superpower status, the disappearance of its sphere of influence in central and eastern Europe, the emergence of newly independent states and the difficult problems of 'transition' in Russia itself. The process of redefinition is obviously highly political; but it also has emotional, psychological and often irrational dimensions. One of the participants in the debate – though now no longer prominently involved in shaping it – has openly acknowledged this, perhaps more courageously than others. He disagreed with the notion that pragmatism should be the guiding principle and confessed that he 'would be very upset if a certain Russian variant of a strictly rational persuasion in foreign policy became predominant. Russia's policies should not only reflect interests but a mission as well.'[3]

The foreign policy of the Russian Federation developed while Yeltsin was president of the Russian Federation – then still called the RSFSR. In June 1990 the Russian Federation declared state sovereignty and began to develop domestic and foreign policy agendas distinct from those of the Soviet Union.[4] Some indications of the new orientation before the attempted coup of August 1991 and the formal end of the USSR in December that year were the conclusion of treaties on interstate relations between the RSFSR and Ukraine, Belarus, Latvia, Estonia, Lithuania, Kazakstan and Moldova; visits by Yeltsin to the European Parliament in Strasbourg and to Paris in April, Prague in May and Washington in June 1991; and the talks between the chairman of the

RSFSR Supreme Soviet's security committee, Sergei Stepashin, and NATO officials in Brussels, with the purpose of achieving observer status for Russia in the Atlantic alliance.[5]

The August 1991 coup reinforced these tendencies. In the period from the end of 1991 to mid-1992, the objectives of the new Russia were devolution of empire; eradication of regional military preponderance; abandonment in most areas of the effort towards military-strategic parity with the United States; pursuit of broad political cooperation with newly found partners in the UN Security Council; full participation in international economic institutions, such as GATT, the IMF and the G7; and – in the long run – NATO membership. Yeltsin's visits to Germany, Italy, France, Britain, Canada, the United States and the UN Security Council, and his planned visits to Japan and South Korea, as well as his participation in the G7 economic summit in Munich, accurately mirrored the new objectives. The same applies to Russia's policies on a number of important issues, including support for UN sanctions against Serbia, Iraq and Libya; negotiation of a START 2 agreement; interest in a global protection system against limited ballistic missile attack; compromises on the export of missile technology to India; and readiness to negotiate with Japan on the southern Kuril islands.

Nationalist, communist and other critics of Yeltsin and the foreign minister of the Russian Federation, Andrei Kozyrev, have charged that a conceptual basis and coherence were lacking in this period of Russian foreign policy. Such charges are ill-founded. Early Russian foreign policy in the near and far abroad was solidly based on a European, transatlantic or Western orientation; it embodied the main principles of the 'new thinking' advocated by Soviet President Gorbachev. Yeltsin clarified in his address to the UN at the beginning of 1992 that Russia regarded the Western countries as 'allies'.[6] His foreign policy adviser, Gennadii Burbulis, explained that none of the pressing domestic problems of the Russian Federation could be 'solved without learning from the European experience' – an unambiguous continuation of Gorbachev's concept of the 'common house of Europe'.[7] Kozyrev warned that yet another failure 'to integrate into the democratic community of states and thus the world economy would amount to a betrayal of the nation and the final slide of Russia down to the category of third-rank states'.[8] Yet the previous foreign minister is also on record as having said: 'There is a habit [in Russia] of thinking in terms of blueprints. We need *Das Kapital* or a CPSU Programme that gives a schematic answer to all questions. But there can be no blueprint. What exist are reactions to a specific situation, and those reactions display Russia's national interests. No country has a description of its national interest.'[9]

Like some of the attacks in the academic world on a scholarly work's apparent 'methodological weaknesses' and lack of a 'theoretical framework', the clamour for codification of national interests and 'conceptual coherence' was hardly motivated by an interest in theory *per se*. It was driven by the desire to change both the theory and the practice of Russian foreign policy – and ultimately to replace its purportedly inept architect. Although there were many points of principle and specific policy issues which ostensibly or genuinely upset the nationalist and communist opposition (including Kozyrev's support for UN sanctions against Serbia, Iraq and Libya, a 'series of unilateral concessions' to the United States on arms control and arms exports policy, and undignified plans for 'trading' Russian territory to Japan in exchange for economic assistance), the main issue which provided the rallying point for its counterattack were Kozyrev's attitudes and policies in the 'near abroad'.

'Eurasianism' and the near abroad

Contrary to the assertions by nationalists, communists, neo-imperialists and great power advocates (*derzhavniki*), Russian policy in the near abroad in 1991–2 rested on elaborate conceptual foundations. It was based on principles similar to those adopted by Gorbachev towards the countries of eastern Europe, including renunciation of the use of force. Thus, in March 1991, when Yeltsin was asked how the problem of Russian communities outside the Russian Federation should be tackled, he replied: 'It is impossible to defend people with tanks. After that their lives would be more complicated. It is necessary to put our relations on a juridical foundation, one of international rights – which we are currently doing.'[10] Similarly, Kozyrev stated in an interview in January 1992: 'After the exclusion of the "elder brother" concept from relations, consultations are now being conducted on the basis of sovereignty, equality and taking account of one another's interests. Russia is not after a special position in the family, nor does it intend to occupy it.'[11]

The difference between this approach and that advocated by its critics, then, does not lie in the presence or absence of a conceptual basis but in how specific policy questions are to be addressed. These are the problems of whether:

(1) the Soviet Union is to be considered irrevocably dead or should be restored in one form or another;
(2) the borders of the newly independent states should be recognized and respected or not;
(3) integration of the post-Soviet geopolitical space is to be instrumentalized, neo-imperialist style, from Moscow, or proceed on a voluntary basis;
(4) integration should be governed by centralizing and authoritarian norms analogous to those of the defunct Warsaw Pact or, following the model of the European Union, market-orientated and democratic principles;

(5) the means to be used in order to achieve a greater degree of Russian influence should be military-political pressures and military force, or inducements and persuasion;

(6) the 25 million ethnic Russians, or more than 30 million 'Russian-speakers' (*russko-yazychnie*), should be used as tools for the reassertion of Moscow's control in a new sphere of influence or encouraged to find a *modus vivendi* with the newly independent states;[12] and

(7) Russian policies in this area should aim at the exclusion of the West as an undesirable competitor or be conducted in a cooperative spirit, with Russia encouraging Western countries and institutions, such as the IMF, the World Bank and the EBRD, actively to involve themselves in reformist processes.

It is a tragedy, and the form in which it occurred a travesty, that the rhetoric of the Russian foreign policy establishment has, on each and every point, embraced the former rather than the latter orientation and that policies have to a some extent followed the rhetoric.

The shift towards a new assertiveness began in earnest in the spring and summer of 1992. By then, the term 'near abroad' (*blizhnoe zarubezh'e*) had crept into the Russian political vocabulary, denoting a peculiar status for and special relations with the newly independent countries. In accordance with this notion, momentum was gathering, notably in the Supreme Soviet of the Russian Federation, for the creation of a separate ministry to deal with Russian–CIS relations, to be headed by state counsellor and special presidential adviser Sergei Stankevich. 'It is apparent', he argued, 'that the CIS calls for a special and independent sphere of Russian foreign policy. The CIS must be dealt with on a daily basis, and not in between trips to London and Paris.'[13] In July, the Russian parliament debated for three days the plight of the Russians in the near abroad, accused the foreign ministry of betraying their interests, complained about 'massive violations of human rights' in the Baltic states and called on the government to apply sanctions against Estonia.[14]

In the same month, the struggle over political leaders and institutions to be involved in policy-making towards the near abroad sharpened as a result of conflicts in the CIS – in Moldova (Transdniestria) and Georgia (Abkhazia and South Ossetia), and between Armenia and Azerbaijan over Nagorno-Karabakh. Yury Skokov, the then secretary of the Security Council, emerged as an ambitious figure who for a time successfully expanded his power base with the apparent intention of establishing a centralized decision-making apparatus.[15] In 1992 the foreign minister still felt strong enough to attack his opponents publicly, warning – in reference to Skokov and his 'national-patriotic' supporters – of the growing influence of a 'war party' and an 'anti-democratic putsch'. He also chastised the hardening of their positions on CIS conflicts as 'political primitivism' and criticized the use of force as a return to the 'Soviet approach' of solving conflict.[16]

The struggle over the authoritative codification of national security interests also sharpened. Three such codifications were emerging and vying for acceptance by the president. The first was that of the foreign ministry, drafted – reluctantly, as we have seen – in response to political pressures exerted by vociferous hard-line factions in the Congress of People's Deputies. The draft document, entitled 'Concerning the Basic Points of the Concept of Foreign Policy of the Russian Federation', was submitted to and discussed by the parliamentary foreign affairs committee in February 1992.[17] It was amended and resubmitted to the committee, without major changes and with detailed explanatory notes, in April.[18] After further discussion, it was approved in October 1992[19] and published in early 1993.[20] The second foreign policy concept was developed by the Council on Foreign and Defence Policy, a group of influential political leaders, administrators, diplomats, military officers and foreign policy experts, established upon the initiative of Sergei Karaganov, the deputy head of the Institute on Europe; it was published in August 1992 under the title *Strategy for Russia*.[21] The third document was written by an inter-departmental commission on foreign policy and security. The commission included all the major institutions involved in foreign and defence policy – the foreign ministry, the ministry for foreign economic relations, the ministry of defence, the intelligence services, the defence council, and the parliamentary committees on foreign affairs and foreign economic relations, and on defence and security. Skokov had overall responsibility for drafting the document, entitled the 'Basic Principles of a Foreign Policy Concept of the Russian Federation'.[22]

The last of these three documents represented official policy. At this time, responsibility for defining the direction of foreign policy rested with the Security Council and not the ministry of foreign affairs. Yeltsin criticized the foreign ministry, charging that its work had been 'lacking consistency and has suffered from too much ad hocism' and had failed to produce a 'well thought out' policy towards the former republics of the Soviet Union.[23] He called for better protection of the rights of Russians in the near abroad and, ignoring almost identical statements by Kozyrev and the foreign ministry, ruled that 'policy considerations in relation to other CIS countries have priority'.[24] In accordance with a decree of 16 December 1992, Yeltsin also gave the Security Council authority over the foreign ministry, thereby further limiting the ministry's authority and influence.[25]

There are similarities between the three documents; but, in comparison with the other two, the concept expressed by the interdepartmental commission is clearly the most assertive and betrays the greatest sense of self-confidence. Russia, the authors state reassuringly, 'remains one of the great powers because of its potential as well as its influence on the course of world events'. Predictably, they declare Russia's relationship with the countries of the former Soviet Union to be of crucial importance. Ordering principles to structure the relations are held to be the 'creation of an effective system of collective defence'; 'ensuring the status of Russia as the single nuclear power in the CIS'; 'strengthening of the external borders of the Commonwealth'; 'maintaining its military infrastructure and installations'; and establishing an 'integral system of military security for its members'. The document also advocates the further development of a 'peace creating mechanism in the framework of a new integration, with the participation of Russia and on the basis of a mandate by the UN or the CSCE'.

Not surprisingly, the Skokov commission's concept contains many formulations similar to those found in the new Russian military doctrine, which was approved in November 1993. The reason for this is simple. In March that year, the Security Council had officially been empowered to work on the doctrine and it incorporated many of its members' ideas on national security.[26] The new doctrine, however, featured an important innovation: the assertion of a unilateral right of intervention in the internal affairs of the CIS countries. The use of force, according to the doctrine, would be proper if it occurred in response to 'suppression of the rights, freedoms and legitimate interests of Russian-speaking citizens in foreign states'.[27]

The reconstruction of the shift in the codification of national interests would be incomplete without reference to presidential statements. Most note worthy in this context are Yeltsin's remarks of February 1993 to a congress of the Civic Union, a centre-right alliance. He suggested that Russia should be granted special rights and privileges to stop ethnic conflicts in the former Soviet Union, claiming that 'the world community is increasingly coming to understand Russia's *special responsibility* in this difficult task'. He also thought that the moment had come 'when responsible international organizations, including the United Nations, should grant Russia *special powers* as a guarantor of peace and stability in the region of the former union. Russia has a heartfelt interest in stopping all armed conflicts on the territory of the former Soviet Union.'[28]

In implementation of what was quickly called internationally the Yeltsin or Monrovsky Doctrine, Kozyrev presented the UN General Assembly in March 1993 with a document outlining the inherent instability of the region, Russia's peacekeeping (*mirotvorcheskie*) operations and the need for a regional peacekeeping mechanism, namely the CIS. The proposal was rejected by the Baltic states, Ukraine and Moldova, which countered that Russian intentions were imperialist rather than humanitarian. Unperturbed, Kozyrev again lobbied the UN in September, contradicting conventional wisdom by asserting that countries with vital interests in a conflict could and should act as peacekeepers.

The 'Monrovsky Doctrine' is part of an overall return to a geopolitical and geostrategic understanding of Russian national interests.[29] The post-1992 Kozyrev is on record as subscribing to it and converting to the traditional realist notions of the importance of armed forces, military bases, spheres of influence, security alliances, power vacuums and buffer states. Russia's interest in the effective management of regional conflicts stemmed from the desire not to 'lose geopolitical positions that took centuries to conquer', he admitted in October 1993.[30] In January 1994, he told Russian ambassadors to the CIS and the Baltic states that 'we should not fear the word "military presence"'.[31] And why not? There was always the risk that, 'as soon as we leave these areas, the ensuing vacuum will immediately be filled by other forces, possibly not always friendly and perhaps even hostile to Russian interests'.[32]

The issue of Russian military bases became a matter of political controversy and embarrassment in April 1994. On 5 April, Yeltsin had issued an 'instruction' approving a defence ministry plan for the creation of 30 military bases in the CIS, ostensibly 'for the security of those states, and for the testing of new weaponry and military technology'.[33] The text of the order, published two days later on the front page of the official government gazette, said it had also been approved by the foreign ministry. But Kozyrev asserted that he had never heard about the order and that the foreign ministry did not 'know where this order comes from or with whom it was agreed'. To add to the confusion, the original list had included the Skrunda early warning radar station in Latvia, prompting Latvian and other Baltic officials to express their concern, eliciting a clarification by Yeltsin's press spokesman to the effect that the inclusion of Skrunda had been a 'technical mistake' and that there was 'no question of creating any kind of bases on the territory of Latvia', and leading the president to amend – but not to retract – his order.[34]

Another presidential order, issued in September 1995, confirmed Russia's 'national interests' in and 'strategic course' towards the CIS. The goals to be achieved, among others, were deemed to be the enhancement of 'integration processes' and the 'strengthening of Russia as the leading force' in the creation of a 'new system of interstate political and economic relations'. In the security realm, the 'national interests of Russia and the common interests of the CIS states' were said to include the 'reliable protection of the borders at the CIS perimeter' and the 'creation of a legal basis for the presence of border troops of the Russian Federation in these countries'.[35] It is important to note in this context the apparently deliberate blurring of the difference between those CIS member states that have acceded to the May 1992 Tashkent agreement on collective security (Armenia, Azerbaijan, Belarus, Georgia, Kazakstan, Kyrgyzstan, Tajikistan and Uzbekistan) and those that have not (Ukraine, Moldova and Turkmenistan).

To summarize, by 1993 – in terms of mood, rhetoric and conceptual approach – the Russian foreign policy establishment had arrived at broad agreement on a view that Russian foreign policy should be based principally on a Realist calculation of national interests. Foreign policy was being realigned with this conceptual shift – but only up to a point. Gaps continued to exist between rhetoric and practice.

Domestic dimensions of the return to geopolitics

What drives foreign policy? Is it ideas that are embodied in institutions and transposed to policy formation? Or do socio-economic interest groups construct ideas and ideologies for the purpose of legitimizing claims to power? Whatever the answer to the question in general, the argument made here is that in post-1992 Russia, socio-economic interests rather than ideas have driven the return to Realist interpretations of the national interest. The following considerations support this argument.

The 'Gorbachev revolution' had elevated a new elite to positions of power and influence. Many of the new actors were young and had made their careers in social and political science and international relations institutes. They were in contact with Western colleagues, spoke foreign languages and had travelled extensively. Their rise to prominence was facilitated by a shift in power to the executive presidency and parliament, relatively free elections, *glasnost'* and *demokratizatsiya*. The Communist Party, unable and unwilling to take a lead in the reform process, was shunted to a siding. The other 'power institutions' – the military, heavy industry, the internal police and the KGB – also lost power and prestige. For the first time in the Soviet era, civilian specialists were able to gain access to, and some leverage over, decision-making on international security matters.

The failure of the August 1991 coup accelerated the process of demoralization and decline of the traditional power elite. The Communist Party was outlawed, the Soviet Union disintegrated and the new elite flocked to the reformist camp under Yeltsin. Protected by presidential power and authority, reformers continued to have a significant role in policy-making: Yegor Gaidar in the overall reform process; Anatoly Chubais in privatization; Boris Fedorov and Andrei Kazmin in financial matters; Andrei Kokoshin in international security; Galina Starovoiteva in nationality affairs; and, of course, Kozyrev and Shelov-Kovediaev in foreign policy. Fatefully, however, the institutionalization of the political and socio-economic reform process had been tenuous. Furthermore, several of the mainstays of Soviet power, although weakened, shaken and adrift, had remained essentially unreformed. This applied first and foremost to the KGB but also to the armed forces, the interior ministry, the military-industrial complex, regional administration and some crucial sectors of the economy, such as agriculture and the oil and gas industry. Their representatives were waiting in the wings for a chance to reassert themselves.

That chance presented itself because of the widespread experience and perception of economic reform as an abysmal failure. Some progress, of course, was made on various dimensions of economic reform.[36] Privatization of industry occurred on a massive scale, prices were freed, export controls were dismantled, market-orientated structures emerged and the rouble stabilized. Yet production fell precipitously in 1992 and 1993, by far exceeding the contraction of the US economy in the Great Depression of the 1930s. Structural readjustment was painfully slow. Investment rates declined. The public international aid effort was high on rhetoric but low on the disbursement of funds.

Most important, however, the shift to the market produced tremendous stress in society. Privatization led to immense discrepancies in income, wealth and economic power. Factory directors of the old regime, conservative regional administrators, influential government officials and members of organized crime groups were able to profit by the new developments and thereby to amass, and ostentatiously to flaunt, huge economic fortunes. The vast majority of the population, in contrast, suffered. This was true in particular for pensioners, blue-collar and farm workers, low and middle-level administrators in central and regional government, and the military. Savings were whittled away by inflation, wages remained unpaid, job insecurity increased and the level of personal safety deteriorated in conjunction with a rise in crime. The absence of a social safety net meant that numerous people were sliding into dismal poverty. As a result, large sections of the population were turning against the reform process. For them, life in the Soviet Union had been more stable, more predictable and more affordable, and the country had been universally respected. They were yearning for a return to a well-ordered life and international respectability.

This mood was exploited to the hilt by nationalists and communists and used as a vehicle for their political comeback. They refused to acknowledge that the communist legacy was primarily responsible for the severe problems of transition towards a new system. Instead, they blamed the reform process itself and the reformers. They attacked the reformers' Western liberal orientation, their atlanticist connections and the 'new thinking', and portrayed the dissolution of the Soviet Union and the Communist Party as part of a huge criminal conspiracy. As for the topic at issue here, they charged that the West was trying to obstruct integration in the CIS and wanted to 'prevent Russia from becoming an economically, politically and militarily influential force and to transform the post-Soviet space into a Western economic and political appendage and its raw material colony'.[37] This approach culminated in the March 1996 resolution of the Duma, which – by a vote of 250 to 98 – declared the dissolution of the Soviet Union legally invalid.

Economic hardship, social stress, disarray and disunity in the government, dissension among political parties, and nationalist and communist propaganda interacted all powerfully and eroded Yeltsin's support in the country. Although the electorate had still been willing to support him in the April 1993 consultative referendum on the government's reform policies, it reacted with cynicism and apathy to the violent confrontation between the executive and the legislature in October of the same year and finally provided the nationalist, conservative, communist and neo-fascist forces with a majority in the December 1993 and 1995 parliamentary elections. The president, sensitive to the realities of power, shifted position – on both policy and personnel.

It is at this point necessary to introduce an important caveat. The advocates and architects of great-power policies and the restoration of the Soviet Union make it appear as if such policies have wide popular support. Such a portrayal of the situation is, however, a gross simplification. It is always difficult in democratic or democratizing countries to ascertain the true meaning of the popular will by means of election results. It is therefore problematic, and often politically fraudulent, to infer from the rejection of one set of policies support for another. The reality of politics is often that everyone, or just about everyone, can agree on what it is they dislike but very few on what they want and – even more to the point – how to go about achieving it. Recent public opinion data would seem to confirm this (see Table 2.1). [38]

The poll results shown in the table reveal that, in popular opinion, ending the war in Chechenia had top priority, followed by the strengthening of law and order and the return of Russia to the status of a great and respected power. However, not only was the support for great-power status and prestige declining, but there was little connection between such a desire and the wish to restore the former Soviet Union.[39]

Table 2.1: Responses to the question 'How can a would-be president win your vote?' (% agreeing; up to five answers allowed, 1996)

	Jan	Feb	Mar
End the war in Chechenia	59	59	60
Strengthen law and order	58	54	51
Return Russia to the status of a great and respected power	54	43	41
Give people back the means of living taken from them by reform	38	36	38
Ensure a fair distribution of income for ordinary people	37	36	36
Press on with reform but with more attention to social protection	35	31	33
Strengthen the role of the state in the economy	37	25	26
Restore the former Soviet Union	13	12	13
Keep Russia on the road of reform	13	11	13
Seek closer ties with the West	6	8	7

Other poll results are consistent with these. The first survey conducted after the Duma had declared the dissolution of the Soviet Union to have been illegal found little support for the resurrection of the Union. Only 14 per cent of the Russian population considered it to be an important task. While 25 per cent of those questioned said the problem deserved some attention, 46 per cent said that since it was impossible to restore the USSR, it would be pointless to devote time to such an aim when it could be spent on more important problems. The same poll found that the Duma vote was supported by less than one-third of those questioned and that 40 per cent of respondents were critical of the move, fearing it would lead only to a deterioration of relations between Russia and the other former Soviet republics.[40] On the basis of such responses, it is fair to conclude that powerful political leaders and groups in Moscow are framing foreign policy issues in such a way as to suit their own purposes.

Policies in the near abroad

To the extent that there is a consensus in Russia about national interests, it is that policies in the near abroad should have top priority. This priority has mainly been interpreted in Moscow as meaning that Russian policy-makers should attempt to achieve some form of 'reintegration' of the post-Soviet geopolitical space. Such attempts have been made, and several instruments are being used in the process. These include the presence of the Russian minority in the newly independent states; the dependence of these states on Russian oil, natural gas and pipelines; Russian military bases, forces and equipment on their territory; the inability of the new states to protect their external borders; and territorial, ethnic and religious conflicts.

The problem which Russia is nevertheless facing in the use of these tools is that the countries in the near abroad, and on the Eurasian continent more generally, differ significantly from one another. They vary in terms of size, population, internal political stability, progress in economic reform, energy dependence, the presence of Russian military bases and forces, and the proportion of ethnic Russians in their midst. Most importantly from the present analytical perspective, they differ in terms of their perceived or actual importance to Russia. It would seem, therefore, that to conduct coherent policies in this area and impose on it a uniform structure is a hopeless endeavour.

Russia's policies have reflected this reality. They have varied from region to region, and even from country to country in the same area. Gaps continue to exist between codifications of the national interest and their realization, rhetoric and practice on the one hand, and ambitions and resources on the other. In Russian policy towards at least some of the areas or countries of the near abroad, the assertive, hegemonist and neo-imperialist bark has been worse than the bite. Furthermore, many actions may have been taken in response to bureaucratic interests in Moscow (e.g. the defence and interior ministries or the security services) or by local actors (units of the armed forces, Cossacks, military districts or regional governors) without the prior knowledge or sanction of the president.

Security 'realism' and economic realities

In his first press conference as foreign minister, in which he reflected on Russian national interests, Primakov also stated that the sovereignty of the former Soviet republics 'cannot negate the need for economic integration'.[41] It may be unfair to impute to this statement the quality of another theory of limited sovereignty. Nevertheless, there are problems with it in the context of his and other Russian leaders' declared objective of 'promoting centripetal tendencies on the territory of the former Soviet Union'.[42]

The first such problem is the discrepancy between political preferences and trade in the CIS. The lion's share of Russia's foreign trade is, and in all likelihood will continue to be in the foreseeable future, with countries *outside* this area. In 1995, its exports to countries other than the newly independent states accounted for 78.4 per cent of the total and imports from these countries for 68.9 per cent.[43] Although Russia's trade with the CIS in that year increased more rapidly than that with other areas, CIS trade statistics released by Russia's State Customs Committee for the first two months of 1996 show both Russia–CIS and intra-CIS trade growing *more slowly* than the overall value of the CIS countries' trade with the outside world. That trend was reported even from the politically loyalist Belarus.[44]

Furthermore, Russia was incurring a *deficit* in its overall trade with the CIS countries, despite its position as energy supplier. The January–February 1996 deficit, $124 million out of a total $5.2 billion Russia–CIS turnover, grew from the statistically insignificant deficit which Russia posted for the first time ever in CIS trade in the last quarter of 1995. Russian imports from CIS countries in January–February 1996 grew by 50 per cent in value, far outstripping the 21 per cent growth in exports – in spite of peak winter energy deliveries. These circumstances suggest that Russian deficits in CIS trade may be turning from a new phenomenon into a trend. Moscow may be tempted to respond by raising protectionist barriers, as it has already done for some major categories of goods despite free trade agreements with CIS partners.[45]

The second problem lies in 'centripetalism'. If economic integration is put into this context, by definition a centre is required – and, possibly, centralism. This carries the risk of a return to what went under the name of 'harmonization of national economic plans' in the Council for Mutual Economic Assistance

(CMEA). It poses yet again the dangers of protectionism, barter trade and subsidization in the service of political interests and strategic objectives. What would seem to be required instead is horizontal rather than vertical integration: the adoption and implementation of a comprehensive package of measures such as unambiguous respect for the independence and territorial integrity of the countries of the CIS and the Baltic states; encouragement of market-orientated reforms; and involvement of Western private investors, governments and international organizations in the reform process. Not only is such a package lacking, its compilation is being deliberately obstructed.

Third, reintegration driven by a centre and emphasis on the political and security aspects of integration benefit the military-industrial complex and impede structural reforms towards a more civilian and consumer-orientated economy. If the armed forces and defence industrialists can shift the agenda in the near abroad towards integrated armed forces, it is obvious that more resources than previously will have to be spent on a network of military bases in the CIS, a single air defence system, joint exercises, common border patrols and standardized weapons. Until now, the armed forces and the military-industrial complex have not fared very well in Moscow's budgetary battles. But they have at least succeeded in arresting the momentum of defence conversion and contraction of arms production and sales.

Fourth, although the application of military-political pressures and manipulation of regional conflicts, notably in the Transcaucasus and Central Asia, will undoubtedly benefit the Russian oil and gas industry, such policies tend to harm economic development and political independence in the countries concerned and to complicate the pursuit of regional stability. They also put brakes on Russia's economic development. While it has been man-oeuvring to regain control over the exploration, production and transportation of oil and natural gas in the near abroad, hoping to secure a dominant position for itself, Russia's own energy industry is a shambles. Oil output is at about half of its mid-1980s peak, and it has taken the country several years finally to enact a production-sharing law, which is still inadequate and unlikely to encourage major Western investment in the Russian energy sector.

Conclusion

In one of the more balanced portrayals of Russian foreign policy, Primakov denied that the foreign ministry had developed no clear strategic concept in the previous five years. 'There has been a concept, and its objective was to end the Cold War by improving relations with the former adversaries.'[46] He also defined Russia's national interests as being the retention of its territorial integrity, provision of foreign policy conditions for economic progress, and advancement of the democratic process in the country.[47] Such sound and sensible views of Russian national interests are unfortunately exceptional. The rule in Moscow at present is simplistic Realist notions of international politics and security, put forward stridently and uncompromisingly, with 'the promotion of the integration processes on CIS territory' as the central focus of national objectives.[48]

The problem with this rule does not rest in the emergence of a consistently applied policy of reintegration of the former Union republics. Nor does it consist in lavish subsidization of imperial holdings, or in overcommitment and overengagement. It lies rather in opportunities lost, time wasted, efforts misdirected, resources reallocated from economic reform to military security, and priorities recast from internal transformation in Russia to restoration of control in the near abroad. It can, finally, be found in the danger that the gap that still exists between the assertive neo-imperialist rhetoric and a more sober and pragmatic policy will be closed.

There are other problems with the current Russian debate and policies in the near abroad. It is disappointing to realize that foreign policy-makers are not only apt to learn but prone to unlearn. One would have liked to think that memories were not so short that the foreign policy elite could forget that the Realist approach had led Soviet foreign policy into a dead end, and that democratization and empire, whether in a near or a far abroad, are incompatible.

Yet another problem with current strands of thinking and policy is their lack of moral quality. One may choose to disregard such excesses as Zhirinovsky's threat to build giant fans to blow radioactive waste towards the Baltic states. But even more responsible attitudes and policies towards the countries of the near abroad reveal an astonishing disregard for the history of tsarist colonization, Soviet repression and Russian ethnic domination. In Moscow today, there is little empathy but many double standards. Cases in point are demands for dual citizenship and claims for the protection of rights of Russians and Russian-speakers in neighbouring countries. Of course, Russian nationalists would consider it to be a preposterous provocation if Ukraine were to assert a right of intervention for ethnic Ukrainians, or Germany for the Volga Germans, in Russia.

One of the many rationalizations of Russia's shift to a new assertiveness is that such a return was inevitable because it was impossible to expect it to remain 'subservient' to,[49] and to 'subordinate' its interests in the near abroad to, cooperative Russian relations with the West. Such rationalizations are a gross misrepresentation of Western intentions and wide of the mark. They proceed from the erroneous assumption, to use the political science jargon, that the games that can be played in the near abroad are exclusively of a 'zero-sum' variety, where one side's gains are the other side's losses. Images such as these ignore the fact that in a sensibly constructed common approach everyone stands to gain – Russia, the newly independent states and the West. It is not subservience and subordination that are needed, but cooperation and coordination of policies.

Notes

1. The Russian quest for 'great power' status was explored by the present author in 'Russia as a "Great Power" in World Affairs: Images and Reality', *International Affairs*, vol. 71, no. 1, January 1995, pp. 35–68.
2. Reuters, 12 January 1996.
3. Sergei Stankevich, 'Derzhava v poiskakh sebya', *Nezavisimaya gazeta*, 28 March 1992. At the time, Stankevich was 'state counsellor' and adviser to President Yeltsin.
4. Text of the Russian sovereignty declaration, as published in *Vedomosti RSFSR*, 14 June 1990.
5. See the apt description and analysis by John Löwenhardt, 'The Foreign Policy of the Russian Federation', unpublished paper presented to the international symposium in Tokyo, November 1991.
6. *Diplomaticheskiy vestnik*, nos 4–5, 19 February–15 March 1992, p. 49.
7. 'Obnovlennaya Rossiya i obnovlennaya Evropa. K poezdke B.N. Yeltsina vo Frantsiyu' (interview with G. Burbulis), *Rossiyskaya gazeta*, 20 April 1991.
8. 'Preobrazhenie ili kafkyanskaya metamorfoza', *Nezavisimaya gazeta*, 20 August 1992; similarly in an interview with *Izvestiya*, 10 October 1991.
9. *Nezavisimaya gazeta*, 1 April 1992.
10. *Komsomol'skaya pravda*, 14 March 1991.
11. Interview with Russian foreign minister Kozyrev conducted by Vladimir Kolistikov, 28 January 1992, Foreign Broadcast Information Service, *Soviet Union, Daily Report*, 30 January 1992.
12. The latter figure is mentioned, for instance, in the 'programme' formulated in the Russian foreign ministry 'for the protection of 30 million Russians in the near abroad'; see 'Moskva razrabotala programmu za zashchitu 30 millionov russkikh v blizhnem zarubezh'e', *Izvestiya*, 17 February 1994.
13. Interfax news agency, 17 July 1992; for details about the plans for the creation of a separate CIS ministry see Suzanne Crow, 'Russia Prepares to Take a Hard Line on the "Near Abroad"', RFE/RL *Research Report*, vol. 1, no. 32, 14 August 1992.
14. As summarized by Leszek Buszynski, 'Russia and the West: Towards Renewed Geopolitical Rivalry?', *Survival*, vol. 37, no. 3, Autumn 1995, p. 107.
15. Skokov fell from presidential grace and resigned from his post of head of the Security Council in May 1993.
16. 'Partiya voiny nastupaet', *Izvestiya*, 30 June 1992. The portrayal of Skokov's rise to power and influence in the summer of 1992 is based on Buszynski, 'Russia and the West', p. 112.
17. Interfax (Moscow), 21 February 1992, reported the content of the document but did not explicitly say that it had been issued by the foreign ministry; see Suzanne Crow, 'Russia Debates its National Interest', RFE/RL *Research Report*, vol. 1, no. 28, 10 July 1992.
18. The documents were entitled 'On Basic Directions of the Foreign Policy Activities of Russia and the Activities of the Ministry of Foreign Affairs of the Russian Federation' and 'On International Relations and the Foreign Policy of Russia, Report by the Ministry of Foreign Affairs of the Russian Federation to the Sixth Congress of People's Deputies of Russia' (both unpublished).
19. 'Foreign Policy Concept of the Russian Federation' (mimeograph); on the background of the foreign policy concept's origins and content see *Nezavisimaya gazeta*, 21 October 1992.
20. *Diplomaticheskiy vestnik*, January 1993.
21. 'Strategiya dlya Rossii. Nekotorye tezisy dlya doklada Soveta po vneshney i oboronnoy politike', *Nezavisimaya gazeta*, 19 August 1992. Nominally, foreign minister Kozyrev was one of the 37 members. Other members have included (positions listed are the most recent known to this author) deputy director of the Institute on Europe at the Russian Academy of Sciences Sergei Karaganov; deputy foreign minister Anatoly Adamyshin; Duma deputy Evgeny Ambartsumov; first deputy defence minister Andrei Kokoshin; chief of general staff of the Russian armed forces Col.-Gen. Kolesnikov; Duma foreign affairs committee

chairman Vladimir Lukin; Duma deputy and presidential adviser Sergei Stankevich; chief of the Russian counterintelligence agency Lt.-Gen. Stepashin; vice-premier Sergei Shakhrai; president of the Russian Union of Industrialists and Entrepreneurs Arkady Volsky; Duma deputy and chairman of the Centre for Economic and Political Research Grigory Yavlinsky; and chairman of the Duma CIS Affairs Committee Konstantin Zatulin.

22. The only publicly available summary of its origins and content is by Vladislav Chernov, 'Natsional'nye interesy Rossii i ugrozy dlya ee bezopasnosti', *Nezavisimaya gazeta*, 29 April 1993. The author is deputy head of the department for strategic security at the Russian Security Council. The commission included foreign minister Andrei Kozyrev, defence minister Pavel Grachev, security minister Viktor Barannikov, head of external intelligence Yevgeny Primakov, external trade minister Sergei Galiev, interior minister Gen. Viktor Yerin, chief of general staff Mikhail Kolesnikov, and UN representative Yuly Vorontsov. Representatives from the Supreme Soviet, the armed forces and other government agencies were also involved.

23. In an address to the Russian foreign ministry, Interfax (Moscow), 28 October 1992.

24. For instance, Kozyrev was on record as having said that 'Russia's main foreign policy priority is relations with our partners in the Commonwealth of Independent States'; see his article, 'Russia: Chance for Survival', *Foreign Affairs*, vol. 52, no. 2, Spring 1992, pp. 1–16. The foreign ministry's draft foreign policy concept also contained references to that effect. Kozyrev was to state later that he devoted 'more than 70 per cent' of his time in office to CIS affairs: Andrei Kozyrev, 'Otkrovennaya diplomatiya', *Argumenti i fakti*, no. 23, June 1993 (interview with V. Starkov, chief editor of the journal).

25. Buszynski, 'Russia and the West', p. 113.

26. See the text of the document, 'Osnovnye polozheniya voennoy doktriny Rossiyskoy Federatsii', *Rossiyskie vesti*, 18 November 1993.

27. Ibid.

28. Yeltsin's speech to the Civic Union, as reported on Moscow television, 28 February 1993, FBIS, *Soviet Union, Daily Report*, 1 March 1993 (italics added).

29. This is true even for such reasonable and sensible international affairs specialists with extensive Western exposure as Alexei Arbatov. He has suggested a trade-off, the 'West leaving the CIS to Russia, and Moscow following the Western lead in other areas'; see his 'Russian National Interests', in Robert D. Blackwill and Sergei A. Karaganov, eds, *Damage Limitation or Crisis? Russia and the Outside World*, CSIA Studies in International Security, no. 5 (Washington, DC: Brassey's, 1994), p. 76, n. 28.

30. Interview with *Izvestiya*, 8 October 1993.

31. Interfax (Moscow), 18 January 1994.

32. Ibid.

33. *Rossiyskie vesti*, 7 April 1994.

34. As reported in detail by Steven Erlanger, 'Yeltsin's On-and-Off Decrees on Bases Cloud the Policy Outlook', *New York Times*, 8 April 1994.

35. 'Ob utverzhdenii strategicheskogo kursa Rossiyskoy Federatsii s gosudarstvami-uchastnikami Sodruzhestva Nezavisimykh Gosudarstv', 14 September 1995, *Dipkur'er* (Moscow), nos 16/18, August 1995, pp. 75–83.

36. Anders Åslund is the chief exponent of this point of view; see his 'Russia's Success Story', *Foreign Affairs*, vol. 37, no. 5, September/October 1994, pp. 58–71.

37. This is the view expressed in a lengthy report drafted by the Institute for Defence Studies (INOBIS), a thinktank closely associated with the military-industrial complex and headed by General Viktor Surikov. The report was published in *Segodnya*, 20 October 1995.

38. The polls were conducted by the All-Russian Central Institute for Public Opinion (Vserossiyskiy Tsentral'nyy Institut Obshchestvennogo Mneniya, or VTsIOM) in January, February and March 1996; the results are reproduced here from *The Economist*, 30 March 1996.

39. The results concerning the low priority given to closer ties with the West are consistent with an earlier poll conducted at the beginning of December 1993. Fifty-four per cent of the respondents were either sure or thought it possible that the West aimed at economically weakening Russia; see *Za rubezhom*, no. 5, 1994, p. 3.

40. Russian radio, 1 April 1996, as reported by Jamestown Foundation, *Monitor: A Daily Briefing on the Post-Soviet States*, 4 April 1996.

41. Agence France-Presse, 12 January 1996.

42. Primakov considered this to be 'the foreign ministry's main task now': Vremya news programme, Russian television, 12 May 1996.

43. According to data compiled by the US embassy in Moscow and transmitted by the Russia/CIS Division, US Department of Commerce.

44. Jamestown Foundation, *Monitor,* vol. 2, no. 84, 13 May 1996.

45. Ibid., based on reports by Itar-TASS, Interfax and *Delovaya Rossiya*, 11 May 1996.

46. Interview in *Komsomol'skaya pravda*, 21 March 1996.

47. Ibid.

48. Ibid. In contrast to many of Primakov's previous portrayals of Russian national interests, however, his statement on this occasion did not list the CIS as being central. This may have been, in part, a reaction to the Duma vote on the dissolution of the USSR as having been illegal.

49. Arbatov, 'Russian National Interests', p. 75.

3 The Russian army in politics

Hans-Henning Schröder

The political forces that gained the upper hand in the Soviet successor states after the liquidation of Soviet statehood at the end of 1991 are now facing the difficult task of building a new order from the ruins of the old. One of the most pressing elements of this task is the integration of the oversized military and security apparatus of the dissolved USSR into the newly emerging political system, and its subjection to the control of democratically legitimized institutions. In the period of transition, the *silovye struktury* – the power structures, i.e. the regular armed forces, the units of the ministry of the interior and the security service, all of which are under the command of people who were socialized during the Soviet era – are a political factor which no government can afford to neglect.

During the difficult transitional period the role played by the armed forces is strangely ambivalent. They guarantee the continuation of Russian statehood and a certain stability; at the same time, however, they constitute a latent threat to democratic development, at least as long as they are not subject to efficient political control. The attempted coup of August 1991, the Moscow autumn crisis of 1993, the conflicts in Nagorno-Karabakh, Abkhazia, Moldova and Chechenia – all these events demonstrated to what degree the governing bodies depend on the support of the military and the internal security organs. This is precisely the reason why the political leadership must, on the one hand, address itself to satisfying the social needs of the military and security apparatus, and, on the other, adapt that apparatus to the new conditions by drastically reducing its size and subjecting it to efficient control. In the face of economic decline and the smouldering crisis of the political system, this task is tantamount to squaring the circle.

The military as a power factor

There are two reasons why the armed forces constitute a primary power factor within Russian society: their ability to use direct force, and their existence as an electorate that can be mobilized through military issues.

By definition, the military wields direct control over the state's instruments of power in the form of troops and weapon systems. This control is of much more than mere theoretical importance. On at least three recent occasions, the conduct of the armed forces determined the outcome of internal political conflicts. The attempted coup of August 1991 failed because important elements within the military leadership – in particular, Grachev and Shaposhnikov – refused to have their troops engage in a civil war. In December 1991, Yeltsin and Gorbachev addressed the military leadership appointed after the August coup and asked them whether or not they were prepared to use force in order to preserve the USSR. The negative response of the military paved the way for the peaceful dissolution of the Soviet state. And despite the fact that during the constitutional crisis of 1992 and 1993, the military leadership tried its best to maintain a neutral stance, in the end, and after much hesitation, it did make the decision to use force against the parliament. The violent intervention of the armed forces at the 'White House' on 3 October 1993 decided the constitutional conflict in favour of the president.

On all these occasions it was typical for the military not to take the political initiative. The armed forces' leadership insisted on the principle of the army 'standing outside politics'.

However, during the years 1991–3, various political groups were constantly trying to bring the military over to their side. In this way, the military was manoeuvred into positions where it had to act politically, whether it wished to or not. In the 'near abroad', the situation was a little different. At least for some periods of time, the Russian commanders gave the impression of carrying out their own policies. The conduct of the 14th Army in Moldova and that of Russian troops dealing with the conflict between Georgia and Abkhazia seemed not always to be in tune with the position of the foreign minister and the president. Outsiders were unable to discern clearly whether the defence ministry and the chief of general staff were following their own policy with the aim of securing Russian hegemony over the CIS or whether local commanders were making independent decisions of their own. In any event the armed forces were of great importance in some crisis situations in the near abroad, gaining a key position through their capability to use force, to deploy troops or weapon systems or simply to threaten to make use of them.

In addition, in the eyes of the Russian political elite the military possesses a certain weight because of the potentially large numbers of voters that can be mobilized through military issues. This became particularly evident during the campaign leading up to the Duma elections in December 1995. For Western observers it came as a surprise to see how many political parties and election groupings hoped to gain an advantage by bringing high-ranking officers to the forefront of their campaigns. For example, Rybkin's centre-left bloc associated itself at least temporarily with Boris Gromov, the last commander-in-chief of Russian forces in Afghanistan, who had been removed from the defence ministry and given an advisory position in the ministry of foreign affairs. He was presented as the top candidate of the election bloc 'My Fatherland'. For his election bloc 'Our Home is Russia', Chernomyrdin won over Lev Rokhlin, commander of the Russian troops deployed in Chechenia. And Polevano's 'New Russia' bloc was said to have contacts with Yevgeny Podkolzin, commander of the airborne troops. An All-Russian Officers' Assembly consisting of extremely conservative officers pledged support for opposition politicians such as Zyuganov, Skokov, Glaziev and Zhirinovsky.[1] Zyuganov, leader of the Communist Party of the Russian Federation, made a personal appearance at the first press conference of this group. The best-known military officer among the general public, Aleksandr Lebed, however, was won over by the 'Congress of Russian Communities' led by Skokov. Lebed, until recently commander of the 14th Army in Moldova, enjoyed great popularity within and outside the army thanks to his skilful handling of the media and his vocal criticism of the president and defence minister.

During the election campaign of 1995, almost all parties and election blocs placed their hopes in active as well as retired high-ranking officers. Apparently, they started from the assumption that the military would help them gain access to potentially large numbers of voters. During the campaign, the weekly *Moskovskie novosti* published a calculation showing that up to one-third of the voters were connected with the military in one way or another: in addition to about 7 million soldiers and their families, there were some 7–9 million employees in the defence industry with their families, and finally some 20–21 million demobilized soldiers and veterans with their relatives – all in all, around 35 million out of the 110 million voters.[2] Even if this estimate is too high, Russian politicians were definitely of the opinion that a quantitatively significant group of voters could be influenced by military policies and attitudes towards soldiers.

The armed forces as a political actor

Given that the Russian political establishment attaches great importance to the stance of the military and that in recent years the military has indeed exerted considerable influence on Russian domestic and foreign policy, we need to ask how the armed forces themselves perceive their role, whether they see themselves as an independent political actor or rather as an instrument of the political leadership. Closely connected to this are the questions whether the armed forces stand for their own institutionally motivated interests, whether they speak with one voice or whether and to what extent the soldiers can be found in opposite political camps, since this will inevitably affect the true weight the armed forces can bring to bear on the process of decision-making.

Institutional interests and interservice rivalry

It is certainly correct to assume that so large and bureaucratic an organization as the armed forces represents institutional interests. Moreover, there are also points of convergence in the fundamental political views of its constituent elements, given the relatively homogeneous socialization of the leading cadres throughout their careers as officers.

With regard to security policy, for instance, there is a basic consensus on the essential elements necessary for the defence of the territory of the Russian Federation against potential threats. Among these elements are maintaining nuclear parity with the United States and safeguarding the strategic glacis. The first objective requires increased financial resources for nuclear and space research; the second is closely connected to the endeavour to preserve the CIS as a 'unified strategic region'. Bilateral military agreements with the individual republics, plans for a collective security system within the framework of the CIS and other activities in the CIS all aim at re-establishing a common air defence, maintaining effective early warning systems and establishing a well-functioning system of leadership.

In questions of social security and financing, too, the military acts in support of collective interests that conflict with those of other groups and organizations. Its main objectives are to guarantee the economic security and well-being of the armed forces and their relatives and to preserve their prestige and social standing. Furthermore, all the armed forces are united in the desire to achieve their 'organizational objective' – in other words, to maintain and build up their fighting capabilities and to proceed with reforms. All of this requires a state order that functions smoothly. Thus, all military men speaking up in public advocate a stable and strong government. All plead for preserving an army that is well taken care of and in possession of full fighting strength. All ask for the necessary means to guarantee the armed forces' economic security and regular maintenance. Moreover, they request additional funding without which the development and acquisition of modern weapon systems are impossible.

As a result of the difficulties in the transition process, however, the armed forces face enormous problems in all of these areas. The daily subsistence of the soldiers is not guaranteed everywhere, and salaries are often paid only after several months' delay. The question of living quarters is unresolved.[3] Regular training cannot be kept up since there are insufficient funds for fuel and spare parts. Pilots spend only 30–40 hours in the air per year instead of the required 180–260. Fewer and fewer modern weapon systems are procured. In 1994, the air force received no more than 50 aircraft; in 1995 the figure was less than half that.[4] Faced with this situation, the Russian armed forces are not completely fit for action and their morale is poor. Against this background, it is more than understandable that all factions within the military demand additional funds and that it is their common concern to push through a higher defence budget. It is this that puts the military in opposition to other interest groups, for example the agrarians, the fuel and energy complex and in part also the defence industries.

While it is true that all factions within the armed forces stand together when it comes to fighting for budgetary funds and securing their position on Russia's international status as a military power, it is also true that the scarcity of funds creates fertile ground for conflicts within the military. The fundamentally changed situation in Europe on the one hand, and the grave economic crisis in Russia itself on the other both make thorough reform of the armed forces essential. A drastic reduction in the size of the army and radical restructuring in all three services are needed to adapt the Russian armed forces to their new environment and maintain their fighting strength. The majority of the leadership and the officers, however, blocked genuine military reform because far-reaching cuts would mean the end of many of their careers. General Igor Rodionov, the newly appointed minister of defence, made a serious attempt to initiate a reform of the military;[5] but from the start he met with great difficulties. The extensive restructuring of the armed forces called for considerable financial means which he did not possess. In addition, the debates led to conflicts between different branches and he had to step in to try to mediate among them. The navy believes that it is being pushed aside by the ground forces, while the spokesmen of the armoured troops are angry about the role the airborne troops want to play within the proposed new mobile forces. These conflicting interests certainly weaken the military's position when it comes to securing a fair share of the budget.

Political fault lines within the armed forces

There is also an emotional factor which should not be overlooked: a basic conservative political orientation shared by many officers. Their sympathy for political forces tending more to the right became apparent as early as the election of December 1993: the percentage of professional officers and non-commissioned officers (*praporshchiki*) voting for right-wing conservative factions such as Zhirinovsky's Liberal Democratic Party was considerably higher than the average of all voters.[6] However, it was also apparent that a cleavage existed within the armed forces: in 1993, the rank and file – whether conscripts or *kontraktniki* (soldiers serving for a fixed period) – voted to a significantly lesser degree than officers for the extreme right. The election results prove that the armed forces as a whole are not a politically homogeneous group. There are fault lines separating the political preferences of different military ranks, often coinciding with different generations.

One can do no more than speculate on the reasons why a strong group of officers and NCOs supported Zhirinovsky's party at the end of 1993. Presumably, a combination of factors was involved. One element seems to have been a wish to register a protest against a political leadership which unscrupulously used the military for political ends. Another factor was Zhirinovsky's clever appeal to nationalistic emotions. Opinion polls, too, confirm the impression gained from reading the military press that the officer corps is dominated by national and conservative sentiments. Most officers dream of a strong state incorporating at least Russia, Ukraine, Belarus and Kazakstan.[7] National and imperial ideas are mixed with calls for a strong state capable of enforcing law and order. Still, the majority of officers are realistic enough to know that there is no going back to the old USSR and that there are major obstacles in the way of unification of the CIS.

The military shows realism, too, in assessing its own role. Only a minority of the officers interviewed at the beginning of 1995 (16 per cent) considered the armed forces to be a political force which could lead the state and maintain law and order. A slightly more numerous group (23 per cent) still clung on to the traditional image of the unpolitical soldier, while a higher proportion (41 per cent) took into account the experience of the preceding four years during which the army was called in time and again to help solve political conflicts.[8] The opinion poll does not reveal a great willingness on the part of the military to take control of the state itself, but is evidence of a general feeling of resignation over the failure of the civilian government to organize a well-functioning political system. This atmosphere intensified after the Duma elections in December 1995 and the presidential elections in the summer of 1996, when neither the new Duma nor the renewed Yeltsin administration took any steps to improve the situation of the armed forces. The new defence minister, Rodionov, initiated an aggressive media campaign in order to draw public attention to the social problems of the soldiers, but his lobbying succeeded only in aggravating the whole situation.[9]

Resignation and disappointment at the failure of the Yeltsin leadership seem to have marked the attitude of many officers in 1994–6. In the preliminaries to the Duma elections of 1995, about one-third of the officers declared their intention to boycott the poll. An equal number wanted to vote for military candidates only. Among the younger officers and the NCOs the proportion of those not intending to go to the polls was even higher, at 40 per cent. On the other hand, only 22–25 per cent of this group declared they wanted to vote for military candidates only.[10] In 1995, too, the basic nationalist and conservative political trend prevailed. Opinion polls revealed that among the officers corps, politicians to the right of the centre enjoyed much more confidence than leftist or liberal ones. Zhirinovsky, the leader of the Liberal Democrats, Lapshin, the president of the Agrarian Party, and the leader of the Communist Party, Zyuganov, were at the top of the list while the reformists Gaidar and Rybkin were low down.[11] It is noteworthy that the popularity of two politicians from the centre of the spectrum – Chernomyrdin and Yavlinsky – has undergone a dramatic change among the military. While Chernomyrdin lost some ground during the summer (one of the reasons possibly being the part he played in the Budennovsk hostages crisis), Yavlinsky climbed to second place in popularity. His image as a man combining authority, competence and the will to reform seems to appeal to a strong minority of officers.

Thus, there are contradictions within the political profile of the officer corps. The most dominant views are a mixture of imperial, anti-capitalist and anti-Western sentiments. But there exists no consensus, nor even strong support for a more important role in politics for the military. Reform-orientated politicians such as Yavlinsky, with their combination of authority and competence, are acceptable to at least some of the officers. It is not clear from the available information whether or not political attitudes have changed since the foundation of the post-Soviet Russian armed forces in the spring of 1991. There is an impression, however, that the growing polarization of society, the doubts about the Yeltsin leadership, the climate of corruption and, last but not least, the continuing material uncertainties have all contributed to an increasing disappointment with the regime.

Representatives of political opinions within the armed forces

Against the background of these generally conservative, although not uniform, political tendencies among the officer corps, the political differences discernible in public statements made by high-ranking military men become more significant. The very fact that during the elections in December 1995 practically every list included well-known generals made it clear to everyone that there exist a number of factions within the military leadership pursuing different political objectives.

In 1995, the group around Grachev exerted great influence. It occupied key positions in the defence ministry but had been subject to increasing criticism from the general public since 1994. Grachev, whose attitude was responsible for the failure of the August coup in 1991, became defence minister of Russia in the spring of 1992. Under his leadership the general staff and the top echelons of the defence ministry were able to build Russian armed forces from the remnants of the Soviet armed forces. The most urgent problems were successfully resolved, namely the establishment of effective control over the troops, the enforcement at unit level of commands given by the headquarters, and the withdrawal of troops stationed abroad. The reorganization of the defence ministry led to a thorough rejuvenation of the military leadership. Grachev was able to keep the armed forces out of political conflicts for almost two years. But the deployment of troops against the parliament in October 1993 and the invasion of Chechenia in December 1994, plus a series of unexplained corruption scandals, cost him his credibility within the armed forces as well as among the public. Some prominent generals, such as Gromov, Mironov and Lebed, spoke out against him in public. His remaining political support came from his closeness to the president, to whose inner circle he seemed to have belonged temporarily. In the summer of 1996, the president finally dismissed Grachev and, after some hesitation, replaced him with Rodionov, an officer highly respected in the army who is closer to the conservative camp politically and who was at first seen as General Lebed's protégé.

The defence minister apart, it was the chief of general staff, Mikhail Kolesnikov, who in the years before his replacement in autumn 1996 began most markedly to emphasize his own independent position. He was able to rely on a functioning apparatus which could look back to four years of considerable achievement. The general staff worked out the outlines of a military doctrine, drew up strategic and operational blueprints adapted to the new situation, produced concepts for future armaments and the revision of military law, and reformed the programmes for military training. Its authority is based on its professional competence. Spokesmen of the general staff have always limited their comments strictly to questions of military and security policy. Since the end of 1994, the general staff has appeared to maintain a certain distance from the defence ministry.

In the spring and summer of 1995, a number of officers close to the general staff advocated a restructuring of the highest military-political authority. This reorganization would withdraw operational control over the armed forces from the defence ministry and put it into the hands of the general staff, which in turn would be under the direct command of the president. This can be interpreted as an attempt to prevent the group around Grachev from influencing military policies. After Grachev's dismissal the general staff was also replaced, and Viktor Samsonov (chief of staff for military coordination within the CIS and a former first deputy defence minister of the USSR) replaced Kolesnikov. This change of personnel, however, seems to have made no difference in the basic attitude of the general staff.

When assessing political actors in the armed forces one should not overlook the individual military men who have come into public view and who seem to follow their own independent political course. The best known among them now is Aleksandr Lebed, the former commander of the 14th Army in Moldova. Within his area of command, Lebed behaved at times like a true warlord, using his military power to meddle in policy-making without any restraint. He even held out against attempts to constrain his conduct from the centre in Moscow.

General Lebed belongs to the generation of officers who gained their most important operational experiences in Afghanistan. In the course of this war, many of the commanders came to the conclusion that military action in low-intensity warfare can lead to success only if it is embedded in the local political context. Commanders in Afghanistan maintained contacts with local rulers wherever possible and adapted their actions to the conditions on the spot. Commands from Moscow or Kabul often bore little relation to the situation at the front and, as the war proceeded, military commanders came to see them as obstacles.[12] These experiences created a type of 'political soldier' who learned to act independently in order to fulfil military tasks. In this respect this 'Afghanistan generation' of officers is reminiscent of the French colonels during the Indochina and Algerian wars. Lebed's conduct in Moldova clearly stems from his experiences in Afghanistan.

Such a situation entails considerable risks: one of the military leaders on the spot could elude political control to become a regional warlord, or a group of officers (like the colonels in the Algerian war) could try to take over the government themselves. In the case of Lebed, however, the defence minister was able to prevail and dismiss the general from his post. Lebed left the army to pursue an active political career. In the first ballot of the presidential elections in June 1996, he succeeded beyond expectation, receiving the third largest share of the vote. As a consequence, the Yeltsin administration offered him the positions of secretary of the Security Council and presidential national security adviser. But Lebed held these positions for only three months before he was dismissed from them, partly because the popularity he gained from brokering a firm ceasefire in Chechenia was politically threatening to Yeltsin's influential entourage.[13]

The breeding ground for political generals like Lebed consists of an officer corps which is extremely dissatisfied with its situation and which has become increasingly critical of the political and military leadership of the country. According to an opinion poll conducted by the German Friedrich-Ebert-Stiftung in the summer of 1994, 52 per cent of the officers interviewed distrusted the defence minister, Grachev. His rival, Gromov, was rejected by only 17 per cent.[14] A similar picture is presented by a poll conducted by Russian military sociologists in the summer of 1995.[15] While the chief of general staff enjoyed a high personal and professional reputation among the large majority of those interviewed, the defence minister was accepted as a person of authority by only one-fifth of the officers. A general of almost Bonapartist calibre, Lebed was seen as possessing only limited professional competence, but personally he scored comparatively well. Thus a large majority of officers had their reservations about the defence minister, while in contrast, a personality like Lebed had the potential to be entrusted with political hopes. The officer corps was by no means a puppet in the hands of Grachev, even if in general it is still integrated into a functioning system of military obedience.

This short survey shows clearly that the Russian armed forces did not speak with one voice. There were a number of individuals and groups who acted politically – at times even against one another – and who relied more or less on support from officers. So far, none of these factions within the armed forces has tried to make use of the military instrument in order to push through its own interests. In 1996, however, discontent among the officers rose considerably. In the autumn, voices were heard calling again, as in 1992, for an all-Russian assembly of officers to provide political expression for the officers' grievances.[16] Published opinion polls indicate that more officers are now prepared to use violence and to organize themselves to defend what they regard as military interests. On the other hand, resignations from the armed forces have also become more widespread: almost 40 per cent of the officers interviewed wanted to leave the armed forces.[17]

Military influence upon Russian politics

Despite the fact that the majority of officers follow national conservative tendencies, and different factions within the army are united by a strong common interest in maintaining well-functioning armed forces, until 1995 the military had not come out actively and in a concerted manner in favour of any particular political objectives. In the process of political decision-making the military have appeared to play a rather secondary role, and quite often were not even capable of pushing through measures to protect their own vital interests. This is clearly apparent when assessing the influence of the military in situations where critical political decisions had to be made. Three examples will be given here, namely the passing of the military budget, the amendment of the conscription law and the issue of the eastward enlargement of NATO.[18] In each case, the issue concerned the core question of how to develop further the armed forces, and also brought the military into conflict with other interest groups.

An increase in the military budget would have consequences not only for the stabilization of the economy on the basis of a successfully implemented policy of 'scarce money' and the reduction of the budget deficit, but also for the funding of social as well as industrial and agrarian policies. On the other hand, the question of military funding was of key importance for the armed forces. The size of the military budget passed by the parliament and its disbursement by the ministry of finance would determine the performance of the armed forces and the social security of the individual soldier. But in its fight for financial means the military had to compete with other important and influential groups. The agrarian and energy-complex lobbies were particularly well organized and pushed aside representatives of the military leadership who had little experience in working within parliamentary committees. The secrecy of the military leadership, who revealed only parts of their expenditure plans, and the lack of a convincing concept for military reform, confirmed the tendency among most of the Duma delegates to reject military demands.[19]

Consequently, the sums earmarked for defence purposes in 1993 and 1994 were well below those sought by the military. Moreover, even these amounts were disbursed only in part. The ministry of finance coupled expenditure with revenue and cut individual budget entitlements accordingly;[20] here the defence ministry fared badly, receiving clearly less than the budgetary average. In the struggle for the allocation of resources in 1994 and 1995, therefore, the defence ministry met with little success. It failed to convince the parliament of its point of view and was not even able to ensure that the ministry of finance paid out the sums that had been legally approved. It is true that the budget for 1996 allowed the situation within the armed forces to stabilize somewhat and that the ministry of finance, in fulfilling the budget, treated the defence ministry with more consideration than in previous years; nevertheless, in comparison with other powerful ministries, the defence ministry still fared very poorly.[21]

The amendment of the conscription law in the spring of 1995 presents a slightly different picture. Unsurprisingly, an expansion of conscription and an extension of the compulsory military service term was not going to meet with much enthusiasm among the young men concerned and their parents, especially since the military leadership seemed incapable of controlling daily violence in the barracks. The old law provided for a whole range of categories – most importantly, students – to be exempted from military service. The result was that only one-quarter of a generation of conscripts was actually called to arms, and in general only youths from the lower classes. Officers spoke cynically of the new 'Peasants' and Workers' Army' because sons of the elite were in general able to avoid conscription quite legally. The armed forces, for their part, complained about the small number and low qualifications of their personnel.[22] In response to complaints by the military leadership the military service term was extended by law and the possibility of having one's service deferred was significantly diminished. On paper, the military had clearly achieved its political objective.[23] In practice, however, there was considerable opposition to this change and soon a number of amendments had been presented to the president. Furthermore, the final passage of the law was delayed for some time by objections raised by the Federation Council (the upper house of the parliament). In the end, however, the military leadership was able to have its way. Undoubtedly, one of the reasons for this success was the fact that the material interests of strong lobbies were not affected, and that the annoyance of conscripts and their parents was not politically significant enough to offset the weight of military opinion.

One area in which the military leadership still exerts considerable influence is the formulation of national security policy,[24] not least because in this respect it is in possession of an information monopoly. In the case of the enlargement of NATO, public statements made by leading military men speaking out against the Western policy – and thereby implicitly also criticizing the former foreign minister Kozyrev – played more than a marginal role.[25] It must be stated, however, that these comments differed only in nuance from statements made by civilian critics of Russian foreign policy.[26] Even the 'new realism' of Russian security policy, as evinced in harsh comments by former defence minister Rodionov on the implications of NATO enlargement, is not monopolized by the military, but has been expressed in similar terms by Foreign Minister Primakov as well as politicians in the president's entourage. It is questionable, therefore, whether the influence of the military was truly decisive in this case. In any event, it must be emphasized that the conceptions of security policy articulated by the military leadership did not have any great effect, since their arguments had no visible impact during the struggle for the distribution of funds and additional resources were in any case not available.

Conclusion

In summary, an analysis of the political influence of the Russian armed forces generates a contradictory picture.

The military possesses considerable potential to intervene in political processes and to contribute to the formulation of policies. There exists a large electorate which is susceptible to military topics or which can be mobilized by the armed forces. In the elections of December 1995, no political alliance could hope to win a majority without the support of this group of voters, Also, in extreme situations of crisis the military leadership is in a position to determine the outcome directly by the use of military means. Theoretically, this capability would enable the military to influence decisions even during the preliminary stages of a conflict.

The basic political consensus among the military with regard to both their conservative patriotic views and their principal interests as an institution would have provided favourable conditions for united political action if conflicting opinions among the officers corps and open clashes between higher-ranking military leaders had not made concerted action impossible.[27] However, it is one of the basic convictions of the officer corps that it is not for the armed forces to engage in politics and decide political outcomes. Deployment against their own – Russian – population is clearly still opposed by most of the officers. In this sense, the Russian armed forces do not comprise a potential civil war army.

When it comes to daily parliamentary routine, however, military officers are currently not particularly successful. Conflicts within the military elite and a lack of experience in the art of lobbying lead again and again to a failure to make their opinion count even on questions relating directly to military or security policy matters. This political weakness was especially characteristic of the group around Grachev, which could not expect support neither from the officers nor from the Duma factions or any of the political movements.

Grachev's successor Rodionov, who was appointed in July 1996, unlike Grachev was respected in the military establishment as a professional soldier. He made great efforts to inform the public about the requirements of the armed forces and to mobilize the Duma in support of the interests of his ministry. However, he had only limited success. The government listened to his dramatic appeals with some scepticism and failed to approve an increase in military expenditure for 1997.[28] Rodionov and Viktor Samsonov, the chief of the general staff, were summarily dismissed by President Yeltsin at a Defence Council meeting in May 1997. This followed Rodionov's presentation of a report to Yeltsin which, in blatant disregard of Russia's financial malaise, projected constant military budgets of 160,000 billion roubles for the next ten years. Rodionov had clashed on this issue with Yuri Baturin, secretary of the new Defence Council (who was subsequently replaced by Andrei Kokoshin), and had argued that the Defence Council should not intercede between the Supreme Commander-in-Chief (the president), on the one hand, and the defence minister and the general staff on the other. The creation of the Defence Council in July 1996 within the Presidential Administration had increased the extent of civilian control over military policy-making. The new defence minister Colonel-General Igor Sergeev (who had commanded the Strategic Missile Troops) and the new chief of general staff, Colonel-General Anatoly Kvashnin (who had commanded Russian forces during the initial part of the Chechenia campaign), rapidly established closer working relations with Yeltsin than Rodionov had achieved.

Overall in the post-Soviet period the influence of the Russian military has been decisive only in situations where the politicians have failed. The inability of Russian politicians to solve the constitutional conflict of 1993 through negotiations and compromise ultimately made it necessary for the armed forces to intervene to resolve the stand-off. In the relative stability of political conditions after the December 1993 elections, the influence of the military declined again. It is true that the majority of the Russian population appears to react positively to 'strong men' from a military background; however, so far this has not led to any attempt by the Russian armed forces to take politics into their own hands.

Appendix

Table 3.1: Attitudes during the December 1993 elections (% of those interviewed voting)

	Turnout of voters	Vybor Rossii	LDPR	Other political parties
Officers		22	45	33
Praporshchiki (NCOs)		16	39	45
Sergeants, rank and file		29	27	44
Contract soldiers		16	25	59
Military in general	56	23	38	39
National results 1993	49	16	23	61

Source: 'Armiya glazami armii', Moskovskie novosti, 1994, no. 36, p. 7 (opinion poll of Gumanitarnaya Akademiya during the first half of 1994).

Table 3.2: Which model of Russian statehood do you prefer? (% of those interviewed)

	Desirable	Probable
Re-establishment of the USSR	20	10
Russia within today's borders	37	60
Union (Russia, Ukraine, Kazakstan)	43	30

Source: A.Golovkov, in Izvestiya, 21 April 1995, p. 4.

Table 3.3: Expectations concerning the relationship between the army and politics (% of those interviewed)

The army remains excluded from politics	23
The army takes over the leadership of the state	16
The army is periodically called in to resolve conflicts	41
None of the above	20

Source: A. Golovkov, in Izvestiya, 21 April 1995, p. 4.

Table 3.4: Confidence in politicians among the military, 1995 (% of those interviewed)

	March 1995	August 1995
Zhirinovsky	15.6	15.8
Chernomyrdin	14.6	9.9
Zyuganov	14.2	14.1
Lapshin	10.3	10.5
Yeltsin	9.8	6.2
Shumeiko	8.7	3.1
Rutskoi	7.4	6.2
Yavlinsky	6.6	14.5
Rybkin	6.5	5.8
Gaidar	6.3	5.2
None of the above	0	8.7

Source: 'Armiya verit tol' ko armii', in *Moskovskie novosti*, 1995, no. 59, p. 6.

Table 3.5: Assessment of higher-ranking military leaders (% of those interviewed)

	Professionality	Personal authority
Kolesnikov	90	77
Nikolayev	80	63
Lebed	26	50
Kvashnin	54	46
Grachev	23	21

Source: A. Golovkov, in *Izvestiya*, 21 April 1995, p. 4.

Table 3.6: Preparedness to resist among Russian officers, 1992–6 (% of those interviewed)

Which form of resistance do you consider admissible?	1992	1993	1994	1995	1996
Complaints according to existing regulations	56	41	41	41	36
Premature leave from the armed forces	23	17	20	24	38
Organizing oneself to defend the rights of the armed forces	21	16	13	19	26
Public appearance in the mass media	22	16	11	23	24
Demonstrative passive fulfilment of duties	2	6	9	14	19
Using force to push through one's demands	10	4	6	18	26

Source: V. Mukhin and S. Solov'ev, 'Protest sluzhashchikh Vooruzhennykh Sil'RF i deyateley kul'tury', *Nezavisimaya gazeta*, 1 October 1996, p. 1.

Notes

1. Members of this Officers' Assembly included Valentin Varennikov, chief of the Soviet ground forces until 1991 and one of the initiators of the attempted coup in August, as well as Dmitri Yazov, who had been Soviet defence minister at the time.
2. 'Armiya verit tol'ko armii', *Moskovskie novosti*, 1995, no. 59, pp. 6–7.
3. At the end of 1994, 132,000 officer families were waiting for proper housing; 52,000 families lived in dormitories and hotels. Another 79,000 families found private quarters on the very expensive housing market.
4. L. Zavarsky, and Y. Ostapova, 'Rossiyskaya aviapromyshlennost' uchitsya salonnym maneram', *Kommersant-Daily*, 30 August 1995, p. 12.
5. 'Vernem liudyam v pogonakh dostoinstvo i uvazhenie', *Krasnaya zvezda*, 7 August 1996, pp. 1, 3; 'Ministr oborony RF Igor' Rodionov: Den' nachinayu i zakanchivayu poiskami deneg dlya armii', *Krasnaya zvezda*, 6 September 1996, pp. 1, 3; 'Ministr oborony Rossii general-polkovnik Igor' Rodionov: Situatsiya v armii grozit vzryom', *Izvestiya*, 2 October 1996, p. 2; V. Chupakhin, S. Knyaz'kov and A. Stasovsky, 'Nado sdelat' vse vozmozhnoe, chtoby armiya bystree vyshla iz krizisa', *Krasnaya zvezda*, 2 October 1996, pp. 1–2.
6. 'Armiya glazami armii', *Moskovskie novosti*, 1994, no. 36, p. 7 (opinion poll of Gumanitarnaya Akademiya in the first half of 1994); see Appendix, Table 3.1.
7. A. Golovkov, 'Za kogo progolosuet leitenant Ivanov?', *Izvestiya*, 21 April 1995, p. 4; see Appendix, Table 3.2.
8. Ibid.: see Appendix, Table 3.3.
9. L. Peven' and S. Popov, 'Sotsiologicheskie oprosy v armii pokazyvayut krayne trevozhnie tendentsii', *Krasnaya zvezda*, 13 September 1996, p. 1; A. Krivolapov, I. Petrov and O. Arin, 'Protivorechiya mezhdu pravitel'stvom i armiey obostryayutsya. Problemy voennogo byudzheta – priznak narastaniya sotsial'no-ekonomicheskoy napryazhennosti v Rossii', *Nezavisimaya gazeta*, 19 September 1996, pp. 1–2; V. Maryucha, 'Chest' imeem? V pis'makh iz voisk vse chashche vyskazyvaetsya ideya ekstrennogo sozyva Vsearmeyskogo sobraniya', *Krasnaya zvezda*, 26 September 1996, p. 1; V. G. Mukhin and S. S. Solov'ev, 'Protest sluzhashchikh Vooruzhennykh Sil' RF i deyateley kul'tury. I te, i drugie bol'she ne khotyat mirit'sya s khronicheskim bezdenezh'em', *Nezavisimaya gazeta*, 1 October 1996, p. 1; S. Solov'ev and S. Popov, 'Vse nizhe i nizhe po dannym voennykh sotsiologov, uroven' zhizni ofitserskikh semey postoyanno padaet', *Krasnaya zvezda*, 15 October 1996, p. 1.
10. 'Armiya verit tol'ko armii', *Moskovskie novosti*, 1995, no. 59, pp. 6–7.
11. Ibid., p. 6; see Appendix, Table 3.4.
12. This general attitude is clearly described in the memoirs on service in Afghanistan by General Gromov, the last commander of the 40th Army; see Boris Gromov, *Ogranichennyy kontingent* (Moscow: Progress, 1994).
13. T. Malkina, 'Aleksandr Lebed' pristupil k obyazannostyam spasitelya otechestva', *Segodnya*, 19 June, p. 1; OMRI Daily Digest, no. 204, part 1, 21 October 1996.
14. *Militareliten in Rußland 1994. Eine Beifragung von 615 Offizieren der Streitkräfte der russischen Armee in den Militärregionen Moskau/St Petersburg, Volga-Ural, Nordkaukasus, Norden/Nordseeflotte, Sibirien, Kaliningrad im Auftrag der Friedrich-Ebert-Stiftung.* Büro Moskau München Moskau. SINUS Moskau: Gesellschaft für Sozialforschung und Marktforschung mbH 1994.
15. A. Golovkov, *Izvestiya*, 21 April 1995, p. 4; see Appendix, Table 3.5.
16. Cf. Maryucha, 'Chest' imeem' p. 1; Mukhin and Solov'ev, 'Protest sluzhashchikh Vooruzhennykh Sil RF i deyatelei kul'tury', p. 1.
17. See Appendix, Table 3.6.
18. Another relevant case, the decision to deploy troops in Chechenia, is discussed in Chapter 13.
19. See S. Rogov, 'Ustoyat li vooruzhennye sily Rossii? Zabytaya voennaya reforma', *Nezavisimaya gazeta*, 3 November 1994, p. 5; see also S. Yusenkov, 'Nad armiey v Rossii nuzhen grazhdanskiy kontrol', *Izvestiya*, 14 October 1994, p. 4.
20. A. Grigor'ev, 'Byudzhet stanovitsya kamnem pretknoveniya pravitel'stvennoy ekonomicheskoy politiki. Byudzhetnyy defitsit snova prevyshit 10% VVP', *Segodnya*, 27 September 1994, p. 1.
21. Cf. Interfax/Interstate Statistical Committee of the CIS Report, 2 August 1996, no. 32 (203), p. 5.; Yu. Golotyuk, 'Minoborony RF trebuet "udovletovoreniya potrebnostey"', *Segodnya*, 18 September 1996, p. 2.

22. See O Falichev, 'Komplektovat' Vooruzhennye Sily dostoynym popolnenium-obshchenarodnaya zadacha', *Krasnaya zvezda*, 23 March 1995, p. 1; concerning the envisaged size of the armed forces see *Rossiyskaya gazeta*, 7 April 1995, p. 4; see also V. Lopatin, 'Manevry generalov', *Izvestiya*, 27 April 1995, p. 4.

23. D. Pushkar, 'Srok posle srochnoy', *Moskovskie novosti*, 1995, no. 65, p. 19.

24. On questions concerning strategic nuclear weapons and the enlargement of NATO see Chapters 4 and 16 by Christoph Bluth in this volume.

25. See e.g. 'Wehe, Wenn die NATO wächst, ZEIT Gespräch mit dem russischen Generaloberst Walerij Manilow', *Die Zeit*, 17 November 1995, p. 12.

26. See e.g. 'Rossiya i NATO. Tezisy Soveta po vneshney i oboronnoy politike' *Nezavisimaya gazeta*, 21 June 1995, p. 2; and, as early as 1993, S. Karaganov, 'Rasshirenie NATO vedet k izolyatsii Rossii', *Moskovskie novosti*, 1993, no. 38. p. 7A.

27. Rodionov's efforts to make the armed forces' positions count in political decision-making were also hindered by conflicts within the military leadership. The dismissal of the commander-in-chief of the ground forces, Semenov, at the beginning of December 1996 has to be interpreted in this context.

28. Cf. 'Finansy, byudzhet i reforma', *Krasnaya zvezda*, 19 November 1996, pp. 1–2.

4 Russian military forces: ambitions, capabilities and constraints

Christoph Bluth

The military policy of a state can be generally understood to be designed as an instrument for safeguarding vital national interests and supporting foreign policy objectives. The perception of threats to national security informs the requirements for military forces to carry out this task adequately. However, it is generally appreciated by students of military affairs that the perception of external threats is only one of the elements that define military policy. The military policy of a state is usually the outcome of a complex interplay among various bureaucratic actors in the domestic political process, including the armed forces and the military industry. Domestic political and economic concerns and vested interests play a significant role. This is certainly the case in Russia, in which the making of policy is a very chaotic process.

Russia inherited a substantial portion of the Soviet armed forces which were largely designed to engage in high-intensity warfare with the West or China. The general staff in Moscow, however, lost control over substantial military assets that had been forward deployed in other republics. The task for the Russian military leadership was to restructure the country's military forces on the basis of this inheritance in a radically different geopolitical environment. The political instability, administrative chaos and economic weakness of the Russian state, furthermore, put severe constraints on the resources available to the military. This chapter seeks to provide an analysis of the military doctrine and force requirements designed to implement national security policy, and of the contradictions between force goals and capabilities. It also examines the extent to which a military capability is being preserved into the next century in view of the political and economic processes of transition that Russia is undergoing.

The Russian military doctrine[1]

During the Soviet period 'military doctrine' expressed the view of the state on the political objectives of war and the military-technical aspects of military policy. The armed forces of the Russian Federation were created in May 1992, but it proved difficult to establish agreement on a military doctrine, which was finally adopted in November 1993. Even then, President Boris Yeltsin made it clear that it was only part of a general security doctrine.[2] It remained unclear throughout the period what this general security doctrine was, although some of the elements were presumably contained in Yuri Skokov's 'The Basic Provisions of a Foreign Policy Concept', which was endorsed by Yeltsin himself.[3]

After the end of the Soviet Union, the traditional perceptions of the international security environment that dominated the Cold War period were abandoned surprisingly quickly by the political elite. The military was somewhat slow to follow a similar path. By mid-1992 the relevance of the 'defence of the Western Perimeter was seriously questioned',[4] but traditional thinking still pervaded the debate until well into 1993. By the time a new military doctrine was approved in November 1993, a radical re-evaluation of the security threats facing Russia had been adopted by the Russian military.[5] The military and arms control policies of Russia under Yeltsin since then reflect the perceptions of the security environment after the Cold War. There is widespread acceptance among the military leadership and the political elite that there is no threat to Russia from the United States and that the principal military threats come from the southern periphery of the Russian Federation and from Third World countries that are acquiring weapons of mass destruction and ballistic missiles. In line with a general restructuring of the Russian military to rapid reaction and crisis intervention roles, there is a fundamental change in thinking about the role of nuclear weapons to meet the new range of threats. The utility of strategic nuclear weapons in this environment is perceived to have declined fundamentally. Russian military research and development efforts are now almost exclusively focused on high-technology conventional weapons. Tactical nuclear weapons were withdrawn from eastern Europe and the non-Russian newly independent states.

As far as the role of nuclear weapons is concerned, the emphasis has been placed squarely on nuclear deterrence. The aim of the Russian Federation's policy in the sphere of nuclear weapons is to eliminate the danger of nuclear war by deterring any aggression against the Russian Federation and its allies.[6] This commits Russia to a policy of extended deterrence against threats to the security of its (unspecified) allies. There is a policy of no nuclear use against non-nuclear states that have acceded to the NPT, but there is no longer such a policy vis-à-vis nuclear weapons states or non-nuclear states which enjoy a nuclear guarantee by nuclear weapons states. This constitutes an abandonment of the pledge not to use nuclear weapons first which some commentators have found alarming. But it should be pointed out that the 'no first use' pledge was made in the context of the confrontation in central Europe, where the Soviet Union was determined to avoid escalation to the nuclear level in any conflict. The new doctrine is more in line with the notion of a deterrent as a last resort in the kinds of conflicts for which Russia is now preparing. It could also be interpreted as a warning to Turkey against any involvement in the conflict between Armenia and Azerbaijan, or to Ukraine as it considers the fate of nuclear weapons on its territory.[7] However, as the capabilities of the Russian armed forces decline, one can detect an increasing emphasis on nuclear forces to compensate for weakness at the conventional level. At present, tactical weapons are not deployed and therefore Russia lacks the instrument to implement a policy of regional nuclear deterrence in any operational sense. There have been suggestions, however, that Russia might redeploy tactical nuclear weapons if NATO expands to include countries of the former Warsaw Pact.[8]

The use of the armed forces in international peacekeeping operations, their deployment outside the national territory and the conduct of peacekeeping operations on the territories of the former Soviet republics together perhaps constitute the most important new element in Russian military doctrine. The doctrine also states that the units of the armed forces can be used in *internal* conflicts to support the forces of the interior ministry of the Russian Federation to localize and blockade the conflict region, to suppress armed clashes and to separate the conflicting parties as well as to defend the strategically important objects.[9] This part of the military doctrine is in conflict with the law on defence, which prohibits the use of regular armed forces inside the Russian Federation.

The military doctrine asserts that Russia does not consider 'any state as its enemy' and will not use its armed forces or other armed formations against any state for any purposes other than individual or collective self-defence in the case of an armed attack on the Russian Federation, its citizens, territory, armed forces or the other Russian armed formations, or its allies.[10]

The potential sources of a military threat towards the Russian Federation from outside include, according the new military doctrine:

- territorial claims to the Russian Federation from the other post-Soviet states;
- existing and potential sources of local wars and armed conflicts, primarily those in direct proximity to the Russian borders;
- proliferation of nuclear and other weapons of mass destruction, the means of delivery and modern military technologies;
- the oppression of the rights, freedoms and legitimate interests of the citizens of the Russian Federation abroad;
- the enlargement of military blocs and alliances (e.g. NATO) in such a way as to violate the military security interests of the Russian Federation.

According to the document, the greatest threat to Russia arises from armed conflicts caused by aggressive nationalism and religious intolerance.

The main objective of the organizational development of the Russian Federation armed forces and other troops is to create and develop forces capable of defending the independence, sovereignty and territorial integrity of the country, the security of the citizens, and the other vitally important interests of society and state in line with the military-political and strategic situation in the world.[11] In view of the absence of an agreed concept of the national security of Russia it is unclear, however, what the vital interests of the Russian Federation are. Such statements in the military doctrine therefore remain open to interpretation.

The military part of Russia's new military doctrine sets out a view of the possible character of future conflicts. Under conditions in which the danger of global war (both nuclear and conventional) is reduced substantially though not eliminated completely, local wars and armed conflicts represent the main threat to stability and peace. Their probability in some regions is increasing.[12]

The doctrine goes on to note that combat action in local war and armed conflicts can be waged by the groups of forces deployed in the region of conflict in peacetime. If necessary, these groups of forces can be reinforced by units redeployed from other regions. The Russian Federation needs to maintain the combat potential of the groups of forces deployed in peacetime at a level sufficient to repulse aggression on a local (regional) scale. The term 'aggression on a local (regional) scale', however, remains vague and is open to a variety of interpretations.

Local wars and armed conflicts are perceived as the most likely source of military threats to Russia. The military doctrine assumes that a wide variety of forces can be engaged in these operations, from a small number of armed units up to operational-strategic groups of forces, along with the use of all types of weapons, from small arms to modern precision-guided 'smart' weapons. The priority is the development of the Russian Federation armed forces and other troops intended for deterrence against aggression, as well as the mobile forces of the Russian Federation Armed Forces and other troops able to redeploy within a short period and to mount and conduct manoeuvre operations in any sector (region) where a threat to the security of the Russian Federation may arise.[13] Furthermore, Russian armed forces can be deployed outside the national territory to safeguard the security of either the Russian Federation or other former Soviet republics.[14]

The document on military doctrine reflects a basic contradiction in the way in which force requirements are defined. On the one hand, local wars and armed conflicts are clearly presented as the principal security threat. On the other hand, the operational strategic concepts and the remarks on practical implementation have the appearance of a guide for preparation for military operations around the globe, based on the acquisition of sea- and airlift capabilities on a global scale. This is also in contradiction to the intention asserted by the Soviet Union in the period of 'new political thinking' of liquidating the capabilities to launch surprise attacks or large-scale offensive operations. The emphasis on the defensive nature of the military-technical aspects of military doctrine thus appears to have been lost.

One possible interpretation is that the military doctrine is designed not only to define the military contingencies with which Russia will most probably have to deal, but also to provide a rationale for the ambitious force goals of the military establishment, which seeks to preserve something as close as possible to the military capabilities of the former Soviet Union.

Strategic nuclear forces

The strategic nuclear relationship with the United States after the Cold War

In the context of the newly emerging pattern of relationships, strategic nuclear forces present a confusing picture. While the transformation of the political relationships between East and West was accompanied by the dismantling of the conventional and nuclear confrontation in Europe, strategic nuclear force postures stayed largely intact even after the disintegration of the Soviet Union itself.

This situation is largely the result of uncertainty about the role of nuclear weapons in an environment that is no longer characterized by a bipolar confrontation. Some significant steps have been taken to reduce the level of strategic nuclear forces. The START 2 agreement will result in the elimination of land-based ICBMs with multiple warheads and reduce the number of strategic nuclear warheads to at most 3,500 on each side.[15] A number of symbolic steps have also been taken to signify that the nuclear confrontation is over, the most recent being the Moscow agreement of January 1994 between the United States and Russia in which the parties undertook not to target strategic nuclear missiles at each other.[16] However, this has not altered the actual situation, namely that two large strategic nuclear arsenals are facing each other, ready to be launched within minutes of warning of an attack.

Russian perspectives on the future of its strategic nuclear arsenal

As in so many other areas Russian voices on strategic arms policy and nuclear arms control are confused and contradictory. One of the few issues on which there is a relatively broad consensus in Russia is that the country should remain a nuclear power for the foreseeable future. The reasons for this are complex and deep-rooted and involve general political considerations as well as economic and military ones.

Remaining a nuclear power: political considerations

From a political perspective, it is believed by most members of the political elite that strategic nuclear weapons are the last remaining symbol of Russia's great-power status. Sergei Karaganov warns of the 'Versailles syndrome' currently experienced by the Russian people.[17] There is a perception that the principal reason why the West, and the United States in particular, is paying so much attention to Russia is that Russia remains a strategic nuclear power. The idea here is not that Russia should rebuild a global role. It is, rather, based on the fear that Russia may become marginalized, and the current political leadership seeks to avoid this at all costs in order to retain and increase the potential for international economic cooperation and aid. These are perceived as essential if Russia is to reverse its sharp political and economic decline and achieve a successful transition to a modern democratic state with a strong economy based on market principles. There is a deep paradox inherent in the maintenance of a substantial arsenal of strategic nuclear weapons on the basis of these considerations. It results from the fact that Russia's strategic nuclear weapons are technically the principal military threat to the United States. This produces a plethora of political efforts to reduce or eliminate the nuclear weapons as a factor in relations with the West. On the other hand, a residual threat based on the mere possession of a substantial arsenal is required to ensure that the West takes Russian concerns seriously.

The political considerations which underlie the preservation of strategic nuclear forces are important in terms of both Russian foreign policy and domestic politics. Russia has absorbed relatively peacefully the enormous shift in the geostrategic balance which has resulted in the loss of its influence in a sizeable part of the Third World, the collapse of the Warsaw Pact and thus the loss of Russian dominance in eastern Europe, not to mention the dissolution of the Soviet Union itself. There is a fear in Russia that without its nuclear status it will lose its last vestige of international influence and respect, given the collapse of the domestic economy, which at least in the short term deprives Russia of other indicators of power and influence.

Nuclear weapons and military security

Are there still sound military reasons for Russia to retain a strategic nuclear arsenal after the Cold War? As we have seen, in the Russian perception the utility of nuclear weapons in the kinds of conflicts it is most likely to have to deal with is extremely low.

Here we encounter the contradiction that despite the acceptance of the political perceptions of the global security environment, strategic analysis in the general staff is still based on the relationship between US and Russian strategic nuclear forces. The objective of strategic arms policy remains that of nuclear strategic parity with the United States. There is, of course, an awareness that third-country nuclear arsenals, such as those of Britain, France and China, remain in place and are even augmented. For Russian strategic planners, the future relationship with China, in an environment where the military-strategic balance and the two countries' relative economic potential are changing substantially, remains potentially the most troublesome. For all these reasons, they perceive the need to guard against nuclear attack or nuclear blackmail in the future. Nevertheless, force requirements are still defined on the basis of US capabilities.

Russian military planners do not base their objectives on the notion of a 'minimum deterrent', such as has been advocated by civilian analysts.[18] For them, strategic parity presupposes the qualitative equality of the strategic capabilities of both sides in their ability to conduct effective operations against each other's strategic offensive forces. It also means that Russia must be sure to maintain, as a minimum, an adequate second-strike countervalue reserve force *vis-à-vis* the United States.[19]

There are various options for the future of Russia's strategic nuclear force posture which are the subject of controversy between the various branches of the armed services and the political leadership. If START 2 is implemented, Russia will have to forgo all its ICBMs with multiple warheads: the ICBM force will consist of the single-warhead SS-25 and/or its successor. If START 2 is not ratified or implemented, then it will be possible for Russia to retain some missiles with multiple warheads. As the SS-18, currently the backbone of the Russian ICBM force, was designed and manufactured in Ukraine, the modernization of that missile is considered an unlikely option. The concept which seems currently to be under most active consideration by Russian military planners is the deployment of a new type of SLBM, which could also be deployed in silos on land as a quasi-ICBM. This missile is being developed as a MIRVed missile with three to four warheads to be based in a new nuclear submarine scheduled to enter service at the beginning of the twenty-first century.[20]

The provisions of START effectively favour the expansion of the sea-based leg of the nuclear deterrent. Russia could maintain virtually all of its most modern missile-carrying submarines – the Delta III, Delta IV and Typhoon – and still remain under the limit of 1,750 SLBM warheads imposed by the second phase of START 2, by 'downloading' some of its MIRVed SLBMs under the agreed rules (i.e. by reducing the number of warheads on each missile). Currently about 30 per cent of Russia's long-range ballistic missiles are deployed on submarines; under START this could increase to over 50 per cent without any new nuclear submarines having to be built or missiles manufactured.[21] Russia's sea-based forces, however, cannot be used to execute the kind of coordinated attack on military targets (e.g. missile silos and command and control centres) which could be mounted by the currently deployed land-based force, and such a shift would therefore require a completely different strategic doctrine and operational plans. The Russian submarine force is also plagued by communications problems which hinder effective command and control in situations of crisis, and is vulnerable to American anti-submarine warfare (ASW). Russia's surface navy, which has a key role in protecting SSBNs, would require substantial rejuvenation, thus raising the cost of rebuilding and expanding the sea-based strategic nuclear forces.

The Russian military leadership is determined to preserve a reserve force at sea. A new type of submarine with a new type of SLBM (similar in characteristics to the Trident C4) is currently being designed. It is believed that three to four boats of the new type will be in operation at the beginning of the twenty-first century. Whether Russia will have the resources to implement these plans is unclear. The currently existing force is deteriorating rapidly for lack of maintenance, and there are only very few sea patrols of Russian SSBNs.

Finally, the strategic bomber forces suffered most from the break-up of the Soviet Union as Russia lost substantial numbers of planes to the other former Soviet republics. President Yeltsin also decided to close down the production lines for Russian strategic bombers. There is not much interest in Russia in rebuilding the strategic bomber force; the most likely scenario is that, despite the fact that START 1 favours deployment of bombers, this leg of the strategic nuclear deterrent force will be abandoned by Russia or at best maintained at a minimal level.

At the Helsinki summit in March 1997 Presidents Yeltsin and Clinton discussed the outlines of a START 3 agreement. The principal elements mentioned were limits for strategic nuclear forces of between 2,000 and 2,500 warheads and the intention of the sides to block ways for circumventing those limits. However, the US side appears less keen to move ahead with START 3 while START 2 has not been ratified.[22]

To sum up, it is evident that there is a consensus in the Russian political and military elite that the country should remain a strategic nuclear power into the next century. The extent to which Russia remains capable of maintaining a nuclear force posture, how it should be constituted and how strategic relations with the United States should be pursued remain controversial. The notion of a complete stand-down between the United States and Russia and a radical move towards a minimal nuclear force posture by both sides has so far not gained substantial support.

Force levels and military reform

The Soviet legacy and Russia's dilemma

When the Commonwealth of Independent States was formed at the meeting in Minsk in December 1991, to be followed soon thereafter by the dissolution of the USSR, there was concern, both at the highest political levels in Russia and in the former Soviet military high command, that the integrity of the Soviet armed forces should be preserved and that the former Soviet Union (except for the Baltic states) should form a common security space. However, it became apparent very quickly that this was incompatible with the requirements of state-building in the NIS, of which the establishment of independent armed forces and the neutralization of former Soviet forces formed a critical element. The principal consequence of these developments was that the integrity of the Soviet military system could not be preserved and a major proportion of the military assets of the former Soviet Union was lost to the general staff in Moscow. For this reason former Russian defence minister Pavel Grachev stated that the Russian armed forces had to be built up from scratch.[23]

Russia inherited armed forces comprising 2.8 million men and large quantities of tanks, armoured vehicles, helicopters, aircraft, artillery and other types of military equipment. Dealing with this legacy in conformity with the security requirements of the post-Soviet state is itself a major task. However, as we have seen, the military doctrine is in many respects rather vague and general. Furthermore, it contains ambiguities which result from the fact that while the Russian military leadership clearly wants to develop the forces and capabilities required to meet the security threats as it perceives them, it would also like to retain as much as possible of the former Soviet capabilities for large-scale, high-intensity conventional warfare. While the military leadership recognizes that the armed forces must be reduced in size, it is unwilling to accept reductions of such a scale as to bring the armed forces to a more sustainable level, at which they could be properly trained, equipped and deployed to meet Russia's security requirements. This recalcitrance is motivated at least in part by a perception of the unacceptable social consequences of decommissioning a large number of Russian officers who would have a hard time finding alternative means of support.

Whatever the ambitions of the military leadership may be, they are subject to some important constraints. One is the Conventional Forces in Europe (CFE) Treaty, which imposes upper limits on the military equipment Russia can maintain. Another is the limit on the resources available for the military from the state. Political attempts to set and maintain a lower ceiling on force numbers as a way of controlling the military's demand for resources have met with limited success. In December 1992 the law on defence set a ceiling on the armed forces of 1 per cent of the population, which means 1.5 million men, to be achieved by the end of 1995. By 1994 the authorized number of personnel was 2.2 million; in 1995 it was reduced to 1.9 million, against strenuous objections from former defence minister Grachev. The state budget for 1995 included a target of 1.5 million for the armed forces by the end of 1995, in line with the law on defence, though this reduction was not fully achieved.

Military organization and structure

The organization and deployment of Russian military forces, it goes without saying, have changed dramatically since 1990. The dismantling of the integrated Soviet military structure resulted in the loss of vital elements of missile early warning, air defence, logistical support and C^3I systems. Because first-echelon forces were deployed at the periphery of the USSR, a high proportion of the most combat-capable and best-equipped units remained outside Russia, even though the forces from Germany and the Baltic states were withdrawn to Russia. Much of the equipment Russia inherited was second-rate or even obsolete.[24] To indicate the shift in the military resources at Moscow's disposal, a simple force comparison can be made. At the end of 1990 the Warsaw Pact could have deployed about 167 divisions after full mobilization. Having lost 60 divisions to the non-Soviet Warsaw Pact countries and 31 to Belarus and Ukraine, Russia now can mobilize the equivalent of 37 divisions west of the Urals.[25]

When Russia formed its own armed forces in 1992, it inherited a force structure developed for the defence of the whole of the Soviet Union. From the perspective of the new strategic situation, therefore, there was a considerable maldeployment of forces on the territory of the Russian Federation. The reorganization of the military district system reflects the endeavour by the military leadership to adapt its force posture to its defence requirements.

In the Soviet period, the defence posture was defined by 'strategic directions' of which the 'Western strategic direction' was the most important. Now the Northern military district (previously known as the Leningrad MD) and the Moscow MD have effectively become the front line. The Baltic MD has been renamed the North-Western Group of Forces. In January 1993 the NWGF had 65,000 men; in 1996 the number of troops deployed in the Kaliningrad MD (the remaining territory of the Baltic MD) had been reduced to 24,000 with two motor rifle divisions (MRDs).[26] The artillery division of the 11th Army from the Baltic MD and all the armed formations stationed in the Baltic states have been disbanded. Some forces from the North-Western Group of Forces, such as the 25th Independent Motor Rifle Brigade and the 11th Army's MRL (multiple rocket launcher) regiment, have been transferred to the Northern MD.[27]

The Northern MD (headquarters at St Petersburg) comprised the 6th Army, the 30th Army Corps and the 26th Army at Arkhangel'sk. Now it has one army headquarters at Petrozavodsk and one corps headquarters at Vyborg (the 26th Army Corps, with only support and logistic units, was disbanded in 1993). There are 52,000 ground troops in the Northern MD, with two motor rifle divisions in the 6th Army; the 30th Army Corps also has two MRDs. There is a total of 870 main battle tanks and 740 ACVs. There is also one airborne division and an independent airborne brigade stationed in the Northern MD.[28]

During the Cold War, the forces in the Moscow and Volga MDs formed part of the central strategic reserve. Now the Moscow MD is a strategically important border district and its forces have been significantly strengthened. The total number of ground troops in the Moscow MD is 82,000. The 13th Army Corps has been upgraded to form the 22nd Army; the 1st Tank Army from the Western Group of Forces has been relocated in the Moscow MD and been converted into an Army. In addition the 20th Army Corps has been formed. There are two airborne divisions: the 106th ABD at Tula and the 98th ABD at Ivanovo (previously located in the Odessa MD). With four tank divisions and two MRDs, there are 1,950 main battle tanks and 3,700 ACVs deployed in the Moscow MD.[29]

The Volga MD has been formed from what was previously called the Volga and Urals MD; the Siberian MD was divided and part of it became what is now called the Ural MD. It is possible that the Volga MD, which now commands the 2nd Army (formerly part of the Western Group of Forces), is being constituted as part of the second strategic echelon.[30] With 46,900 ground forces, two tank divisions, one MRD and one ABD, it deploys 1,100 main battle tanks and 1,840 ACVs.

The North Caucasus MD, previously a rear echelon district, is now at the front line against instability and conflict at the southern periphery of the Russian Federation. One MRD was redeployed there from the Western Group of Forces in 1994.[31] There are now 65,000 ground forces, two MRDs and one ABD in the North Caucasus MD, though the attempts to build a strike grouping of mobile forces in that military district were not very successful, as the war in Chechenia dramatically revealed.

Given the vagueness about the political foundations of national security policy, the military doctrine leaves open several crucial questions about the most probable number, geographical location and scale of the conflicts in which Russia could be engaged and which it should prepare to wage simultaneously. Nevertheless, some elements of the planned Russian military posture can be extracted from the public statements of top military officials. Speaking about the size of the future Russian armed forces, former defence minister Grachev stated that Russia is now unable to deploy military units 'under each bush' alongside its longest borders. In this situation Russia can rely only on the rapid deployment forces.

Mobile forces are a key element in the restructuring of Russia's armed forces. Russia inherited about 60 per cent of the airborne forces of the Soviet Union (five divisions and two to three brigades).[32] By the end of 1993 it was reported that Russia was planning to organize two types of mobile forces: for immediate deployment and rapid deployment. The first must have an alert status of ten hours, that is, be ready to act within ten hours of receiving its orders. The second type will need several days to be deployed and be ready to act, and will consist of MRDs and reinforcement units. In view of the changes in the military-political situation and the geostrategic posture of Russia, new approaches towards the organization of groups of forces are considered necessary. It is no longer considered reasonable to deploy groups of forces along the whole border. The structural reform is based on the principle of a mobile defence, presupposing an organization of smaller forces, powerful enough and ready to be used operationally wherever a real threat to Russia's security appears.

In this context, the Russian military leadership's insistence on the need for revision of the rules in the CFE Treaty governing the 'flanks' is very important.

Financial aspects of military reform

On 16 May 1996, at the height of the presidential election campaign in Russia, President Yeltsin announced an end to military conscription. He signed a decree according to which the Russian armed forces would, by April 2000, consist entirely of professional officers and contract soldiers. With one stroke of the pen he thereby seemed to have resolved a controversy over the future of the Russian armed forces. It is a testimony to the unpopularity of military service and the low status of the once revered armed forces that Yeltsin believed this measure would add a major impetus to his campaign. The disastrous intervention in Chechenia has done much to deepen popular disdain for the military and has further reduced the public acceptability of military service. Military affairs continued to be subordinated to the requirements of electoral politics. After narrowly topping the poll in the first round of the election ahead of his main rival Gennady Zyuganov, Yeltsin sacked the unpopular defence minister, Pavel Grachev, and appointed his erstwhile rival, General Aleksandr Lebed as national security adviser, only to dismiss him after he successfully negotiated a ceasefire in Chechenia. Igor Rodionov, who replaced him as defence minister, had sought to oversee the process of military reform, until in turn he was replaced in May 1997 by the former commander of the Strategic Rocket Forces, Igor Sergeev.

It is clear that Yeltsin pronounced an end to military conscription without any clear concept of how the armed forces are to be restructured and how the various demands of force requirements and budgetary constraints are to be reconciled. The principal reason why Yeltsin announced the move to a professional army is evidently the unpopularity of conscription. Yet the financial constraints that will apply for the foreseeable future mean that the implementation of the measure will require serious choices to be made as regards the mission and overall size of the armed forces.

The overall GDP of the Russian Federation can be taken as a measure of the resource base which limits the options for the development of the armed forces. When the Soviet Union was dissolved, Russia accounted for 61 per cent of the GDP of the former Soviet Union. This has fallen precipitously, and by the end of 1995 Russian GDP amounted to only 36 per cent of the last figure for the Soviet Union. The maintenance of military forces and capabilities on anything approaching the scale of those of the former Soviet Union on such a reduced and falling resource base is clearly an untenable position. Since 1992, the GDP of the Russian Federation has fallen relentlessly (see Table 4.1).

Table 4.1: Changes in Russian GDP

Year	1992	1993	1994	1995	1996
% change	−14.5	−8.7	−2.6	−4.0	−6.0

Source: *Country Profile Russia 1997-98*, Economist Intelligence Unit, London, 1997, p. 41.

The most optimistic forecasts have predicted that during the period 1997–2000 Russia will experience economic growth of the order of 5 per cent per annum. This forecast already looks too optimistic for 1997 when Russia is likely to have at best zero growth. Even if this rather optimistic scenario is realized, by the end of the decade Russian GDP will still amount to only about 40 per cent of the last Soviet GDP figure.[33]

The key question is, of course, what share of the national income the political elite is willing to allocate to the military. There have been vigorous internal debates in Russia about the appropriate share of resources for the military so that it can adequately provide for the security of the state. Former defence minister Pavel Grachev and his deputy Andrei Kokoshin fought hard to maximize the resources allocated to the military. Two concerns were uppermost in their minds. One was that although the defence industrial base clearly has to contract, it should not be allowed to wither away. Russia must remain at the leading edge of military technology. There must also be sufficient funds to permit the maintenance of military hardware. Military industries are a major employer, and the social consequences of their closure must also be considered. The other concern was that the personnel of the armed forces should have proper living conditions and that military infrastructure and weapons should be properly maintained to retain their operational capability. If the living conditions and the pay of personnel in the armed services were allowed to deteriorate even further, control over substantial portions of the armed forces might be lost. At a minimum, their combat-readiness would seriously decline.

On the whole, it must be said that Grachev and Kokoshin were not very successful. Despite very vigorous lobbying of parliament, almost to the point of blackmail, military spending has steadily declined as a percentage of GDP. According to IMF estimates, Russian defence expenditure in 1992–5 amounted to between 4.4. and 5 per cent (compared with at least 15 per cent for the Soviet era). It is quite clear that there has been a consensus in the legislature since 1992 that military spending should not exceed 5 per cent of GDP – despite the predominance of communists and nationalists in the Duma.

This can be explained by the competing political influences on government spending. The defence budget is drawn up by the ministry of defence, but has to be approved by the government in the first instance. It is evident that the ministry of finance has the backing of the president and the prime minister in imposing severe limits on all government spending, including military expenditures, in order to keep inflation in check and satisfy the IMF that Russia is moving towards a sound financial policy. The draft state budget is subsequently submitted to parliament. The Duma imposes a limit on the overall budget deficit, thereby further reducing the scope for lobbying by special interests. Moreover, here military industry has to compete with other important interest groups, such as the gas and oil industries and the agricultural lobby.

Another important aspect of Russian budgetary politics is the underfulfilment of public spending plans. Even when the military can persuade the Duma to agree to a higher military budget, this does not mean that the monies authorized will also be available. The persistent shortfall between projected tax receipts and actual revenues means that military expenditure tends to be a good deal less than is budgeted for. This shortfall is added to the arrears from previous years, which spills over into the next federal budget. As a consequence the government debt to the armed services and defence industries increases, while actual expenditures amount to only about half the amount that the military leadership considers to be the bare minimum. Indeed, at the end of the year the Duma typically makes additional emergency appropriations of the order of 2–3 trillion roubles to prevent mass starvation in the armed forces.[34]

The defence budget for 1996 reflected the priorities of the political elite. Defence spending was reduced from 21.3 per cent to 17 per cent of the federal budget. This implied a reduction from 5.5 per cent to 3.8 per cent of GDP. Social costs (salaries, pensions, housing, etc.) accounted for most of the budget; a mere 10 per cent was to be spent on procurement. In view of the large sums required by the ministry of defence to pay off its debts to military enterprises, this meant that actual procurement was virtually reduced to zero.

For the 1997 budget, the military had to go around the same loop again. The request for minimum sufficient financing exceeded the government draft figure by 40–50 per cent. The 1997 federal budget submitted by the government allocated about 104.3 trillion roubles for the item 'national defence'. This amounts to 19 per cent of the entire federal budget for 1997, or 3.7 per cent of the forecast GDP of Russia. This total amount represents an increase over the 1996 allocation equal to the rate of inflation. However, again it can be assumed that not all of these funds will actually become available, and moreover substantial sums are owed to banks and military enterprises. A closer analysis of the defence budget (as close as the limited information published permits) shows that again most of it goes on the maintenance of the armed forces. Procurement of weapons and military equipment and, even more importantly, research and development are to get even fewer resources than in the previous year. As a consequence, Alexei Arbatov has painted a vision of the Russian army in ten years' time, facing new military threats on Russia's geostrategic borders without a modern military, without state-of-the art weapons technology and without a mobilization base.[35]

Experts in the Russian general staff have calculated on the basis of relatively sophisticated models the relationship between the share of GDP allocated to the military and the size of the armed forces that can reasonably be maintained.[36] Their figures are based on two assumptions. One is that Russia's economy will stabilize and by the year 2000 its GDP will have increased by 20 per cent over the level of 1994. The other is that Russian forces are maintained at a level of training and equipment comparable to Western forces. The results are as shown in Table 4.2.

Table 4.2: Russian troop levels and military share of GDP

No. of troops (million)	0.5	1	1.5	2
% of GDP	3.9	7.7	11.6	15.5

This means that the two fundamental tenets of Russian military force planning – armed forces with 1.5 million troops, funded by at most 5 per cent of GDP – are incompatible. Russian planners conclude that there are three alternatives:

(1) a well-equipped army of at most 650,000–750,000 men;
(2) a poorly equipped army of 1.5 million men;
(3) a substantial increase in the military share of national income.

It is important to add that the general staff's assumption about the level of Russian GDP in the year 2000 appears optimistic at best. Furthermore, the current levels of training and equipment are much lower than assumed. The military would quite clearly prefer option 3 and remains unwilling to contemplate option 1, with the result that, so far, option 2 is the actual policy being implemented.

The Russian debate about the size and structure of the armed forces is hampered by a lack of consensus on its future role and missions. The military doctrine does not identify a potential adversary and remains vague on the threats or security risks that Russian armed forces are likely to face. The question as to whether the armed forces are purely to serve the territorial defence of the Russian Federation, whether they are also to provide for the security of all signatories to the Tashkent collective security agreement or the entire Commonwealth of Independent States, or whether they are to be used as an instrument to sustain geopolitical objectives further afield, has not been resolved, or even openly debated. Nevertheless, it is critical to the issue of force planning.

In view of the end of the Cold War and partial normalization of relations with the West, some prominent analysts, including military leaders, have argued that the size of Russia's armed forces should be assessed according to criteria applicable to a 'normal' civilized state. A comparison with other OSCE countries would lead to the conclusion that, taking into account Russia's territory and population, the size of its armed forces should be about 0.9 million men. The majority view in the general staff, however, seems to be that Russia has special problems and that such criteria are not applicable.

There is a wide range of views among the opposition parties. Vladimir Zhirinovsky's Liberal Democratic Party, which has very ambitious views about Russia as a regional and global power, advocates a minimum target of 3 million men, of which 1 million should be officers. This is obviously completely unrealistic. The most detailed proposals have been put forward by the Yabloko coalition. They advocate a target of between 1 million and 1.2 million men. This is based on the view that Russia is not going to be embroiled in a regional conflict with another major power in the near future. Russia will not attempt to play the role of a great military power; however, it will be responsible for the security of Russia and the signatories to the Tashkent collective security agreement. A vital part of this programme is the formation of a number of elite forces which are fully manned and equipped and combat-ready. Support for the most important branches of military industry is also considered essential. The emphasis is on focusing resources so that at least some parts of the armed forces are capable of realistically implementing their tasks. The Yabloko programme is perhaps the most thorough attempt yet made in Russia to deal with the implications of the reduced resource base for military policy and to match requirements with capabilities.[37]

Yeltsin decided, after much internal debate, that the nominal level of the armed forces should be 1.7 million by the end of 1995 and 1.5 million by the end of 1996. This objective has now been postponed until 1998. However, it is also quite clear that Yeltsin wants to reduce the armed forces further. He is conscious of the budgetary limitations and supports drastic reductions in military expenditures.

Military reform appears to have received more high-level attention since the presidential elections in 1996. Grachev's successor as defence minister, Igor Rodionov, made frequent speeches emphasizing the need for military reform and for a solution to be found to the problem of the chronic underfunding of the armed forces. He went so far as to say that the projected 1997 defence budget covered only a third of the necessary expenses on the armed forces and added that if it were not corrected, Russia might finally lose the armed forces as an integral and capable state structure.[38]

Plans for military reform continue to be hampered by a lack of clear direction at the highest level about Russia's security interests and force requirements. In order to provide a more unified approach to policy on the armed forces, a Defence Council (an institution which previously existed in the Soviet Union) was established with Yuri Baturin as secretary (until he was replaced by Andrei Kokoshin during summer 1997). During its first session on 4 October 1996, Prime Minister Viktor Chernomyrdin described the four aims of restructuring the armed forces as:

- adjusting the composition, structure and size of the armed forces to the existing political and military situation and the economic possibilities of the situation;
- developing a core of technically well-equipped and well-trained armed forces capable of removing threats emerging in key strategic directions;
- the full and unconditional provision of the armed forces and other troops with funding, armaments, combat and other hardware, material and technical means;
- keeping troops in high readiness for defence.[39]

However, Chernomyrdin gave no indication of how these objectives were to be achieved. It soon emerged that Baturin had views on military reform which were at odds with those in the military establishment. Having been tasked with monitoring implementation of the presidential edict 'On Measures to Ensure Military Organizational Development in the Russian Federation', he began to advocate the concept that military reform should be started now, using existing resources, while simultaneously cutting the country's power structures by an average of 30 per cent.[40]

On 7 February 1997 Rodionov and Baturin gave a press conference designed to dampen press speculation about disagreements between the ministry of defence and the Defence Council on military reform. Rodionov affirmed his support for a three-stage programme advocated by Baturin. The first phase, until 2000, would consist in a reduction in the size of the armed forces; the second phase (2001–5) would deal with qualitative problems; the third phase (after 2005) would involve large-scale rearmament. According to Rodionov, the size of the of the armed forces was to be reduced by 200,000 to 1.5 million.[41]

However, it was clear that Rodionov and Baturin disagreed quite fundamentally about the future of military reform.[42] The disagreement focused around three different issues. The first was the very existence and the role of the Defence Council, which increased the civilian influence over military policy, an area in which the general staff continued to claim unique expertise and competence. Although Rodionov had initially supported its creation, he gradually became increasingly vocal against such an alternative locus of decison-making on military affairs. The second was the financial allocation to the military. Rodionov forcefully advanced the view that the military needed to be financed properly and, moreover, that substantial resources needed to be made available to implement military reform. The defence allocations for the 1997 budget amounted to only 104.3 trillion roubles, even though the military had asked for 160.3 trillion roubles. In February 1997, Rodionov went as far as to raise questions about the safety and secure control over the Russian strategic nuclear arsenal, thereby breaking a major taboo, in order to highlight the desperate need for more funds for the military. Moreover, as Rodionov also pointed out on various occasions alongside other military experts, there are also structural problems about implementing military reform. A reduction in the number of officers does not save money immediately if the social obligations (redundancy payments, pensions, housing, etc.) are taken into account. Some analysts believe that savings will not become significant until five years have passed. Indeed, the initial costs of military reform have been another obstacle to prevent this issue from being dealt with in a rational and decisive manner.

The secretary of the Defence Council on the other hand clearly maintained the position that there was no possibility of increasing the proportion of the federal budget allocated to the military. Indeed, in February 1997, when Rodionov made a desperate plea for more funds, Baturin stated bluntly that there could be no increase in the military budget,[43] and given the problems of achieving the tax income targets on which the budget was based, further reductions in allocations were likely. Armed forces planning and military reform would have to be carried out within the financial constraints of the budget.

The third area of disagreement related to military doctrine. In November

1996, Yuri Baturin called for a revision of Russia's military doctrine in view of the changes in its economic and geopolitical situation. Rodionov's response was to reaffirm the military doctrine adopted in November 1993, only to publish an outline for a new doctrine shortly thereafter, presumably in order to pre-empt a revision of military doctrine by the Defence Council.[44]

Clearly there was a power struggle between the ministry of defence and the Defence Council. In the absence of clear guidance from the president, no progress was made on any of these issues, and indeed in the first five months of 1997 the Defence Council did not meet.

When Yeltsin had seemingly recovered sufficiently from the consequences of his multiple heart bypass operation and other medical problems, a meeting of the Defence Council was held on 22 May 1997. Two days prior to this Rodionov submitted a report to the president which projected constant military expenditures at 160,000 billion roubles for the next ten years. Yeltsin was angered by this apparent unwillingness to accept the fiscal realities, as well as by the failure to make any progress with regard to military reform and by the criticism of the decision to establish the Defence Council as an institution. At the meeting of the Defence Council on 22 May 1997, Yeltsin berated the military high command and Rodionov personally for their obstructive behaviour. He expressed the view that military expenditure at a level of 5 per cent of GDP was unsustainable and higher than the military expenditure anywhere in the 'civilized world'. He set a target of 3–3.5 per cent of GDP for defence expenditure in the future.[45] Yeltsin's intention to bring the leadership of the armed forces into line was dramatically demonstrated by the dismissal of both Rodionov and the chief of the general staff, Viktor Samsonov, from their posts. Igor Sergeev, commander of the Strategic Rocket Forces, was named defence minister, and Anatoly Kvashnin, commander of the North Caucasus military district, was appointed chief of the general staff.[46] Two commissions were set up by the Defence Council to further the work on military reform, the first chaired by prime minister Chernomyrdin. Its membership includes the new defence minister, the first deputy prime minister Boris Nemtsov, and the deputy defence minister Andrei Kokoshin. Its task is to prepare a planning document on military development. The second commission is to deal with military financing and economic services.

The consequence of these developments is that with regard to the arguments about military reform the political leadership has firmly come down on the side of the Defence Council and the reformers against the military leadership. Moreover, some momentum was injected into a process of pushing the reforms forward. Thus on 18 July 1997 Yeltsin signed a decree on 'urgent measures to reform the armed forces of the Russian Federation and to improve their structure'. The main elements of the decree were:

- The authorized strength of the armed forces of the Russian Federation is to be established at 1,200,000. A reduction of 500,000 in the number of servicemen is to be carried out by the ministry of defence during 1997–8.
- The structure of the armed forces will be reorganized. By 1 January 1998, the Strategic Rocket Forces, the Military Space Forces and the Anti-Ballistic Missile Forces (PRO) of the Air Defence Forces (PVO) are to be united to form one service – the Strategic Missile Troops. The directorate of the Ground Forces commander-in chief is to become the Main Directorate of Ground Forces. By 1 January 1999, the Air Forces and the Air Defence Forces are to be united into a single service called the Air Force (VVS).
- The military districts are to be given a new status. In future they will be operational strategic commands of the armed forces of the Russian Federation in their strategic sectors.[47]

The secretary of the Defence Council, Yuri Baturin, clarified that the armed forces would be reduced by 500,000 servicemen, and that the civilian personnel in the armed forces would be cut to a maximum of 600,000 (from at least 760,000).[48] An important element of the strategy to implement military reform is the effort to reassign marginal, non-military functions away from the ministry of defence. For example, the federal road-building directorate, which was part of the ministry of defence, is being transferred to the civilian Federal Road Service.

The reorganization of strategic and missile defence forces is aimed at streamlining the infrastructure (where there is some duplication between the different branches of the armed services as hitherto constituted) and operations, and at eliminating interservice rivalry. In terms of the military operations of the strategic nuclear forces, such a reorganization makes sense and removes anomalies which arose during the Soviet period.[49] For this reason the new commander-in-chief of the Strategic Rocket Forces, Colonel-General Vladimir Yakovlev, welcomed this plan which will enhance his role considerably.[50] It has the additional merit that up to 25 positions at the level of general and 10–15 per cent of the entire strength of the combined services will be eliminated.[51]

The overall thrust of the reform is to decentralize and reduce the costs of the central administrative apparatus of the ministry of defence. For example, the central office of the commander-in-chief of the Ground Forces will be abolished and its functions will be delegated to local territorial military districts. Likewise operational control over the combined air defence and air force troops will be delegated to the military districts. These reforms, if and when implemented, will have quite a fundamental impact on the organization of the armed forces of the Russian Federation. Critics have argued that these changes have not been properly thought through and that the commanders of military districts may not be ready and able to discharge the new functions, which would lead to a breakdown in the organizational coherence of the Ground Forces.[52]

On 25 July 1997, defence minister Sergeev presented the government commission on military reform chaired by prime minister Chernomyrdin with the ministry of defence blueprint for military reform up to the year 2005. This was a comprehensive document covering Russia's military security at a global and regional level and its future development, the economic basis for Russia's military security, as well as the future development of Russia's armed forces and the military-industrial complex.[53]

It remains unclear, however, to what extent there is political will to face the hard issues. There is considerable opposition in the Duma to Yeltsin's renewed drive for military reform on the grounds that instead of reducing the military budget, substantial resources should be allocated to deal with the crisis in the armed forces and military industry. The critics fear that instead of genuine military reform Yeltsin's programme will turn out mostly to consist of cuts in the officers' corps, leading to the breakdown of the structural coherence of the armed forces of the Russian Federation. Lev Rokhlin, chairman of the State Duma's Defence Committee, has formed a movement in support of the army and defence sector and has campaigned in military districts and military-industrial facilities.[54] Ousted defence minister Igor Rodionov has allied himself with Rokhlin on this issue.

While the seriousness with which the government moved on military reform during spring and summer 1997 was unmistakable, it is not clear whether it is willing to make the required resources available. The cost of just implementing the mandated reduction of the armed forces by 500,000 is estimated at 30 trillion roubles.[55] Moreover, the armed forces have a huge payment arrears crisis of about 44 trillion roubles for food and salaries (not counting arrears to the military industry). In July 1997 first deputy prime minister Boris Nemtsov announced that 1.8 billion roubles would be made available to pay off wage debts. Yeltsin ordered that all overdue wages to military servicemen should be paid by 1 September 1997.[56] However, this only scratched the surface of what is required to implement military reform. While substantial cuts in the number of personnel in the armed forces now appear likely, it remains to be seen whether the political will exists to reorganize the Russian armed forces in a coherent manner to meet the challenges of the next decade and beyond.[57]

Christoph Bluth

The future of conscription in Russia

The problem becomes more complicated if conscription is entirely abolished. There has been a steady professionalization of the army, which continued until the finance ministry declared in 1995 that the limits of the affordable had been reached. The military leadership is also opposed to the concept of a smaller professional army, even though Grachev himself at one stage advocated an all-volunteer army of 1 million men as the ultimate goal of military reform.[58] After that point, attitudes changed; the military leadership took steps to increase the number of conscripts by removing many exemptions from military service and lengthening the period of the draft from eighteen months to two years. This, however, is bound to increase the personnel costs of the forces, and, without concomitant increases in the military budget, the consequence is likely to be a further deterioration in the living conditions of troops and an even greater squeeze on funds available for procurement. If action is taken to implement Yeltsin's election promise to abolish conscription, then the direction of policy is going to be reversed once again.

As the preceding discussion makes clear, such a move can only be contemplated if accompanied by a very substantial reduction in the level of forces. A professional army of more than 600,000 men cannot be sustained at present levels of military expenditure. Even this may be an overestimate. A professional army is currently not sustainable because of the severe shortage of junior officers and the large number of officers reaching retirement age. It is quite clear that unless service conditions and remuneration are substantially improved, it will be impossible to recruit sufficient personnel of adequate quality to create a viable professional army.

At the same time, conscription itself is becoming less tenable. For one thing, popular resistance to conscription means that President Yeltsin will find it difficult not to live up to his election promise to abolish it. More important are the demographic trends which indicate a sharp reduction in the pool of available conscripts. Despite the measures taken to extend the period of conscription from eighteen to twenty-four months, most units of the armed forces are far below nominal strength because of a lack of conscripts. The airborne forces, which are the best-organized elite force in the Russian military, have only 85 per cent of their nominal authorized level of troops. At the same time, Russian military expert Dmitri Trenin reckons that only one-third of the troops can be relied on in an emergency.[59] The Strategic Rocket Forces, another elite force which has a far higher ratio of officers to enlisted men than other forces, is also experiencing a serious shortfall in personnel because of declining numbers of conscripts and a large number of junior officers leaving the service. Missile crews are generally staffed at only 50–60 per cent of their required level. This raises problems of security, safety and combat readiness. The situation is generally far worse in other branches of the armed forces. Substantial parts of the armed services, especially the Pacific Fleet, but also the ground forces and part of the air force, are subject to material and social decay. Equipment is not properly maintained, there is a shortage of fuel and spare parts, and the living conditions of servicemen are often extremely poor. Sixty per cent of pilots receive no systematic flight training because of the lack of fuel. It is estimated that only 250,000 of the Russian armed forces are ready for military action. Modern weapons account only for 30 per cent of the Russian arsenal, whereas in west European armies the figure is typically about 70 per cent. The Russian army is also in danger of losing the traditional advantage of conscript armies of a large pool of reservists, as no call-up has taken place since 1991.

In summary, the only way out of this situation is a determined effort to phase out conscription and reduce the size of the armed forces very considerably, to about 500,000, and make the appropriate investments in social infrastructure, training and military procurement. However, the most likely outcome at present is that the situation will be allowed to continue to drift on, thereby increasing the cost of military reform in the future.

The other forces

One aspect of this debate which confuses the situation further is the exclusion of many important items from the military budget. Funding to maintain the twenty-five closed cities and towns under the jurisdiction of the ministry of defence and the ministry of atomic energy is not included. Troops and civilian staff of the ministry of interior, the federal security service and the border guards (otherwise known as 'the other forces') are also excluded. The costs of the Chechenia operation are likewise not included in the regular military budget. Thus total military outlays for 1995 are estimated to amount to 7 per cent of GDP.

The most controversial aspect of this are 'the other forces'. Military leaders criticize their expansion while regular forces have been run down. They are better financed and serviced, and personnel are better paid and looked after. Their total numerical strength has reached a level of between 700,000 and 800,000 men, i.e. about half of the nominal size of the regular armed forces. However, they are not integrated into the operational plans of the regular forces. The consumption of resources by these forces is considered to be partly responsible for the neglect of the regular armed forces. They are not sufficiently regulated by the state, and because of their sheer size constitute a challenge to the regular armed forces.[60]

It is quite clear that there are political reasons why the 'other forces' have become so important. In a country where the principal security threats originate internally, this is not necessarily to be deplored. It is, however, an issue that needs to be addressed when looking at military reform more generally. There are some indications that the Russian government has decided to do this. When Viktor Samsonov replaced Mikhail Kolesnikov as chief of the general staff in October 1996, Defence Minister Rodionov expressed the view that all military units in the country had to be brought under the control of the general staff.[61] In December 1996 Rodionov resigned his commission to become a civilian minister of defence. This was seen as indicative of a package of reforms whereby the ministry of defence would be separate from the general staff, and the general staff would be in charge of all military structures. The secretary of the Security Council, Ivan Rybkin, reaffirmed that this should be the new role for the general staff.[62] How this will be translated into practice remains to be seen. For example, given that the minister of the interior, Anatoly Kulikov, was promoted to vice-premier, it is unlikely that MVD troops are going to be subordinated to the general staff in the foreseeable future.

Conclusion

Russia's military policy reflects the different world-views and institutional interests that inform its foreign and security policy after the Cold War. On the one side there is a strong commitment to join the international community, to adhere to international norms, to support arms control and a close partnership with the West. On the other side there is the assertion of national interests, however they may be defined. The latter are often associated with an assertion of Russian dominance in the former Soviet space and cooler relations with the West. In terms of military policy, adaptation to the international environment would require the renunciation of a global role, drastic reductions in nuclear weapons, the downsizing of the armed forces and the development of highly trained, well-equipped and organized mobile forces. But many in the military establishment see Russia's strategic nuclear forces as the guarantor of the country's great-power status and seek to maintain as much as possible of the former Soviet Union's capabilities for large-scale conventional warfare. The larger ambitions of sections of the political and military elite have blocked a determined and radical approach to military reform, which would also be unpopular as a result of its social consequences. These obstacles have prevented the development of a coherent approach to military policy based on the actual requirements of national security and the nation's ability to provide the resources for its implementation. The severe financial restraints that exist make a deterioration in the situation inevitable. This prospect is fraught with great danger, as the social cohesion of the armed forces may break down to the point where both civil and military control over the armed forces are lost. There are clearly potential catastrophic outcomes which would have grave ramifications for European security. The adaptation to the realities of the post-Soviet era has only begun. It is vital for European security that it continue.

Notes

1. This section is based in part on a paper commissioned for the purposes of this study from the Institute for Defence Research (INOBIS), Kaliningrad, Moscow Oblast: *Russia's Conventional Forces: Military Doctrine, Capabilities and Force Structures*, 1995.
2. Charles J. Dick, 'The Military Doctrine of the Russian Federation', *Journal of Slavic Military Studies*, vol. 7, no. 3, September 1994, pp. 481–506; for an analysis of the Soviet concept of military doctrine, see Christoph Bluth, *Soviet Strategic Arms Policy before SALT* (Cambridge: Cambridge University Press, 1992), pp. 83–123.
3. This document was never published. For discussion, see Pavel K. Baev, *The Russian Army in a Time of Troubles* (London: Sage, 1996), p. 31.
4. Ibid., p. 28.
5. *Izvestiya*, 18 November 1993, p. 4.
6. *Voennaya mysl'*, Special issue, May 1992. 'Osnovnye polozheniya voennoy doktriny Rossyskoi Federatsii', pp. 3–23 at p. 5. Note that only a description of the basic provisions of the military doctrine of the Russian Federation has been published. Any reference to the military doctrine in this chapter is to that description as published in *Voennaya mysl'*.
7. For analysis see Charles Dick, 'The Military Doctrine of the Russian Federation', *Jane's Intelligence Review*, special report no. 1, January 1994.
8. Interviews in Moscow, April 1996.
9. *Voennaya mysl'*, p. 16.
10. Ibid., p. 4.
11. Ibid., p.16.
12. Ibid., p. 12.
13. Ibid., pp. 17–18.
14. Ibid., p. 18.
15. See Christoph Bluth, 'Arms Control and Nuclear Safety: The National and International Politics of Russia's Nuclear Arsenal', *Government and Opposition*, vol. 30, no. 4, Autumn 1995, pp. 510–32.
16. Christoph Bluth, 'American–Russian Strategic Relations: From Confrontation to Cooperation?', *The World Today*, vol. 49, no. 3, March 1993, pp. 47–50.
17. Sergei A. Karaganov, *Russia: The New Foreign Policy and Security Agenda* (London: Brassey's, 1992), pp. 24, 25. It should be added that Karaganov supports the scrapping of all tactical nuclear warheads and some reductions in strategic nuclear forces.
18. See Committee of Soviet Scientists for Peace, Against the Nuclear Threat, *Strategic Stability under the Conditions of Radical Nuclear Arms Reductions* (Moscow: Novosti, 1987); Alexei Arbatov, 'Strategic Equilibrium and Stability', in Yevgeny Primakov, ed., *Disarmament and Security 1987 Yearbook* (Moscow: Novosti, 1988), pp. 239–63.
19. This means that even in the event of the worst case of a first strike by the United States, Russia would still retain sufficient nuclear weapons for use against soft targets (cities and industry) to be able to inflict what is called 'unacceptable damage' to the United States.
20. For more detail see Christoph Bluth, 'The Russian View of its Strategic Nuclear Arsenal', *Jane's Intelligence Review*, vol. 6, no. 6, June 1994, pp. 263–7; Joshua Handler, 'The Future of Russian Strategic Forces', *Jane's Intelligence Review*, vol. 7, no. 4, April 1995, pp. 162–5.
21. Alexei Arbatov, 'START II, Red Ink and Boris Yeltsin', *Bulletin of the Atomic Scientists*, April 1993, pp. 16–21 at p. 20.
22. 'Russia: Rodionov Voices "Concern" Over US Calls To Leave ABM Treaty' Interfax, 14 May 1997.
23. *Izvestiya*, 1 June 1992.

24. Roy Allison, 'The Russian Armed Forces: Structures, Roles and Policies', in V. Baranovsky, ed., *Russia and Europe: The Emerging Security Agenda* (Oxford: Oxford University Press/SIPRI, 1997).

25. Andrew Duncan, 'Russian Forces in Decline – Part I', *Jane's Intelligence Review*, vol. 8, no. 9, September 1996, pp. 404–10. This estimate of current Russian force levels and mobilization capabilities indicates not only the losses due to the break-up of the Warsaw Pact and the Soviet Union, but also the shift of large quantities of military equipment to east of the Urals to preserve it from destruction under the CFE (Conventional Forces in Europe) agreement, the reductions in forces by way of implementation of CFE and the declining ability of the Russian military to maintain its force levels.

26. *The Military Balance 1996/97* (London: International Institute for Strategic Studies/Oxford University Press, 1996), p. 114.

27. Andrew Duncan, 'Russian Forces in Decline – Part 2', *Jane's Intelligence Review*, vol. 8, no. 10, pp. 442–7.

28. Duncan, op. cit.; IISS, *Military Balance 1996/97*.

29. Andrew Duncan, 'Russian Forces in Decline - Part 3', *Jane's Intelligence Review,* vol. 8, no. 11, pp. 491–7; IISS, *Military Balance 1996/97*.

30. Allison, 'Russian Armed Forces', p. 21.

31. Baev, *The Russian Army in a Time of Troubles*, p. 134.

32. John W. R. Lepingwell, 'Restructuring the Russian Military', RFE/RL *Research Report*, vol. 2, no. 25, 18 June 1993, pp. 17–24 at p. 20.

33. Dmitri Trenin, 'Russia's Military Resources', paper presented at a BIOst conference, November 1995.

34. Alexei Arbatov, *Obshchaya gazeta*, 31 October 1996.

35. Ibid.; see also 'Russia's Military: The Politics of Reform', *Strategic Comments*, vol. 2, no. 2, October 1996.

36. V. Andreevsky and V. Tkachev, 'Chtochto kasaetsya voprosa opredeleniya moshchnosti lichnogo sostava Vooruzhennykh Sil', *Voennaya mysl'*, no. 2, 1995, pp. 25–30.

37. See I. Rodin, *Nezavisimaya gazeta*, supplement, 14 December 1995, for an overview of the attitudes of different political groupings with regard to military reform and military policy.

38. Moscow Interfax, 'Defense Minister Says Russian Armed Forces in 'Crisis'' ', 25 October 1996, cited from FBIS-SOV-96-208.

39. Interfax, 4 October 1996, cited from FBIS-SOV-96-195.

40. *Rossiyskaya gazeta*, 17 January 1997, p. 5.

41. *Omri*, Daily Brief I, 10 February 1997.

42. The following section is in part based on a paper by Dov Lynch, 'A New Era in Russian Civil-military Relations and Military Reform?', to be published in 1997.

43. *Nezavisimaya gazeta,* 8 February 1997.

44. This is the view of Dov Lynch; see Lynch, 'A New Era in Russian Civil-military Relations'. Lynch refers to the following source: *Nezavisimoe voennoe obozrenie,* no. 22, 28 November 1996.

45. 'Russia' TV Channel, 22 May 1997 cited from Lynch, 'A New Era in Russian Civil-military Relations'.

46. *Nezavisimaya gazeta*, 23 May 1997.

47. 'Yeltsin Decrees Urgent Army Reform Measures', Interfax news agency, 18 July 1997, cited from *BBC Summary of World Broadcasts - Former Soviet Union* (henceforth SU) SU/2975 S1/1, 19 July 1997.

48. 760,000 is the official number, but Defence Council Secretary Baturin believes the real number to be far higher. See 'Defence Council Secretary Yuri Baturin Interviewed on Army Reforms', *Ekho Moskvy radio*, 17 July 1997, cited from SU/2975 S1/6, 19 July 1997.

49. During the Soviet period there was often intense rivalry between the anti-missile forces of the PVO and the Strategic Rocket Forces, duplication of resources (for example missile ranges and launchers) and overlapping areas of responsibility. For more detail see Bluth, *Soviet Strategic Arms Policy Before SALT* pp. 199–242.

50. ITAR-TASS news agency, 23 July 1997.

51. Mikhail Urusov, 'A Dangerous Breakup', *Moscow News*, 31 July- 6 August 1997, p. 3.

52. Urusov, op. cit.

53. ITAR-TASS news agency, 23 July 1997.

54. NTV, Moscow, 22 July 1997, cited from SU/2979 S1/3, 24 July 1997.

55. *Obshchaya gazeta*, 29 May 1997 (interview with Rodionov) .The figures given in that source have been adjusted for the level of reductions now required.

56. Interfax news agency, 22 July 1997, cited from SU/2989 S1/4, 24 July 1997. Nemtsov mentioned that revenue from the sale of shares in the Tyumen Oil Company would be used to repay wage arrears.

57. Judith Perera, 'Russian Forces Edge Closer to Financial Ruin', *Jane's Intelligence Review*, no. 2, February 1997, p. 69.
58. ITAR-TASS, Moscow, World Service, 7 May 1993, in SU/1684 C1/2, cited from Allison, 'Russian Armed Forces', p. 26.
59. Trenin, 'Russia's Military Resources'.
60. G. Borzenkov, *Krasnaya zvezda*, 30 June 1995.
61. ITAR-TASS, Moscow, 22 October 1996, FBIS-SOV-96-205.
62. *Rossiyskie vesti*, 15 December 1996.

5 The future role of the Russian defence industry

Julian Cooper

Since 1991 the Russian defence industry has experienced dramatic contraction and largely spontaneous restructuring under the combined impact of the break-up of the USSR, severe budgetary stringency and systemic transformation. The unstable economic and political environment, coupled with uncertainties about the security policy of the new Russian state, have rendered the pursuit of a coherent strategy for the contraction and reform of the defence industrial base almost impossible. Nevertheless, in a halting fashion, at considerable economic and human cost, a new Russian defence industry is beginning to emerge. Although reduced in scale, it should retain the capability to supply the Russian armed forces with modern weapons and to remain competitive in the world arms market. Contrary to the predictions of many observers both within Russia and abroad, there is now a prospect that this fundamental restructuring will be achieved without destabilizing social and political conflict. Many problems remain, however, not least in attitudes and expectations: aspirations have yet to be aligned fully with material possibilities.

The post-Soviet inheritance

While Russia inherited most of the Soviet defence-industrial base, including almost all the nuclear weapons development and production facilities, some significant capabilities were lost with the collapse of the USSR. Ukraine was left in possession of a major development and production centre for strategic missiles, one of the principal tank design and manufacturing bases, unique facilities for the building of heavy surface naval vessels, ship propulsion units and heavy transport aircraft, the USSR's largest manufacturer of aero engines and important centres for radar and optical systems. Lost to Belarus were major manufacturers of electronic components, optical and radar systems, and missile transporters; to Kazakstan, less strategically sensitive but nevertheless important producers of infantry weapons and naval armament; to Georgia and Uzbekistan, enterprises building combat and transport aircraft; and to the Baltic states, some significant suppliers of precision components and systems.

Thus whereas the Soviet Union's defence industry had a genuine across-the-board capability, this was lost to Russia from the end of 1991. The impact of fractured supply links was blunted, however, at least in the short term, by the existence of stockpiles of materials and components and also by the ability of enterprise directors to draw on long-standing personal contacts in order to maintain supplies, often on a barter basis.

In the Soviet Union most production of weapons and military equipment was undertaken by organizations subordinate to a set of powerful industrial ministries, eight or nine in number in the final years of the regime. Under Yeltsin this ministerial system was disbanded and control of the Russian defence industry passed to a much weaker Committee for the Defence Industry, upgraded in 1993 to a state committee, Goskomoboronprom. The internal organization of Goskomoboronprom reflected its Soviet origins in so far as it had eight branch departments, similar in scope to the disbanded ministries. Only in the nuclear industry was a Soviet-style ministry retained in the shape of the ministry of atomic energy (Minatom). Of the other agencies with some involvement in military production, the two most important are the Russian Space Agency, which by the end of 1995 had taken over almost forty facilities from the missile-space department of Goskomoboronprom, and the Committee for Machine Building, although military work represents only a small proportion of the latter's total output.[1] As discussed below, in May 1996 Goskomoboronprom was upgraded to create a ministry of the defence industry (Minoboronprom).

Contraction

Since 1992 budget allocations for the armed forces of the ministry of defence have been reduced to less than 4 per cent of GDP. Price liberalization and reduced levels taken by procurement have had a dramatic impact on the structure of the defence budget: the shares taken by procurement and R&D have fallen sharply, with particular pressure on the latter, at least until 1995, probably because it has been unable to mobilize political support as effectively as the production sphere (see Tables 5.1 and 5.2). To make matters worse for the defence industry, actual budget outlays have consistently fallen below planned levels of expenditure and payments have been made only after long delays, during which their value has been eroded by inflation. While much depends on the general state of the economy, there is little prospect of any appreciable relaxation of budgetary stringency for the remaining years of the century.

The output of the Russian defence industry has declined inexorably since 1992, when procurement was cut at a stroke by two-thirds, and showed no sign of recovery even by mid-1996. By 1995 total military output was barely one-

Table 5.1: Procurement and R&D within the budget for national defence (% total budget for 'national defence'), 1991–6

	1991[a]	1992	1993	1994	1995	1996
Procurement	37.3	16.1	18.3	20.8	17.3	16.5
Military R&D	16.7	10.6	7.2	6.0	8.3	8.1
Minatom[b]	1.9	2.8	1.6	2.1	1.7	1.9

[a] USSR.

[b] Expenditure of the ministry of atomic energy on the development and production of nuclear weapons.

Sources: 1991–3: *SIPRI Yearbook 1994* (Stockholm/Oxford: SIPRI/Oxford University Press, 1994), p. 426; 1994: *SIPRI Yearbook 1995*, p. 406; 1995: final version of budget, as approved 27 December 1995 (*Rossiyskaya gazeta*, 4 January 1996); 1996: budget as approved 31 December 1995 (*Rossiyskaya gazeta*, 10 January 1996).

Table 5.2: Defence expenditure as % GDP, 1992–6[a]

	1992	1993	1994	1995	1996
'National defence' as % GDP	4.5	4.2	4.4	2.9	3.5

[a] Data refer to actual defence expenditure. For 1992–3 the revised GDP series (*Finansovye izvestiya*, 29 September 1995) has been employed.

Sources: 1992–5: *Russian Economic Trends*, various issues; 1996: budget as approved and GDP estimate, 2,300,000 billion roubles (*Voprosy ekonomiki*, 1996, no. 2, p. 114).

fifth of the level of output of 1991 (see Table 5.3). For Goskomoboronprom, military output in 1996 was a mere 13 per cent of the 1991 level (see Table 5.4). The civilian output of the defence industry has also fallen sharply, especially in 1994/5, with the result that for Goskomoboronprom civil output in 1996 was barely 30 per cent of the 1991 level. The decline in output of consumer goods has been especially marked: almost 38 per cent in 1995 alone.[2] However, the figure for the defence industry as a whole conceals the differential performance of Minatom and Goskomoboronprom: output of consumer goods rose by 15 per cent in the former, but fell by approximately 50 per cent in the latter.[3] The factors responsible for this substantial contraction of civil output include foreign competition, a sharp decline in the demand for investment goods and a severe reduction of funding for national and local government procurement of such items as transport equipment and medical instruments.

There has been considerable variation in the fortunes of the different sectors of the defence industry under the impact of procurement cuts, an abrupt

Table 5.3: Russian defence industry: output and employment, 1991–5 (index, 1991 = 100)

Branch	Output				Employment[a]		
	1992	1993	1994	1995	1992	1993	1994
Nuclear	102	105	84		97	94	88
Missile-space	100[b]	95	67	61[c]	100[b]	89	77
Aviation	84	68	36	31[c]	91	82	70
Armaments	84	69	43	33[c]	93	85	73
Munitions	70	57	36	31[c]	92	82	67
Shipbuilding	89	78	58	64[c]	90	81	70
Radio	84	78	49	33[c]	87	75	62
Communications equipment	74	58	32	21[c]	87	71	57
Electronics	72	48	26	22[c]	92	75	57
All defence industry including	82	69	45	39	91	80	67
military production	62	43	26	22	63	49	
civilian production	93	83	56	48	108	100	

[a] Employment data for 1995 not available.
[b] 1992 = 100 (data for 1992 cf. 1991 not available).
[c] Eleven months.
Sources: 1992–4: Tsentr ekonomicheskoi kon'yunktury pri Sovet Ministrov, *Rossiya* – 1994, vyp.1, p.193; *Rossiya* – 1995, vyp.1, p. 139 (data for Goskomoboronprom and Minatom); 1995: *Segodnya*, 27 December 1995; BBC, *Summary of World Broadcasts*, SUW/0421 WD/16, 9 February 1996.

Table 5.4: Output of Goskomoboronprom, 1991–6 (index, 1991 = 100)

	1992	1993	1994	1995	1996
Total output	80.4	64.6	39.2	30.9	22.5
Military	49.5	32.5	19.9	16.6	12.8
Civilian	99.0	85.6	52.6	40.4	29.3[a]

[a] January to October only.
Source: *Krasnaya zvezda*, 17 February, 22 June 1996 and 23 January 1997.

contraction of deliveries to foreign clients, and declining civilian output (see Table 5.4). Exploiting civil nuclear possibilities, Minatom has fared relatively well, achieving a modest growth of output in 1994/5. By early 1996 civilian production is reported to have accounted for 90 per cent of Minatom's total output.[4] The shipbuilding industry has also maintained activity by securing foreign civil contracts. The aircraft industry, unable to find many customers for

Table 5.5: USSR Russian Federation: production of major weapons systems: Western estimates (units), 1990–94

	1990	1991	1992	1993	1994
Strategic missiles	190	100	65	35	25
Fighters/ground attack	575	225	150	100	50
Transport aircraft[a]	n.a.	70	60	60	35
Helicopters[a]	n.a.	350	175	150	100
Main battle tanks	1,300	900	500	200	40
Infantry fighting vehicles	4,400	3,000	750	300	400
Submarines	12	6	6	4	4
Major surface ships	8	3	1	1	0

[a] Includes civilian production.
Source: USSR, 1990: US Department of Defence, *Military Forces in Transition 1991*, pp. 22–3; Russian: UK ministry of defence estimates (as published in *Moscow Times*, 9 April 1996, p. 11).

Table 5.6: Employment in the Russian defence industry ('000 employees), 1991–5[a]

	1991	1992	1993	1994	1995	% change 1991—5
Goskomoboronprom (GKOP) Industry	4,440	3,990	3,440	2,820	2,500	-44
R&D	980	885	765	680	500	-49
Total employment[b]	5,440	4,890	4,225	3,500	3,000+	-45
Minatom[c]	960	930	905	850		
GKOP+ Minatom						

[a] Data for 1992–4 refer to November of each year; 1995, October; 1991, approximate end of year totals.
[b] Includes a small residual of other unidentified types of employment.
[c] Minatom data are less accurate as based on an approximate total for 1991 and 1994 and reported annual changes in the number of 'industrial productive personnel' (excluding R&D). *Sources*: Goskomoboronprom: 1992 and 1993: *Segodnya*, 1 February 1994; 1994: calculated from percentage changes in employment, November 1993 to November 1994 (*Krasnaya zvezda*, 28 January 1995); 1991: calculated from total employment in 1991 minus Minatom employment; total employment derived from November 1992 total (GKOP plus Minatom) using 9% overall decline in 1992 (see Table 5.3). Both industrial and R&D employment are assumed to have declined in 1992 by similar c.10%. 1995: *Delovoi mir*, 27 December 1995, *Segodnya*, 27 December 1995. Minatom: Based on total employment of c.800,000 early 1995 (*Rossiyskaya gazeta*, 25 February 1995) and c.1 million in 1991/2 (*Delovoi mir*, 27 May 1992); annual percentage change 1991–4 as Table 5.3.

civil transports, suffered a severe downturn in 1994 which continued to 1996, when for the first time the industry received no orders from domestic airlines for new aircraft.[5] Most severely hit has been the electronics industry, reduced by 1995 to a mere one-fifth of its 1991 output. Given the opportunity to buy foreign components of higher quality, Russian producers of electronic equipment have deserted the domestic industry *en masse*. The same applies to the Russian computer and communications equipment industries: the former has almost completely disappeared, surviving only as a small-scale assembly industry based on imported components.

In most cases official Russian data are not available, but an indication of output trends for major weapons systems is provided by the estimates presented in Table 5.5. The figures for 1995 are likely to be even lower. With the exception of strategic missiles, the major factor sustaining output since 1992 has been export orders.

The labour force of the defence industry has declined since 1991, but not to the same extent as output. The directors of enterprises and institutes have shown great ingenuity in maintaining employment, but nevertheless, by the end of 1995, in the main by voluntary means rather than enforced redundancies, the Russian defence industry had lost almost 2.5 million employees (see Table 5.6). For Goskomoboronprom the decline has been more severe than for Minatom, amounting to 44 per cent for the former and probably little more than 10 per cent for the latter. Employment in the R&D sector has been maintained more successfully, possibly because research personnel have proved to be better equipped to earn a living without leaving the military sector. At least until Gorbachev came to power, the defence industry was one of the best-paid industrial sectors, but since 1991 pay levels have declined steadily in relation to the average industrial wage. The nuclear and ship-building industries have been the most successful in maintaining their levels of pay, the hard-pressed electronics-related branches the least successful. These figures must be treated with caution, however. The defence industry is characterized by an extraordinary degree of intra-branch variation in pay between enterprises. Furthermore, average rates of pay conceal a reality familiar to many workers: wage arrears are common, at times amounting to several months, as enterprises experience long delays in receiving payment from customers, above all the ministry of defence, which is kept on an impossibly tight budgetary rein by the ministry of finance.

The financial fortunes of significant arms producers are now linked to arms exports (see Table 5.7). According to the former deputy prime minister Oleg Soskovets, in 1995 the sale of weapons abroad exceeded domestic procurement by 60 per cent.[6] Whereas in the past most of the proceeds from foreign arms sales went directly to the state budget, now the producers gain a larger share of the income. At an official level there is still considerable optimism

Table 5.7: Russian arms exports (US$ billion, current prices), 1992–6[a]

	1992	1993	1994	1995	1996[b]
Arms exports	2.3	2.5	1.7	3.05	3.5—3.6

[a]Data from Russian sources. For 1994–6 (forecast) the series appears to be consistent, but may not be fully compatible with 1992–3.
[b]Forecast.
Sources: 1992, 1993: *Izvestiya*, 19 April 1994; 1994: *Segodnya*, 30 December 1995; 1995: *Krasnaya zvezda*, 13 April 1996 (including Rosvooruzhenie, $2.8 billion); 1996 forecast: *Finansovye izvestiya*, 4 April 1996 (forecast of Kotelkin, general director of Rosvooruzhenie); in June 1996 the forecast was revised to $3.0–3.5 billion (*Kommersant-Daily*, 29 June 1996).

with regard to export prospects. Whether this is justified in the face of greater competition from the United States, which may now begin to extend even into the former Soviet space, remains to be seen.[7]

Conversion

Since 1992 Russia has maintained a policy commitment to the conversion of part of the capacity of the defence industry to civilian purposes.[8] In practice, notwithstanding the adoption of state programmes and the provision of budgetary allocations to fund conversion activities, the results have not been impressive. A fundamental problem has been inadequate funding: actual budget disbursements have consistently fallen far below planned allocations. Other serious obstacles have been the collapse of the domestic market and changes in the structure of demand arising from the opening up of the Russian economy and shifting relative prices.

In an attempt to focus conversion activity on a limited number of fields considered to have national importance, in December 1995 the government adopted a new federal conversion programme for the period 1995–7, consisting of seven sub-programmes for Goskomoboronprom (civil aviation, shipbuilding, fuel and energy sector equipment, medical equipment, electronics, consumer goods, and communications and information technology) and one for Minatom. Total planned funding is 18.6 trillion roubles to the end of 1997, including direct state budget funding of 7.4 trillion roubles.[9] Also in December 1995 a decision was taken to create a new state conversion fund, with income from diverse sources, including the state budget and dividends accruing to the state-held shares of firms undergoing conversion.[10]

It would be a mistake to characterize all conversion activities in Russia since 1992 as unsuccessful. In some fields there have been genuine achievements, above all in those sectors of the economy in which there has been relatively strong domestic demand backed by real purchasing power. While the civil aviation and shipbuilding programmes have experienced considerable difficulties, enterprises developing and manufacturing equipment for the fuel and energy sector have found customers for their new products. Many new producers of equipment for the oil and gas industry have appeared, although frustration has been openly expressed that Russian oil and gas companies have shown a preference for imported technology, and there have been calls for better coordination of the new producers to enhance their strength as a lobby.[11] There has been state support for one project of vital concern to the Severodvinsk State Centre for Atomic Ship Building: the supply of equipment for the exploration and exploitation of the offshore oil and gas resources of the Pechora and Barents seas. To the fore in this project is the joint-stock company AO Rosshel'f, led by Academician Yevgeny Velikhov, who has become a vigorous advocate of dual-use technologies. Drilling rigs and specialized ships are now being built using capacities previously devoted to submarine construction.[12]

On a more modest scale, but apparently successful, has been a programme to develop and manufacture equipment for the coal industry. This is an import substitution programme to provide Russian sources of supply for the technology previously acquired from producers in Ukraine and Kazakstan, in Soviet times responsible for 60 per cent of all coal industry equipment. Some 20 defence industry companies are involved, including the missile industry's Yurga machine-building works in Siberia, the principal producer of equipment for missile launch silos and rail mobile launchers, AO Nizhne-gorodski mashinostroitel'nyi zavod, producing nuclear technology and also large-calibre guns, and the Volgograd Barrikady, which builds missile transport erector launchers. Representatives of the coal industry have praised the quality of the new equipment that has been developed and see promising export possibilities.[13]

The building of transport equipment has also provided conversion opportunities. One of the most significant projects is the proposed building of a high-speed railway between St Petersburg and Moscow, which will reduce the journey time to three hours. More than 50 defence industry companies are involved in the design and building of equipment, in particular the Rubin Central Design Bureau of St Petersburg, the principal Russian design organization for nuclear submarines, which together with the Yakovlev aircraft design organization is responsible for the design of the Sokol high-speed train (up to 250 km per hour). Also involved in design work on this project is the country's principal research institute for armoured vehicles, the St Petersburg VNII Transmash. The train itself is being built at the Tikhvin AO Transmash, a defence industry company previously part of the tank- and tractor-building concern Kirovskii zavod. By April 1995 more than 17,000 people were reported to be employed on the project.[14]

An issue of serious concern to the government and the ministry of defence is the collapse of the Russian electronics industry. The federal programme for its revival has been starved of funding and does not appear to have achieved much success. More promising has been the conversion programme of Minatom, which has a strong focus on the development of microelectronics, including the production of materials for the manufacture of advanced components and fibre optics, and the development of new supercomputers. In effect, a new microelectronics industry is appearing alongside the specialist branch overseen by Minoboronprom. A great advantage of Minatom is its ability to fund conversion activities from its substantial export earnings: planned funding for Minatom's conversion programme for 1995/7 is almost three times that allocated to the programme for the development of the electronics industry, and has much greater credibility, as two-thirds is to be derived from non-budget sources, as opposed to only one-third for the latter.[15]

Working for the future

Research and development in the defence industry has been cut back sharply since 1991 and the number of personnel in institutes and design organizations attached to Goskomoboronprom has fallen by nearly 50 per cent. For a long time the situation was exacerbated by the lack of a coherent policy for restructuring and also by the failure to agree a medium- or long-term armaments programme that would clarify priorities for the industry's R&D system. Some institutes have sought salvation through privatization, but such hopes have rarely been fulfilled. For many research and design organizations, privatization presented new problems as it was associated with the break-up of the Soviet-era corporate structures, the production and science-production associations. Institutes previously linked to the enterprises were transformed into free-standing organizations, and in some cases the experimental production facilities attached to institutes or design organizations were split off and privatized separately. In these circumstances, it is not surprising that many R&D organizations of the defence industry have attempted to remain in the state sector and to lobby for continued budget funding.

In order to provide some protection for major centres of research, in June 1993 Yeltsin approved the formation of state research centres (GNTs). Such centres could expect to receive at least part of their funding from the state budget.[16] Understandably, many industrial R&D organizations have applied for this status, but the ministry of science and technology policy, from whose budget the funding is provided, has maintained a selective policy. By 1996

61 GNTs had been created, 25 (40 per cent) of them in, or closely related to, the defence industry. These included seventeen under Goskomoboronprom, six under Minatom and two non-affiliated: the Moscow Kurchatov Institute of the nuclear industry and the St Petersburg Institute of Applied Chemistry, a major centre for research into liquid propellants for missiles. The GNT scheme has provided a measure of protection for such leading research institutes as the Central Aerohydrodynamics Institute (TsAGI), the Krylov Institute of the shipbuilding industry and the Vavilov State Optical Institute.[17]

Another form of state-supported R&D organization has been created specifically for the defence industry: the federal research and production centre (FNPTs), granted formal status by a decree of October 1995. These centres are to be created on the basis of research and manufacturing facilities responsible for what are considered to be the most important types of military hardware. Their ownership can be of any form, but the designation of FNPT indicates that they are eligible for special state support.[18] By the end of 1995 five centres with FNPTs status had been created, including the Severodvinsk State Centre for Atomic Shipbuilding, the Moscow Khrunichev Centre for space equipment and the Miass (Urals) Makeev Centre for sea-launched missiles. It has been reported that the creation of more than 50 FNPTs is under consideration.[19]

Reduced funding, loss of personnel and general disorganization suggest at times that the Russian defence industry has lost its capability to work for the future. This impression is distinctly misleading. In fact, an extraordinary resilience has been shown and it is clear that there are many new development programmes under way, especially in those organizations able to export, or those considered so vital to Russia's national security that funding of programmes has been maintained. However, there is little doubt that the range and diversity of development programmes have been reduced, with reports that a significant number of programmes in progress in the final days of the Soviet Union have been curtailed. Nevertheless, given the substantial duplication and redundancy characteristic of the Soviet military R&D effort, this narrowing of focus is not necessarily detrimental to Russia's ability to develop new weapons.

Prominent among the domestic programmes not driven by export earnings or prospects is the work of the Moscow Institut Teplotekhniki on the Topol-M2 strategic missile, which in both mobile and silo form will become the mainstay of the country's land-based nuclear deterrent. It has been emphasized that this is a purely Russian ICBM, with no Ukrainian input.[20] It can be assumed that similar development work is being undertaken at the Miass Makeev design bureau on submarine-launched missiles. In addition, as acknowledged by the minister of the atomic industry, Viktor Mikhailov, work continues on the development of nuclear weapons to improve safety and to enhance their ability to counter anti-missile defence systems.[21]

New military aircraft under development include the MiG-AT and Yak-130 trainers, the former with French participation, the latter with Italian; the Su-39 ground attack aircraft (a modernization of the Su-25); the Su-37 fighter; and a new MiG multi-role fighter, known in the West as project I-42. Both Mil and Kamov have new helicopter programmes, including the Ka-52, a two-seater version of the Ka-50 combat helicopter. The Nizhnii-Tagil Uralvagonzavod design bureau has developed the T-90 tank, although this is more of a modernization of the T-72 and T-80 than a new model.[22] It has been acknowledged that work is continuing on the development of a new generation strategic nuclear submarine: after the year 2002 it is planned to deliver to the navy one boat per year.[23] There have been tests of what is claimed to be an original, high-precision, operational–tactical missile system for the ground forces. This appears to be a development by the Kolomna machine-building design bureau, previously responsible for the Oka (SS-23) system – scrapped, mistakenly in the view of many Russian observers, under the terms of the INF Treaty.[24]

It should not be overlooked that in developing new systems Russian firms can exploit possibilities not previously open to them. Access to foreign technology is no longer impeded by the COCOM system, direct links can be established with Western defence contractors, and regular participation in the principal arms fairs and displays provides opportunities for Russian designers and engineers to keep abreast of developments.

Concerned to protect the country's technological base in order to maintain a capability to develop new weapons at the forefront of technology, the defence community has increasingly focused policy on two related issues. First, in 1994 work began on a programme of measures to develop critical technologies. This federal programme, the National Technological Base, has been promoted by the leadership of Goskomoboronprom and also by Andrei Kokoshin, first deputy defence minister. It gained government approval in August 1996.[25] Secondly, the development of dual-use technologies has moved to the forefront of the policy agenda, perceived by many as a means of maintaining advanced skills and capabilities vital to military work while enhancing the civil economy's technological level. Funding considerations are not entirely absent: by promoting dual-use technology programmes, some within the defence sector clearly hope to gain access to a larger share of the civilian science budget.

Two of the most prominent advocates of the development of dual-use technologies have been Yevgeny Velikhov and Zinovii Pak. Velikhov, president of AO Rosshel'f, succeeded in putting the issue on the agenda of the presidential Council on Science and Technology Policy at its very first meeting in August 1995 and has been campaigning for the adoption of a very ambitious federal programme for the development of dual-use technologies.[26] Pak, until

May 1996 general director of the Lyubertsy Soyuz science-production association, a major centre for the development of solid-propellant missile propulsion systems, was one of the first Russian defence sector directors to promote dual-use technologies. In June 1994 Yeltsin visited Soyuz and was evidently impressed by Pak and his work. In the following year Yeltsin approved the organization at Soyuz of a federal centre for dual-use technologies of defence enterprises, with Pak as director. Later in the year Pak was made a member of the presidential Council on Science and Technology Policy and also accompanied Yeltsin on his trip to Washington. In May 1996 the 56-year-old Pak was appointed chairman of Goskomoboronprom, where from the very beginning, evidently with Yeltsin's approval, he put the development of dual-use technologies at the centre of his policy agenda.[27]

State or private?

Since 1992 one of the principal issues for the Russian defence industry has been that of ownership. Should enterprises engaged in the development and manufacture of armaments remain in state hands, or should they be permitted to privatize? After initial resistance, by the end of 1993 the leadership of the defence industry had accepted that many firms could be transformed into joint-stock companies, but it had been agreed by the government that a set of core facilities considered essential to the country's national security would remain in full state ownership, or would retain a controlling state shareholding, at least for a transitional three-year period.[28] This state participation could take the form of a single so-called 'Golden Share', giving the state a right to veto any decision of the company considered detrimental to the country's national security. A draft list of 474 facilities of Goskomoboronprom not to be privatized in 1993–5 was set out in a government decree of 19 August 1993, and a revised final version was approved in December that year.

Contrary to a widely held, but inaccurate, stereotype of the 'red director' allegedly typical of the Russian defence industry, many leaders of enterprises favoured privatization, as they perceived it as a means of escaping from administrative intervention by Goskomoboronprom and other state agencies. This applied above all to those enterprises that appeared to have some chance of commercial success, especially those with export prospects. In some cases enterprises had to fight for this right in the face of opposition from Goskomoboronprom. On the other hand, directors of less favourably placed enterprises, as well as old-style Soviet-era leaders unable or unwilling to adapt to the new conditions – some of whom were still, and are still, to be found – fought to be placed on the 'no-privatization' list. In these circumstances, it is not at all clear that national security needs have predominated in deciding which enterprises are to remain in state hands.

Privatization changed the relationship of enterprises to Goskomoboronprom. Four categories of enterprise were created. Some fully privatized facilities, usually those no longer engaged in military work, left the state committee altogether. By agreement, other fully privatized companies maintain collaborative relations with Goskomoboronprom and are still considered to come under its supervision. This also applies to joint-stock companies in which the state holds a stake. Finally, there are the fully state-owned enterprises which remain subordinate to the state committee. By the end of 1995, almost 13 per cent of Goskomoboronprom's total number of facilities, had left, 24 per cent had been fully privatized and remained under its supervision, 28 per cent had a state ownership stake and 35 per cent remained in state hands.[29] In the aviation industry only 21 per cent of enterprises were state-owned; the corresponding proportions were 35 per cent in the armaments industry, producing infantry weapons, armoured vehicles, optical equipment and solid-propellant missiles, 40 per cent in the shipbuilding industry, 54 per cent in the missile-space industry and 82 per cent in the munitions and special chemicals industry.[30]

The privatization of defence enterprises has generated considerable controversy. A number of individual cases have received extensive attention in the media, notably that of the Rybinsk aero-engine works, one of the largest producers of aircraft engines in Russia. After a prolonged struggle, the government was forced to retreat from its attempt to sell its shareholding, an intention opposed by Goskomoboronprom and the company's management because they feared that the company would fall into the hands of AO Gazprom, which would, they believed, sooner or later withdraw from the building of aero engines. Eventually, in the spring of 1996, AO Rybinskie motory was placed on the list of strategic enterprises, whose federal shareholding cannot be sold prematurely.[31] More heat has been generated by the issue of foreign participation in the ownership of defence sector companies, which has been made the subject of a campaign against the government by communists and nationalists. The biggest scandal related to a small US company, Nick and C Corporation, which succeeded in buying shares in nineteen Russian defence companies, mainly in the aerospace industry, including some heavily engaged in military work. In this case the campaign was successful: in March 1996 the Moscow Arbitration Court ruled that Nick and C Corporation's purchases of shares were illegal and ordered their surrender.[32] It is clear that there will be considerable reluctance in Russia for the foreseeable future to permit a foreign ownership stake in firms with any serious involvement in military work.

In a bid to calm agitation from communists and other critics, who had been alleging that privatization of defence enterprises presented a threat to Russia's national security, in April 1996, in the run-up to the presidential elections,

Yeltsin established a federal commission to review privatization in the defence industry.[33] This initiative was also related to work then under way to draw up a list of defence enterprises not subject to privatization. In February 1996, before the creation of the federal commission, the then chairman of the State Property Committee, Aleksandr Kazakov, had spoken in terms of 400 defence enterprises which would not be privatized; in the event, in July, the government approved a list of 480 such enterprises, suggesting that the commission to some extent yielded to conservative and nationalist pressure.[34]

The 480 enterprises and organizations of the ministry of the defence industry that will remain in full state ownership according to the government decree of 13 July 1996 include 45 in the aviation industry, 60 in the missile-space industry, 60 in the armaments industry, 93 in the munitions and special chemicals industry, 54 in shipbuilding, 51 in the communications equipment industry, 73 in the radio industry, and 44 in electronics. As a proportion of the total number of facilities in each branch, by far the highest share of state-owned enterprises will continue to be in the munitions industry. Overall, the state-owned facilities represent almost 30 per cent of Minoboronprom's 1,700 enterprises.[35] In addition there are fully state-owned facilities in both Minatom and the Russian Space Agency. If account is also taken of those firms in which the state will retain a controlling interest, there remains little doubt that in Russia the development and manufacture of weapons is set to remain an activity of the state sector of the economy to a much greater extent than is typical of most market economies.

Policy for restructuring: corporatization

During the first three years of the new Russian regime inaugurated in 1991 there was no coherent policy for restructuring the defence industry. To a large extent enterprises were left to find their own place in the emerging market economy. A policy for restructuring was finally set out in a government decree of 19 December 1994, dealing specifically with measures to stabilize the economic situation of enterprises and organizations in the defence complex.[36] Three lines of restructuring were established: first, as discussed above, the creation of state scientific and production centres for the development and production of the most important types of military hardware; secondly, the formation of so-called 'treasury' factories, i.e. fully state-owned facilities; thirdly, the transformation of other enterprises into joint-stock companies. The decree called for the completion of this restructuring during the first half of 1995, but by early 1997 it had hardly begun, hampered above all by the inability of the government to secure adequate state budget funding to support the state centres and treasury factories.

Since 1994 the principal thrust of restructuring in practice has been the formation of new corporate structures, bringing together related design and manufacturing facilities in companies, corporations, military-industrial companies or financial-industrial groups. One of the first advocates of such a policy was the first deputy defence minister, Andrei Kokoshin, who, as early as the autumn of 1992, had promoted the creation of financial-industrial groups (FIGs) in the defence industry, modelled on the South Korean *chaebols*. These FIGs, uniting enterprises, R&D organizations and financial institutions, would, he argued, develop and produce competitive military, civilian and dual-use goods, and would play the role of 'locomotives' of the Russian economy.[37]

While the number of officially registered FIGs in the defence sector remains small, a very active process of corporatization is under way, driven to a large extent by export possibilities. This policy has been promoted vigorously by Boris Kuzyk, Yeltsin's adviser on the arms trade, Andrei Kokoshin, Oleg Soskovets, and also the new minister of the defence industry, Zinovii Pak. The most striking example of this process to date is the formation of the 'military-industrial company' (*voenno-promyshlennaya kompleks* – VPK) MAPO, created in the first half of 1996 following a presidential decree in late January. The organization of this state-owned company, uniting twelve enterprises together employing 100,000 people, marks a major step in the restructing of the Russian aviation industry. It includes not only the MiG design organization and its associated MAPO production plant, but also the Kamov helicopter design organization, the St Petersburg Klimov aero-engine design bureau, major manufacturers of systems, and Aviabank.[38] With its strong export orientation, VPK MAPO clearly has the potential to become a significant force in the world military aircraft industry. A similar aviation corporation, Sukhoi, was organized at the end of 1996.

Other initiatives in the aviation industry include the creation of the Il'yushin transnational FIG, bringing together the Moscow design organization and the two largest plants building Il'yushin planes: Voronezh and the Tashkent Chkalov plant in Uzbekistan, which builds the Il-76T, widely used as a military transport aircraft. This FIG has encountered difficulties, and in the absence of firm orders for its products from Russia, the Tashkent plant has shown an interest in finding alternative partners.[39] The Tupolev design organization has formed a link with its Ukrainian counterpart Antonov to form the Mezhdunarodnye aviatsionnye proekty group,[40] and is also a member of the Rossiiskii aviatsionnyi konsortium FIG organized for the production of Tupolev civil aircraft. The Yakovlev aviation design organization now forms part of the Yak corporation, together with production plants in Saratov and Smolensk.[41] This example is being followed by the Mil company, AO Moskovskii verto-letnyi zavod M L Milya, which plans to link up with the two leading companies building its helicopters, the Rostov and Kazan plants, and banks, to form the helicopter corporation Mil.[42] Clearly, then, restructuring is well under way in the aviation industry; further rationalization can be expected, however, as by international standards the Russian industry still has excess capacity and too many competing design organizations.

Two substantial corporations now dominate the development and manufacture of air defence systems, a field in which Russia is optimistic of substantial export sales. The AO Promyshlennaya Kompaniya Kontsern Antei was created by government decree in December 1994 on the basis of the Antei research and production organization, with Veniamin Efremov as director and general designer. It unites more than fifteen development facilities and manufacturing plants responsible for such systems as the S-300V, Tor and Krug.[43] A more recent development is the creation of AO Oboronitel'nye sistemy which brings together the country's principal facilities for the design and production of anti-missile air defence systems. Marketing and improved systems integration are to the fore in this initiative, which involves the Almaz and Fakel design organization and associated facilities involved in the development and manufacture of the S-300PMU-1 (the Russian equivalent of the US Patriot system, claimed to be superior by its producers and Rosvooruzhenie) and other air defence systems. The organization of this joint-stock company appears to represent a market-driven development from below, and not the product of a central state initiative.[44]

In the missile-space industry the Kompomash corporation, created in November 1994, links fourteen state enterprises and joint-stock companies in order to enhance their ability to diversify into the production of high-technology equipment for the fuel and energy, transport, agriculture and medical sectors. Companies involved include the Miass KB V P Makeeva, the principal design organization for submarine-launched ballistic missiles; Energomash, the leading design organization for rocket engines; Tekhnomash, the missile industry's main institute for production technology, and Kompozit, a major centre for advanced materials. One of Russia's leading banks, Imperial, is also involved. The intention is that defence orders will constitute no more than one-fifth of the total volume of work. Kompomash employs some 70,000 people. Again, this new corporation appears to be a product of enterprise from below, although initially a 51 per cent state ownership stake has been retained.[45]

Some regional corporate groupings are also appearing. A notable example is FIG Aviatsionnya promyshlennost' Sibiri, bringing together all the principal aerospace facilities of the Omsk region, in particular the vast Polet concern, where Kosmos space launchers and satellites and also the An-74 aircraft are built, and the Baranov aero-engine plant, which produces engines for the MiG-29.[46] Transnational groupings are still few in number. One of the first to be formed was the interstate joint-stock corporation (MAK) Vympel, a Russian–

Belarusian company employing more than 35,000 people and, bringing together the principal facilities of the CIS involved in the creation and manufacture of missile early warning radar systems, although in the absence of new orders it has been actively diversifying into telecommunications.[47] Given its profile, it is likely Vympel will play an important role in the new transnational FIG Granit, which is to be created to provide equipment for the common air defence system, to the creation of which all CIS member countries are now committed.[48]

Restoring broken links

Strenuous efforts have been made since 1992 to restore fractured defence industry links within the framework of the CIS. Russia has concluded a series of bilateral agreements with all CIS member states to maintain such links and to provide possibilities for collaboration on military technological projects. It is clear that the Russian defence industry has been relatively successful in this endeavour. To its advantage has been its superior bargaining power: Russian defence plants can find ways of substituting for inputs from other CIS states, but enterprises in the CIS beyond Russian borders have poor prospects if they are deprived of their Russian partners. As Alexei Shulunov, president of the Russian League in Support of Defence Industry Enterprises, has observed, many enterprises outside Russia have faithfully maintained their supply links with Russian enterprises, 'living on vague hopes' in the absence of any payment.[49]

Information revealed by Viktor Glukhikh, former head of Goskomoboronprom, in December 1995 indicates the extent to which supply links have been retained or restored. He noted that Goskomoboronprom worked with all CIS member countries within the framework of 25 intergovernmental and seventeen interministerial agreements. These agreements made provision for enterprises involved in the production of military hardware to work together without customs tariffs or taxes on interstate transfers. In 1995 440 Russian enterprises involved in military production had received deliveries from 1,033 enterprises located in CIS member countries.[50]

There has been much discussion of the creation of transnational financial-industrial groups in the defence industry as a means of strengthening links within the CIS, but, as noted above, to date there has been only limited practical implementation of this concept. The examples of Ilyushin and Vympel have been cited, but the most significant is the Russian–Ukrainian FIG Mezhdunarodnye aviatsionnye motory, which brings together almost 40 design organizations and enterprises engaged in the development and manufacture of aero engines, the principal members being the Zaporizhzhia Progress design bureau and AO Motor Sich, the biggest aero-engine factory of the FSU. This transnational FIG was under discussion for over a year before it was finally established in April 1996.[51]

Alongside efforts to maintain links within the CIS, the Russian defence industry has also been pursuing an import substitution policy, which appears to have been directed above all towards eliminating dependence on external sources of supply for systems, components and materials considered vital to Russia's national security. This balance is likely to be maintained, taking advantage of links that can be developed, but insuring against their possible future breakdown.

A new stage?

Developments in the first half of 1996 suggested that the Russian defence industry had embarked on a new stage of development. There is little doubt that Yeltsin decided to take action to strengthen the position of the defence sector following the poor performance of reform-orientated parties in the elections to the State Duma in December 1995. The first sign of change was the abrupt dismissal in January of Glukhikh as leader of Goskomoboronprom and his replacement by, as noted above, Zinovii Pak.[52]

From the start it was clear that Pak had his own views on a development strategy for the defence industry and also that his thinking had much in common with that of Kokoshin of the ministry of defence, who was given state secretary status immediately after Pak's appointment, and Kuzyk, Yeltsin's personal adviser on the arms trade and defence industry matters. At a meeting with Yeltsin shortly after his appointment, Pak is reported to have urged a transition to smaller but better-equipped armed forces.[53] He has also advocated a higher profile for the defence sector within the structures of government, the creation of larger, state-owned, corporate structures, including FIGs, increased expenditure on military R&D, and measures to reduce the burden on enterprises of having to maintain spare capacity for potential mobilization.[54]

No doubt influenced to a large degree by the forthcoming presidential election and the need to win the support of employees in the defence sector, between January and June the government adopted a series of measures to support defence industry enterprises in particular regions, including Sverdlovsk and Khabarovsk, and the republics of Marii-El, Tatarstan and Udmurtia. Yeltsin, Chernomyrdin, Soskovets, Pak and Kokoshin also visited major centres of the industry, including, in the president's case, the Energomash rocket engine centre at Khimki, Severodvinsk, the Kapustin Yar missile test range, Ekaterinburg and Khabarovsk.

At the end of 1995 a law for which the defence industry had been campaigning since 1992 was finally adopted. The law on the state defence order codifies the contractual relations between the ministry of defence as purchaser and the firms of the defence industry as suppliers, although its full im-plementation will probably have to wait until the budget situation has improved.[55]

Yeltsin also indicated that another controversial issue was under consideration, arguing with Pak for a reduction in the scale of mobilization capacities required of enterprises, freeing space and equipment for civilian work. For many enterprises, the stipulation that they maintain these mobilization capacities has contributed to their financial difficulties, given that state budget support for the mobilization system has to a large extent collapsed since the end of the Soviet regime. A decree of July 1994 permitted some reduction in the scale of mobilization capacities and reserves, but this proved inadequate.[56]

This new level of official attention to the defence industry reached its climax shortly before the first round of voting in the presidential election. On 8 May 1996 Yeltsin signed two important decrees. The first transformed Goskomoboronprom into a ministry of the defence industry (Minoboronprom), and Pak accordingly gained ministerial status and became a full member of the government; the second outlined a series of measures to support enterprises of the ministry. The latter included a requirement that the government should settle all the debts accumulated by defence enterprises since 1994, with an assurance that they would be exempt from taxation until the debts had been paid, and also give some assistance in meeting energy costs. An important measure designed to stimulate investment was a decision to make joint-stock companies in the defence industry owners of the land on which their enterprises are located.[57] To underline the new concern for the industry, at the end of May more than 500 representatives of the defence industry gathered for an all-Russian convention addressed by Yeltsin, Kokoshin and other leading figures. Extra support was promised and Kokoshin indicated that the long-term programme for armaments, extending to the year 2005, would soon gain government approval, thereby providing a stable framework for the future work of the industry.[58]

The results of the second round of the presidential election provide some evidence that this campaign was successful. Yeltsin received strong backing in most of the principal centres of the Russian defence industry: the republics of Tatarstan, Bashkortostan and Udmurtia and the regions of Sverdlovsk, Perm, Chelyabinsk, Moscow, Samara, Tula, Khabarovsk, Nizhnii Novgorod, Arkhangelsk (Severodvinsk) and Vladimir, not to speak of the cities of Moscow and St Petersburg. However, the results were not as favourable for Yeltsin in some other centres, including Novosibirsk, Omsk, Marii-El and Volgograd.[59] With some exceptions, then, a strategy aptly summed up by a headline in the newspaper *Segodnya*, 'A strong MIC – a strong president' (17 April 1996), proved its worth. In Yeltsin's second term, however, there will be an expectation that the defence industry will occupy a higher place in the ranking of policies than during the initial formative period of the new Russian state.

Prospects beyond the millennium

Painfully, out of the legacy of the Soviet system, a new Russian defence industry is beginning to emerge. No longer a privileged sector of the economy confident of political support, the emergent defence industry has adapted with striking enterprise to the new situation. Above all, it has proved able to exploit its fundamental strength, namely its technological capability, now enhanced by easier access to foreign technology. Whereas in the initial period of post-communist transformation it was a valid question whether Russia would be able to retain its arms production capability, by early 1997 this was no longer in doubt.

Nevertheless, while the technological capability of the Russian defence industry may not be an issue of dispute, the country's economy remains weak and its growth prospects uncertain. It is worth speculating on the possible trajectory of the Russian defence sector to the year 2000 and beyond. Given a plausible forecast of GDP growth of 4 per cent per annum to the year 2005, and a 5 per cent share of GDP for military expenditure (ministry of defence only), by the year 2000, in real terms, military expenditure could reach 95 per cent of its 1992 level, rising to almost 120 per cent by 2005. However, in the latter case, military expenditure would still amount to less than two-thirds of its 1991 level.[60] Forecasting the growth of output of military hardware is more difficult, but given the above assumptions and a plausible scenario that arms exports will grow, but to no more than double the 1995 level by the end of the century, the level of military output could reach 60 per cent of the 1992 level by the year 2000 and 80 per cent by 2005, although this would represent only 40 per cent of the 1991 level. Thus, while Russia has a realistic prospect, other things being equal, of substantially enhancing its military capability by the early years of the next century, without a crippling diversion of resources to the military sector there is little or no prospect of a restoration of the levels of military spending and output characteristic of the late Soviet period.

The most likely outcome is the evolution of a slimmed-down, more competitive, Russian defence industry, predominantly in state hands, possessing strong capabilities in certain fields, with the partial restoration of links with the industries of other CIS states, and the development of collaborative relations with foreign partners beyond CIS borders. However, Russia may find itself no longer able to meet all its military hardware needs from domestic sources of supply, and thus forced to consider imports. There is a distinct unwillingness to contemplate this option, but attempts to maintain an across-the-board capability would require the protection of relatively backward, inefficient and non-competitive sectors of the defence-industrial base, putting pressure on the budget, with potentially damaging consequences for the country's economic revival.

For the future development of the Russian defence industry, much now depends on the process of military reform and the extent to which the new military leadership is willing to scale down the armed forces substantially in terms of personnel, not only in the ministry of defence, but also in the many other military formations. This would create conditions for a re-equipping of the forces in the early years of the twenty-first century. After a troubled transition, Russia now has the prospect of remaining a major force in the global defence industry, and it is entirely credible that the former superpower could regain a position second only to the United States in the world arms market.

Appendix: Producers of Russia's exportable weapons

This list is illustrative only and makes no claim to comprehensive coverage. Compiled by the author from Russian press sources.

MiG-29: Moscow, MiG-MAPO; St Petersburg, Zavod im. V Ya Klimova and AO Krasnyi Oktyabr (engines); Omsk, Zavod im. Baranova (engines) (now united with other enterprises in the vpk MAPO).

MiG-29 UB (training variant): Nizhnii-Novgorod, AO Sokol.

MiG-31: Nizhnii-Novgorod, AO Sokol.

Modernized MiG-21 (Kop'e): Nizhnii-Novgorod, AO Sokol.

Su-25UB and Su-25UTG (training variants): Ulan-Ude, AO Ulan-Udenskii aviatsionnyi zavod (the standard combat variant of the Su-25 is still being built by the Tbilisi aviation works in Georgia).

Su-27: Moscow, AO OKB Sukhogo, Komsomol'sk-na-Amure aviatsionnoe ob'edinenie Yu A Gagarina.

Su-27UB: Irkutsk, AO Irkutskoe aviatsionnoe proizvodstvennoe ob'edinenie.

Mil helicopters: Moscow, AO Moskovskii vertoletnyi zavod im. M L Milya; Rostov, AO Rosvertol (Mi-24, Mi-25, Mi-26, Mi-28, Mi-35); Kazan; AO Kazanskii vertoletnyi zavod (Mi-8, Mi-17); Ulan-Ude, aviatsionnyi zavod (Mi-8, Mi-171).

Ka-50 helicopter: Arsen'ev, AO Arsen'evskaya aviakompaniya Progress.

S-300PMU-1 air defence system: Moscow, TsKB Almaz; St Petersburg, Gospred. Leningradskii severnyi zavod and other enterprises of AO

Oboronitel'nyi sistemy.

S-300V air defence system: Moscow, APK Kontsern Antei.

Tunguska and Pantsir air defence systems: Tula, KB priborostroeniya; Ulyanovsk, mekhanicheskii zavod; Mytishchy, AO Metrovagonzavod.

BUK-1M air defence system: Ulyanovsk, Mekhanicheskii zavod; Mytishchy, AO Metrovagonzavod.

Tor air defence system: Moscow, APK Kontsern Antei, Izhevsk, Mekhanicheskii zavod.

Shilka air defence system: Mytishchy, AO Metrovagonzavod.

Rif and Shtil' ship air defence systems: Moscow, NPO Al'tair.

Igla portable anti-aircraft missile system: Kolomna, KB mashinostroeniya; Kovrov, AO Zavod im. Degtyareva.

Missile systems for aircraft and ships: Khimki, KB Fakel; Dubna, OKB Raduga and AO Dubnenksii mashinostroitel'nyi zavod; Korolev (formerly Kaliningrad), OKB Zvezda and Strela factory; Moscow, KB Vympel; and NPO Al'tair.

Ground and airborne radar systems: Nizhnii Novgorod, AO NITEL; Moscow, Liazanovskii elektromekhanicheskii zavod, MAK Vympel and Moscow NPO Vega-M.

T-72S tank: Nizhnii-Tagil, Uralmashzavod.

T-80U tank: Omsk, PO Zavod transportnogo mashinostroeniya; Kaluga, AO Kaluzhskii motorostroitel'nyi zavod (engines).

BMP-2 and BMP-3 infantry combat vehicles: Kurgan, AO Kurganmashzavod.

BTR-80 armoured personnel carrier: Arzamas, AO Arzamaskii mashinostroitel'nyi zavod (Nizhegorodskaya oblast).

MSTA-S and Giatsint-S self-propelled 152 mm howitzer and gun: Ekaterinburg, Gospred. Uraltransmash.

Grad, Smerch and Uragan multiple rocket launcher systems: Tula, GNPP Splav and Shtamp zavod; Perm, AO Motovilikhinskie zavody.

Metis-2 and Vikhr anti-tank systems: Tula, KB priborostroeniya.

RPG anti-tank weapons: Moscow, NPO Bazal't.

Kalashnikov and SVD infantry weapons: Izhevsk, AO Izhmash.

Varshavyanka diesel-electric submarine (Kilo class): St Petersburg, Rubin Central Design Bureau; Nizhnii-Novgorod, AO Zavod Krasnoe Sormovo.

Patrol boats and air cushion naval craft: St Petersburg, Almaz TsKB.

Julian Cooper

Notes

1. A reported 4.5 per cent in 1992, falling to 3.9 per cent in 1995 (*Finansovye izvestiya*, 5 July 1996).
2. BBC, *Summary of World Broadcasts*, SUW/0421 WD/16, 9 February 1996.
3. *Konversiya*, 1996, no. 3, p. 33; *Krasnaya zvezda*, 17 February 1996.
4. *Finansovye izvestiya*, 19 April 1996.
5. The current plight of the Russian aviation industry can be appreciated from the following: the figures for orders for new aircraft from domestic airlines: 1992 292, 1993 180, 1994 47, 1995 28, 1996 0 (*Inzhenernaya gazeta*, 1996, no. 31).
6. BBC, *SWB*, SU/2549 C/4, 1 March 1996.
7. This issue is discussed in more detail in Chapter 14.
8. For a more detailed account, see Julian Cooper, 'The Conversion of the Former-Soviet Defence Industry' in D. Dyker, ed., *Investment Opportunities in Russia and the CIS* (Washington, DC: Brookings Institution/ RIIA, 1995), pp. 127–74.
9. *Sobranie zakonov Rossiyskoy Federatsii*, 1996, no. 3, art. 183.
10. *Rossiyskaya gazeta*, 18 January and 25 July 1996.
11. See the many articles by Aleksandr Romanikhin of AO 'Soyuzneftemash', e.g. in *Segodnya*, 26 April and 13 May 1996; *Krasnaya zvezda*, 27 May 1995; *Trud*, 11 April 1996.
12. *Krasnaya zvezda*, 17 December 1994, 19 December 1995, 29 May 1996; *Rossiyskaya gazeta*, 30 May 1996.
13. *Finansovye izvestiya*, 22 March 1996, 20 June 1996; *Rabochaya tribuna*, 14 June 1996.
14. *Krasnaya zvezda*, 29 April, 29 December 1995; *Rossiyskaya gazeta*, 4 July 1995; BBC, *SWB*, SUW/ 0428 WD/1, 29 March 1996.
15. *Sobranie zakonov Rossiyskoy Federatsii*, 1996, no. 3, art. 183.
16. *Rossiyskaya gazeta*, 2 July 1993.
17. *Konversiya*, 1995, no. 12, pp. 11–13; *Scientific and Technical Complex of Russia: Outline of Development* (Moscow: Ecolink, 1995), pp. 52–3. The aviation and shipbuilding industries each have six GNTs, the armaments (optical) industry three, and the munitions and electronics industries one each.
18. *Rossiyskaya gazeta*, 18 October 1995.
19. *Konversiya*, 1996, no. 1, p. 3.
20. *Krasnaya zvezda*, 21 December 1994, 6 September 1995.
21. BBC, *SWB*, SU/2553 S1/1, 6 March 1996.
22. *Krasnaya zvezda*, 5 September 1995.
23. BBC, *SWB*, SU 2653 S1/1, 2 July 1996.
24. BBC, *SWB*, SU/2445 S1/2, 27 October 1995; *Ogonyek*, 1995, no. 41, p. 63; *Rabochaya tribuna*, 19, 25 July 1996.
25. *Krasnaya zvezda*, 29 April 1995, 5 June, 26 October 1996.
26. *Izvestiya*, 16 August 1995; *Inzhenernaya gazeta*, 1995, no. 88, August, 1996, no. 3, January.
27. *Rossiyskaya gazeta*, 30 June 1994; *Nezavisimaya gazeta*, 18 August 1994; *Kommersant-Daily*, 9 February 1996; *Rossiyskie vesti*, 30 May 1996.
28. The first stage of Russian defence industry privatization and post-privatization restructuring is discussed in Antonio Sanchez-Andres, 'The First Stage of Privatization of Russian Military Industry', *Communist Economies and Economic Transformation*, vol. 7, no. 3, 1995, pp. 353–67, and Yevgeny Kuznetsov, 'Adjustment of Russian Defence-related Enterprises in 1992–94: Macroeconomic Implications', ibid., vol. 6, no. 4, 1994, pp. 473–513.
29. *Voprosy ekonomiki*, 1996, no. 4, p. 63.
30. Ibid.
31. *Kommersant'*, 1995, no. 31, 29 August, pp. 20–5; *Rossiyskaya gazeta*, 28 May 1996; *Kommersant-Daily*, 6 July 1996.
32. *Business in Russia*, March 1996, pp. 55–8; *Chas pik*, 27 March 1996; *Rossiyskaya gazeta*, 12 March 1996.
33. *Ekonomika i zhizn'*, 1996, no. 20, *Vash partner*, p. 25. For examples of the strident campaign, see the report of the Russian Audit Chamber (*Sovetskaya Rossiya*, 11 April 1996); also *Pravda-5*, nos 2, 3, January 1996, and *Sovetskaya Rossiya*, 16, 18 April 1996.
34. The Jamestown Foundation, *Monitor*, 23 February 1996; BBC, *SWB*, SU/2671 C/1, 23 July 1996.
35. *Rossiyskaya gazeta*, 30 July 1996.

36. *Ekonomika i zhizn'*, 1995, no. 1, *Vash partner*, p. 7.
37. See Julian Cooper, 'Transforming Russia's Defence Industrial Base', *Survival*, vol. 35, no. 4, Winter 1993–4, pp. 147–62.
38. *Krasnaya zvezda*, 1 June 1996; *Kommersant-Daily*, 28 May 1996.
39. *Kommersant-Daily*, 27 April, 23 May 1996.
40. *Komsomol'skaya pravda*, 5 September 1995; *Segodnya*, 16 September 1995.
41. *Kommersant-Daily*, 1 December 1994. the president of Yak is now Viktor Glukhikh, until January 1996 chairman of Goskomoboronprom (*Kommersant-Daily*, 20 July 1996).
42. *Kommersant-Daily*, 25 August, 1 September 1995.
43. *Sobranie zakonov Rossiyskoy Federatsii*, 1994, no. 33, art. 3456.
44. *Krasnaya zvezda*, 28 October 1995, 14 April 1996.
45. *Rabochaya tribuna*, 29 June 1996; *Krasnaya zvezda*, 23 September 1995; *Komsomol'skaya pravda*, 25 June 1996.
46. *Delovaya Sibir*, 1996, no. 15, April, p. 2; *Rossiyskii vesti*, 19 April 1996; *Finansovye izvestiya*, 29 February 1996.
47. *Nezavisimaya gazeta*, 3 March 1993; *Segodnya*, 9 August 1994. In July 1996 the president of MAK Vympel, Nikolai Mikhailov, was appointed deputy secretary of the Security Council.
48. BBC, *SWB*, SU/2557 S1/1, 11 March 1996.
49. *Pravda*, 20 March 1996.
50. V. Glukhikh, press conference, Moscow, 25 December 1995 – text as issued by Federal News Service.
51. *Krasnaya zvezda*, 20 July 1996.
52. The Russian press offered two competing explanations of Glukhikh's downfall: it was an expression of Yeltsin's dissatisfaction with Glukhikh's apparent failure to work actively for votes for the 'Our Home is Russia' bloc in the Duma elections, or, alternatively, it was linked to the scandal surrounding the inclusion in, then later withdrawal from, the 'shares-for-loans' scheme, of the Sukhoi company in late 1995 (see *Komsomol'skaya pravda*, 24 January 1996; *Izvestiya*, 25 January 1996; *Segodnya*, 2 February 1996.
53. BBC, *SWB*, SU/2525 S1/1, 2 February 1996.
54. *Kommersant-Daily*, 9 February, 25 May 1996; *Krasnaya zvezda*, 18 May 1996; *Business in Russia*, July 1996, pp. 20–2.
55. *Rossiyskaya gazeta*, 4 January 1996.
56. *Segodnya*, 17 February 1996. On the mobilization system, see Dyker, ed., *Investment Opportunities*, pp. 158–9.
57. *Rossiyskaya gazeta*, 13, 14 May 1996.
58. Shortly thereafter, as if to underline the break in policy, the death was announced of Mikhail Malei, Yeltsin's adviser on conversion from late 1991 to September 1993 and subsequently chair of the Security Council's interdepartmental commission on scientific and technical questions of the defence industry. It was the misfortune of Malei, who became widely known at home and abroad as a vigorous advocate of the technological possibilities of the Russian defence industry, to have had responsibility for conversion at a time when the preconditions for a viable policy were almost totally absent (see *Delovoy mir*, 8 June 1996).
59. *Rossiyskaya gazeta*, 16 July 1996, final presidential election results.
60. Yeltsin's election programme included reference to a 4 per cent annual rate of growth of GDP by the end of the century; Kokoshin has revealed that he has been campaigning for a defence budget share of GDP of between 5.2 and 6 per cent; and, more realistically, a draft bill on military reform prepared by the defence and security committees of the two chambers of parliament provides for a defence share of GDP of at least 5 per cent (Jamestown Foundation, *Monitor*, 31 May 1996; *Voennaya mysl'*, 1996, no. 5, p. 9; BBC, *SWB*, SU/2670 S1/1, 22 July 1996).

Part II

Ukraine, Belarus, Central Asia and the Caucasus states

6 Ukraine: national interests between the CIS and the West

Alexander Goncharenko

The successor states of the Soviet Union are attempting to come to terms with what it means to become an independent state. This involves an articulation of national interests to provide a conceptual basis for independent foreign and security policies. Such interests are based on a society's understanding of the nature of its own identity as a people and a state, and on basic values, such as 'democracy', 'freedom' and 'independence'. Among the significant factors influencing this process are threat perceptions, analyses of the current political and economic situation, and also more traditional conceptions of a role in the international system. The principal objective of Ukrainian foreign policy is to assert the independence of the state in the international community and especially *vis-à-vis* Russia. The dispute with Russia since 1991 has been largely rooted in Russia's failure to treat Ukraine as an independent sovereign state and its assumption that Russia is the successor state to the USSR. Ukraine has thus challenged Russia's attempt to assume a leadership role in the CIS and to institutionalize such a role.

Defining the national interest

The task of defining and articulating the national interest was to prove difficult for Ukraine, unprepared as it was for independence and lacking a single, unified national 'outlook' and system of values and interests. The nation was, indeed, deeply divided, in political, economic, ethnic, social and religious terms. Ukraine was thus caught in a vicious circle: the building of a national state necessitates a national consensus on the identity of the state and its people which sets the framework for the definition of the national interest; and yet the consolidation of such a consensus is difficult, if not impossible, without a strong unified state, especially in a newly formed entity with a heterogeneous population. Ukrainian attempts to resolve this dilemma were painful and sometimes counterproductive. As a result, after almost four years, Ukraine has only just begun to form a unified system of national interests and a consistent national strategy.

Attempts to this end, however, were made earlier – even before Ukraine became independent. Several articles by the present writer, published in mid-1991 both in Ukraine and in the West, defined the basic national interests of a sovereign Ukrainian state as the maintenance of its sovereignty and territorial integrity by all possible means, including military, if necessary; the establishment of adequate national security, including its political, economic, legal and socio-cultural dimensions, and integration into regional and global security structures; gradual but total nuclear disarmament; and the development and maintenance of a socio-cultural and spiritual revival as the foundations of a national state system.[1] In 1991–2, the present writer also joined in elaborating the main principles of a concept of national security for Ukraine.[2]

The first official version of a concept of national security for Ukraine was prepared by the state's National Security Council in 1993 and discussed by the parliament in October of that year. A revised version of this concept was approved, narrowly, by the parliament in May 1995. The primary national interests of Ukraine outlined in this document can be summarized as ensuring the state's sovereignty and territorial integrity; overcoming the nation's economic crisis and developing a market economy; creating a civic society subject to the rule of law; and integration into the European and world community. The document stressed that accurate assessment of real and potential threats to national security was vitally important for the formation of an adequate development strategy and domestic and foreign policies. The main political threats to Ukraine's national security cited were interference by other states in Ukraine's internal affairs; territorial claims and other encroachments on Ukrainian sovereignty by other nations; and the existence of separatist trends in some regions, along with the aggravation of inter-ethnic and inter-confessional conflicts.[3]

Kiev's perception that outside interference in its internal affairs and violation of its territorial integrity constitute one of the major potential threats to Ukrainian national security was shared by many Western analysts. A joint policy statement by the Atlantic Council of the United States and the Ukrainian Institute of World Economy and International Relations on 'The Future of Ukrainian–American Relations' outlined the threat to Ukraine of an internal conflict provoked from outside.[4]

The persistence of Ukraine's economic crisis poses another major threat to the state's equilibrium. Domestic economic instability, together with external factors, could have devastating consequences for Ukraine's national security. As Strobe Talbott has pointed out, 'Ukraine's many friends around the world feared that the greatest jeopardy to Ukraine's independence and sovereignty came not from beyond its borders but from within.'[5]

By the beginning of 1994, the ruling elite of Ukraine at last understood that political independence would be impossible without real economic independence. The previous inability of the parliament and government to undertake the radical reforms needed to attract Western investment, to pay world prices for energy and to revive the economy had brought the country to the brink of catastrophe. The continuation of this indecisive policy could have led only to the progressive disintegration of productive forces, actual deindustrialization, social unrest and the growth of regional separatist tendencies – and, most importantly, would have increased Ukrainian vulnerability to Russian economic blackmail and domination. These factors forced President Kuchma and his team to put a programme of economic reform at the centre of domestic policy and to proclaim it the primary means for Ukraine's survival. In cooperation with the International Monetary Fund and other financial institutions, a comprehensive reform programme was drawn up. Its provisions included measures for price and exchange rate stabilization, a drastic reduction of the budget deficit, tight monetary policy and wide-ranging privatization.

Some initial effects of the implementation of this policy were evident by the end of 1995. These included the beginning of the socio-political stabilization of Ukraine; the creation of an efficient economic and financial system; price liberalization; the elimination of subsidies; and overall macroeconomic stabilization. The monthly inflation rate fell from 21.1 per cent in January 1995 to 11.4 per cent in March 1995 and to 5 per cent by the year's end. The decline of GNP (23 per cent in 1994) slowed. Preliminary indications of gradual economic recovery could be observed in the last quarter of 1996. In view of these achievements, the IMF granted Kiev a $1.5 billion standby credit. International financial support for Ukraine in 1995 amounted to nearly $6 billion.[6]

Two main obstacles to the progress of the economic reform programme nevertheless persist. These derive from the powerful agrarian lobby in parliament, whose activities may lead to massive agricultural subsidies, and the as yet unresolved problem of Ukraine's debts for gas and oil supplies. To minimize the risks deriving from these problems and enable the implementation of the tough and consistent policies necessary for radical economic transformation, legislation was enacted providing for the establishment of strong and competent executive power. The constitutional agreement of 9 June 1995 between the Supreme Council and the Ukrainian president created the legal basis for the reorganization of state power and the radical economic reform programme. It may be considered as a point of no return in Ukraine's long and difficult struggle towards a market economy and overall stability.

Alexander Goncharenko

Ukraine in the former Soviet space

One of the key elements for a successful outcome of this struggle, cited repeatedly in statements by President Kuchma, is Kiev's development of a so-called 'strategic partnership' with Russia and the CIS countries. However, no member of the Ukrainian political elite, including President Kuchma himself, has given a clear definition of this 'strategic partnership' – and indeed, it is easier to define what 'strategic partnership' in this context does *not* mean. According to numerous explanations given by key ministers and the president, it does not comprise any kind of active military cooperation or attempt to form a military alliance. For clarity, let us assume here that a 'strategic partnership' with Russia, *à la* Kuchma, would exclude military and geopolitical dimensions but include all other aspects of interstate cooperation, taking primarily economic and cultural forms.

Would such a partnership be beneficial or detrimental to Ukraine? In view of the severely distorted economic structure which Ukraine inherited from the Soviet Union, the nation's dependence on gas and oil supplied by Russia and other CIS countries, the traditional orientation of the majority of Ukrainian goods to CIS markets and the tough protectionist policies of Western countries, most notably those of the United States, against Ukrainian goods, the effect could only be positive. However, while emphasizing this reorientation of foreign and domestic policy, Kuchma is consistently very cautious, even sceptical, in his estimation of the potential of the CIS. He continually stresses that relations with Russia and the CIS should not be developed at the expense of Kiev's relations with the West, and vice versa. According to the president, 'The continuation of the previous policy of self-isolation is economic and political suicide' and Ukraine will make special efforts to increase cooperation with Western countries and its integration into international economic organizations.[7] Kuchma also stressed, 'Unfortunately the CIS at present is an amorphous organization that adopts many decisions, which, it is true, are not implemented.'[8]

This attitude towards the CIS on the part of Ukraine, shared by some other newly independent states, accords with apparent differences between them on the one hand, and Russia on the other, regarding the aims and role of this organization. For Russia, the CIS is a tool for the reintegration of the FSU and a vehicle for Moscow's renewed territorial ambitions. Originally founded as an organization of independent states, the CIS has gradually been transformed into a proxy for Russia, and Moscow openly strives for full domination of this organization. The Russian vision of the CIS, as presented at the October 1994 CIS summit in Moscow, clearly involves a long-term programme for the reintegration of the FSU.[9] Contrary to previous agreements, Moscow has become the centre for all CIS activities: all of the organization's major committees and ruling bodies are run by Russians; the completely Russified

CIS Defence Council has evolved into a puppet body used to confer formal approval of the Kremlin's military operations within the CIS states; Moscow has secured 50 per cent of the votes in the interstate economic committee. Russian attempts to push through the United Nations its idea of granting UN observer status to the CIS could be used to claim UN funding and sanctions for peacekeeping operations and could potentially transform the CIS into a powerful tool for the promotion of Russian interests within and even beyond the geopolitical space of the FSU.

In contrast, the primary *raison d'être* of the CIS for Ukraine, Moldova, Azerbaijan and other former Soviet republics is to liquidate a centre. These countries are not ready to accept the resurrection of a central FSU authority in Russia. Ukraine accordingly has limited its presence in the organization to associate membership and has carefully avoided any participation in political and military cooperation. Moldova has restricted its involvement to the economic sphere; Turkmenistan and Azerbaijan more often abstain or refuse to sign agreements than willingly participate. As a result, many CIS agreements exist only on paper.

The CIS summit in Belarus in May 1995 ended in complete failure. Leading Ukrainian ministries considered CIS proposals for a customs and monetary union and the Russian Federation's recommendation that Ukraine join the agreement as a full member. Kiev concluded that full membership would be premature given that Ukrainian recommendations for the protection of its economic sovereignty were not taken into account during the preparations for the agreement. In a special statement, the ministry of foreign affairs declared that while Ukraine's participation in the CIS economic union at the level of associate membership would allow Kiev to develop relations both within the East and with the West, full Ukrainian membership in this union could be perceived as a change in its foreign policy and affect the perception the EU countries had of Ukraine as an independent nation. Moreover, according to the statement, 'should Ukraine sign the above mentioned document, this could be viewed by Russia as a pretext for putting pressure on our state to enter military and political structures within the framework of CIS'. Ukraine's full membership could thus result in its alienation, both politically and economically, from central European countries.[10]

Further developments, in particular President Yeltsin's decree of 14 September 1994 entitled 'The Strategic Course of Russia towards CIS Countries', showed that Kiev's fears were not unsubstantiated. This document, issued by the leader of one 'equal' CIS member, unilaterally assumed the Russian president's right to regulate by decree the flow of integration processes within the entire geopolitical space of the FSU and that this would be determined primarily by the national interests of Russia.

The primary strategic priority of the Russian Federation, according to the decree, is to strengthen Russia as the 'leading force of economic and political relations in the former Soviet space, and to stimulate integrative processes in the CIS'. Moscow should simultaneously make efforts to gain the understanding of other countries that the CIS 'is first of all the sphere of Russian national interests'. Other CIS states are to be 'passive objects of this integration', diligently fulfil their obligations to Russia and abstain from participation in blocs and alliances other than those with Russia.[11] Yeltsin's decree thus confirmed that Russia has no intention of building relations with other CIS nations on the basis of equality and respect for economic and political sovereignty. In the words of the Ukrainian minister of foreign affairs, Hennady Udovenko, in a confidential letter to President Kuchma, '"Integration", the necessity and usefulness of which is declared in the decree, in practice means the demolition of the sovereignty of CIS countries, subordination of their activities to Russia's national interests, and the revival of the centralised superpower.'[12]

Ukrainian disillusionment with the CIS at the official level corresponds to the low profile of this organization in public opinion. According to a 1995 opinion poll, only 17 per cent of the population foresee a future for the CIS as a single union with joint bodies of power; 17 per cent believe that the CIS has no future; only 1 per cent think that the organization will become a military union, 1 per cent a political union. The prevailing view (42 per cent) is that the CIS will survive as an economic union.[13] This opinion generally accords with Ukraine's current status as an associate member of the CIS.

The future of this organization in many aspects depends upon the ability of Moscow to treat the newly independent states as equal partners. If it cannot do so, the contradictions existing on many levels of the CIS combined with increasingly assertive Russian policies will probably stimulate its disintegration.

It is clear that a worldwide tendency towards integration exists, particularly in the economic sphere. It would, however, be a grave mistake to exaggerate the process of global and regional integration and to base upon it, in theoretical and practical terms, the reconstruction of a unified post-Soviet entity on the territory of the FSU. An example of such an ideologically driven approach was the Russian Foreign Intelligence Service (FIS) report 'Russia and CIS: Does the Western Position Need Correction?', presented by the former FIS director and present Russian foreign minister, Yevgeny Primakov. This report is also well known as the ideological background for Moscow's 'new' foreign policy *vis-à-vis* CIS countries. According to Primakov, the 'objective' tendencies towards reintegration would inevitably lead to the restoration of some form of 'new economic and defence zone' under Russian leadership within the CIS. The scenarios elaborated clearly suggested two alternatives: total integration in the economic and military spheres and the formation of a 'common defence zone' with sub-units under a unified command, which would guarantee stabilization, democratization and the advancement of reforms; or overall destabilization of the CIS, which would pose a threat to the entire world community and lead to increased problems such as socio-political tensions, nationalistic, anti-democratic tendencies, the criminalization of society, and the infringement of the rights of ethnic minorities.[14] In other words, *with* Russia, one-sixth of the world is predestined to enjoy stability and prosperity; *without* Russia, the nations of the FSU, many with a history of more than 2,000 years of statehood, are doomed.

Obviously, within the geopolitical space of the FSU, the interaction of the processes of integration and disintegration involves many other factors, such as national and ethnic conflicts, which complicate such one-sided and politically motivated conclusions. But attempts to use these conclusions to determine Russian state policy intensified considerably at the end of 1995 and in the period leading to Yeltsin's re-election as president in summer 1996. After Yeltsin's decree on 'The Strategic Course of Russia towards CIS Countries' and the general shift to the left in the post-communist world, Moscow launched an active campaign to use the Inter-Parliamentary Assembly of the CIS (IPA) as a tool to expedite the integration of the countries of the CIS. Under the Kremlin's initiative, the original agreement which established the IPA in 1992 would be replaced by a so-called convention which would trans-form the IPA into a supranational body with broad powers, including those of a sovereign state subject to international law. With the communist majority in the Russian Duma having proclaimed its intention to press for the revival of the Soviet Union by all possible means, including by referendum, it is clear that Moscow needs the IPA to secure the denunciation of the 1991 Belovezhskaya Puscha Agreement and to legalize the process of restoration of the USSR.

In December 1995, an open row erupted in the Ukrainian parliament over the IPA. As an associate member of the CIS, Ukraine participated solely as an observer in the assembly's work. It was repeatedly stressed that, with the Russian initiative, Ukraine's full membership in the IPA could substantially limit its sovereignty and political independence. In contrast to other interparliamentary institutions, such as the parliamentary assembly of the Council of Europe and the parliamentary assembly of Black Sea collaboration, the CIS's IPA became a body aimed at legitimizing the domination of one member state over the others. In a joint letter to the then prime minister, Yevgen Marchuk, the Ukrainian ministers of foreign affairs (Hennady Udovenko), justice (Sergiy Holovaty) and foreign trade (Sergiy Osyka) stated that it was necessary to preserve Kiev's current observer status in the IPA, as joining the assembly would conflict with Ukraine's basic laws and its national interests.[15]

Since 1991, despite differences between representatives of various political parties and groups, Russia has developed a policy *vis-à-vis* Ukraine which comprehends both maximum and minimum strategic aims. The maximum consists of the complete subordination of Ukraine and its return to its former semi-colonial status, with full Russian control over Kiev's foreign, military and economic policy; the minimum includes the 'Finlandization' of the republic, with its official 'neutral' status closely supervised by Moscow. Gradual Russian economic and cultural expansion in Ukraine would ensure Kiev's political obedience and economic dependence.

There are, of course, other interpretations of Moscow's intentions towards Ukraine and its other neighbours. These include the various versions of 'geopolitical pluralism', a concept first propounded by Zbigniew Brzezinski. According to this approach, which is popular in the West but which is usually denounced by Russians, Moscow will not cease to safeguard its vital interests in the 'near abroad' but will abstain from attempts to build a new superstate structure or alliance under the cover of a process of 'natural historic integration'. Rather, Russia will focus on its core interests, of maintaining its influence and preventing the transformation of any new states, through either instability or outside intervention, in such a way as to constitute a threat. Moscow will regard its neighbours' sovereignty as beneficial in the quest for regional stability.[16] This interpretation presupposes that Russia is now, or soon will be, able to give up its role as the 'great protector' of the post-Soviet space and start to interact with its neighbours as a 'normal' state.

This theory can arguably be seriously considered only as a classic example of Western 'wishful thinking' which underestimates the tradition of 200 million people with a 400-year history of permanent expansion and domination of other nations.[17] This has been clearly demonstrated by Russia's conduct in Tajikistan, Chechenia, Moldova, Belarus and Crimea. The possibility that Russia will adopt a strategy of 'geopolitical pluralism' in the years to come will thus be excluded from the following consideration of Ukraine's policy options in view of Russia's 'maximum' and 'minimum' programmes.

An adequate Ukrainian response should be well balanced and take into account not only economic, political and military factors, but also the strategic priorities and expectations of both Russia and the West. Integral to such a response must be clear answers (at least for the Ukrainian political elite) to questions regarding its future role in European security structures, including its relations with NATO and its attitude towards the process of NATO enlargement.

Options for Ukrainian security policy

In current circumstances, Ukraine has four major policy options in pursuing its national security at the international and regional levels: reliance on its own forces; membership of existing security alliances; the creation of a regional security structure within the framework of a broader, pan-European security system; and neutrality.

These options are not mutually exclusive; some may be realized or may develop in combination with others. Some, of course, are more probable than others; some are precluded by existing economic and political realities or by Ukrainian legislation. For example, the first option, that of reliance on national forces, is not feasible as the security of a state with the size and geostrategic position of Ukraine can be ensured only by possession of a strong, preferably nuclear, deterrent or by participation in a powerful military alliance. Kiev's rejection of nuclear deterrence and its adherence to the nuclear Non-Proliferation Treaty (NPT) in effect eliminate that possibility as economic constraints preclude the development of an adequate conventional deterrent.

Ukraine's second policy option, alliance, is also currently 'forbidden' by Kiev's declaration of independence. According to this document, the republic should become a 'non-nuclear and permanently neutral state which does not take part in military blocs'.[18] Although this determines policy for the near future, the stipulation could change: the majority of the Ukrainian elite recognizes the danger of excessively restricting the nation's security options.

The state of European security today is generally determined by the existence of NATO and the Tashkent agreement on collective security. Thus far, however, the latter has primarily been of symbolic, rather than practical, value. Internal instability in Russia, the weakness of existing CIS mechanisms, and the open or clandestine opposition of some FSU countries, including Ukraine, inhibit Moscow from transforming the CIS collective security system into one equal in authority to NATO. The persistent threats of some Russian leaders to create a new military alliance in response to NATO enlargement is more a bluff than a real possibility. More dangerous for Ukraine would be a decision to accede to the Tashkent Treaty since this would eventually lead to the end of its independence while its membership of NATO or the WEU will not be possible for at least ten to fifteen and fifteen to twenty years respectively.

The creation of regional security structures in central and eastern Europe – Kiev's third security policy option – has been under discussion since the disintegration of the Warsaw Pact. In response to the perception of a growing security vacuum in the region, various proposals were put forward by political leaders in the affected countries. These included that of Poland's president, Lech Walesa, in 1992–3 for the establishment of 'NATO Mark Two'; the suggestion of the former Ukrainian president, Leonid Kravchuk, for the creation of a 'zone of stability and security' in eastern Europe; and numerous propositions for the formation of a 'Baltic–Black Sea confederation' security belt. None of these initiatives was aimed against any particular state or intended as a substitute for existing institutions. The proposed regional security systems were instead envisaged as potential sub-units of a more comprehensive European security system, able to make a substantial contribution to a better division of labour among NATO, the UN, OSCE, WEU and other organizations within a general framework of interlocking institutions.

Unfortunately, NATO's Partnership for Peace programme (PfP), along with plans for enlargement of the alliance, have in some way undermined the idea of regional security structures. The countries of central and eastern Europe, especially those of the Visegrad Group (the Czech Republic, Hungary, Poland and Slovakia), have lost any interest in this idea and instead have lobbied for NATO membership. Ukraine and the other countries of the region which could not expect to be admitted into NATO in the near future have been the main losers. Although the idea of regional security structures is not completely dead, discussion now centres on structures for regional and sub-regional economic cooperation. These include bodies such as the Association of Black Sea Economic Cooperation, the Central European Free Trade Association and the Central European Initiative. Kiev expects to secure full membership of the last two organizations during 1996 and has begun active cooperation with the Baltic and Northern Councils. In spite of numerous conferences and international consultation in recent years about the possible creation of a Baltic–Black Sea security belt (involving at least Ukraine, Belarus and the Baltic states), no one in the countries concerned has shown interest at the official state level and Belarusian participation in such a scheme has seemed even more remote since Belarus and Russia signed their bilateral treaty to establish a 'Community of Sovereign States' in April 1996. A change in the European political climate and geopolitical situation could, however, lead to a revival of this idea.

Ukraine's fourth security policy option, neutrality, could be realized in at least three different forms. The weakest would be a continuation of Kiev's existing self-proclaimed neutrality. In the event of NATO expansion and a de facto Western recognition of the CIS as a sphere of Russian 'special interest' and 'special responsibility', Ukraine would become very vulnerable to Russian political, military and economic pressure and could be forced into closer political and military alignment with Moscow. Much more profitable in terms of Ukraine's national interests is the second possible form of neutrality, that of permanent neutrality guaranteed by the world's nuclear powers, similar to that assumed by Austria in 1955. Kiev received security assurances from the nuclear powers in 1994 at the OSCE summit in Budapest. In view of the geopolitical importance of Ukraine, a further consolidation of these obligations could be regarded by the West as a reasonable and useful step towards strengthening this region's security. The problem is that Russia will apparently block any attempt to grant this status to Ukraine as too far-reaching, even for the proponents of a 'Finlandization' of Ukraine. Of course, such Russian conduct could push Ukraine further towards closer relations with other military alliances.

The most reasonable and potentially best possible strategic solution for Kiev could be a third type of neutrality: 'active' neutrality, including 'special relations' with NATO. A formally neutral Ukraine would increasingly cooperate with NATO within the framework of the North Atlantic Council and the PfP, and would develop special relations and special agreements – similar to those proposed to Russia – with the alliance. The adoption and implementation of such a strategy would have to allow time for the population to become accustomed to the idea of close cooperation with NATO, though an opinion poll of December 1995 revealed that Ukrainians in general already view NATO favourably. According to this poll, 33 per cent of the population support the idea of close cooperation with NATO and 25 per cent favour immediate membership of the alliance, while only 14 per cent categorically oppose membership.[19] For many reasons, however, the question of Ukrainian membership of NATO should remain open for at least a decade. Its eventual resolution will depend upon the success of economic reforms in Ukraine and the general development of the geopolitical situation in Europe and in Russia.

The Ukrainian political elite continue to debate the enlargement of NATO. Some officials, without rejecting such enlargement entirely, have repeatedly expressed fears that an artificially accelerated process could trigger thinking analogous to that of the Cold War among some sectors of the population. As Foreign Minister Udovenko commented, 'Ukraine would like to avoid these fears becoming transformed into reality and finding itself – even hypothetically – in a position of a "buffer zone" or a *cordon sanitaire* between the two military groupings.'[20] Former prime minister Marchuk put it more bluntly: 'The major task of Ukraine is not to become a buffer between NATO and non-NATO'.[21] Alternative approaches have therefore been proposed. According to the national security adviser to the president, Volodymir Horbulin,[22] 'Ukraine has only two choices – to become a buffer or a crossroad with two way movement.' During his visit to London in December 1995, President Kuchma stressed that 'Ukraine does not want to be an apple of discord between NATO and Russia. Ukraine wants to become a bridge that unites both sides. It should therefore be non-allied.'[23]

Whether it likes it or not, Ukraine's current and, no doubt, future role is that of a buffer, or, in Kuchma's words, a 'bridge', between Russia and the CIS and the West. Ukraine's primary national interests – its political survival and economic development – depend upon this: a fact which is well understood by both the CIS and the West. Ukraine thus finds itself in an almost classic situation: as a smaller country, wanted not just by one but by two large powers or blocs, the newly independent state has a chance to survive. Conversely, any premature attempt to choose one side could have very unpredictable consequences and would almost certainly undermine Kiev's independence and efforts to build a comprehensive system of European security.

This dilemma manifested itself in a very acute manner as the Helsinki summit in March 1997 resulted in a process to establish in a short space of time the conditions whereby Russia would acquiesce in the enlargement of NATO in return for a special charter that would establish a new framework for relations between Russia and the NATO alliance. This created the paradoxical situation for Ukraine that while on the one hand it was coming under renewed criticism by Russia for its positive stance towards NATO,[24] on the other hand it was now lagging behind Russia in terms of developing a formal relationship with the alliance. For this reason the Ukrainian government initiated negotiations with NATO for an agreement on mutual cooperation that would mirror the accord envisioned with the Russian Federation.[25] On 9 July 1997, at the NATO summit in Madrid where the invitation was issued to Poland, the Czech Republic and Hungary to apply for NATO membership, NATO leaders and Ukrainian President Leonid Kuchma signed a charter setting out a 'special partnership' between the alliance and Ukraine. The five-page document calls for consultation and cooperation between NATO and Ukraine and is similar to the one signed between the alliance and Russia in May.[26] The result of these developments is that while Ukraine continues to seek closer cooperation with NATO rather than actual membership, this path has become easier to pursue given the new framework of cooperation between Russia and NATO which makes it more difficult for Russia to object to Ukraine's policy *vis-à-vis* NATO.

The maintenance of Ukraine's territorial integrity and independence has become one of the central components of the contemporary Western vision of a unified European and Atlantic community. Ukraine's future security orientation will undoubtedly have substantial consequences for the emerging European security structures. Kiev's orientation will in many respects depend not only upon Western professions of support for the territorial integrity of Ukraine and the inviolability of its borders, but also upon Western actions to promote Ukraine's integration into European political, economic and security structures. Ukraine has always been and will continue to be a part of Europe and the European cultural tradition. The republic's integration into European political, economic and security structures is historically preordained by virtue of its national and cultural development. Unfavourable developments in the international environment and/or the policies of certain countries could slow down or delay this process. But its artificial termination in the present atmosphere of national revival in Ukraine, including the increasing understanding of the Ukrainian people of their national identity and their basic national interests, is no longer possible.

Notes

1. Alexander Goncharenko, 'Ukraine: National Interests and Geopolitics', *Vechirniy Kyiv*, 20 June 1991; *Suchasnist'* (Newark, NJ), October 1991.
2. Alexander Goncharenko, 'National Security of Ukraine', *Vechirniy Kyiv*, 11 April 1991; O Bodruk, A. Goncharenko and E. Lisitsin, 'About the National Security of Ukraine', *Narodna armiya*, 18 June 1992; 'Ukraine's National Security Concept', *Narodna armiya*, 8 July 1992; 'Possible Ways of Securing Ukraine', *Narodna armiya*, 29 July 1992; 'Social, Economic and Ecological Aspects of National Security', *Narodna armiya*, 19 August 1992.
3. 'Concept of National Security of Ukraine' (draft), *Verkhovna Rada Ukrainy*, 21 March 1995.
4. 'The Future of Ukrainian–American Relations', joint policy statement prepared by the Atlantic Council of the United States and Institute of World Economy and International Relations (Academy of Sciences, Ukraine), Washington, DC, 5–12 November 1994.
5. European Wireless File News Alert, 21 November 1994.
6. *Kievskie vedomosti*, 9 June 1995.
7. BBC, *Summary of World Broadcasts*, U/2125 D/8, 13 October 1994.
8. BBC, *SWB*, SU/2163 D/3, 1 December 1994.
9. *Wall Street Journal*, 22 September 1994.
10. BBC, *SWB*, SU/2307 D/5, 19 May 1995.
11. *Golos Ukrainy*, 22 December 1995.
12. *Zerkalo nedely*, 7 October 1995.
13. Based on a SOCIS–Gallup poll of 1,200 residents of Ukraine conducted in January 1995, reported in *Ukrainian Weekly*, 19 February 1995.
14. BBC, *SWB*, SU/2110 B/8, 26 September 1994.
15. *Zerkalo nedely*, 18 November 1995.
16. Sherman Garnett, 'Integration and the FSU', *Washington Quarterly*, Spring 1995, p. 42.
17. See discussion in Mark Smith, *Ukraine–Russian Relations: An Unequal Partnership*, Whitehall Paper (London: Royal United Services Institute, 1995).
18. *Literaturna Ukraina*, 19 July 1990.
19. Statistical Survey of the International Institute of Sociology, Kiev Mohyla Academy, December 1995.
20. *NATO Review*, November 1995, p. 17.
21. *Holos Ukrainy*, 15 September 1995.
22. *Ukraina moloda*, 26 May 1995.
23. *Holos Ukrainy*, 16 December 1995.
24. *Rossiyskaya gazeta*, 2 April 1997 p. 7.
25. See the interview with the Ukrainian foreign minister for more details in *Holos Ukrainy*, 27 March 1997, pp. 1 and 2.
26. Kitty McKinsey, ' NATO/Ukraine: New Accord Begins "Special Partnership"', RFE/RL Special Report on the NATO Summit, http://www.rferl.org/nca/special/madrid-nato/index.htm

7 Ukrainian security planning: constraints and options

Taras Kuzio

Russia's military intervention in Chechenia between 1994 and 1996 has turned a spotlight on the socio-economic crisis affecting its armed forces, whose performance has been poor.[1] The Russian Council on Foreign and Defence Policy found the Russian army to be a 'catastrophe' which, 'has long ceased to be a guarantee against external threats'.[2] The socio-economic crisis affecting Ukraine's armed forces appears to be as bad, if not worse, and reflects the large Soviet inheritance bequeathed to Ukraine at the time of independence as well as the poor economic situation in Ukraine.[3] The Institute of Sociology of the Academy of Sciences believed 'that it does not differ from the situation in Ukrainian society in general. It exists in some kind of undetermined state.'[4] And according to President Leonid Kuchma, 'The main outcome of the past three years of military development is our realization that one can destroy the old only when there are opportunities for its effective replacement.'[5]

This chapter surveys the socio-economic and political constraints which influence the evolution of Ukraine's security forces, drawing upon previous material published by the author as well as recent developments in the country.[6] It analyses the security options open to Ukraine in the light of its capabilities, particularly with a view to current plans for military reform and a new military doctrine. Finally, the implications for European security of these domestic constraints and options in the formulation of Ukrainian security policy will be investigated.

The armed forces: constraints

Budgetary problems

By February 1994, according to the then head of the economic-financial directorate in the ministry of defence, General Ivan Shtopenko, only 10 per cent of the $1.8 billion (63.7 trillion *karbovanets*) requested by the ministry of defence for the armed forces that year had been allocated.[7] The Ukrainian parliament voted in favour of its first real budget on 6 April 1995, by a vote of

238 to 53, in order to qualify for an IMF stabilization loan of over $1.5 billion essential for President Kuchma's economic reform programme. Ukrainian expenditure was cut by 4 per cent in every field, but the greatest cut was in funding for the armed forces,[8] 'a threat to our national security,' independent parliamentarian Oleksandr Ihnatenko believed.[9] Viktor Suslov, the former head of the parliamentary commission on questions of finance and banking activity, criticized the threat to Ukrainian sovereignty posed by the IMF criteria. 'After all, it is our internal affair how much we allocate for defence and education.'[10]

Total defence expenditure in 1995 was only $757 million (106 trillion *karbovanets*); of this, the army would obtain $657 million, which represented only 4.3 per cent of the total Ukrainian budget.[11] This compared unfavourably to 21.3 per cent or $8.6 billion in Russia (the Russian ministry of defence had asked for $15 billion). The proportion of the total Ukrainian budget allocated to defence was one of the lowest in the world.[12]

During 1992–5 the defence budget had never covered more than 35 per cent of the armed forces' needs. In 1995 the budget met only 16.9 per cent of financial needs; this represented a declining trend since 1992, when it received 34 per cent of its needs, through 1993–4, when it received 28 per cent.[13] Colonel-General Anatoly Lopata, former first deputy defence minister, believed that the allocation in the 1996 budget would cover only 18.5 per cent of the military's needs.[14] Ukraine's 1997 budget was not adopted by parliament until July of that year and it only provided approximately $850 million for the armed forces (or 1.43 billion *hryvna*, just slightly more than the 1.25 billion allocated the previous year). Only the air force, missile units, communication units, the air defence forces, radio-electronic units and the navy can count on an infusion of extra funds.[15]

Ukraine's former defence minister, Valery Shmarov, complained that the budget allocation for 1995 was insufficient to allow for even elementary modernization of weapons and equipment and he feared that the armed forces would 'become unfit for action'.[16] He claimed: 'For three years the military budget has covered only 25–30 per cent of needs. We have therefore been unable to pay sufficient attention to scientific trends and purchase new weaponry,' and warned that 'funds are barely sufficient to maintain the armed forces, let alone develop them. If we continue to act in this way we risk crossing a Rubicon beyond which the negative processes now under way will be irreversible.'[17] Shmarov calculated that 141.1 trillion *karbovanets* was required to finance fully all of the armed forces' needs and that only 5–12 per cent of the funds required for training and new technology were forthcoming – sufficient only for salaries and provisions with no allocation for the purchase of military hardware.

The lack of funds has meant reductions in personnel – by 65,000 in 1995 –

and the proposed sale of military installations (garrisons, airfields, firing ranges, etc.) and land. The term of conscription may be reduced from two years to eighteen months. But, as Ukrainian military commentators have pointed out, reducing numbers also has costs, for example in housing and social adaptation. The financial crisis also made it difficult to plan ahead: financially the ministry of defence had to operate on a monthly or, in some cases, even a daily basis because of the lack of stability.[18]

The most successful branch of the armed forces, having become commercialized to gain access to additional sources of funds, is transport aviation, which earned $1.5 million in 1994; another $3 million was owed to them by civilian airlines. Some regions have provided foodstuffs free of charge to the Ukrainian navy, while others have agreed to purchase apartments for naval officers. The armed forces had to sell off surplus military equipment to cover the gap in their budgetary needs. In 1996 these sales brought in $17.7 million in revenues which were used to build housing for officers. The armed forces will obtain their main extra-budgetary needs from two sources: from railroad troops who will work on national economic projects, and from military transport aviation. The priorities for these extra revenues will be geared towards housing and training for flight personnel.[19]

According to Anatoliy Kovtun, chairman of the parliamentary commission on budget affairs, Ukraine's 1995 budget met only 50 per cent of the needs of the ministries of defence and the interior. 'Such a considerable reduction in spending on these ministries has to do with the reduction of state budget income which is currently a third of expenditure owing to the decline in output,' Kovtun said.[20] The greatest cuts would be to the security service, the State Customs Committee and the border troops. The head of the main ministry of defene financial-economic directorate, General-Major Hryhorii Kucharskyi, outlined the general declining trend in funds for the armed forces since 1992, and pointed out that the 1995 budget allocation would meet only the most basic needs – foodstuffs, salaries and communal utilities.[21]

Socio-economic crisis

A poll conducted at the end of 1993 found that 93 per cent of officers in the Ukrainian armed forces were dissatisfied with their financial status. The poll, taken on the eve of the Congress of Servicemen and Businessmen (established to link together the newly developing private sector with retired or demobilized officers), also found that one in two young army officers would like to quit the armed forces.[22] Half of all military officers did not want their children to serve in the armed forces. In 1993 alone 9,000 officers, a third of them from the younger generation, had voluntarily resigned from the armed forces. Many of these included specialists vital for the efficient functioning of the armed forces: doctors, lawyers, economists, topographers, communications specialists and radio electronics engineers.

An opinion poll of the officer corps of the Ukrainian armed forces, dividing its members according to their attitudes and performance, published in the organ of the Congress of Ukrainian Nationalists in 1995,[23] revealed some uncomfortable facts:

- Officers who took an active part in the building of the Ukrainian armed forces accounted for just 17 per cent of the total.
- Many officers (18 per cent) had no housing; of those who obtained accommodation, over half then resigned their commissions.
- Twenty per cent of officers worked in commercial organizations and used the army as an additional source of income.
- Nine per cent were drunken and lazy officers who could not find employment outside the armed forces.
- Twenty-four per cent of officers were preparing for civilian life.
- 'Fifth columnists' – officers who were disloyal, unpatriotic or even working for a foreign power – were also to be found.

A survey of officers in a Kiev military garrison found that 51 per cent were only serving in the armed forces as a route to a new profession. Salaries and conditions were so poor that 37 per cent relied upon help from family and relatives. One-fifth of the officers believed the general regime was too strict,[24] and there was disaffection with commanding officers. These problems are clearly seen in the results of a poll among officers in different regions of Ukraine and the navy conducted by the Ukrainian Centre for Economic and Political Research (see Table 7.1).

Table 7.1: 'What factors are keeping you in the armed forces of Ukraine?'[a]

	Centre	West	East	South	Navy
Military oath	23.7	25.7	18.6	14.8	17.4
Fear of unemployment	28.3	29.6	32.7	49.1	39.1
Family situation	14.9	20.1	15.5	38.9	19.1

[a] Copy of extensive polling of attitudes towards the military and within the armed forces by the Ukrainian Centre for Independent Economic and Political Research in 1996 in the possession of the author. This centre was headed by Oleksandr Razumkov, formerly an adviser to President Kuchma who was promoted to the position of Deputy Head of the Ukrainian National Security and Defence Council in summer 1997.

The socio-economic crisis affecting Ukraine's armed forces influenced their commitment to the Ukrainian state. Among those who, in a referendum, would still vote in favour of Ukrainian independence, trust in the armed forces was far higher than among those who would vote against independence. The building of the armed forces, therefore, is closely tied to the existence of the independent Ukrainian state.[25] Relative to other institutions of that state, the armed forces achieve a high ranking in public confidence: in 1995 they scored 24 per cent, only just below the presidency at 28 per cent.[26] However, in the same year the Ukrainian popular movement, Rukh urged President Kuchma and parliament to discuss the claim that 'pro-communist and pro-imperial forces are becoming more active in the Ukrainian armed forces' and demanded that the authorities 'interfere in the situation and put an end to anti-state actions in the Ukrainian armed forces.'[27]

Low morale

Morale in the armed forces is at an all-time low. The ministry of defence has admitted to growing shortcomings in combat training and army discipline arising from the socio-economic situation, attributing low morale also to the 'decline in the prestige of the defenders of the motherland'. A shortage of housing and delays in the payment of salaries also affected morale among officers.[28] Volodymyr Sytnyk, head of the directorate for education in the ministry of defence, analysed the problem:

> The overall situation remains difficult. The unbalanced relationship between society, the state and the armed forces causes a lack of direction in military education and ideological passivity. Furthermore, crumbling army welfare has led to apathy among servicemen which affects relations between them.[29]

When Kuchma became president in July 1994, he said the dominant mood in the armed forces was 'a lack of perspective, a loss of direction and loss of faith in the future'. Nearly 60 per cent of officers took a negative view of their situation (compared to 37.7 per cent taking a positive view). By the end of 1995, the greater attention paid to the economy and to social problems in the armed forces by President Kuchma and former defence minister Shmarov respectively had improved morale among officers, reducing the proportion viewing their conditions of service negatively to just over 40 per cent. However, among sergeants and conscripts the corresponding proportions were as high as 61.36 and 61.17 per cent respectively.[30] Only just over half of all officers were glad to be in the armed forces, an attitude influenced by the socio-economic situation they found within the military.[31] Nearly 40 per cent of all officers (including warrant officers and both older and younger generations) placed their material and personal situation as the top priority to be addressed.[32]

The popularity of the armed forces among young people eligible for the draft has remained low. Forty per cent of army draftees do not want to serve in the armed forces because of poor conditions.The socio-economic crisis also affected these draftees by increasing the number among them who had criminal records, were alcoholics and underweight. Enrolment in military academies was over-subscribed, however, 'because young people are eager to be educated at the expense of the state'.[33]

The main reasons given by young people for their negative image of military life in 1994 were:

- desire to serve close to home with friends rather than being posted with strangers (28 per cent);
- desire to enter higher education (24 per cent);
- *didovshchina* (bullying of new recruits, 21 per cent);
- fear of losing civilian jobs (17 per cent).[34]

The factors influencing these negative views about the military were found to be:

- family (38 per cent);
- the media (22 per cent);
- schools (19 per cent).

Corruption and lack of discipline

The combat capability of the armed forces depends heavily on discipline and the psychological condition of personnel. The number of cases of breach of regulations by servicemen grew by 47 per cent between 1993 and 1994. In 1994 criminal proceedings were instituted in 215 cases, compared to 147 in 1993. The decline in discipline in the armed forces was blamed on the socio-economic crisis which, as noted above, produced a large number of social problems, low salaries and low morale. Another poll found that 60 per cent of all military personnel felt that low discipline was due to non-military factors.[35] As in the Soviet era, those with family connections continued to ensure that their children escaped the draft; consequently, 98 per cent of conscripts are from the ranks of the peasants and workers. The numbers of conscripts from the families of the higher ranks of the state administration or the wealthy was 'miserable'.[36] Only 1.3 per cent of conscripts had university degrees, and 23 per cent had not even completed secondary school, while nearly 90 per cent had gained no work or university experience prior to entering military life.[37] Only 57.92 per cent of military personnel admitted that they followed military regulations and laws, while 27.33 per cent admitted to breaching them.[38] In addition, only 21 per cent of conscripts admitted that they even knew or had read the statutes and laws which governed the armed forces, a figure which suggests that abuses by officers of the rights of conscripts are made easier by the latter's ignorance of those rights.[39]

Lieutenant-General Kobzar, former head of the educational directorate of the ministry of defence, pointed to six areas which had led to a weakening of discipline:[40]

- the crisis affecting the state, which limited the funds allocated to the armed forces, leading to poor day-to-day provision for personnel combined with lax implementation of legal guarantees for servicemen;
- loss of professional interest on the part of officers, for whom military service had ceased to be their main activity (an officer's salary is enough on average for only two weeks' food for a family of three);
- an outdated system of responsibility for discipline;
- insufficient team spirit and internal accord;
- occasionally, the poor quality of officers;
- lack of patriotic feelings and attitude.

Former defence minister Shmarov had complained that the armed forces were infested with bribery, corruption and theft. During 1995 there were 250 inspections aimed at rooting out corruption within the armed forces: together these returned to the state 96 billion *karbovanets* and US$104,000. Often, military units were signing contracts to lease or sell military property with dubious commercial enterprises; the problem, as military commentators have acknowledged, was that military officers were simply not prepared for dealings with the business world, elements of which have links with organized crime. Sometimes 'senior defence officials are forced to seek aid from other ministries and departments, as well as private companies who are sometimes willing to help the army out.'[41] Unfortunately, this was not always without complications. As one military commentator explained:

Some contracts are perfectly explainable. Some military installations are being reprofiled in the course of the reduction of the Ukrainian army and some cantonments are being 'mothballed', remaining on the balance sheets of the defence ministry. The army needs money to keep them in proper order, which it cannot get from the budget and this often gives rise to situations when the military, willingly or un-willingly, get tied up with dishonest lessees and even with obviously roguish firms.[42]

Impact upon the capability of the armed forces

The socio-economic crisis, low morale and corruption has taken its toll upon the armed forces. During the first ten months of 1996, over 3,000 crimes were committed in the armed forces. Perhaps the worst outcome was that the armed forces themselves were an obstacle to reform because they had vested interests in a continuation of the current situation. One member of parliament, complaining about rampant corruption in the armed forces, wrote that:

> The central apparatus of the defence ministry still comprises a group of generals and officers who, irrespective of a regular replacement of defence ministers, manage to keep in their hands threads of management over 'critical' positions and over the entire defence ministry. There are rumours in the officers' corps that precisely this defence ministry's clan that managed to obtain everything they wanted – villas, luxurious duplex apartments, cars, and an opportunity to trade in weapons[43] – hinders all progressive reform in the armed forces.[44]

A review of the state of combat capability of the armed forces by the Collegium of the Defence Ministry (which brought together all high-ranking officers) found the following disturbing facts:[45] that not a single one of the 190 mechanized and tank battalions was combat ready; that only one out of every three bomber units was combat ready; that only three out of 45 flight units were fully combat ready because 2,500 pilots had resigned; and that border troops only possessed 74 per cent of their required weapons.

The armed forces: options

Military reform

Only since 1994–5, under President Kuchma and the civilian former defence minister Shmarov – both of whom have had long careers in the military-industrial complex – has Ukraine committed itself to a serious programme of military reform. Plans for restructuring the armed forces place greater emphasis upon the socio-economic capabilities of the Ukrainian state and a more sober assessment of the domestic and external threats to its security. The Ukrainian government asserted that 'maintaining the army must not be a great burden for the country'.[46] Defence ministry spokesman Valery Korol said: 'The current situation requires armed forces which are not large, but battle ready. This is tied to Ukraine's economic capabilities.'[47] The Ukrainian leadership since 1994–5 has also been more attentive to the social and financial problems faced by the armed forces (discussed above). One of Shmarov's main functions was to implement restructuring of the armed forces in the teeth of military and nationalist opposition, which in the absence of a clear division of functions caused tension in his relations with the general staff.[48]

Ukraine inherited 726,000 service personnel from the former USSR, a total which is to be reduced in two stages – by 1995 and by 2000 – according to its military doctrine of 'reasonable defence sufficiency' and limits imposed by the Conventional Forces in Europe (CFE) Treaty. By 1995 the armed forces had been reduced to 420,000 (a reduction of nearly 50 per cent within four years). It was planned to carry out a further reduction to 350,000 by the end of 1996–7. This was postponed until the year 2005, however, on the grounds that the state lacked the necessary funds to return servicemen to civilian life and that previous statements on force reductions had been based on political populism rather than real calculations.[49] One of the first areas to be targeted for a reduction in military staff would be the central apparatus, which has many personnel opposed to reform. This apparatus would be reduced by 1,000 generals and other officers. Defence Minister Kuzmuk admitted that any transition to a professional army could only occur after the fulfilment of the reform programme that is due to be completed in the year 2005.[50]

While Ukraine's armed forces are being reduced, the number and range of domestic security units (such as the National Guard and State Protection Force) are growing. This trend reflects the views of the Ukrainian elite that domestic factors pose a greater threat to independence than external factors. In addition, as pointed out earlier, the navy continues to receive additional budgetary resources probably because of the importance of this branch of the armed forces for projecting Ukraine's sovereignty in Crimea. In June 1997 the first ever naval parade on land and on water was held in Sevastopol attended by the Ukrainian leadership. A rapid reaction force will be established, composed of airborne, air force and air defence units, that is expected to be on constant alert to 'rebuff any aggression immediately'.[51]

At the same time as Ukraine's armed forces are being drastically reduced, there are growing calls for them to be placed on a professional footing. This is unlikely in the short term, for two reasons. First, the state budget could not finance a professional army and therefore only a small proportion of the armed forces would be on a contract system. Secondly, the conscript armed forces are a useful incubator in which to develop patriotism and loyalty to the independent Ukrainian state. They are therefore an important component and symbol of state-building.

The reduction of the armed forces to 350,000 by 2005 will make possible a more effective use of the military budget and will yield a net gain in terms of battle-readiness.[52] The Ukrainian authorities argue that these leaner armed forces will be more mobile, better armed and more professional, with Soviet-era armies and divisions replaced by corps and brigades in appropriate numbers for the tasks assigned to them. Organizational and structural changes will be put into effect only after pilot schemes have been run at the tactical or operational level, according to the first deputy defence minister, Colonel-General Ivan Bizhan. Operational commands will in future have more power than the current corps possess, and the powers of the general staff and defence ministry will be increased.

The reform plans would reduce the number of cumbersome staff structures inherited from the Soviet era, which include a large number of surplus senior staff officers while there is a shortage of young officers at the company and platoon level. The programme of reform will be implemented over ten years, and its progress is dependent upon financial resources. The military reform plans aim to create a 'closed cycle' for producing and maintaining weaponry and equipment. Where required, Ukraine would also launch joint projects for the production, development and modernization of weapons systems with other countries. A Central Scientific-Research Institute devoted to armaments and military technology, headed by the deputy defence minister in charge of armaments, Anatoly Dovhopol, was established within the armed forces. It has been created to implement the state programme on the modernization and development of military equipment. Between 30–80 per cent of the armaments of the Ukrainian armed forces are physically outdated and 3–10 per cent of them deteriorate beyond repair each year. The armed forces aim to possess about 80 per cent of their equipment as new by the year 2005.[53] The priorities will be the development of fighter aviation and an overhaul of medium-sized naval vessels equipped with missiles and guns.

In December 1996 the National Security and Defence Council approved a 'State Programme for the Building and Development of Ukraine's Armed Forces to the Year 2005', the sixth such programme to be elaborated since independence. Three operational and command directorates would be established on the basis of the inherited Carpathian command (based in L'viv), the Odessa command and an experimental Northern command (based in Chernihiv and focusing on Ukraine's eastern border which was not adequately covered by the former Soviet military command structure, which had been oriented westward). These commands are not very different from the inherited Soviet military districts. Therefore Shmarov's proposals to replace them with 'Operational-Territorial Commands', a proposal heavily criticized by nationalists (see below), were abandoned. Each of the three commands is intended to possess mobile rapid-reaction units capable of quickly responding to crisis situations.

The armed forces would continue to be organized into four branches – the ground forces, air force, air defence forces and the navy. The air force and air defence forces would consist of two aviation corps, based upon a brigade and regimental structure, and three brigade-based corps respectively. The navy would be distributed between the eastern and southern districts within the Odessa military command. The general staff, which will be drastically reduced in size, will now be given the task of defence planning. The chief of the general staff will be directly subordinated to the minister of defence. The general staff will also co-ordinate the functions of non-military units (for example, the national guard, border troops and ministry of interior internal troops). It is currently staffed by 3,500 officers and warrant officers and this number will be reduced to a maximum of 1,500 personnel. Civilian control of the armed forces, which had always been ephemeral under Shmarov and heavily criticized by officers and nationalist groups, is now postponed indefinitely.[54]

Opposition to reform

Plans for reform and reduction of the armed forces were not welcomed by all military officers. In February 1996 President Kuchma sacked Colonel-General Lopata for criticizing the plans.[55] Five commanders of the general staff resigned in support of their former chief, who had supported the preservation of a larger Ukrainian army on the Soviet model. Nationalist political parties, civic groups and publications regularly denounced Shmarov and demanded his resignation.[56] This nationalist campaign gathered momentum after the November 1995 military agreements signed between Russia and Ukraine in Sochi.[57] This mounting domestic criticism of Shmarov led to his dismissal as Ukraine's defence minister in July 1996 and his replacement by Lieutenant-General Kuzmuk. Hostility to Shmarov had come not only from nationalist quarters but also from within the officer corps of the armed forces which preferred to see a military (not a civilian) person as defence minister. Lopata's opposition and his championing by Ukrainian nationalists was countered by a carefully orchestrated open letter in support of military reform signed by 700 generals and officers.[58]

Reform of the armed forces has continued to be criticized by the Union of Ukrainian Officers, which complained that it had not received any replies to proposals it had sent to the ministry of defence.[59] The head of the union, member of parliament Vyacheslav Bilous, believed that, 'instead of reforms there have been irresponsible discussions'.[60] Among the public at large only 19 per cent agreed that reforms were leading to an improvement in the military capabilities of the armed forces (another 33 per cent believed they were having a negative influence while 22 per cent thought they were having no influence whatsoever).[61] Major-General Vadym Hrechanynov, formerly President Kuchma's adviser on military affairs and currently the military expert at the Centre for

Economic and Political Research, held similar views to these. He claimed that the state programme for military reform to the year 2005 was principally a political measure aimed to ease tension among the officer corps and to raise Ukraine's international image (Ukraine was the first CIS country to launch such a programme). In his view it merely set out the guidelines (not a programme) for constructing the armed forces and its implementation would be hamstrung by the usual lack of financial resources.[62]

Towards a new military doctrine

The new draft military doctrine drawn up in November 1995 to replace the October 1993 doctrine is divided into two parts: military-political and military-technical. The new military doctrine was due to be put to parliament for its approval after the adoption of a new constitution on 28 June 1996; to date this has not happened. The main military threats to Ukraine are international political crises which fan economic, territorial, inter-ethnic and religious conflicts which could in turn lead to aggressive designs upon Ukraine by a single state or a coalition of states. These could take the form of political or economic pressure, territorial demands, anti-Ukrainian propaganda and/or the inciting of inter-ethnic hatred.

The military-technical part of the new military doctrine describes the character of possible wars, the strategic tasks of the armed forces and the principles on which the military reconstruction is based, and continues to emphasize defence sufficiency as its objective.[63] The new military doctrine does not envision any radical change in the current system of military districts. However, these districts, inherited from the Soviet era, are too cumbersome as a system of administration, and Shmarov had said that his ministry had been 'working on making the districts smaller and more efficient'.[64]

The main challenges facing Ukrainian security, according to Shmarov, included the completion of denuclearization (which occurred in 1996), the fulfilment of CFE Treaty obligations, the final division of the Black Sea fleet and the terms on which the Russian portion of the fleet will be stationed on Ukrainian territory, as well dealing with the security vacuum in central and eastern Europe after the disintegration of the Warsaw Pact.

Changes in Ukraine's military doctrine will have to take into account its security predicament in the light of the expansion of NATO to its western borders and of the CIS military-political union to its eastern borders. In contrast to the feelings that prevailed when the 1993 current military doctrine was adopted, Ukraine's current leaders do not perceive a serious external threat emanating from any neighbouring country, much less from distant ones. Ukraine, it is felt, should dispense with Soviet-era assumptions that it was surrounded by hostile forces. As President Kuchma pointed out at a two-day seminar entitled 'The Transformation Processes in Ukraine in the Context of World Development', the exaggerated external threat perceptions in the October 1993 military doctrine implied that 'one should dig trenches on the country's borders, sit in them and defend the land'.[65]

This feeling of greater security is founded on the greater political support and security assurances granted by the West since 1994, a more optimistic assessment of domestic stability, the erosion of support for separatism and greater confidence in the ability to deal with any threat from Russia (fostered by the poor performance of Russian forces in Chechenia). In addition, in contrast to Russia, Ukraine does not perceive NATO as an antagonistic bloc and a threat to its security. Ukraine's conclusion of interstate treaties with Russia and Romania in May–June 1997 also signalled that all its borders were finally recognized by its neighbours.

The new military doctrine outlines Ukraine's attitudes to the CIS (which are less hostile under President Kuchma than under his predecessor) and NATO as well as towards nuclear weapons (the 1993 military doctrine was adopted prior to Ukraine's ratification of START 1 or the Non-Proliferation Treaty). It supports efforts at arms control (such as START 2 and CFE) and the reduction of 'aggressive weapons'. The new military doctrine will also have to elaborate Ukraine's attitude to participation in peacekeeping duties.

The doctrine of non-bloc status outlined in the July 1990 Declaration of Sovereignty and the October 1993 military doctrine are unlikely to be altered in any new military doctrine. Ukraine, therefore (unlike the three Baltic states), is not officially applying to join NATO until 2010, hoping to maybe become a member in the second tier. It has also ruled out membership of the CIS collective security treaty. Its policy of neutrality could be dropped in the new military doctrine (Ukrainian experts believe this would not conflict with maintaining the country's non-bloc status). As it is, Ukraine's 'neutrality' allows it to undertake joint military exercises within NATO's Partnership for Peace (PfP) while rejecting similar exercises within the CIS collective security treaty. 'Neutrality' has also allowed Ukraine to be a member since February 1995 of the CIS joint air defence agreement (with reservations) and would permit the establishment of a foreign base on its territory (by Russia in Sevastopol). The June 1996 constitution provided for the temporary stationing of foreign bases on Ukrainian territory; clauses which were used to negotiate the final solution to the dispute over the Black Sea fleet in May 1997, the Russian portion of which is to be mainly based in Sevastopol for twenty years.

Conclusions

The socio-economic crisis in Ukraine has affected its security forces in many different ways. Certainly it is the case, as Martyrosian has argued, that 'we are still not ready for a professional army, primarily for economic reasons.'[66] Ukrainian security planning is hampered in particular by:

- inadequate financing to meet the existing needs of the security forces inherited from the former USSR, to transfer the forces to a professional contract system, and to provide proper training and new technology;
- the lack of a closed domestic military cycle, necessitating bilateral and, in one case, multilateral military cooperation within the CIS;
- inadequate provision of housing for officers, including those returning to Ukraine from the former USSR, and low and late payment of salaries compared to Russia and some other CIS states;
- the low educational level of conscripts and lack of specialist skills;
- the poor health and low morale of conscripts, leading to lack of attention to military duty, resignations and even suicides;
- a lack of adequate budgetary provision, leading to corruption, poor discipline and nihilism.

The analysis in this chapter indicates the limited options available to Ukraine and their significant implications for its security policy.[67]

First, Ukraine is constrained to maintain good relations with its neighbours, particularly Russia; the Ukrainian security forces are in no condition to back an antagonistic foreign policy *vis-à-vis* Russia. Ukraine will also continue to support the territorial status quo in central and eastern Europe and to oppose border changes. Ukraine's security policy will therefore be non-radical (neither the radical right nor the radical left has any realistic chance of coming to power), conservative and in favour of only evolutionary changes (for example, in respect of the expansion of NATO).[68]

Secondly, Ukrainian military reform efforts are also subject to constraint. Ukraine cannot afford to be a nuclear power, and the last nuclear missile was removed in May 1996. Denuclearization has been a financial drain on the state and a socio-economic problem. It is accepted by the government that a reform of the armed forces is necessary 'which takes into account the state's defence needs and economic possibilities'.[69] However, such reform, including a reduction in manpower from 420,000 to 350,000 by the year 2005 and an evolution from a Soviet organizational system to one of corps, brigades and battalions, will be staunchly opposed both within and outside the armed forces.

The new military doctrine will take into account Ukraine's security capabilities enshrined in its reform plans, as well as changes to the external and domestic security environment for Ukraine since the adoption of the previous October 1993 doctrine, which will define the security options available to its leadership. The conclusion of a treaty with Russia and the negotiation of a solution to the Black Sea fleet dispute also reduced the likelihood of an actual threat coming from Moscow, although these events have not yet altered the Ukrainian *perception* of threat. Even after the Russian–Ukrainian treaty had been signed, 48 per cent of Ukraine's elites continued to perceive Russia as the country's greatest threat (the country which was viewed as most threatening after Russia was the United States but only 11 per cent of the sample regarded it as a threat).[70]

Despite the advantages of possible reductions in military expenditure, Ukraine is not likely to join the CIS collective security treaty or any Russian-dominated military bloc which would be aimed against the West and NATO. Ukraine will continue to drift westwards, therefore, which will serve to balance its relations with Russia.

Appendix: The security forces of independent Ukraine

Numbers

Armed forces	Strength
Navy	420,00
Air force	40,000
Ground forces 220,000	160,000 (includes air defence forces)
Security service	5,000 (approx.)
Border troops	50,000
National Guard	30,000
Internal troops	50,000
State Protection Force	180,000
Berkut (Special Purpose Militia Units)	5,000 (approx.)
Directorate for State Protection	n.a.

Functions[71]

Armed forces These include the ground forces, the navy (independent of the Black Sea fleet) and the air force (including air defence forces and air forces). Ukraine received a substantial number of small and medium-sized vessels of the Black Sea fleet after its final division in 1995–7, but it remains unclear how many personnel will be transferred to the Ukrainian navy. The navy includes a western naval command, southern maritime district (formerly the Crimean naval base of the Black Sea fleet), a river fleet and a directorate of naval aviation. The creation of western, southern and central operational commands in summer 1992 out of the Carpathian, Odessa and Kiev military districts was reversed in autumn 1993 when they reverted to their old designations. According to the new reform programme the navy will consist of two districts.

Security service[72] This was formerly the Ukrainian Republic branch of the Soviet KGB. Its functions are mainly domestic, with little foreign capability. The only militarized directorate within the security service is that controlling government communications. The other main directorates of the security service are intelligence, counter-intelligence, defence of the constitutional order, organized crime and corruption, information, and analysis and investigation.

Border troops The main directorates of the border troops include border control, treaty law, operational-investigative and personnel. The border troops are divided into five regional directorates: northwestern, southern, southeastern (a new directorate since January 1993 along the Russian border), maritime and Odessa border patrol ship formation.

National Guard[73] The internal riot police units of the National Guard were transferred to the internal troops of the ministry of internal affairs and the National Guard's functions are now mainly geared towards backing the border troops against external aggression, although they have also been deployed in Crimea as a symbol of Ukrainian sovereignty in view of the unreliability of the local ministry of internal affairs. The National Guard are stationed throughout Ukraine (Kiev, Donets'k, L'viv, Odessa, Crimea, Kirovohrad and Kharkiv) and are divided into the following main directorates: operational, organizational-mobilization, communications and automization, education, military preparation and military technology.

Internal troops These troops have similar functions to the internal troops of the ministry of internal affairs in the Soviet era: protecting prisons, nuclear power stations, and the military-industrial complex, and as riot control units who would back the Berkut police units (see below) in the event of major civil disturbance.

State Protection Force This comprises a large new unit of the ministry of internal affairs which protects lower-ranking officials and government buildings other than those top officials and central government buildings assigned to the Directorate for State Protection (see below).

Berkut (special purpose militia units) These are geared to dealing with organized crime and demonstrations. Formerly they formed the OMON (in Ukrainian, ZMOP) riot police of the late Soviet era.

Directorate for State Protection This has the function of protecting top state officials and central government buildings, with a similar role to the ninth directorate of the Soviet KGB. In 1997 it was transferred to the security service.

Notes

1. See Mark Galeotti, 'Russia's Rotten Army', *Jane's Intelligence Review*, vol. 8, no. 3, March 1996.
2. *The Ukrainian Weekly*, 2 March 1997.
3. See Taras Kuzio, 'Ukrainian Armed Forces in Crisis', *Jane's Intelligence Review*, vol. 7, no. 7, July 1995 and 'Crisis and Reform in Ukraine – Parts 1 and 2', *Jane's Intelligence Review*, vol. 8, nos 10 and 11, October and November 1996.
4. *Narodna armiya*, 6 April 1994.
5. UNIAN news agency, 2 December 1994
6. See T. Kuzio, 'Ukrainian Civil–Military Relations and the Military Impact of the Ukrainian Economic Crisis', in Bruce Parrott, ed., *State Building and Military Power in Russia and the New States of Eurasia: The International Politics of Eurasia*, vol. 5 (Armonk, NY/London: M. E. Sharpe, 1995), pp. 157–92.
7. *Narodna armiya*, 16 February 1994.
8. *Washington Post*, 7 April 1995.
9. Reuters, 22 March 1995.
10. UNIAN, 5 April 1995.
11. *Holos Ukraiiny*, 22 March 1995.
12. Ibid.; *Narodna armiya*, 29 March 1995.
13. *Kievskie vedomosti*, 3 March 1995. The figures are provided by the head of the main financial-economic directorate of the ministry of defence, Hryhoriy Kukharskyi.
14. UNIAN, 24 January 1996.
15. *Demokratychna Ukraiina*, 7 June 1997.
16. UNIAN, 30 March 1995; *East European Report*, 9–15 April 1995.
17. Reuters, 27 March 1995.
18. *Narodna armiya*, 19 April 1995.
19. *Demokratychna Ukraiina*, 7 June 1997.
20. UNIAN, 25 January 1995.
21. UNIAN, 13 February 1995.
22. ITAR-TASS news agency, 22 November 1993.
23. *Shliakh peremohy*, 18 March 1995.
24. *Narodna armiya*, 15 February 1995.
25. *Narodna armiya*, 21 February 1995.
26. The results of an opinion poll published in *Narodna armiya* (21 February 1995) found the following levels of trust in the armed forces among political groupings: social democrats 37 per cent; national democrats 36 per cent; radical left 29 per cent. A more recent poll found that 52 per cent of the public had trust in the armed forces, with 33 per cent holding the opposite view (and the remainder holding no opinion), *Den'*, 8 May 1997.
27. Interfax news agency, 17 February 1995.
28. Radio Ukraine world service, 14 February 1996.
29. UNIAR news agency, 6 February 1996. The education directorate was previously named the socio-psychological service between 1992 and 1994. It retains its old functions, namely to 'Ukrainianize' the armed forces and instil patriotic values among officers and conscripts.
30. *Narodna armiya*, 3 August 1995.
31. Ibid.
32. Ibid.
33. Itar-Tass news agency, 26 March 1997.
34. *Narodna armiya*, 29 July 1994.
35. *Robitnycha hazeta*, 31 March 1994.
36. *Narodna armiya*, 29 July 1994. See also *Narodna armiya*, 21 February 1995.
37. UNIAR, 6 February 1996.
38. *Narodna armiya*, 3 August 1995.
39. *Narodna armiya*, 29 July 1994.
40. UNIAR, 12 December 1994.
41. UNIAR, 6 February 1996.
42. ITAR-TASS news agency, 25 November 1994.
43. See T. Kuzio, 'Ukraine's Arms Exports' and 'Ukraine's Arms Exports Continue to Expand', *Jane's*

Intelligence Review, vol. 6, no. 2, February 1994 and vol. 9, no. 3, March 1997.
44. *Holos Ukraiiny,* 22 July 1997.
45. *Uryadovyy Kuryer,* 17 December 1996. See also the comments by the member of parliament, Mykola Porovsky, in *Ukrayina moloda,* 12 June 1997.
46. Reuters, 26 September 1995.
47. Reuters, 13 March 1996.
48. See Yuri Sandul, 'Derzhava kydae armiyu naprysvolyashche', *Ukrainske slovo,* 19 March 1995.
49. Reuters, 28 December 1996.
50. Reuters, 28 December 1996.
51. UNIAN, 16 January 1997.
52. Interfax-Ukraine and Reuters, 13 March 1996.
53. *Den',* 31 January 1997.
54. See Serhii Markov, 'Ukraine Adopts Military Reform Program', *Prism,* Jamestown Foundation, vol. III, no. 3, Part 1, 21 March 1997 and Bohdan Sambirsky, 'Ukraine Adopts Program for Military Reform', *The Ukrainian Weekly,* 2 March 1997.
55. These reforms were agreed upon at a session of the National Security Council the previous month (see ITAR-TASS and UNIAN, 12 February 1996). The nationalist defence of Lopata is typified in the highly alarmist article entitled 'Derzhavnyi perevorot. Ministr Oborony Shmarov Die Proty Ukraiiny', *Vechirniy Kyiv,* 8 February 1996.
56. See 'Komu sluzhyt Valeriy Shmarov', *Chas,* 16 February 1996.
57. 'Provodeno Analiz Sochyns'kykh Domovlenostei', Institute of Statehood and Democracy, press release no. 9 (5 February 1996).
58. *Uryadovyy kuryer,* nos 32–3, 17 February 1996; *Kievskie vedomosti,* 21 February 1996 and *Shliakh peremohy,* 24 February 1996.
59. See T. Kuzio, 'Ukraine's young Turks – The Union of Ukrainian Officers', *Jane's Intelligence Review,* vol. 5, no.1, January 1993.
60. UNIAN news agency, 14 December 1996.
61. The poll was conducted by SOTSIS-Gallup (*Den',* 12 June 1997). The remainder of the sample held no opinion on the matter.
62. UNIAN news agency, 13 January 1997.
63. *Ukrainske slovo,* 12 November 1995.
64. *Halychnya,* 11 November 1995.
65. *Narodna armiya,* 20 October 1995.
66. *Holos Ukraiiny,* 13 May 1995.
67. See also T. Kuzio, *Ukrainian Security Policy.* Washington Paper no. 167 (Washington DC: Praeger Center for Strategic and International Studies, 1995) and 'Ukraine's Security Dilemmas', *Jane's Intelligence Review,* vol. 8, no. 1, January 1996.
68. See T. Kuzio, 'Ukraine and the Expansion of NATO' and 'The Baltics, Ukraine and the Path to NATO', *Jane's Intelligence Review,* vol. 7, no. 9, September 1995 and vol. 9, no. 7, July 1997.
69. Russian NTV, 17 February 1996.
70. *Den',* 18 June 1997. The poll was conducted by the Independent Experts Fund among Ukraine's political, economic, civic and media elites.
71. See T. Kuzio, 'The Organization of Ukraine's forces', *Jane's Intelligence Review,* vol. 8, no. 6, June 1996.
72. See T. Kuzio, 'The Security Service of Ukraine – A Transformed Ukrainian KGB?', *Jane's Intelligence Review,* vol. 5, no. 3, March 1993.
73. See T. Kuzio, 'The Ukrainian National Guard', *Jane's Intelligence Review,* vol. 5, no. 5, May 1993.

8 Belarus: in search of a security identity

Vyachaslau Paznyak

More than any other of the former Soviet republics, Belarus was unprepared for the dissolution of the Soviet Union and remains uncertain about its status as an independent country and about its national identity. Because of this uncertainty it is difficult to apply conventional approaches to the analysis of national security policy in the case of Belarus. The problems attached to the formulation and conduct of Belarusian security policy are exacerbated by, among other things, a lack of tradition, the small size of the community dealing with this field at a professional and competent level, and a tendency for conceptual choices to be largely preordained by the government's political preferences and for alternative suggestions to be disregarded. Security perceptions have also been influenced by the limited international experience of the new members of the government.

Challenges for the creation of a Belarusian security culture[1]

In the first years of Belarusian independence, redefining the identity of the state of Belarus and its security interests posed a major challenge. The search for a consensus on a new identity among plural, sometimes incompatible belief systems and political forces met many stumbling blocks. However, since 1994 the country's political leadership has been vigorously trying to restore the old Soviet state and the identity associated with Slavic civilization. There has been an attempt under the leadership of Aliaksandr Lukashenka (who was elected president in July 1994) to impose a new conformity through an officially sanctioned view of foreign policy.

The theme of independence and statehood has been downplayed in official statements. A form of societal inferiority complex has been imposed on Belarus. The official rhetoric about Belarus has been full of references to it as 'an unhappy patch of land', 'an impoverished republic', to its 'all-out corruption', its 'inability to survive without big brother Russia', its enormous dependence on Russian energy sources, and so on. The break-up of the former Soviet Union has been pointedly recalled as the major cause of Belarusian enterprises lying idle, the lack of markets for the goods produced and the overall 'historical tragedy of the peoples of the FSU, staged by modern feudal princes and their nationalist elites'.[2] Belarus's sovereignty and independence have been described as a heavy burden exacting extraordinarily high costs.[3]

From the standpoint of traditionalist political forces in Minsk, Belarusian security policy may still seem to be as artificially imposed and uncomfortable as Belarusian sovereignty itself. The best solution for them would be to get rid of the problem altogether by relinquishing independence and reverting to the customary pre-independence security perceptions based on the concept of a great power with its decision-making centre in Moscow. However, although the 'down-with-sovereignty' attitude has seemed to be politically dominant in Belarus, even if more implicitly than explicitly, differing opinions have been voiced by some other major political players and officials, ranging from the Belarusian Popular Front and several newly formed political parties to the chairman of the old parliament, Mecheslau Hryb. Hryb has stressed the values of independent statehood. Former foreign minister Uladzimir Syanko, who described as fortunate the failure of the monetary union between Belarus and Russia because it endangered Belarus's sovereignty,[4] was playing the difficult role of moderating inappropriate or haphazard pronouncements and actions on the part of the president's office. Former prime minister Nikolai Chigir was also balancing the president's pro-integration declarations with positive statements on sovereignty.

Belarus continues to be dominated by the political and security culture of the former Soviet Union, although this is gradually weakening. Although not a single candidate from the Belarusian Popular Front (known for its controversially radical nationalism) was elected to the parliament in the December 1995 elections, its candidates came second in many constituencies by winning 20–30 per cent of the vote, which signals a growing degree of support for its aims across the country.[5] Since this is a transitory phase, the prevailing situation may be termed the 'post-Soviet political and security culture'.

Is Belarus in fact a sovereign state at all? It may indeed lack a 'community of sentiment', and has only a weak national identity to 'form the political basis on which state authority rests' – one of the two basic foundations of sovereignty in international relations. But it definitely fulfils the other basic precondition of sovereignty, namely a territory over which institutional authorities exercise legitimate control.[6] At the same time, international relations constitute a basis for the development and existence of state sovereignty which is, consequently, dependent on them.[7] In this respect, the diplomatic recognition of Belarus and the establishment of Belarusian diplomatic relations as well as the state's participation in international organizations are both expressions and reinforcements of sovereignty.

Belarusian security policies and decision-making

A newly independent state such as Belarus would naturally experience many difficulties in generating political strategies and deciding on particular lines of action. A modern independent state needs teams of experts, established bureaucracies with differentiated professional skills, to formulate, elaborate and implement policies in the domestic and international domains. Clearly, a period of five years or so has not been long enough to create such teams of professionals, even for the most vital structures. This is one of the reasons why security policies in Belarus often remain undifferentiated from other elements of 'syncretic' strategic policy, both at home and internationally. The list of the so-called 'foreign policy priorities' for Belarus in 1991 reflects this mix of goals. These priorities included 'achieving real independence and sovereignty; interacting in the creation of a common economic space within the new community of sovereign states; mobilizing international support for the solution of the Chernobyl problem; transforming Belarus into a nuclear weapon-free zone and a neutral state; integrating Belarus into the pan-European process; creating conditions for the formation of market structures in Belarus, and for its economic development; ensuring ecological security and ensuring free interaction of world cultures'.[8]

National interests and foreign policy[9]

Although Belarusian national interests have been defined by Belarusian leaders as the sole motivating criterion of foreign policy,[10] foreign and security policies should be distinguished from the former, since national interests are neither consistently perceived nor formulated as a concept. Their crystallization is one of the many challenging tasks facing a young state where drafts of foreign policy and national security doctrines are being continuously revised without being adopted, either because of a lack of consensus or because of realignments of power resulting from political struggles over the strategy on which further development needs to be based.

The first attempt to draft a comprehensive foreign policy programme dates back to 1992–3, when 'foreign policy guidelines' were prepared by the foreign ministry. They were heavily criticized in 1993 by the then chairman of the Supreme Council, Stanislau Shushkevich, and returned to the drafters for revision. The first version was aimed at covering the transitional period and did not offer any concrete options, simply describing what foreign policy should be like. Attempts to bring together versions prepared by several teams at the foreign ministry and the Supreme Council failed. The second draft, prepared early in 1994, was not discussed and had to undergo yet another revision as a result of the adoption of the new constitution and the election of the first president in July 1994, which led to a reformulation of domestic and foreign policies and government reshuffles. Shortly after taking office, President Lukashenka issued instructions for the elaboration of a state concept of foreign policy. The consequent work, finished by the foreign ministry in mid-1995, brought the existing number of versions of the foreign policy programme to about five. All of them, with the exception of the first, feature the same foreign policy objectives, differing mainly in specific formulations and details.

The last version defined the objectives of the state's foreign policy and the methods to be used to achieve them.[11] Like the national security concept it has not been made public, and has been awaiting official adoption by the parliament.

President Lukashenka rejected the doctrinaire approach to foreign policy and concluded that none of the alternative foreign policy programmes of which he was aware bore any relation to the real life and interests of ordinary people. Consequently he proclaimed the ultimate goal of Belarusian foreign policy to be the 'well-being of the man, the citizen of Belarus'. Lukashenka defined this approach as representing the 'human dimension of foreign policy', in contrast to abstract ideas or short-term calculations.[12] Yet neither the Belarusian public nor the political elite has had much influence on the framing of this policy. Especially since the closure of the last session of the old Belarusian parliament, foreign and security policy has been monopolized by the president and his office. No one else – what remained of the old parliament, political parties, authoritative personalities or, for that matter, the public – has had any means of influencing decision-making. Indeed, even the ability to air views through the mass media has been limited. The presumption of the equality of the branches of power was replaced by a metaphor that 'every society must have a pillar, a trunk, from which these branches grow. And this trunk is the head of state.'[13] According to the new interpretation, 'the state can and must have only one foreign policy. The legislative power is also taking part in shaping it by its proper methods. However, this foreign policy is proposed and executed by the president.'[14] The priority area of activity of the foreign ministry and its permanent missions abroad was designated as the promotion of the republic's economic interests.[15]

Threat perceptions and national security[16]

The Belarusian foreign minister has characterized the republic as a medium-sized European state which does not have global interests.[17] This means that its security depends largely on the regional security environment. Until recently, however, security issues in Belarus seem to have been addressed more thoroughly in the domestic sphere (for example, in respect of crime and ecology) than on the military-political plane (except for the sensitive areas of nuclear disarmament and arms control). Internal security threats that have been officially identified include the ecological consequences of the Chernobyl disaster, social problems related to growing unemployment, the shortage of housing, illegal immigration, drug-trafficking, and military issues related to the demilitarization of the country.[18]

It now appears that the issue of state security has been somehow substituted by the themes of 'public safety', combating crime and corruption, and, ultimately, the safety of the new leadership. The actions taken against the opposition, the parliament and the mass media, and the strengthening of security measures for the president's office, all testify to a remarkable emphasis on this meaning of security. The presidential decree 'On Some Measures for Ensuring Stability in the Republic of Belarus', a ban on a strike by the metro workers in Minsk on the pretext of an alleged threat to public security, newly introduced restrictions on public demonstrations and on the transfer across the Belarusian border of information materials 'damaging the state interests' and numerous other developments also point in this direction.

President Lukashenka believes that Belarus is encircled by intelligence services, because 'the West fears restoration of the "evil empire", and it is the Belarusian President who is the most consistent in raising the issue of integration. Therefore there is a strong pressure [on Belarus]. . . There are similar trends also in Russia'.[19] The West is also suspected of intentions to 'finally dismember' the Slavic peoples and 'turn them into a raw materials appendage'.[20] Nevertheless, despite a mistrust of the West, Belarus is developing relations with it in a pragmatic way. According to Lukashenka, 'Western states have always built their policy primarily on their states' interests and have protected the interests of their producers. No one is waiting for us in the Western markets. Moreover, we are being pushed out of those places where we fought our way in through tough competition...'.[21] However, the republic's geopolitical position compels it to 'operate on the two fronts' simultaneously. It is thought to be unwise not to exploit its position at the world's crossroads of both trade routes and military-political interests.

On a number of key international security issues Belarus has tended either to avoid taking a clear stand or cautiously to follow Moscow's line, as in the case of the Balkan crisis, which prompted only one official foreign ministry statement expressing concern over 'the escalation of military involvement in the situation in Bosnia and Herzegovina'.[22] At the same time, the attention paid by the Belarusian authorities to the activities of the Catholic church has raised this matter to the level of a national security issue. Apparently, the tightening of regulations for Polish missionaries and appeals to the Vatican to send preachers to Belarus from America and Africa, as well as the official visit to Belarus of the Russian Patriarch Alexei II, demonstrate official uneasiness over signs of a growing influence in Belarus of Catholicism, Poland and the West, as against the Russian Orthodox Church, Russia and the civilization kinship represented by the former Soviet Union.[23]

The national security concept

Lukashenka accepts that 'the primary concern remains the protection of the country's security'.[24] At the end of March 1995 the Belarusian Security Council approved the first draft of a national security concept. Unlike the former Soviet view of national security, which was based on the sources of threats and reduced to military-political factors, the Belarusian security concept is centred on the objects to be protected. National security is defined as the condition of protection of the vital interests of the individual, society and state from internal and external threats. The vital (national) interests are grouped into political, economic, ecological, humanitarian and information categories. The actual and potential threats in each category are defined, as well as the priority activities of the state to ensure the country's security in the corresponding spheres. Special attention is paid to the protection of the nation's security in the humanitarian sphere, namely the development of physical, intellectual, moral, cultural and other aspects of the individual and society as a whole. The concept does not provide concrete advice but serves as a basis for elaborating specific approaches and programmes.[25]

Belarus's military interests are defined as: (1) the maintenance of an optimal correlation between the needs of defence, determined according to the principle of defence sufficiency, and the interests of the country's socio-economic development; (2) the. enhancement of international cooperation, partnership and confidence in the military sphere; (3) keeping the republic's armed forces out of direct or indirect involvement beyond the country's borders. The concept is based on the understanding that the republic is not seeking enemies and does not view any state as an 'enemy', but seeks to have good relations with all countries, above all with neighbouring ones. At the same time the concept provides for military cooperation, both with Russia and the CIS member states and with other countries.[26]

The concept has been adopted by the National Security Council but it still awaits the approval of the parliament. The Council plays a special role in the formulation of foreign and security policy. At present it is a 'constitutionally established consultative body, helping the President in decision-making'. It consists of two main elements: members of the Council itself, and the staff. The latter are extremely important, given their task of drawing together departmental interests into state ones.[27]

The goal of neutrality

By 1994 the officially accepted Belarusian goal of neutrality had come to be interpreted in such a way that, unlike an actual constitutionally and internationally established neutral status, it would not constrain Belarus's conduct of security policy. No conflict is perceived between the goal of neutrality on the one hand and the republic's participation in collective security systems on the other: 'From a security perspective it would be practical for Belarus to participate most actively in all security structures.'[28] This position reflects a rationale according to which Belarus should not be kept in isolation, but should take part in pan-European processes and where possible influence them.[29]

The most elaborate exposition of this interpretation and attempt to create a kind of guiding concept was made by the Belarusian Supreme Council. It posited that 'in today's world, state neutrality must be a neutrality of taking part in all available non-antagonistic alliances which do not stand against each other, it must be a neutrality of integration and mutual integration in all global and regional alliances and relations'.[30] In keeping with global integration processes, Belarus can easily combine membership of the UN, the OSCE, the CIS Tashkent collective security agreement, the NATO Partnership for Peace programme, the cooperation agreement with the EU and economic union with Russia. The result of such participation and reciprocal integration, it is claimed, will be the creation of a new type of neutrality, described as active neutrality, whereby, on the basis of mutual interests, no state is confronting any other but all are cooperating with one another.[31] However, after the Supreme Council was virtually disbanded on the pretext of the results of the referendum held in November 1996, the National Assembly that replaced it has followed the line taken by the president's office.

Security policy: security revisionism

Belarus's most significant policies in the security sphere have been those relating to the assumption and implementation of commitments on denuclearization and conventional arms reductions (see below). Membership of the OSCE, NACC, and PfP has been necessary, but less demanding. The country's involvement in CIS defence activities and the decision to sign the Tashkent agreement have been based on a combination of pragmatism and recognition of the important symbolic political significance of demonstrating loyalty to Russia.

Although during the pre-independence period the Byelorussian Soviet Socialist Republic joined some arms control agreements (see Appendix), which facilitated the creation of an initial base for security policy, these early steps were not aimed at the formulation of an independent security policy. The cornerstones of Belarus's security policy were laid down in 1992–4 and resulted in the adoption of the constitution containing provisions on Belarus's neutral and non-nuclear-weapon status. The denuclearization process depended on the ratification of the NPT and the START 1 Treaty, which aroused little argument. On 4 February 1993 the Belarusian parliament ratified START 1 and the Lisbon Protocol (which laid down the procedure for the redeployment of the 81 SS-25 strategic nuclear missiles on Belarusian soil to Russia, and thereby committed the country to disarmament and eventual non-nuclear status, with very little opposition. It also voted to join the NPT as a non-nuclear state.

In contrast, the neutrality of Belarus has been repeatedly questioned, even if under the guise of other issues. The heated debate on whether to join the CIS Tashkent collective security agreement during 1993 (Belarus was not among the original signatories in May 1992) culminated in a decision to accede to the agreement and the ousting of the parliamentary speaker Stanislau Shush-kevich, who opposed this step.[32] The Belarusian legislature successfully stipulated an amendment to the treaty, however, whereby Belarusian military personnel would not have to undertake service outside Belarus unless the parliament gave specific approval. For this reason Belarusian troops have not been engaged in CIS peacekeeping operations, nor have they participated in UN peacekeeping operations in former Yugoslavia, unlike Russian and Ukrainian troops.

Indeed, the real core security issue which determines all concomitant ones has been whether Belarus should consistently adhere to the goal of neutrality or depart from it in some way. The period since autumn 1994 constitutes a distinct stage in the shaping of Belarus's security policy. Along with the first wave of reshuffles in the presidential team, the official strategic discourse started to change noticeably, becoming more straightforward and categorical. There has been a visible departure from constitutional provisions in the foreign and security policy practice of the executive, and contradictions between the president and the outgoing parliament have increased. Official statements by the Belarusian leadership in 1995 to the effect that Belarus was doing every-thing possible to consolidate its independence and that its prestige in the world was growing have only underscored the gap between words and deeds.[33]

The military-political dimension of security has only been defined either superficially or in a biased manner, whereas economic problems have been considered to be of paramount security concern. Belarusian state sovereignty, as a security value to be protected from possible risks, is clearly missing from the developing security outlook. In fact, Belarus's security policy is its own greatest security threat.

Along with the exacerbation of the socio-political and economic crises in Belarus, the 'funnel' through which political decisions and options emerge has narrowed further. Under these circumstances the foreign and security policies of the republic have become more of a political instrument of the incumbent leadership, a means for the realization of their narrow perceptions and preferences, which apparently differ from national or state interests. While there has been a gap between theoretical constructs of national security and Belarus's actual security policies, there has been at the same time a perfect correlation between the latter and the present Belarusian leader-ship's own security identity. As Dawisha and Parrott write, 'which features come to be accepted as key markers of national [and, we might add, security] identity in a particular case depends not only on objective social conditions but on the political entrepreneurship of the governmental and cultural elites that seek to shape the nation according to their own political agendas'.[34]

In the Belarusian case, its leadership's political and security self-identification is conspicuously ideological, founded on a mixture of socialist and pan-Slavic ideals, concepts and sentiments which may be embraced by a broader (albeit unfortunately rather vague) definition of 'nostalgia for the FSU'.[35] This means that foreign and security policies are in large measure ideologically motivated. Observers have discussed speculations on 'Belarusian imperialism' and the alleged ambitions of President Lukashenka to make Minsk a centre for the integration of the Slavic peoples and himself the leader of the confederation.[36] Sardonic comments in both Belarus and Russia forced the president's office to disavow such speculations as 'provocation'. In response to further moderate accusations of 'surrendering' Belarus's sovereignty, the president said that the process of building closer relations between Belarus, Russia and other CIS states might emulate the EU model.[37]

It would hardly be possible, therefore, to identify specific security ambitions of the incumbent Belarusian leadership. The ambitions of the leadership are much broader. Generally speaking, one may identify two major goals pertaining to the security sphere: (1) the revision of the constitutional goal of neutrality (and in that sense the redefinition of the whole notion of security for Belarus); and (2) a vigorous effort to integrate with Russia, which goes far beyond security needs and makes an independent security role for Belarus altogether meaningless in the context of a hypothetical merger with Russia. There have been overt attempts to restore another state, which was not Belarus, or was much more than Belarus, and of which Belarus was only one peripheral part, albeit an important one.

Belarus has taken a dual approach to defence policy. On the one hand, after the military doctrine was approved, the reform of the army and reductions in military equipment, and conversion of the military sector of the economy, continued along with the building of independent Belarusian military forces. At the same time, expanded military contacts and cooperation agreements with newly independent central and west European states and the United States were coupled with fostering 'special relations' with Russia in the military sphere (see the section below on 'The interaction of Belarusian and Russian security policies'). If the present trends continue, the military doctrine will soon have to be revised. The provision of defence *de tous azimuts* (with the assumption that potential attack may originate from any direction) is being replaced by alliance obligations.

On 23 February 1995 President Lukashenka announced a temporary suspension of the CFE Treaty final-phase weapons reductions which were due to be completed by 15 November 1995. Initially this decision was coupled with claims of an 'imbalance of forces' linked to the prospective NATO expansion. Since this echoed Russian concerns expressed about NATO creeping eastward and closer, it prompted many analysts to interpret Belarus's move as a test to see whether its 'elder brother' Russia might adopt a tougher posture on revising the CFE and other issues.[38] Some time later, however, the delay was explained by reference to the $33 million financial burden of the reductions, and subsequently only financial problems have been cited. In March 1994 the United States pledged to give Belarus $5 million for purposes related to CFE weapons destruction, but Belarus claimed that these funds, which did not go directly to CFE weapons destruction, were insufficient.[39]

During his meeting at the end of June 1995 with Coit Blacker, special adviser to the US president and chief director for Russian, Ukrainian and Eurasian affairs of the US National Security Council, President Lukashenka stated that no elimination of armaments would take place at the expense of the Belarusian people: 'The situation is such that we are not going to give our arms to anyone free of charge. This is the property of Belarus.'[40] One option was to raise funds for disarmament from arms sales. According to some estimates, in autumn 1995 almost 30 per cent of the state budget came from arms sales.[41] Contracts relating to the shipment of Belarusian military equipment to Iran, Iraq, Sudan and other countries were reported in the press that year. Eventually, however, after receiving pledges by the West to provide additional assistance and after a delay of ten months, in October 1995 Belarus resumed the implementation of its obligations under the CFE Treaty and completed the process in April 1996. In meeting the CFE Treaty limits Belarus was left with a maximum of 1,000 tanks, 1,615 artillery pieces, 2,600 ACVs, 260 combat aircraft and 80 attack helicopters. These quotas were favourable to Belarus since it was assigned 12 per cent of the total former Soviet entitlement of treaty-limited equipment. In principle, therefore, it was permitted an arsenal significantly stronger than any of the other former Soviet republics apart from Russia and Ukraine.

Vyachaslau Paznyak

The Belarusian military forces

In reality, however, such high force levels are economically unsustainable. Since Belarusian national forces and CIS forces were divided in April 1992 Belarus has had to make adjustments to match its resources, with a considerable reduction of the military assets located in the former Soviet Belorussian military district (abolished in May 1992). Defence spending is severely constrained and virtually no arms or hardware have been procured for the Belarusian army since it was created and there have been serious problems in funding any defence research programmes. Funds have not been properly allocated even for the acquisition of spare parts or the repair of military hardware. This has undermined the technical sophistication and combat training of the armed forces overall.[42] In 1996 the Belarusian defence ministry requested 6.418 trillion Belarusian roubles but received only 2.231 trillion. In 1997 it appeared it would need to content itself with only just over two trillion.[43] But despite financial difficulties, the defence ministry has made some progress in professionalizing the armed forces. By early 1996 some 40 per cent of those serving in the armed forces were on contracts; this increased to 50 per cent by spring 1997 and by 1998 it is hoped to increase this figure to around 70 per cent.[44]

By early 1995 the former Soviet force levels in Belarus had been cut by a half and a corps/brigade system adopted (three army corps were created as well as detached mechanized brigades each with 3,000–5,000 men). This reduction was encouraged by the limit of 100,000 personnel Belarus accepted in the CFE1A Treaty (an agreement on military personnel which followed the CFE Treaty) and by the fact that the concentration of military forces Belarus inherited when it achieved independence exceeded that of any other former Soviet republic. A session of the Collegium of the Belarusian defence ministry in January 1996, chaired by President Lukashenka, agreed to reduce the strength of the armed forces from 85,000 (the level to which they had been cut at that time) to 60,000. It also agreed to reduce the number of services to two: ground forces and air defence forces, the latter to combine air forces and air defence forces under one command. The ground forces would remain the basic arm of service and comprise army corps, mobile forces, reserve formations and other elements.[45]

It appears that the bulk of the Belarusian armed forces will remain concentrated in the western regions of the country. Belarusian officials have emphasized that in keeping with its military doctrine Belarus regards no state or group of states as a potential enemy (despite their objections to the enlargement of NATO – see below). The troops remain deployed in the regions where the necessary infrastructure for them exists.[46] But the fact that a core of these forces and the basis for new mobile forces are derived from elite former

Soviet airborne troop formations, which were intended for offensive operations in the former Soviet western military theatre, may create uneasiness in Belarus's western neighbours.

There is a declared emphasis on small, flexible and highly combat-ready forces, centred on ground force brigades. Lukashenka issued a decree in June 1995 requiring the rapid creation of mobile forces. With a strength of around 5,000, these forces now include two former air assault brigades, from the former 103rd Vitebsk Guards Airborne Division, now converted to independent mobile brigades, and the 38th Independent Mobile Brigade, the former 38th Air Assault Brigade. It is not yet clear whether the basic operational principles for these mobile forces have been developed, but the general intention is that they would move rapidly to any threatened axis and win time for the deployment of the Belarusian army's main forces.[47] The Russian military command has taken a close interest in the evolution of these new forces, with a view to cooperation, and joint operations by the mobile forces of both Russia and Belarus cannot be ruled out; whether such an outcome will occur depends on the nature of future security policy interaction between the two neighbour states.

The interaction of Belarusian and Russian security policies

The nature of and prospects of Belarusian integration with Russia have been a particularly controversial security issue since 1992. After the dissolution of the USSR the dynamics of disintegration prevailed until the first major reintegration attempt between the two states was undertaken on 20 July 1992, when more than twenty agreements on economic, military and other issues were signed in Moscow. This coincided with the fulfilment of one Russian priority: the withdrawal of tactical nuclear weapons from Belarusian territory to Russia for their eventual destruction.

The subsequent ratification by the parliaments of Belarus (on 4 February 1993) and Russia of the Treaty on the Coordination of Activities in the Military Sphere and of the Agreement on the Strategic Forces Temporarily Stationed on the Territory of Belarus, signed on 20 July 1992, legally defined the status of the nuclear forces and the further commitments of the parties thereto, and allowed them to coordinate the timetable for the withdrawal of nuclear armaments. According to those agreements, Russian troops were to be withdrawn from Belarus by 1997. As a result of prolonged negotiations, the Treaty on the Status of the Military Units of the Russian Strategic Nuclear Forces Temporarily Stationed in Belarus, and the Agreement on the Procedure for the Withdrawal of Military Formations of the Russian Strategic Forces with the attached schedule, were signed on 24 September 1993 and ratified by the Belarusian parliament on 25 November 1993.[48]

In 1993–4 attempts were made to create an economic union within the CIS and a monetary union between Russia and Belarus, but these eventually failed. Nevertheless, during the 1994 elections both presidential candidates, Prime Minister Vyacheslav Kebich and Aliaksandr Lukashenka, competed in their support for closer Belarusian–Russian ties. The election of the first Belarusian president in July 1994 and the creation of new executive structures initially brought a pause in the process, but did not remove the integration issue from the political agenda.

From the summer to the autumn of 1994 Belarusian–Russian relations made notable progress, from tough bargaining over the exchange of debts for energy sources to preparing several dozen joint documents. Relations with Russia at the beginning of 1995 were described by President Lukashenka as representing the real beginning of integration processes in the CIS, a breakthrough to a qualitatively new level of relations along the road to Slavic unity.[49]

On 6 January 1995 a number of important agreements were signed in Minsk by Belarus's prime minister Mikhail Chihir and Russian vice-premier Alexei Bolshakov.[50] Belarus renounced the right to levy rent and raise taxes from Russia, except for 'taxes on economic activities', for the next 25 years. Agreement was reached on using and maintaining the Vileika radio station and the Baranovichi missile early warning facility in Belarus (which would be under Russian jurisdiction), but in each case it was stated ambiguously that 'nothing... should imply that the facility in question shall be granted the status of a military base'.[51] One of the documents contains a provision for the participation of the two states 'in the formation of a system of collective security' whereby 'the defence of the external borders will be carried out by joint forces'.[52] This wide-ranging accord on border security and its subsequent refinements would prove to be particularly sensitive. In return, Russia promised to give Belarus a credit worth 150 billion roubles on favourable terms and supply oil and gas at reduced prices.[53] It also pledged to provide equipment and material resources at its internal prices for the protection of Belarusian borders. These offers were exploited by President Lukashenka to dissipate doubts and criticisms expressed in the parliament about the military agreements. However, little has been done so far to implement those commitments.

Further major developments with regard to integration took place on Belarusian soil during President Yeltsin's official visit to Minsk in February 1995, when another package of major agreements was signed. These included the Treaty of Friendship, Good-Neighbourly Relations and Cooperation between Belarus and Russia (ratified in April 1995 by the Belarusian Supreme Council, and next month by the Russian Duma), the Agreement on the Joint Management of the Customs Services of the two states, the Treaty on the Joint

Efforts in Guarding Belarus's State Border, and an intergovernmental agreement on cooperation in the group of member states of the Open Skies Treaty. A symbolic demolition of a checkpoint on the Belarusian–Russian border was performed by President Lukashenka and Russia's prime minister, Viktor Chernomyrdin in Belarus in May 1995.

The withdrawal of the SS-25 missiles from Belarus has been among the problems highlighted in bilateral security relations. According to press reports in July 1995, President Lukashenka suspended the withdrawal of the Russian Strategic Rocket Forces from Belarus. He was cited as criticizing the decision of the former Belarusian leaders to conduct this withdrawal as a major political mistake in view of the envisaged future complete merger of Belarus and Russia.[54] Although all subsequent comments referred to these reports as a misunderstanding arising from purely technical and financial difficulties, some analysts suggested that Belarus was again acting as a 'testing ground' for Russian plans to renege on arms control obligations in response to the plans for NATO enlargement. Although the Russian side has been ready to withdraw its nuclear weapons from Belarus ahead of schedule, it is indicative that a member of Russia's Presidential Council, Andranik Migranian, stated in early 1994 that 'Russia should not go out of its way to impose a non-nuclear-weapon status on Ukraine.... In the event of a closer integration of the two states nuclear weapons may only enhance the combined power of these two states or the CIS as a whole.'[55] Similar scenarios may exist for Belarus.

On 9 December 1995 Russian defence minister Pavel Grachev and his Belarusian counterpart Leanid Maltsau signed eighteen documents on bilateral military cooperation. Among them were the schedule for the withdrawal of the remaining two regiments of the Russian Strategic Rocket Forces from Belarus (completed on 27 November 1996), the agreement on the joint arrangement of regional security (for the signatory states of the CIS Tashkent agreement, to be further signed at the head of state level), the protocol on the joint activities of air defence forces, the protocol of intentions on military-technical cooperation, and the protocol of intentions on training personnel and the procedure for transferring officers between the two military forces.[56]

Military-technical cooperation between the two countries is being revitalized. Its significance was characterized by the Belarusian president as 'strategic' and Russian military orders as 'saving our defence enterprises from being closed down'.[57] Undoubtedly there are some economic incentives to such cooperation; the Belarusian military command claims that it could be used to build up their armed forces more cheaply and efficiently. Yet it also has a politico-strategic dimension. Grachev's comments during his visit at the end of 1995 to the effect that Russia was beginning to work seriously on the realization of the collective security agreement and attached a special importance to bilateral cooperation with Belarus in that respect, as well as his statement on the need to take 'adequate measures' should NATO attempt to move its borders eastward, indicated an intention to go ahead with the creation of a military alliance which would include Belarus.[58] President Lukashenka, for his part, argued that the talks sought to ensure that both Belarusian and Russian concepts of military construction would definitely be directed at enhancing the trends towards integration between the two states.[59] One may suggest that the whole issue of security for Belarus has been tightly linked to the task of integration with Russia. NATO enlargement provides a convenient pretext for a renewed enthusiasm about such bilateral integration.

In autumn 1995 Russian general staff officers raised the possibility that in the event of NATO enlargement a major military force could be developed on the basis of a Russian–Belarusian military-political alliance and deployed on the borders of Poland and Lithuania.[60] However, when pressed on the matter in April 1996 the Belarusian defence minister Maltsau argued that to permit foreign (Russian) military bases on Belarusian territory was complicated from the legal point of view and that to concentrate troops on the border with Poland would be a drastic step which could only be taken 'if all political methods of sorting out the problems connected with the military-political balance in Europe are exhausted'. He stated that there were no plans to create a joint command of Russian and Belarusian armed forces, that each side would be entitled to define independently what kind of army it needed to have. Even in the case of joint combat actions, he claimed, 'there will be no coalition command of the two countries' armed forces'; rather, 'each country will command its own army, but the operational plans will be coordinated'.[61]

Despite these qualifications, the goal of military coordination was reinforced by a meeting between Grachev and Maltsau in May 1996 which led to agreements on the principles of jointly providing for regional security. The concept for a joint defence policy would be prepared as well as common principles on a build-up of the Russian and Belarusian armed forces and cooperation between them.[62] This expressed a quite different spirit in bilateral defence relations from that prevailing only a few years before, when there had been numerous disputes connected with breaches of agreements reached on the withdrawal of Russian troops from Belarusian territory. It was also agreed at the May meeting that the two countries would maintain defence plants cooperating in the production of military equipment and spare parts, and Maltsau emphasized that the two countries' air defences had begun joint combat duty. The Belarusian air defence system has been presented as crucial for the defence of central Russia, although Belarus still carries the financial burden of maintaining this system.[63] Grachev evoked an alarmist scenario at the May 1996 meeting in the event of NATO enlargement: 'the possibility of a "powerful" Russian–Belarusian military grouping being set up on the territory of Belarus'. He claimed that this was also viewed as a possibility by President Lukashenka.[64] In fact, this option assumes a commitment of Russian military and military-economic resources for the re-creation of some kind of 'Western military axis', which, given the financial and structural crisis of the Russian military organization, is unlikely in the next few years even if Lukashenka were to approve such a scheme.

Russian military resource constraints are reflected in Russian equivocation over the issue of financing the protection of Belarusian external borders (those with non-CIS states). Lukashenka claimed in autumn 1996 that Russia would take on this financial responsibility, but in intergovernmental agreements at that time Russia had offered Belarus only some funds towards new equipment for Belarus's new interstate borders.[65] Clearly, Russian economic difficulties limit practical efforts at military-security integration with Belarus. In this context it should be recalled that the fate of Belarusian sovereignty in 1991 was determined not by Belarus itself, not by its political choice, long-time aspirations or a struggle on the part of a majority of its people, but by external factors. Similarly, given the residual nostalgia over the USSR, the possibility of forgoing this sovereignty will depend largely on outside political players, above all Russia.[66] Russian political ambitions and economic capabilities alike, therefore, are crucial for the future of Belarus.

The problems Belarus is experiencing in its relations with the West naturally encourage it to look for other partners. As President Lukashenka observed in an interview with the German newspaper *Handelsblatt*, it is the position of the West that may bring about integration in the East, because Western markets are closed to Belarus. Being denied assistance, the East is forced to create an integrated economic system: 'The longer Western governments play the role of observers, the faster this integration process may proceed.'[67]

Belarusian–Russian relations, including those in the security field, are intended to serve as a model for other CIS states. However, given the varied interests of different member states, Belarus has in reality a limited influence over decisions on security issues in the CIS. According to what may be termed the Migranian Doctrine (after the Russian Presidential Council member Andranik Migranian), the whole of the CIS space comprises an area of Russian national interests, which should be promoted by political, economic and cultural pressure and influence without creating any new interstate unions. By leaning on Belarus, and through the example of Russian–Belarusian relations, Moscow would like to influence other CIS countries.[68] Lukashenka has stated that 'by strengthening ties with Russia the republic facilitates the task of building new relations with other CIS countries. And these countries are acquiring their own spheres of interests and influence beyond the borders of the FSU. And cooperation with the main Eastern neighbour is objectively increasing our capabilities on the world arena.'[69] Although it has refrained from sending its troops on peacekeeping missions, Belarus has otherwise supported and joined all recent military agreements within the CIS.[70]

Political manoeuvres around the nature of integration between Belarus and Russia continue. In contrast to many of his previous pronouncements, in autumn 1995 President Lukashenka claimed that so long as he remained president there would be no merger of the two countries, since he viewed this move as neither necessary nor beneficial to either Belarus or Russia. Nor, he stated, did he contemplate any longer the creation of a monetary union: 'At present the two countries are seeking to establish a payments union akin to the one existing in the European Union.'[71] Despite these reservations about political and economic integration, the initial differences between Belarus and Russia over military cooperation have been superseded first, as described above, by a coordinated approach to security policy, and then by Belarusian dependence on the security policy of Russia.

Indeed, on 2 April 1996 a broad treaty on union between Belarus and Russia was signed in Moscow by Presidents Lukashenka and Yeltsin to create a Community of Sovereign States. The way this developed suggested that once again Belarus was promoting the integration agenda, although Yeltsin was also using the integration rhetoric of the treaty to bolster his presidential election campaign. Aiming at the deep economic and political integration of the two states, the treaty stipulated that the parties would 'coordinate their foreign policy, common positions on their main international issues, cooperate in maintaining security, protecting borders and combating crime'. Further, it committed the parties, 'with a view to ensuring reliable security', to 'elaborate common principles of defence building and the use of military infrastructure in accordance with national legislation' (Article 3). By this time over twenty military agreements had been signed between Belarus and Russia and a number of others were being negotiated.

However, the April 1996 treaty is only a framework treaty and was concluded principally with domestic political functions in Belarus and Russia in mind. It contains no timetable for its implementation or sanctions in the case of the non-implementation of its provisions. The foreign policy provisions are vague and declaratory, while the substance of military-political cooperation is to be found in separate bilateral treaties (as discussed above). Moreover, it is unclear how the complicated decision-making structure envisaged by the treaty would relate to existing CIS structures and committees. In 1997 there were further integration efforts between the two states. The Treaty on the Union of Belarus and Russia and its Statute, which was confirmed, generally emphasized integration trends in the military sphere. On 2 April the Supreme Council of the Community of Belarus and Russia adopted a document on 'The General Principles of the Military Construction of Belarus and Russia and the Use of Elements of the Military Infrastructure', which provides for close bilateral military interaction and a procedure for financing and implementing joint defence programmes. A concept for a joint defence policy has been elaborated and submitted for approval to the Executive Committee of the Community of Belarus and Russia. It envisages, among other things, the formation of a single system of air-defence and anti-missile defence, and coordination of procurement from defence industries.[72] To implement this concept changes will have to be made by the two countries' legislatures in their national military doctrines and defence-related laws. Meanwhile, a new interstate treaty on cooperation in the military sphere is being drafted. Also, there have been press reports that a joint Belarusian-Russian working group has prepared a draft concept of safeguarding regional security (by implication it applies to the western 'outer borders' of the Community, and now the Union, of the two states).[73]

Ultimately, however, momentum towards substantive integration between Belarus and Russia will depend on firm political will towards that goal within the leaderships of both countries and a Russian readiness to accept the costs that this would entail. Despite constant rhetorical statements on the issue, it is not clear that Russia considers itself to have the resources available to absorb Belarus.

Belarus and NATO

Belarus's approach to relations with the West and NATO has been marked by contradictions similar to those characterizing its attitude to independence. The PfP programme, which Belarus joined in January 1995, has been viewed positively, even as a 'humanistic programme', and Belarus joined it to avoid being left out of European and global integration processes. Initially Belarus intended to address only minor, financially unburdensome issues, such as information, conversion, ecology and so on, within the PfP programme. But in November 1995 Belarus decided to activate its participation in the PfP programme, and the National Security Council of Belarus has elaborated a programme of cooperation under the PfP. Military cooperation with the United States has also been developing within the framework of a bilateral memorandum on understanding and cooperation in the military sphere, signed in October 1993.

Despite these links, NATO enlargement has been perceived by Belarusian leaders as an unwelcome development, because of an assumed negative reaction from public opinion in Russia, Belarus and Ukraine arising from NATO's 'hostile image among their people'.[74] Belarusian officials have repeatedly referred to greater insecurity arising for Belarus in the event of a new confrontation between military alliances in Europe.[75] From the perspective of the concept of 'active sovereignty', according to Mecheslau Hryb, Belarus could in principle combine membership of the CIS Tashkent agreement and of NATO. However, the inertia of Cold War thinking, it is claimed, drives 'certain forces' into pushing forward NATO enlargement towards the western borders of Belarus and Russia. The conclusion is that NATO is a manifestation of 'an old atavism of the bipolar confrontation', and that Belarus should oppose its eastward expansion.[76]

NATO enlargement has also been associated with an increased nuclear threat. At the NPT review and extension conference in April–May 1995, Belarus's concern 'about possible risks of more and more places in Europe being used for nuclear weapons deployment in the event of NATO's geographical expansion'[77] apparently drove it into resurrecting the idea of creating a nuclear-weapon-free zone in central Europe. This idea, however, met with a lukewarm response even from Russia.[78]

The chief of the Belarusian president's secretariat, Ural Latypov, has claimed that NATO enlargement may lead to a new confrontation, in which case the 'line of fire' would be drawn across Belarus. He has further pointed to the possible negative effect of such an enlargement on the domestic political situation, on the shaping of democratic institutions and the public attitude, which in turn will affect the European security context. The main merit of the PfP agreement for Belarus, in his opinion, has been access to full information on NATO development. In the event of NATO enlargement this partnership would be considerably devalued for Belarus.[79]

Since Belarus has indicated its readiness to side with Russia in creating another defence alliance, this means it is prepared to contribute to its own insecurity. A policy of pursuing balance between Russia and NATO might be a better idea, but it would require a much higher degree of sophistication, uncharacteristic of Belarus's current foreign and security policy. In any case, if Belarus is the only strategic ally of Russia at its western border, as both Belarusian and Russian officials stress, and there is no other state to join it in creating a military alliance counterbalancing NATO expansion, the prospects for the alliance depend specifically on Belarus. In this respect Belarusian security policy looks like a projection of Russian security policy in the region, or at least a representation of some influential political currents in Russia.

The Belarusian position has been further complicated, however, by the conclusion in May 1997 of the NATO-Russia Charter and the creation of the Permanent Joint Council for NATO and Russia to manage situations threatening peace and stability. Belarus was isolated from the negotiations leading to the NATO-Russia Charter and has no reliable guarantee that its interests will be represented by Russia in the future in the new structure of relations with NATO. Belarus would be further disadvantaged if a new geopolitical axis is formed between the Baltic States, Poland and Ukraine. In these circumstances Belarus may be compelled to develop its own dialogue with NATO if it is to have any role in shaping a new European security system and if it is to avoid further damage to its relations with the West.[80]

Conclusion

For some sceptics, such as the Czech deputy foreign minister Alexander Vondra, Belarus's transition from a former Soviet republic to an independent state is over; it has simply failed.[81] However, any transition, even if it is being reversed, should feature some of the momentum previously gained from the 'big bang' disintegration. This should result for a period of time not in a state of transition 'from–to' but in a 'transition adrift' (the latter has already been expressed in Belarus's controversial statements and moves in the security sphere). Time will eventually show if the idea of reintegration with Russia, whether under a pan-Slavic banner or otherwise, will come to fruition or will become a second utopia (in its literal meaning as a 'non-existent place' or an unrealistic project) after independence. If such full reintegration does not materialize, then the third option could be for Belarus to remain as a quasi-state in the centre of Europe with the formal attributes of sovereignty and a low profile, enjoying little attention or interest from the international community and treated as a would-be and de facto province of a powerful neighbour.

Appendix

Belarusian participation as an independent state in international security arrangements and international arms control agreements

Security arrangements	Date	Arms control agreements
CD	1996	CTBT
PfP	1995	CWC
CIS Tashkent agreement	1993	NPT
		START–1
NACC	1992	CFE Treaty
OSCE		
CIS	1991	

Vyachaslau Paznyak

Notes

1. In using the term 'security culture' the author draws on the definition of 'strategic culture' as a milieu of ideas which limits behavioural choices, an integrated 'system of symbols (e.g. structures for argument, languages, analogies, metaphors) which act to establish pervasive and long-lasting strategic preferences by formulating concepts of the role and efficacy of military force in interstate political affairs, in a manner which makes the strategic preferences seem uniquely realistic and efficacious'. See Clifford Geertz, *The Interpretation of Cultures* (New York: Basic Books, 1973), p. 90. Cited in Alastair Iain Johnston, 'Thinking About Strategic Culture', *International Security,* vol. 19, no. 4, Spring 1995, p. 46. In addition to the military dimension, security culture would also include other aspects of national security. For a discussion of various aspects of security see Barry Buzan, *People, States and Fear: An Agenda for International Security Studies in the Post-Cold War Era,* 2nd edn (Hemel Hempstead: Harvester Wheatsheaf, 1991).
2. President Lukashenka, cited in *Zvyazda,* 4 November 1995.
3. See Aliaksandr Lukashenka, 'Lichu syabe dzyarzhaunym chalavekam', *Zvyazda,* 8 July 1995.
4. *Zvyazda,* 18 February 1995.
5. See *Svobodnye novosti-plus,* no. 50, December 1995, p. 3.
6. See J. Samuel Barkin and Bruce Cronin, 'The State and the Nation: Changing Norms and the Rules of Sovereignty in International Relations', *International Organization,* vol. 48, no. 1, Winter 1994, pp. 110–11.
7. See Anthony Giddens, *The Nation-State and Violence* (Berkeley: University of California Press, 1987), p. 263. Cited in Barkin and Cronin, 'The State and the Nation', p. 110.
8. See *Statement by Pyotr K. Krauchanka, Minister of Foreign Affairs of the Republic of Belarus in the General Debate at the 46th Session of the United Nations General Assembly* (Minsk: Republic of Belarus, 1991), pp. 21–30.
9. For a discussion of the broader foreign policy decision-making process and structures see Vyachaslau Paznyak, 'Belarus's Foreign Policy Priorities and Decision-making', in Karen Dawisha and Adeed Dawisha, eds, *The Making of Foreign Policy in Russia and the New States of Eurasia* (Cambridge, MA: M. E. Sharpe, 1995).
10. See President Aliaksandr Lukashenka, 'My spadzyaemsya na kanstruktyunaye supratsounitstva z usimi palitychnymi silami', *Zvyazda,* 29 July 1994; Mecheslau Hryb, 'Zneshniya Palityka Buduetsa na Padstavah Natsyyanalnaha Intaresu i Natsyyanalnaiy Byaspeki', *Narodnaya hazeta,* 16 August 1994; also, Belarus's foreign minister Uladzimir Syan'ko, 'My ne planuyem radykalnyh zmen u zneshnyay palitytsy', *Zvyazda,* 9 August 1994.
11. See 'U Belarusi stvorana kantseptsiya zneshnyai palityki', an interview with the first deputy foreign minister of Belarus, Valeri Tsepkalo, in *Zvyazda,* 10 August 1995, and Ural Latypov, 'Vazhno naiti svoyo mesto', *Belorusskaya delovaya gazeta,* 6 February 1995.
12. See Aliaksandr Lukashenka, 'Dabrabyt chalaveka, hramadzyanina Belarusi, z'yaulyayetsa vysheishai matai nashai zneshn'yai palityki', *Zvyazda,* 5 August 1995.
13. See Aliaksandr Lukashenka, 'Ya vymushany prymat' zhorstkiya rashenni, kab zakhavat' dzyarzhavu', *Narodnaya hazeta,* 25 October 1995.
14. See Aliaksandr Lukashenka, 'Dabrabyt chalaveka'.
15. *Zvyazda,* 4 August 1995.
16. On some theoretical issues of the national security of the newly independent states see Vyachaslau Paznyak, 'National Security of the Newly Independent States', in idem, ed., *European Integration and Military and Political Aspects of National Security of the Newly Independent States: Proceedings of the International Conference, 10–12 June 1993* (Minsk: National Centre for Strategic Initiatives 'East-West', 1994), pp. 22–4.
17. Uladzimir Syanko, 'Kiraunitstva Belarusi dalyokaye ad papulizmu', *Zvyazda,* 30 July 1994.
18. See Belarus foreign minister Pyotr Krauchanka's statement at the Conference on Stability in Europe, *Narodnaya hazeta,* 31 May 1994.
19. *Narodnaya hazeta,* 1 December 1995.
20. See *Zvyazda,* 5 May 1995.
21. See Lukashenka, 'Ya vymushany prymat' zhorstkiya rashenni'.
22. *Vo slavu rodiny,* 15 September 1995.
23. See, e.g., *Svaboda,* 31 October 1995.

24. *Zvyazda*, 11 May 1995.
25. See Anatoli Tozik, 'V kontseptsii natsional'noy bezopasnosti razrabotchiki postavili tochku', *Narodnaya hazeta*, 6 June 1995.
26. Ibid.
27. See Ural Latypov, 'Vazhno naiti svoyo mesto', *Belorusskaya delovaya hazeta*, 6 February 1995.
28. See Valeri Tsepkalo, 'Stremlenie Belarusi k neitralitetu ne zapreshchaet ey ukreplyat' mir vo vsem mire', *Narodnaya hazeta*, 10–12 September 1994.
29. *Zvyazda*, 20 January 1995.
30. Mecheslau Hryb, 'Respublika Belarus u intahratsyynym pratsese suchasnasti', Statement by the Chairman of the Supreme Council of the Republic of Belarus at the 93rd Conference of the Interparliamentary Union in Madrid, *Zvyazda*, 7 April 1995.
31. Ibid.
32. On the debates in Belarus on joining the CIS Collective Security Treaty see Frank Umbach, *Back to the Future? Belarus and its Security Policy in the Shadow of Russia* (Cologne: Berichte des Bundesinstitut für Ostwissenschaftliche und Internationale Studien, No. 10/1993) and Paznyak, 'Belarus's Foreign Policy Priorities'.
33. See e.g. statements by President Lukashenka, *Zvyazda*, 4 August 1995, and Prime Minister Chihir, *Zvyazda*, 29 July 1995.
34. See Karen Dawisha and Bruce Parrott, *Russia and the New States of Eurasia: The Politics of Upheaval* (Cambridge: Cambridge University Press, 1994), p. 57.
35. There are interesting parallels with the so-called 'Third World cultures' here. In such states political groups 'owe allegiance to and act for interests other than the national interest. Instead of identifying with the state, individuals identify with ethnic, religious, or regional groupings. . . Rather than transcending the differences among these different groups, the state is often simply the representative of the group that holds power in the capital.' See Steven R. David, 'Explaining Third World Alignment', *World Politics,* vol. 43, no. 2, January 1991, pp. 233–56, cited in Stephen Peter Rosen, 'Military Effectiveness: Why Society Matters', *International Security*, vol. 19, no. 4, Spring 1995, p. 28. In the present case the Belarusian leadership holds allegiance to and acts in the name of the political and psychological idiosyncrasies of the FSU shared by a majority of the country's population.
36. See e.g. Yuri Drakohrust, 'Sil'niee zverya koshki nyet', *Belorusskaya delovaya gazeta*, 20 July 1995.
37. *Narodnaya hazeta*, 10 October 1995.
38. See e.g. Arkadi Dubnov, 'Kazus Lukashenko', *Russian Daily-Novoe Russkoe slovo*, 14 March 1995.
39. See Sarah Walking, 'Belarus Suspends CFE-Required Weapons Reductions', *Arms Control Today*, April 1995, p. 19.
40. *Zvyazda*, 30 June 1995.
41. *Svaboda*, 4 August 1995, p. 6.
42. See article by N. Kuznetsov in *Sluzhba*, no. 10, June 1995, p. 6.
43. *Belorusskaya delovaya gazeta*, 6 February 1997.
44. According to the Organization-Mobilization Directorate of the Main Staff, *Vo slavu rodiny*, 1 March 1996; also in interview of the defence minister, Lieutenant General Alexander Chumakov, *Krasnaya Zvezda*, 23 April 1997.
45. By February 1997 the armed forces had been reduced in strength only to 83,500 according to Chumakov, *Sovetskaya Belorussia,* 22 February 1997.
46. Interview of the then defence minister of Belarus, General Anatoli Kostenko, in *Vo slavu rodiny*, 17 June 1994.
47. For a description of these forces see V. Kovalov in *Krasnaya zvezda*, 13 October 1985. See also description of report by President Lukashenka at the defence ministry's Collegium session in June, in *Vo slavu rodiny*, 29 June 1995.
48. On Belarus's nuclear policies see Vyachaslau Paznyak, 'Belarus's De-nuclearization Policy and the Control of Nuclear Weapons', in George Quester, ed., *The Nuclear Challenge in Russia and the New States of Eurasia* (Cambridge, MA: M.E. Sharpe, 1995).
49. *Zvyazda*, 11 May 1995.
50. These included: the Agreement on the Customs Union and the Protocol on the Introduction of a Free Trade Regime, the Agreement on the Principles of the Establishment of Financial and Industrial Groups, the Agreement on Trade Non-payments, a Memorandum on Broadening and Deepening Belarusian–Russian Cooperation, the Agreement on the Procedure for the Use and Maintenance of

the Vileika Radio Station, the Agreement on the Procedure for Completing the Construction, the Use and Maintenance of the Baranovichi Centre of the Early Warning System, and the Agreement on the Matters of Jurisdiction and Mutual Legal Aid Concerning the Temporary Stationing of Russia's Military Forces.

51. *Belarus News/National Weekly,* no. 1, March 1995.
52. Ibid.
53. *Zvyazda,* 22 March 1995.
54. *Izvestiya,* 6 July 1995.
55. *Nezavisimaya gazeta,* 18 January 1994.
56. See *Nezavisimaya gazeta,* 14 December 1995.
57. *Zvyazda,* 21 February 1995.
58. See *Svobodnye novosti-plus,* no. 50, December 1995, p. 4; *Zvyazda,* 9 December, 1995; *Svaboda,* 12 December 1995, p. 2.
59. *Vo slavu rodiny,* 12 December 1995.
60. Interview with high-ranking officer of the Main Operations Department of the Russian general staff, in *Nezavisimaya gazeta,* 7 October 1995.
61. Interview in *Vo slavu rodiny,* 19 April 1996.
62. *Segodnya,* 17 July 1996.
63. Interview of Belarusian air defence forces commander, Lieutenant General V. Kostenko, *Rossiyskaya gazeta,* 12 May 1997.
64. Interfax news agency, in BBC, *Summary of World Broadcasts, Former Soviet Union,* SU/2612 S1/1, 15 May 1996.
65. Article by Y. Golotyuk in *Segodnya,* 11 September 1996.
66. The results of elections to the Russian Duma in December 1995 (in which the Russian Communist Party gained the largest share of the vote) emphasize the potential Russian role. The communist factions of both newly elected parliaments, the Belarusian and the Russian, indicated their intention to coordinate activities. However, the failure of the Russian Communist Party leader Zyuganov to unseat Yeltsin in the summer 1996 presidential elections moderated the Russian impulse towards integration with CIS neighbours.
67. Cited in *Narodnaya hazeta,* 23 November 1995.
68. See *Zvyazda,* 23 February 1995.
69. Aliaksandr Lukashenka, 'Dlya myane halounym u zneshnyay palitytsy z'yaulyayetsa intaras Belaruskaha hramadzhanina', *Zvyazda,* 26 October 1995.
70. See the description of CIS agreements signed by Belarus by Colonel Dmitry Shilo, chief of the Belarusian foreign ministry's Department for Foreign Relations, in *Vo slavu rodiny,* 24 May 1996.
71. *Narodnaya hazeta,* 23 November 1995.
72. See interview of Defence Minister Alexander Chumakov, *Krasnaya zvezda,* 23 April 1997; and Colonel B. Bikkinin in *Vo slavu rodiny,* 16 May 1997.
73. See S. Anisko, *Belarusskaya delovaya gazeta,* 13 March 1997.
74. See Tsepkalo, 'Stremlenie Belarusi k neitralitetu'.
75. *Zvyazda,* 21 February 1995, 11 May 1995.
76. Hryb, 'Respublika Belarus u intahratsyynym pratsese suchasnasti'.
77. See Uladzimir Syanko, Minister of Foreign Affairs of the Republic of Belarus, at the NPT Review and Extension Conference Plenary Meeting, New York, 18 April 1995, p. 3.
78. For a Russian analysis of this idea see A. Portnov, *Nezavisimaya gazeta,* 19 September 1996.
79. *Narodnaya hazeta,* 18 October 1995.
80. On this issue see I. Karmanov, *Nezavisimaya gazeta,* 5 June 1997; L. Sayenko, 'Lukashenka Has His Own Answer to NATO', *Moscow News,* no. 23–24, 19 June–2 July 1997, p. 4.
81. Mr Vondra said that 'Already Belarus has not succeeded as an independent state . . . Belarus is a model of reintegration and of an increase of Russian influence in the Western direction at the smallest cost.' Cited in *Komsomol'skaya pravda,* 15 August 1995.

9 The Caucasus states: the regional security complex

Jonathan Aves

Questions of national security in the three former Soviet Transcaucasian republics of Georgia, Azerbaijan and Armenia have been dominated by the state of their relationship with Russia. In all three republics, to a greater or lesser extent, attitudes have veered from viewing Moscow as the most serious threat to national security to viewing it as a key partner in enhancing national security, and vice versa. These dramatic changes in perception have been in part the product of a lack of any relevant experience in foreign policy. Not only were these new states, they had emerged out of a totalitarian regime where it was simply impossible to discuss in any serious manner what the optimal national security policies of future independent states should be. The only partial exception to this is Armenia, where such debates were conducted with intensity in the large diaspora; but their usefulness is open to question because, since independence, Armenia has been governed by a home-grown political party.

The development of national security policies can conveniently be divided into three phases which did not always chronologically coincide in the different Caucasian (Transcaucasian) states. In the first phase, attitudes to Russia were dominated by the struggle for independence. Not surprisingly, Moscow was seen at this time as the principal obstacle in the drive for independence and was widely accused, with some justice, of fomenting ethnic conflict. In these states more tangible threats to their national security than facing republics in any other region of the Soviet Union, in the form of ethnic secessionist movements – or, in the case of Armenia, the need to protect the Armenian minority in Azerbaijan – the rise of mass nationalist movements was accompanied by the formation of unofficial armed militias.

In the second phase, the nationalist movements stood at the head of formally independent states but, ironically, now faced a Russia which had identified the South Caucasus region as a region where its vital 'national interests' were at stake. The nationalist movements in power identified the militias with which they had earlier been closely identified as an obstacle to the consolidation of their power. In the third phase, it became clear that the three republics were moving in different directions. National security policies in Georgia and

Armenia were similar in that they were based on a strategic relationship with Russia, although in the case of Armenia there was a much more sincere acceptance than in Georgia that it did have real common security interests with Russia. Moreover while in Armenia the new domestic regime, with the militias successfully subordinated, had been consolidated at a very early stage, in Georgia regime consolidation proved to be a much more drawn-out process. Azerbaijan, meanwhile, had successfully resisted being drawn back into a tight security relationship with Russia and was continuing to keep a range of options open in formulating its external relationships.

The first phase

Of the three Caucasus states, Georgia adopted the most radical stance in asserting its independence from Moscow. Although the nationalist movement came to power relatively late, in multi-party elections in October 1990 the clear winner was the radical Round Table–Free Georgia bloc headed by Zviad Gamsakhurdia, a former dissident nationalist. Georgia was the first Caucasus state to declare full independence, on 9 April 1991. This act was in contravention of the Soviet law on secession and was not recognized by any foreign government, but was prompted partly by the signs that Mikhail Gorbachev, the Soviet president, was successfully rallying support for a new union treaty, with the signing of the 'nine plus one' agreement, and partly by a desire to prevent Moscow intervening on the side of separatists in the autonomous region of South Ossetia.

The Georgian government sought to back up its drive for independence by forcing the withdrawal of all Soviet forces from the country. The Georgian parliament had declared Georgia an 'occupied country' as early as February 1990, and nationalist rhetoric which depicted the Soviet military as 'occupiers' led to mass evasion of the draft and increasing harassment of Soviet military personnel. In November 1991 the parliament began nationalizing Soviet military equipment in the country and demanded the withdrawal of Soviet troops.[1] As relations between Georgia and Moscow deteriorated rapidly, the Georgian government claimed that Moscow had imposed an economic blockade on the country. Gamsakhurdia showed himself to be unskilful in exploiting the rivalry in Moscow between Gorbachev, who headed the Soviet government, and Boris Yeltsin, who headed the Russian Federation government. In the spring of 1991 he was able to extract a degree of support from Yeltsin over South Ossetia, but in the autumn he angered the Russian government with his statements of support for the separatist movement in Chechenia in the Russian Federation.[2]

Armed militias began appearing in Georgia in 1989. Although they usually claimed a patriotic mission to protect Georgian independence and defend the rights of Georgians living in non-Georgian areas, they were chiefly preoccupied with the internecine squabbles of the fractious nationalist movement.[3] The most powerful of the militias was the Mkhedrioni (Knights) led by Jaba Ioseliani. The Mkhedrioni first appeared in 1989, and in September 1990, on the eve of the elections which brought the nationalist movement to power, was registered by the government as a civil defence organization. Though reliable figures do not exist, membership soon ran to several thousands. It also began to acquire heavy equipment, such as rocket-propelled grenades and armoured personnel carriers. The evidently substantial funds at its disposal suggest that links between the Mkhedrioni and the shadow economy were present from an early stage, and talk of its participation in protection rackets, control of commodities (such as petrol) and involvement in arms and drug trafficking soon became common. Ioseliani was an uncompromising opponent of Gamsakhurdia;[4] in early 1991 he was arrested and the Mkhedrioni temporarily suppressed.

In January 1991 the Georgian government decided to set up its own military force, the National Guard, to act as a deterrent to possible Soviet military intervention and to combat secessionist movements and the opposition militias. According to the relevant law, service in the National Guard was to be obligatory for all Georgian men of draft age, giving it a total potential strength of 12,000.[5] Formally, the National Guard was subordinate to the Georgian ministry of internal affairs, but in practice it turned out that the first loyalty of most of the guardsmen was to Tengiz Kitovani, who had been appointed leader of the National Guard by Gamsakhurdia rather than a professional Soviet military officer because he was regarded as more politically reliable. Tension between Gamsakhurdia and Kitovani grew quickly. In August 1991, during the attempted coup in Moscow, Gamsakhurdia, under pressure from the Soviet military, ordered the disbanding of the National Guard and its tighter subordination to the ministry of internal affairs, but Kitovani refused to obey orders and joined Gamsakhurdia's political opponents. In December 1991 the National Guard headed the armed groups which overthrew Gamsakhurdia.

Azerbaijan was the slowest of the Caucasus states to move towards independence because of the crushing of the Azerbaijani Popular Front (APF) by Soviet troops in January 1990. Ayaz Mutalibov, the new Azerbaijani leader, sought with some success to swing Moscow's support behind Azerbaijan in its struggle with Armenian separatists in the autonomous region of Nagorno-Karabakh, by demonstrating his support for a renewed Soviet Union just as Armenia was asserting its independence. Particularly in the spring of 1991, Soviet forces supported operations by troops from the Azerbaijani ministry of internal affairs to remove the Armenian population from villages in the Shaumian district.[6]

Mutalibov's strategy was blown completely off course by the August 1991 coup in Moscow, which he openly supported. The failure of the coup meant that he lost his backers among 'conservative' elements in the Soviet leadership and he now had to set off unwillingly down the path of independence, making a formal declaration in October 1991. Azerbaijan now faced the Armenian separatists in Nagorno-Karabakh without the clear support of the Soviet military and without having begun to establish its own armed forces. The power of militias, mainly loyal to the APF, expanded greatly in this vacuum. The inability of Azerbaijan to resist the Armenian guerrillas further undermined Mutalibov's position, and after a massacre of Azerbaijani civilians in the village of Khojaly he was forced to resign as president at the beginning of March 1992. The militias played a key role in foiling an attempt by Mutalibov to return to power in May, paving the way for Abulfaz Elchibei, leader of the APF, to win presidential elections in June.

During the first phase Armenia pursued a median path in its relations with Moscow. The Armenian National Movement (ANM) came to power following parliamentary elections in June 1990 and immediately announced its intention to take Armenia out of the Soviet Union but to follow the procedures laid down by Soviet law. Thus it was the last of the Caucasus states to declare independence, doing so after a referendum, in November 1991.

Nonetheless, in the meantime its stance was clearly more anti-Soviet than that of Azerbaijan under Mutalibov and, as a result, it experienced intense pressure from Moscow. This was manifested not only in the form of Soviet military support for Azerbaijan in the Nagorno-Karabakh conflict, as described above, but also in the form of an ultimatum delivered to the new ANM government in July 1990 demanding the disbanding of militias within fifteen days on pain of Russian military intervention.[7] The struggle of the Armenians of Nagorno-Karabakh for self-determination had produced a proliferation of militias. The most powerful of them was the Armenian National Army, which was formally closely associated with the ANM. Levon Ter-Petrosian, the leader of the ANM, handled the crisis with consummate skill by persuading the militia, which numbered about 10,000 men, to hand over quantities of weapons, but at the same time beginning to bring them under government control.[8] By no means all the militias were subdued at this time, and they continued to cause tension in Armenia's relations with Moscow; in May 1991 one Soviet general threatened to 'wipe Armenia off the face of the earth' after Armenian guerrillas kidnapped a group of Soviet army officers,[9] but the suppression of the Armenian National Army helped ensure an enviable civil peace in Armenia during the transition to independence and even during the Nagorno-Karabakh conflict.

The second phase

In the second phase the three Caucasus states were faced with the rapid and seemingly irreversible collapse of Russian authority in the region. In this situation they began an intensive search for new strategic partners to bolster their independence and strengthen their hand in ethnic conflicts. By the end of this phase, however, a new Russian interest in the region was apparent, particularly signalled by the decision to replace the moribund Soviet Transcaucasus military district with a new permanent Russian military presence, the Russian group of forces in the South Caucasus region, in January 1993. While Georgia and Azerbaijan attempted to resist Russian expansionism, Armenia welcomed the return of Russia as a counterbalance to Turkey.

In this second phase, the nationalist movements were also preoccupied with consolidating their hold on power. A crucial element in this process was the formation of unified national armies. The decision to establish national armies raised important questions about relations with Russia, which was the only real source of relevant expertise and still controlled the main sources of hardware, but, even more importantly, it brought relations with the militias to a crisis. These militias, which during the first phase in the development of national security policies had been seen as the first line of defence in ethnic conflict, were now seen as a threat to the consolidation of the new nationalist governments.

In Georgia, the military council which assumed power in January 1992 moved quickly to improve relations with Russia, and especially the Russian military, by immediately withdrawing the law labelling Soviet forces as 'occupiers'. There is evidence of a quid pro quo; the deputy commander of the Transcaucasus military district, Lieutenant-General Sufian Beppaev, directed Soviet forces to give support to the National Guard during the coup which overthrew Gamsakhurdia.[10] By the end of May, Pavel Grachev, the Russian minister of defence, reported to the Russian parliament that the situation for Russian soldiers based in Georgia had improved considerably and that he had recommended that some military equipment should be handed over.[11] Georgia's relationship with Russia was further improved by the signing of the Dagomys agreement in June which led to Russian peacekeeping forces being deployed in South Ossetia. The Dagomys agreement meant that Georgia lost effective sovereignty over South Ossetia but ensured that it continued to receive the share of equipment from the Soviet army which was agreed at the CIS summit in Tashkent in July 1992.

In the autumn of 1992, however, relations between Georgia and Russia deteriorated rapidly. The reason for this was Georgia's determination to resist subordination to Russian ambitions in a region where Moscow had decided that its national interests were at stake. The outbreak of war in Abkhazia in August was only an exacerbating factor in this more fundamental conflict. At the beginning of October Georgia suffered its first severe defeat in Abkhazia, with the loss of Gagra and the withdrawal of its forces to the Gumista river just north of Sukhumi. Georgian claims that the assault on Gagra had been spearheaded by Russian tanks appear to have some justification.[12] Georgian indignation at Russian intervention led to the Georgian parliament passing a law nationalizing all Soviet military equipment on its territory, and by the spring of 1993 Eduard Shevardnadze, the new Georgian leader, was describing the Abkhazian war as a conflict between Russia and Georgia.[13]

Despite a statement by Grachev in May 1993 that Russia would withdraw all its forces from Georgian territory by the end of 1995, Russian intentions towards Georgia had been more clearly laid out during his visit to Russian military commanders in the sensitive autonomous regions of Abkhazia and Ajaria in February, when he emphasized that Russia had vital strategic interests in the country.[14] When the Abkhazians renewed their final, successful offensive in September, Grachev refused to do anything to prevent local Russian commanders lending their support and urged Georgian forces to withdraw from Sukhumi.[15] By the end of September Georgia had to cede control of Abkhazia, and its prostration appeared complete when an insurgency in western Georgia, launched by supporters of Gamsakhurdia, swept all before it in October. In order to avoid the complete collapse of the Georgian state, barely a week after accusing the Russian military of masterminding the capture of Sukhumi Shevardnadze took Georgia into the CIS and agreed to the deployment of Russian marines in western Georgia.[16]

Numerous attempts to bring the Georgian militias to heel were made after the autumn of 1991, culminating in the arrest of Ioseliani in November 1995. The first moves in this direction were begun under Gamsakhurdia when a ministry of defence was established in September 1991 and formally given control of the National Guard.[17] After the coup the new government attempted to enforce control of the militias by appointing Lieutenant-General Levan Shareshanidze, a professional Soviet army officer, to the post of minister of defence. The prominent role played by the militias in the coup, followed by the swift outbreak of war in Abkhazia, meant that, in practice, it was the militias which ended up taking control of the military. In May, Kitovani removed Shareshanidze in peremptory fashion and had himself appointed minister of defence; and in October Shevardnadze set up a powerful national security and defence council, with Kitovani and Ioseliani as joint deputy chairmen, to organize the military effort in Abkhazia. In May 1993 Shevardnadze made a new attempt to rein in the militias, replacing Kitovani as minister of defence and abolishing the national security and defence council. This work was once again undone during the military emergency in Abkhazia and western Georgia in the autumn, when the militias were able to make a comeback. The failure of the Georgian government to impose a monopoly of the legitimate means of coercion on its territory had a debilitating effect on its national security, leaving it weak in the face of secessionist movements and providing a lever by which hostile external forces could attempt to exert pressure.

In Azerbaijan the APF had the misfortune to come to power just as Russia was attempting to re-establish its position in the region. In summer 1992 Moscow had still not formulated its policy towards the South Caucasus region and evidently did not oppose the widespread hiring of Russian mercenaries by Azerbaijan or the seizure of large quantities of weaponry from Soviet bases, ostensibly in accordance with the Tashkent agreement,[18] both of which paved the way for a string of Azerbaijani military victories in Nagorno-Karabakh. Even more dramatically, worn down by the constant harassment of the Soviet 7th Army based in Azerbaijan by Azerbaijani fighters, the Russian ministry of defence agreed that all CIS joint armed forces would be withdrawn from the republic by the end of 1993.[19] The APF government pinned great hopes on Turkish assistance in bolstering its military effort. Turkey did sanction the secondment of 'retired army officers' to Azerbaijan and turned a blind eye to shipments of weaponry, but was unwilling to force a confrontation with Russia over the issue, particularly after the death of President Turgut Ozal in April 1993.

The impact on Azerbaijan of the Russian resurgence in the South Caucasus region became apparent in early 1993. There were widespread claims by the Azerbaijanis that Russian forces based in Armenia supported the Armenian offensive which led to the capture of the Kelbajar district in March. Russia increasingly sought to reinforce its position in Azerbaijan by demanding that its troops be deployed in the country to carry out peacekeeping functions. The last Russian military contingent in Azerbaijan, the 104th Parachute Regiment based in Ganje, the republic's second city, issued an ultimatum to Elchibei in January demanding that it be allowed to remain in the republic as a 'peace-keeping force'.[20] In February Yeltsin made his notorious demand for Russia to be granted an exclusive peacekeeping mandate in the CIS. The Azerbaijani government refused to yield to Russian pressure and insisted that the Russian forces in Ganje leave as agreed. As they did so, the Russian military commander handed over quantities of weapons to Suret Husseinov, a prominent militia leader, who was engaged in a serious confrontation with the government.

When it was in opposition the APF consistently criticized Mutalibov and Iagub Mamedov, his interim successor, for their failure to create a national army. The decision to set up an Azerbaijani national army was made in October 1991, and in March 1992 Rakhim Gaziev, who was associated with the APF, was appointed minister of defence.[21] In fact these were cosmetic measures designed to impress public opinion, with both Mutalibov and Mamedov concerned that an army could become a source of political opposition and hopeful that political pressure on Russia would be more effective in turning the scales in Nagorno-Karabakh.[22] When the APF came to power in June the army was in disarray, with the ministry of defence estimating that it would take until the year 2000 to bring it up to strength.[23] Over the summer Elchibei ordered that measures be taken to enforce conscription, but, in October, he was still lamenting that there was no coordination between the military and civil authorities in the regions to round up draft dodgers.[24]

In reality, by the end of 1992 the Azerbaijani army was still composed of various militias loyal to their local commanders rather than the unified military command (which, situated in Baku, was out of touch anyway). In November 1992 Elchibei appointed 'Colonel' Suret Husseinov his personal envoy in Nagorno-Karabakh. Husseinov did not have a professional military background but had gained a reputation by equipping a military formation at his own expense; he had amassed a large fortune from his wool-processing factory in Ganje as well as other business dealings. After a bungled operation in the winter which paved the way for the Armenian capture of the Kelbajar district, Elchibei tried to recall Husseinov; he refused and took refuge in his home town. At the beginning of June Elchibei launched a pre-emptive strike against Husseinov's stronghold in Ganje, but the government troops were beaten back with heavy loss of life.[25] Husseinov decided to capitalize on his victory and began to march on Baku: on 18 June, Elchibei fled the capital. In theory Azerbaijan had substantially more human and material resources than Armenia to devote to the struggle over Nagorno-Karabakh, but its inability to obtain Russian assistance or even to ensure political control over the military made its defeat inevitable.

Armenia was the first Caucasus state to move back into a close relationship with Moscow. In contrast to Georgia and Azerbaijan (which joined the CIS in November 1993), there was a considerable area of common interest on which good relations between Armenia and Russia could be established. Armenia was, from its inception, an enthusiastic member of the CIS and alone of the three Caucasus states signed up to the CIS pact on collective security at the Tashkent summit in May 1992. Furthermore, harassment of Russian forces stationed in Armenia did not reach the proportions experienced in Georgia and Azerbaijan. The turning point in the relationship came in May 1992 when Turkey began to threaten Armenia after fighting broke out in the Azerbaijani enclave of Nakhichevan. In the same month a Russian government delegation, including Grachev, flew to Yerevan for talks. Afterwards an Armenian foreign ministry spokesman said that the Russians had given assurances that they were not about to withdraw their forces from the country.[26] This visit marked the beginning of a close strategic relationship between Armenia and Russia, with Russian bases in the country providing a convenient source of military expertise and acting as a conduit for supplies of equipment for the embryonic Armenian army.

Despite Russian reassurances Armenia stepped up its efforts to establish a unified national army in the autumn of 1992.[27] The Armenian government had originally set up a ministry of defence in November 1991, but progress was slow.[28] This was partly for political reasons; in December 1991 Ter-Petrosian said that Armenia should create a national guard, not an army, and expressed the hope that CIS military bases would remain on Armenian territory.[29] The appointment of Vazgen Manukian as minister of defence at the end of September 1992 marked the beginning of a period of intensive activity to strengthen the army. At the end of November Ter-Petrosian issued a series of decrees on the formation of the army, including measures to enforce the draft.[30] Backed up by the country's alliance with Russia, Armenian efforts to set up the army appear to have been remarkably successful. In December 1993 Sergei Sarkisian, the new minister of defence, boasted that the draft was over 100 per cent fulfilled and, with 60,000 men under arms, Armenia had the strongest army in the region.[31]

The suppression of the Armenian National Army in the summer of 1990 did not end Armenia's militia problem. Much of the work in organizing the 'self-defence' detachments in Nagorno-Karabakh had been undertaken by diaspora Armenians associated with political parties, particularly the Armenian Revolutionary Federation (Dashnaktsiutiun), which controlled the government of the self-proclaimed Nagorno-Karabakh Republic (NKR). In the summer of 1992 Ter-Petrosian took measures to bring the NKR government under closer control from Yerevan and succeeded in having his supporters appointed to key positions in the NKR government. In September 1993 he replaced Manukian with Sergei Sarkisian as minister of defence. Previously, Sarkisian had been minister of defence of the NKR and his appointment ensured that the NKR military would adopt an approach more in line with Yerevan's wishes.[32] It seems that the various militias in Nagorno-Karabakh did not put up any real resistance to their incorporation into formal military structures, although deals must have been made with individual commanders, and, in stark contrast to the situation in Georgia and Azerbaijan, they have not subsequently played an independent role in Armenian political life.[33]

The third phase

In the third phase the national security policies of the three Caucasus states began to follow different patterns. The return of Shevardnadze to Georgia had raised hopes that Western states would take a greater interest in the country. By the spring of 1994 it was obvious that these hopes had been groundless, perhaps even counterproductive in terms of stoking up Russian suspicions. The failure of any foreign country to offer peacekeeping forces to monitor the ceasefire in Abkhazia, and the introduction there of a purely Russian contingent in May 1994,[34] was the final nail in the coffin of Georgia's attempts to use Western countries as a counterbalance to Russia. Georgia thus had no choice but to enter into a close partnership with Russia which imposed real limitations on its sovereignty.

In February 1994 Yeltsin travelled to Tbilisi to sign a wide-ranging treaty on friendship, good-neighbourliness and cooperation, and detailed negotiations on a military treaty were set in train.[35] This led to the signing of an agreement in March 1995 which allowed for the establishment of four Russian military bases on Georgian territory: one just outside Tbilisi, the others at Akhalkalaki on the Turkish border, and Batumi and Gudauta in Abkhazia.[36] Georgia still had to persuade Russia that it would be a reliable partner and, drawing parallels with the situation in Abkhazia, gave strong support to Yeltsin during the Russian military intervention in Chechenia. In return, Georgia received Russian help with the establishment of a new unified army; in April 1994 Lieutenant-General Vardiko Nadibaidze, formerly serving with the Russian army in Georgia, was appointed minister of defence.[37] Russia also began to put pressure on Abkhazia to accept the return of Georgian refugees and to agree to a federation with Georgia.[38]

From the end of 1993 a new series of moves was initiated to bring the militias under control. In October 1993 Igor Giorgadze, a former KGB officer, was appointed head of a new, reinforced ministry of state security to carry out this task.[39] The power of the National Guard had waned rapidly after Kitovani was sacked as minister of defence in the spring, but the Mkhedrioni was able to force the government to give it legal status as the Rescuers Corps, ostensibly a sort of civil defence organization, which allowed it to retain its weapons, in August 1994.[40] However, at the beginning of May 1995 Shevardnadze revoked his decree allowing the corps to keep its weapons. It was clear that far from all of the Mkhedrioni's weapons were handed over to the government and relations with Shevardnadze remained tense. At the end of August the government implicated Ioseliani in an assassination attempt on Shevardnadze, but his status as a candidate in the parliamentary elections postponed his arrest for several months.[41]

Alone of the three Caucasus states, Azerbaijan managed to remain outside the new *pax russica*. It was widely expected that the return of Aliyev to power in Baku would signal a new pro-Russian orientation in Azerbaijani foreign policy, a view that was backed up by Aliyev's decision to take Azerbaijan into the CIS. However, he resisted pressure from Moscow to allow Russian forces back on to Azerbaijani territory either in the form of peacekeeping troops in Nagorno-Karabakh or in the form of guards on the Iranian border. Instead, he skilfully played off Iran and Turkey against Russia and sought to engage Western interests in Azerbaijan by signing the 'deal of the century' in September 1994 which gave the contract for exploiting Azerbaijan's offshore oil reserves to a consortium of Western companies.[42] Subsequently, Azerbaijan resisted Russian pressure for the route of the pipeline which would carry the oil from Azerbaijan to pass across its territory. With Turkish and American support the oil companies agreed in October 1995 that there should be two pipelines: one through Russia and one through Georgia.

In the summer and autumn of 1993 Aliyev carried out a thorough purge of the army and in the winter of 1993–4 a new purpose was evident in the Azerbaijani offensive in Nagorno-Karabakh. Even so, Azerbaijani forces had to be bolstered by contingents of Afghan mercenaries and they failed to make a breakthrough. Strains in Aliyev's relationship with the military have continued to make themselves felt. In February 1995 he replaced Mamedrafi Mamedov, whom he had appointed minister of defence in September 1993, with Lieutenant-General Safar Abiev.[43] In the summer of 1995 an arrest warrant was issued for Vahid Musaev, another former minister of defence. Aliyev also moved to eliminate Suret Husseinov, the militia leader who had effectively brought him to power, in September 1993.[44] In March 1995 he disposed of another potential threat, Rovshan Javadov, the deputy minister of internal affairs, who headed a paramilitary police force and was alleged to have prepared a coup.[45]

By the summer of 1995 the ANM could boast that Armenia was more secure than could have reasonably been hoped for five years previously. It had cemented a close relationship with Russia: on 16 March 1995 Presidents Ter-Petrosian and Yeltsin signed a treaty which would allow Russia to maintain a military base near Gyumri, close to the border with Turkey, for the next 25 years – an agreement based on a degree of real mutual trust and common interest.[46] Unlike its regional neighbours, Armenia's military was both effective and firmly under political control.

Conclusion

The environment in which the leaderships of the three Caucasus states had to operate from the late 1980s was both dangerous and unpredictable. Success in enhancing national security was often a matter more of luck than of judgment. But for the farce of the August 1991 Moscow coup, Mutalibov's strategy of eschewing independence in favour of obtaining Moscow's support in Nagorno-Karabakh might now seem like the policy of a far-sighted statesman. Similarly, Elchibei was not the only politician to believe that Russia's withdrawal from the South Caucasus region was not permanent. Nonetheless, what does stand out from this analysis of the development of national security policies in the South Caucasus region is the high price that has been paid by Azerbaijan and especially Georgia for the loss of political control over the militias which arose in the first phase of their transition to independence. By the time the three Caucasus states marked five years of independence, however, the international environment in which they were operating had become more predictable. The issue of pipeline routes could still provoke a new round of instability, but it appears that Russia had achieved its main strategic aims in the region by securing a decisive measure of influence in Georgia and Armenia. Furthermore, violence had subsided in both Abkhazia and Nagorno-Karabakh. By August 1997 a political settlement of the Abkhazian conflict finally appeared possible, although a solution to the Nagorno-Karabakh conflict still seemed remote. The nature of the security threat faced by the Caucasus states at the end of the 1990s is likely to be determined primarily by economic questions, such as pipeline routes and energy supplies, and social issues, such as organized crime and emigration.

Notes

1. BBC *Summary of World Broadcasts*, 16 November, 6 December 1991, citing Georgian media.
2. Ronald Grigor Suny, *The Making of the Georgian Nation*, 2nd edn (Bloomington: Indiana University Press, 1994), p. 327.
3. Jonathan Aves, *Paths to National Independence in Georgia* (London: School of Slavonic and East European Studies, 1991), pp. 42–3.
4. A faction of the Mkhedrioni loyal to Gamsakhurdia, the Society of White Georgia, broke away in 1990. See *Moscow News*, 1991, no. 9.
5. *Independent*, 30, 31 January 1991.
6. Radio Free Europe/Radio Liberty, *Report on the USSR*, 24 May 1991.
7. *Independent*, 10 August 1990.
8. *Independent*, 9, 13, 31 August 1990.
9. *The Times*, 3 May 1991.
10. *Moscow News*, no. 57, 20–27 December 1992. Beppaev retired from the army in the autumn to take over the leadership of the National Council of Balkar People. In 1992 he had been in charge of allocating weaponry to the armies of Georgia, Azerbaijan and Armenia and his presence was missed by the Georgian government. *Russia Briefing*, vol. 3, no. 3, 25 March 1995.
11. BBC *SWB*, 1 June 1992, citing Russian television..
12. *Guardian*, 5 October 1992, *Moskovskie novosti*, no. 42, 18–25 June 1995.
13. *Guardian*, 6 October 1992; *Independent*, 17 March 1993.
14. BBC *SWB*, 4 March 1993, citing Interfax, Russian television and *Krasnaya zvezda*; *Reuters*, 18 May 1993.
15. *Guardian*, 21 September 1993.
16. *Guardian*, 29 September 1993; *Associated Press*, 8 October 1993.
17. BBC *SWB*, 11 September 1991, citing Georgian radio.
18. Foreign Broadcast Information Service, 2 September 1992, citing *Nezavisimaya gazeta*.
19. BBC *SWB*, 5 May 1992, citing Russian radio.
20. *Nezavisimaya gazeta*, 26 February 1993.
21. *International Herald Tribune*, 12 October 1991; BBC *SWB*, 19 March 1993, citing Azerbaijani radio.
22. In March 1993 Mamedov told a Russian journalist that Azerbaijan would continue to rely on self-

defence units in Nagorno-Karabakh and not call a general mobilization: BBC, *SWB*, 28 March 1993, citing *Izvestiya*.

23. FBIS, 17 June 1992, citing *Krasnaya zvezda*.
24. FBIS, 7 October 1992, citing *Bakinskiy rabochiy*.
25. *Guardian*, 8 June 1993.
26. *Guardian*, 25 May 1992.
27. Ter-Petrosian said in a speech in October that Armenia's failure to secure support under the Tashkent mutual security pact had made the creation of a national army essential: BBC, *SWB*, 31 October 1992, citing Armenian radio.
28. BBC *SWB*, 25 November 1991, citing *Izvestiya*.
29. BBC *SWB*, 30 December 1991, citing TASS.
30. FBIS, 23 December 1992, citing *Krasnaya zvezda*.
31. *Armenian International Magazine*, August–September 1994.
32. Ibid., February 1994.
33. One of the reasons given by Ter-Petrosian for banning the Armenian Revolutionary Federation at the end of December 1994 was that it was running an underground terrorist organization called Dro; but the evidence for the existence of such an organization has yet to be produced and on the information which is available it does not appear to be related to the militias which took part in the Nagorno-Karabakh conflict. See *Armenian International Magazine*, November–December 1994.
34. *Georgian Chronicle*, May 1994.
35. Ibid., March 1994.
36. Ibid., March 1995.
37. Ibid., April 1995.
38. *Reuters*, 23 August 1995.
39. *Georgian Chronicle*, October 1993.
40. Ibid., August 1994.
41. *Guardian*, 1 September 1995.
42. *Transition*, 15 February 1995.
43. *Jane's Sentinel: CIS Newsletter*, vol. 1. no. 9, 1994.
44. Laura le Cornu, *Azerbaijan's September Crisis: An Analysis of the Causes and Implications* (London: RIIA, 1995).
45. *Guardian*, 18 March 1995.
46. *COVCAS Bulletin*, 29 March 1995.

10 Central Asia: national, regional and global aspects of security

Oumirserik Kasenov

The contemporary international significance of the new Central Asian states of Kazakstan, Kyrgyzstan, Tajikistan, Turkmenistan and Uzbekistan reflects their economic and demographic potential, their geographical location and the character of their relations with other states, primarily neighbouring ones, as well as their role in regional and global international organizations. Over 55 million people live in the region of former Soviet Central Asia, which is quite rich in natural resources and in terms of its economic, scientific and technological potential.

The strategic significance of the region derives from the fact that it borders two of the five nuclear states of the world, Russia and China, and through Iran and Afghanistan has access to the Persian Gulf and Indian Ocean. With the completion of trans-Asian railway projects and the development of road and air communications, the geostrategic trade and economic significance of Central Asia will rise further, for it will start to serve as a route for considerable cargo flows from Asia and the Pacific region to Europe and western Asia, as well as from west to east.

Potential military threats

The official documents on military policy of the CIS Central Asian states do not specify probable enemies, although CIS documents signed by these states suggest in broad terms the sources of potential military danger.

In October 1993 in Bishkek, Kazakstan, Kyrgyzstan, Uzbekistan and Tajikistan signed an agreement on the concept of military security of the CIS member states. This document considers as a major source of potential military threat for member states of the CIS the instability of the social, economic, military and political situation in a number of regions, the existence of strong military potential in certain states which exceeds their defence needs, and the proliferation of nuclear and other weapons of mass destruction.[1]

On February 1995, at a CIS summit, a declaration of member states of the collective security agreement and a concept of collective security were adopted.

This concept, which of course was not meant to apply only to the Central Asian region (and Turkmenistan has not signed the original collective security agreement), defines major sources of military danger, and factors which might contribute to military dangers evolving into a direct military threat, as follows:

- the build-up of military capabilities in regions neighbouring member states to levels which disturb the existing balance of forces;
- the formation and training on the territory of other states of armed forces intended for use against member states;
- the exacerbation of border conflicts and undertaking of armed provocations from the territory of bordering states;
- the transfer of foreign troops on to territories neighbouring the member states (unless connected with peacekeeping measures in accordance with the resolutions of the UN Security Council or OSCE).[2]

A significant handicap for the CIS Central Asian states is the fact that their armed forces are still at an early stage of formation. They are fragments of the collapsed armed forces of the former Soviet Union and therefore do not yet have a single internal system which includes command and control, communications, a comprehensive supply system, mobilization readiness, the training of personnel and defence production. Nevertheless in the period of independence to date the Central Asian states have determined the general structure of their armed forces. Command and control bodies, military doctrines and military policies as a whole are being worked out.

Does a military threat to Central Asian states arise from regional states beyond the CIS region such as China, Afghanistan, and Iran? Among the latter only China has a powerful military potential which includes nuclear weapons. The Lanzhou military district bordering Central Asia is the fourth largest Chinese military district; twelve Chinese land divisions are deployed there and the Lop-Nor nuclear test site is also situated in the district.

Referring to a seminar organized by the Rand Corporation in Almaty in October 1992, S. Kurginian maintained in *Nezavisimaya gazeta* that the 'Lanzhou military district, if aimed directly at Kazakstan, can deploy about 400,000 soldiers, 500 tanks, 5,000 artillery pieces and mortars, and 480 aircraft in the event of a conflict'. He argued that the 40th Afghan Army, which was left as a legacy to Kazakstan by the Soviet forces deployed in the republic, would not be sufficient even to guard the border more or less effectively.[3] This analyst noted not only the increasing military force of China, but also unsettled border issues and a form of ethnic expansion by the infiltration of Chinese into other countries with the intention of establishing permanent residence.[4]

Another part of the claim about the Chinese threat is that Beijing can accuse the Central Asian states of allowing their territories to be used by some Uighur organizations for subversive activities against China.[5] In both the Russian and the Western press a number of publications have reported that the appearance of newly independent states in Central Asia has stimulated the struggle of Turkic Muslim peoples in China, mainly Uighurs, for their national independence. However, in Central Asia there are no signs of any pan-Turkic or pan-Islamic solidarity. The Central Asian states maintain the principle of non-interference in the internal affairs of other states and do not permit any organizations to undertake activities which would damage their relations with other states, including China. The registration of such organizations is not permitted and their activities are prohibited.

An agreement on strengthening confidence-building measures in the military arena, signed at the end of April 1996 in Shanghai by the leaders of Russia, China, Kazakstan, Kyrgyzstan and Tajikistan, was of particular significance in enhancing stability and developing neighbourliness among these states. The agreement stipulates the withdrawal of armed forces and armaments, except border forces, from a zone 100 km from the border between the CIS states and China, the cessation of military exercises directed against the other side and limitations on the size and number of forces participating in military exercises, as well as a requirement for the states to inform each other about such exercises. It also establishes friendly relations between the border troops and provides for the mutual invitation of observers to military exercises.

Iran, which ranks as one of the world's top oil-producing states after Saudi Arabia and raises about $20 billion a year from oil sales, has considerable armed forces and is conducting a large-scale programme of rearmament. Western states accuse Iran of creating an infrastructure for the production of nuclear weapons, with assistance mainly from China. However, it can be affirmed with full confidence that Iran is not and will not become a source of military threat to the Central Asian states. Iran is increasing its military potential in order to become a major regional power centre in the Persian Gulf. This is a long-term goal of its external policy. Even though Iran has interests in the northern and northeastern perimeter of its borders with the Caucasus states, central Asia and Afghanistan the lessons of the Iran-Iraq War suggest that Iran will not use force, let alone armed aggression, against any of its neighbours, at least in the foreseeable future.

The real threat to the security of the newly independent states of Central Asia is the situation on the Tajik–Afghan border, which poses the danger to Central Asia at large of 'Afghanization': the possibility of the new Central Asian states cracking at their ethnic seams, as is occurring in Afghanistan. This could come about if the Tajik–Afghan border were to disappear. Iran, Pakistan, Russia and Uzbekistan, the states bordering on Afghanistan and involved in Afghan affairs, have all declared their interest in the integrity of Afghanistan, since its fragmentation could become a serious source of destabilization in the region.

The fracturing of the CIS Central Asian states along ethnic lines is a potential danger for Russia itself since, as noted by many Russian analysts, this region forms the 'soft underbelly' of Russia. In response, Russia would have to build new state borders in an attempt to contain what is viewed as 'Islamic fundamentalism'. Yet neither Russia nor the Central Asian states are able to equip new intra-CIS state borders. According to Russian estimates, the equipment for one kilometre of border would cost no less than 1 billion roubles. The decision whether to continue to guard the 1,300 km Tajik–Afghan border, or to leave Tajikistan and to start the construction of a new 6,200 km Russian–Kazak border, is an acute question for Russia. It is influenced by the fears noted above and by the fact that the Central Asian states themselves cannot afford the construction and equipping of new state borders. Therefore, it is in the interests of both Russia and the Central Asian states to leave 'transparent' borders between themselves, but to strengthen the protection of the outer borders of the CIS, especially the Tajik–Afghan section.

It is in Russia's strategic interests to strengthen the state sovereignty and territorial integrity of the Central Asian states, to promote the development of their economic and defence potential, and to engage in military and political cooperation in order to protect the common borders of the CIS by means of joint forces. A coincidence of strategic interests underlies the treaties of friendship, cooperation and mutual assistance signed by Russia and the Central Asian states. These treaties presuppose mutual defence obligations in the event of aggression against any one of the parties. Similar interests underpin more specific treaties on military cooperation.

Kazakstan

The core elements of the defence policy of the Republic of Kazakstan may be summarized as follows. First, the formation of Kazak armed forces capable of defending the sovereignty and territorial integrity of the country is under way. Secondly, in May 1992 Kazakstan and Russia concluded an agreement on friendship, cooperation and mutual assistance, by which they are obliged to render each other military assistance in case of aggression against one of them. A supplementary agreement on military cooperation was signed in December 1994 together with a package of documents on military issues in January 1995.[6] Russia is leasing the Baikonur space facility from Kazakstan. There remain forces and military sites on the territory of Kazakstan under Russian jurisdiction. Thirdly, also in May 1992, Kazakstan signed the CIS collective security agreement and is making every effort to create a joint defence space aimed at the coordination of defence activities with its CIS partners.

One of the important factors reinforcing the security of Kazakstan after its Supreme Council ratified the nuclear Non-Proliferation Treaty (NPT) as a non-nuclear state in December 1993 was the acceptance of formal affirmations of security from Russia, the United States and the United Kingdom. In December 1994, in Budapest, during the OSCE summit, presidents Yeltsin and Clinton and prime minister John Major signed the memorandum on security guarantees, confirming their commitment to respect the independence, sovereignty and existing borders of Kazakstan and to avoid the threat or the use of force against the territorial integrity or political independence of Kazakstan, as well as to avoid exerting economic pressure against it.

If Kazakstan becomes a victim of aggression or an object of threats to use nuclear weapons, then Russia, the United States and the United Kingdom will demand immediate action from the UN Security Council to render assistance to Kazakstan as a non-nuclear member state of the NPT.[7] The Chinese government has also offered Kazakstan guarantees of security. As expressed by the Xinhua agency on 8 February 1995, China fully understands the desire of Kazakstan to obtain security guarantees. To abstain unreservedly from the use of nuclear weapons or the threat of their use against non-nuclear states and non-nuclear zones is the consistent position of the Chinese government. This position of principle applies to Kazakstan.[8]

Kazakstan's armed forces

When the Soviet Union was dissolved in December 1991, the armed forces on the territory of Kazakstan consisted of 440,000 military personnel. About 95 per cent of the officers were from Russia, Ukraine and Belarus. President Nazarbayev expressed a clear preference for the preservation of unified CIS forces when Russian President Yeltsin created the armed forces of the Russian Federation in spring 1992. Consequently the process of separating armed forces under the jurisdiction of Russia, the CIS and Kazakstan was undertaken, although Nazarbayev still emphasized that Kazakstan would not be able to implement military reform in the absence of close partnership with the armed forces of Russia.[9] Second World War veteran Sagadat K. Nurmagambetov was appointed defence minister, to be replaced by Alibek Kasimov in 1995. A republican guard of 2,500 men to protect the president and the parliament was created. Initially, force planning by the Kazak ministry of defence was based on the criterion that troop numbers should be at least 0.5 per cent of the state's population (i.e. about 83,000). This proved to be unrealistic, given the shortage of funds and the inability to enforce conscription consistently. The other serious problem for the Kazak armed forces is the lack of experienced Kazak leadership personnel. About 6,000 Russian troops from the former Soviet 40th

Army remained in Kazakstan to provide military training, and according to bilateral agreements with Russia, 500 officers from Kazakstan are sent to Russian military schools each year. Nevertheless, Kazakstan still has to rely on ethnic Slavs for most of its officer corps. The departure of many non-indigenous officers has resulted in a shortage of cadres of more than 50 per cent. By early 1996 the ratio between ethnic Russian and Kazak officers in the Kazak armed forces was about 50:50.[10] In 1993 the International Institute for Strategic Studies' *Military Balance* estimated the strength of the army at 44,000 troops. In 1995 this estimate had declined to 25,000 (with an estimated figure of 40,000 for the armed forces in total). The air force (personnel estimated at 15,000) has 37 fighter and 71 ground attack aircraft at its disposal. The social conditions of the army are very poor; soldiers are said to suffer from infectious diseases and lack of food. Despite official rhetoric, the army exhibits all the signs of severe neglect. Much of the equipment inherited from the Soviet armed forces is deteriorating due to lack of maintenance. Landlocked Kazakstan has no navy but intends to form a maritime force of coast-guard vessels.[11]

Kazakstan accommodates on its territory a wide range of former Soviet missile testing grounds, bombing ranges and so forth, covering some 4 per cent of its land surface, which have been the subject of negotiations with Russia. The most important Soviet strategic assets on Kazak territory were the ICBM bases, with 104 SS-18s, the Semipalatinsk nuclear test site, the Baikonur space launch centre and the ABM radar site. The disposition of these assets raised major difficulties, since on the one hand Kazakstan could not integrate them into its own military forces, but on the other hand it had an interest in getting the most out of their presence on its soil. Furthermore, President Nazarbayev insisted that all military installations in Kazakstan were the property of Kazakstan. In the event, the strategic nuclear missiles were stood down as part of the START process and all the nuclear warheads were transferred to Russia as Kazakstan joined the NPT as a non-nuclear power.[12] The Semipalatinsk site was closed. After much political wrangling, the Baikonur space complex was made available to Russia on the basis of a twenty-year renewable lease.[13]

Kyrgyzstan

The Russian–Kyrgyz military relationship centres on border protection. An intergovernmental agreement concluded in October 1992 stipulated that Kyrgyzstan, to ensure its own security, the security of the Russian Federation and the collective security of the CIS member states, delegated the issue of protecting its state border with China to Russian border troops. A subsequent agreement in April 1994 established the terms of recruitment and military service of citizens of Kyrgyzstan in the Russian border troops deployed on the territory of Kyrgyzstan. Russia covers 80 per cent and Kyrgyzstan 20 per cent of the expenses of these troops. Russia has undertaken to help Kyrgyzstan to form its own border troops during a transitional period. However, the duration of this transitional period has not been specified.

Uzbekistan

The Uzbek president, Islam Karimov, has explained the framework of Uzbek security policy in the following terms: in the unstable world surrounding us we have friends, but there are those as well who would like to drag Uzbekistan into their sphere of influence. And those forces may use any available methods, including military ones. Therefore, we must have a mobile, well-trained and equipped army, capable of defending our borders, our independence and sovereignty.[14]

The key elements of the concept of national security, as declared by Karimov, are as follows:

- Uzbekistan occupies an extremely favourable geographical location, in the centre of the transport and autonomous energy and water systems of the region.
- Uzbekistan's population outnumbers those of its neighbours, and Uzbekistan surpasses them in its scientific and technical potential and other capacities.
- Uzbekistan possesses those resources which are the backbone of any economy, oil, oil products and gas; it has every chance to increase its economic potential.
- Uzbekistan occupies a deserved place in human civilization; it exerts a strong influence on various spiritual and political processes not only in the region, but all over the world.
- Taking these assets into account, Karimov believes, Uzbekistan could emerge as a centre of integration in Central Asia.

At the 48th session of the UN General Assembly, Karimov proposed the establishment in Tashkent of a permanent UN seminar on issues of security, well-being and cooperation in Central Asia. In this connection he claimed that 'the republic could serve as an outpost in Asia, a bridgehead of cooperation of the OSCE and the United Nations in the provision of regional security and cooperation, preventive diplomacy and conflict prevention'.

Uzbekistan is a fully-fledged member of the Non-Aligned Movement (NAM). It could be claimed that this membership, which stipulates non-participation in military blocs, contradicts Uzbekistan's commitments in the collective security agreement which it signed in Tashkent in May 1992. However, as the NAM does not intend to undertake any actions against any member of the CIS, and as the 1992 Tashkent agreement cannot serve as a basis for the formation of military blocs, participation in it does not contradict the objectives of the NAM, for which the criteria for membership are not, in any case, clear-cut.

Uzbekistan's armed forces

Uzbekistan faced the familiar problem of building up its armed forces out of the Soviet heritage. In 1992 70 per cent of the officer corps was still Russian speaking and only 6 per cent of officers were ethnic Uzbeks. At the same time about 7,000 Uzbek soldiers and non-commissioned officers were serving in the armed forces of the Russian Federation. But by 1996 the officer corps in the Uzbek armed forces was 80 per cent ethnic Uzbek.[15] The declared target for the Uzbek armed forces according to the Law on Defence is 25,000–30,000 men plus a national guard of about 1,000.[16] The most important difficulties are the shortages of funds and trained personnel. In March 1994 Presidents Yeltsin and Karimov signed a treaty on military cooperation according to which Uzbekistan would receive help with training, logistics and equipment, although this military relationship has deteriorated subsequently.[17] Uzbekistan continues to be part of the CIS peacekeeping force in Tajikistan and 500 Uzbeks participate in guard duty at the Tajik–Afghan border. The armed forces of Uzbekistan have 280 main battle tanks, 780 armoured vehicles, 265 fixed wing aircraft and 24 helicopters.[18]

Military integration in Central Asia

During the summit of the presidents of Kazakstan, Kyrgyzstan and Uzbekistan held in Bishkek on 29–30 April 1994, Kyrgyzstan joined the agreement on the creation of a single economic space previously signed by Kazakstan and Uzbekistan. It is noteworthy that the integration of these three Central Asian states is deepening not only in the economic field, but also with regard to defence issues. During a session of the Interstate Council of Kazakstan, Kyrgyzstan and Uzbekistan held in December 1995 in Jambyl, the three states approved a regulation on a joint council of defence ministers to guide the development of concrete proposals on military cooperation. The regulation specified that the council, as a working body of the interstate council, would consider all relevant issues of regional security, defence coordination and cooperation. In pursuit of such cooperation it is given the tasks of coordinating military exercises, air defence and mutual supplies, as well maintaining arms and equipment, military research and other activities.[19]

To ensure national and regional security, the three states should in the view of this author direct and coordinate their efforts on the following levels:

- Individual defence: forming and strengthening national armed forces.
- Collective defence: forming a system of collective security within the framework of the CIS (since the agreement on collective security, signed in Tashkent in May 1992, still does not have mechanisms for its realization and so is not in effect on the ground, Kazakstan, Kyrgyzstan and Uzbekistan have to proceed with efforts aimed at the coordination of their defence activities in Central Asia).
- The creation of a system of Euro-Central Asian security: the coordination of defence policies and cooperation, as well as peacekeeping activities, jointly with member states of the OSCE and NATO.
- The creation of an Asian system of security: the strengthening of cooperation and confidence-building measures jointly with the Asian states.
- The creation of a global system of security: jointly with all the UN member states, primarily with the members of the Security Council.

Turkmenistan

Turkmenistan did not sign the October 1993 agreement on the concept of military security, the February 1995 agreement on collective security or a number of other CIS documents related to issues of military policy. Consequently it remains outside the Council of Collective Security of the CIS States and has distanced itself from multilateral CIS defence or security policy coordination. The state maintains a posture of 'positive neutrality' and according to its military doctrine does not view any state as an enemy. In September 1996 Turkmenistan's parliament amended the Essentials of Turkmenistan's Military Doctrine (originally adopted in May 1994) to emphasize that the country does not take part in any military blocs, alliances or interstate associations involving rigid mutual obligations or providing for collective responsibility of members, that the state shall not allow foreign military bases on its territory, but would take part in world community efforts designed to prevent wars and armed conflicts and in peacekeeping efforts.[20]

In his earlier speech at the international conference on 'Neutrality of Turkmenistan and International Relations in Asia' held in Ashgabat in September 1995, the president of Turkmenistan, Saparmurad Niyazov, had formulated the neutrality policy of the country as follows: 'Having today over 30 per cent of the world's reserves of natural gas, up to twelve billion tons of oil in the Caspian shelf alone, owning a huge territory and a population of almost five million, it is impossible to do without neutrality, it is impossible to join any group of countries for that would lead to the creation of blocs and weaken neutrality'.[21] Turkmenistan's status as a permanently neutral country was recognized by a UN General Assembly resolution of 12 December 1995.

In conformity with these principles, Turkmenistan has distanced itself from CIS multilateral security arrangements, but has still been prepared to enter into a bilateral relationship of strategic partnership with Russia to tackle certain defence issues jointly with it, including the protection of its 2,300 km southern border with Afghanistan and Iran.[22] The number of border incidents on the Afghan section of this border has significantly increased since 1995. The growing tension there has compelled Turkmenistan to strengthen its border defences jointly with formations of Russian border troops.

Niyazov declares that Turkmenistan is committed to the principle of positive neutrality, but emphasizes that this goal will be achieved with the support of Russia. Overall, Turkmenistan's armed forces are about 35,000 strong, and include an army, air force, air defence force and rear services. President Niyazov has stated that the national armed forces' strength will not exceed one per cent of the population, which suggests an upper limit of about 45,000 men (from a Soviet inheritance of about 108,000 personnel in the republic, most of whom were placed under Russian jurisdiction).[23] It is noteworthy that these armed forces employ many Russian military officers. Indeed, the Defence and National Security Council of Turkmenistan includes a Russian officer who represents the Russian defence ministry at the defence ministry of Turkmenistan, Major-General V. M. Zavarzin; the commander of border troops, K. Kabulov, and his first deputy, V. S. Grishchak, are also Russian. However, Turkmenistan's officers are being trained in military schools not only in Russia, but also in Turkey, and Ashgabat has concluded agreements on the training of its officers with the defence departments of Iran and Pakistan as well.

Russia's national interests: a threat to Central Asia?

There is no question that Russia considers Kazakstan and the rest of Central Asia to be in its own sphere of national interest. What kind of interests, then, does it have in Central Asia? On the basis of statements by Russian politicians, Kazak experts have come to the conclusion that while the Russian approach towards Central Asia has not yet taken shape, there is a framework for the definition of policy. The most important points are the following:

- The Russian military considers the loss of Kazakstan and the whole of Central Asia as a threat to Russian state security.[24]

- Central Asia is at the periphery of the global economy and will always remain so. However, Russian economic interests have to be protected, especially in Kazakstan, by the following measures: the end of direct control from Moscow, but the preservation of some Russian assets and rights; support for the economic interests of ethnic Russians; and the support and preservation of the economic system in the Ural, western Siberia and northern Kazakstan regions.[25]
- Russian influence in central Asia should not be allowed to diminish to the point where more dynamic economies could gain a stronger foothold. The usual contenders are Turkey and Iran.[26]
- Russia is the last bastion capable of stopping the spread of Islamic fundamentalism.[27]
- Russia cannot permit the reinforcement of China's position in Central Asia. China could extend its influence through economic pressure, the presence of nuclear weapons and ethnic infiltration. The last possibility is the most dangerous from the Russian point of view.

This conception of interests at stake has external and internal dimensions. Externally, Russia wants to demonstrate to the world that Central Asia belongs exclusively in the sphere of Russian interests, and will therefore not allow any rival powers to emerge. Internally, this conception aims at convincing the newly independent states of Central Asia (as well as public opinion in Russia) that there is an external threat from other regional powers and that only Russia is capable of protecting them against absorption by these powers.[28]

In Kazakstan, it is believed that this conception will govern Russian foreign policy in the future. There are important reasons for this conclusion. The best-known factor is the Zhirinovsky phenomenon. Although his declarations regarding foreign policy, Russia's national interests and the fate of Kazakstan clearly cannot be part of any responsible approach to foreign policy, Kazak analysts believe that despite his political decline in 1996 the demagogy of Zhirinovsky reflects not merely the opinion of political extremes, but also the ambitions of Russia's ruling elite. The next factor is Solzhenitsyn. This modern Russian prophet declared some years ago that the northern part of Kazakstan belongs to Russia because these territories were colonized and settled by Russians for a long period in history. Such views were also evident in statements by the former Russian defence minister Pavel Grachev in the spring of 1994, and the then foreign minister Andrei Kozyrev in 1995, to the effect that the CIS is the Russian sphere of influence, and Russia will protect the Russian population anywhere, with the use of force if it considers this necessary.

Although the concept of Russia's national interests has not yet been officially declared, it can be discerned in various documents, most notably that concerned with Russia's military doctrine. Kazak experts have concluded that the new military doctrine of Russia is radically different from the former Soviet one. Whereas the USSR had proclaimed it would never use nuclear weapons first, the new Russian doctrine allows the use of nuclear weapons in specific situations, namely aggression against a state which is party to the NPT, or against an ally of the Russian Federation. This is a policy of nuclear deterrence. It extends nuclear deterrence to the parties of the collective security agreement signed in Tashkent in May 1992. Therefore one could say that Kazakstan is under some sort of nuclear umbrella.[29]

However, Russia's new military doctrine also implies, at least in principle, that Kazakstan could be the object of political, military and nuclear blackmail. The doctrine considers the subversion of strategic stability as a result of the violation of international arms reduction and limitation agreements as a source of military danger to the security of the Russian Federation. This point is exemplified by the START 1 agreement. Russia, the United States, Ukraine, Kazakstan and Belarus are party to this treaty. If Kazakstan had not joined the NPT by December 1993, it could have been considered a military threat. Likewise, when the Ukrainian parliament (the Supreme Rada) declared Ukraine a de facto nuclear state, Ukraine became a potential military threat to Russia, giving rise to a whole range of potential actions to coerce Ukraine into denuclearization. Russia also considers the violation of the rights of Russian minorities as a potential military threat, justifying military intervention. Moscow regards the so-called Russian population in Kazakstan (i.e. those speaking Russian as a first language, about 50 per cent of the total) as Russian citizens. From 1993 to 1994, Moscow demanded that Kazakstan recognize the principle of dual citizenship for Russians in Kazakstan.

It is also clear from the Russian military doctrine that the preservation of administrative and military control over strategic nuclear forces, space assets (such as Kazakstan's space launch centre at Baikonur) and any installations which are part of the system of control over strategic nuclear forces is central to Russian national security interests. The Russian military doctrine defines the security space of the Russian Federation, which is supported by the collective security treaty within the framework of the CIS. Russia has used the treaty only once, in the case of Tajikistan. But to support the treaty commitments fully requires expenditure, in the view of the government of Kazakstan, which Russia cannot at present afford.

The adoption of the Russian military doctrine and its place in Russian foreign and security policy permits the following conclusions to be drawn:

- Russia insists on the right to follow its own policy in the field of security; that is why by spring 1993 it rejected the formation of unified armed forces of the CIS.
- Russia estimates that various sources of threats to its national security

will emerge. To deal with some of these problems, Russia will sacrifice the sovereignty of its allies.

- The fundamental paradox of Russian–Kazak relations, as exemplified by the Russian military doctrine, is that Russia is both the guarantor of Kazakstan's security and the principal threat to it. Russia views Kazakstan both as an ally, as part of the sphere of Russian national interest, and as a potential military threat.

Central Asian peacekeeping forces

During the meeting of the interstate council of Kazakhstan, Kyrgyzstan and Uzbekistan held in Jambyl on 15 December 1995, a resolution was signed on the formation and organization of a joint peacekeeping battalion of the three countries under the aegis of the United Nations. The three presidents appealed to the UN Secretary-General to send a UN mission for consultations with representatives of their ministries of foreign affairs and defence, and requested the preparation of the necessary documents in order to join the Agreement on Reserve Forces of the UN. This decision to form a joint peacekeeping battalion separate from CIS peacekeeping efforts (see Chapter 11) reflected concern over the situation in Tajikistan and Afghanistan and probably an appreciation of the inefficiency of collective peacekeeping forces within the CIS framework. This battalion, CentrasBat, has taken part in joint military exercises with United States and NATO units.

The OSCE and Central Asia: from a European to a Euro-Central Asian security space

The role and responsibilities of the OSCE in respect of the territory covering all of Europe, Euro-Asian Russia, the Caucasus and Central Asia (an area one could describe geographically as the Euro-Central Asian region) are very great. For the OSCE is the only organization which unites all states of the region and is charged with the provision of security and cooperation. However, the avalanche of conflicts within the post-communist space has highlighted the OSCE's lack of a mandate, funds, or its own peacekeeping forces to control the situation, especially in cases of armed conflict. The UN has such a mandate, funds and peacekeeping forces; but it is experiencing serious difficulties in maintaining and supplying its present operations, and it is unrealistic to anticipate its involvement in settling conflicts in the vast Euro-Central Asian space.

NATO has offered its military potential, under the aegis of the UN or OSCE, for the resolution of critical situations beyond its zone of responsibility. The option of referring to NATO in critical situations and strictly in accordance with the mandate of the UN Security Council or OSCE should not be ruled out. However, NATO is a military and political alliance of sixteen states which has its own interests, and it is unlikely that any involvement of its military potential beyond its zone of responsibility would be accepted positively by all its members, let alone that any such agreement could be sustained.

At the same time, Russia's attempt to obtain a mandate and funding from the UN and OSCE for the use of its armed forces for peacekeeping purposes on the territory of the former USSR is unacceptable. Russia, which insists on the recognition of its priority role in settling conflicts in the CIS region and the conferral of a peacekeeping status on its armed forces, seeks to promote its own interests in so doing since it envisions that it will become the most influential power in the region if its armed forces serve as the basis of regional peacekeeping forces.

Instead of looking to NATO or Russia, the optimal solution would be to create multinational peacekeeping forces of the OSCE itself. In contrast to organizations such as NATO and the WEU, the OSCE is the only institution in which all the states of Europe (including Turkey), Euro-Asian Russia, the Caucasian states and the Central Asian states are represented on an equal basis. Of course, this should not exclude the possibility of the creation of CIS collective peacekeeping forces, which are indeed in the process of formation. The most important element in the creation of peacekeeping forces of regional organizations is to avoid the watering-down of the universal role of the UN in respect of peacekeeping operations. Such operations should be conducted only under the UN mandate, in strict compliance with the established rules, and on the basis of two major principles: neutrality and multinationality.

The Central Asian states gained CSCE, then OSCE membership not by virtue of their geographical location but as a legacy of their position in the former Soviet Union. As a result they were positioned in a space of security and cooperation much broader than the post-Soviet space, reinforcing their sovereignty. Since the strengthening of security and cooperation is the major mission of the OSCE, the Central Asian states are very interested in contributing to the success of this mission. The active participation of the Central Asian states in the activities of the OSCE helps to bolster their security, sovereignty and territorial integrity, economic and social progress, development of legislative and democratic political institutions, and respect for human rights and the rights of national minorities.

The creation of a united Euro-Central Asian space of security and cooperation (if one takes into account the participation of the United States and Canada in the OSCE, then it would be more accurate to talk about a North

Atlantic and Euro-Central Asian space) is not at cross-purposes with the efforts of Kazakstan to convene a conference on cooperation and confidence-building measures in Asia (CCCMA). The latter initiative is derived from the experience of the European CSCE/OSCE security process and has many similarities with the CSCE/OCSE experience of collaboration with certain Mediterranean countries which are not members of that organization. The situation not only in Central Asia itself, but also in neighbouring regions which do not participate in the OSCE – China, Afghanistan, Iran, Pakistan and India – is of concern in efforts to strengthen the stability of the OSCE space. In this context the OSCE should welcome the efforts of Kazakstan aimed at the convening of the CCCMA. The OSCE should also accept positively the processes of regional integration in Central Asia and in the CIS as a whole, as well as within the framework of the Economic Cooperation Organization, which groups the Central Asian CIS states with Azerbaijan, Turkey, Iran, Afghanistan and Pakistan (and which seeks to stimulate economic cooperation in the region with a special emphasis on transport and communications).

The following arguments in favour of the realization of the idea of a Euro-Central Asian system of security may be advanced.

- It would place the Central Asian region in the field of European processes of security and extend on to its territory the common principles of inviolability of frontiers and territorial integrity, as well as other basic principles enshrined in the OSCE (former CSCE) process.
- The Central Asian states would thus be entrenched in a broader security space than the post-Soviet space, which would reduce the domination of Russia in the Central Asian region and increase the opportunities of the OSCE to implement or control peacekeeping operations on their territory.
- It would put an end to disputes about the possible expansion of NATO and diminish frictions between Russia and NATO, Russia and the United States, and Russia and the West as a whole, in connection with Russia's policy in eastern Europe and the post-Soviet space. The border between the 'far' and 'near' abroad would be eliminated in favour of the single Euro-Central Asian security space.
- There would emerge a reasonable balance of mutual relations between the OSCE, NATO, EU, WEU and CIS, which as a whole and under the aegis of the UN might characterize the Euro-Central Asian system of security.
- The creation of the Euro-Central Asian system of security would not run counter to Kazakstan's efforts to create a system of security on the Euro-Asian continent, but would contribute to that process.

The security strategy of the Central Asian states would be effectively realized within a number of concentric circles, with the system of national security placed within regional Central Asian and CIS security frameworks which in turn are built into the Euro-Central Asian and global systems of security. In foreign policy and economics alike, it is very important for the central Asian states, whose armed forces never will be comparable with those of such neighbours as Russia and China, to be able to rely for the most part upon effective cooperation with other states, above all with neighbouring countries.

NATO and the Central Asian states

At the beginning of the independent existence of Kazakstan, President Nazarbayev declared that:

> The North Atlantic Treaty has a suitable goal for our rapprochement – to assist the democratic development of the states of central and eastern Europe and the CIS, and to prevent regional conflicts as far as possible ... NATO member states for the purposes of cooperation with these states have committed themselves to providing their accumulated experience and considerable expert potential in defence policy ... Considering all this, we will broaden contacts with NATO, provided their sphere and limits are strictly determined and they are not damaging for military cooperation within the CIS framework or bilateral military ties.[30]

NATO responded to the dissolution of the Warsaw Pact and the Soviet Union by establishing the North Atlantic Cooperation Council, on the basis of which a completely new form of cooperation, the Partnership for Peace (PfP) programme, was developed. These activities were conditioned by the following well-defined NATO objectives:

- to prevent the emergence under conditions of political uncertainty and economic chaos of new totalitarian regimes and militarized states;
- to prevent the creation within the CIS framework of a new anti-NATO military bloc;
- to prevent the merger of Central Asian states with the Islamic world, especially with the countries where the ideology of orthodox Islam prevails;
- to assist the mutual cooperation of the new states in order to provide regional and global security;
- to help create the necessary conditions for the democratization of societies in these states.

NATO has devoted considerable efforts to implementing these objectives, as a result of which its contacts with Central Asian states are developing and joint programmes in the sphere of security are being carried out. Within a year of NATO inviting the new Central Asian states to cooperate under the PfP programme the framework document was signed with all these states except Tajikistan. The interest of these states in developing a partnership with NATO is also conditioned by their belief that it will create options for military, political, economic and technical cooperation with the alliance in establishing and developing their national armies. It is believed that such partnership will promote the creation of armed forces in these countries that will comply with democratic principles and world standards, and be able to participate in UN peacekeeping operations.

Modern conflicts, irrespective of their geography, increasingly often have an ethnic origin, and in such cases the priority is to extinguish the flames of conflict promptly. To assist this goal, NATO has at its disposal certain military, material, technical, human and financial resources as well as the means to create data banks and monitoring services to help resolve conflicts.

Since the PfP programme was initiated, military and civil representatives of the new Central Asian states have taken part in the majority of events conducted within its framework: in seminars and conferences concerning security problems and the principles of constructing armed forces in democratic societies, and in various NATO training activities during which the objectives of peacekeeping activities have been elaborated. Military officers from Kazakstan, Kyrgyzstan and Uzbekistan have also been welcomed to military schools in NATO member states. In August 1995, some military units of Central Asian states participated alongside military units of the United States and Canada at military exercises conducted in Louisiana. To deepen this cooperation, NATO headquarters agreed to prepare similar exercises in August 1996 in North Carolina. Kazakstan, Kyrgyzstan and Uzbekistan opted to send a unit of the Central Asian peacekeeping battalion, which was still being formed, to take part in these exercises. The consolidation of cooperation with NATO permits the conduct of similar exercises on the territory of the Central Asian states. Plans for such an exercise on the territory of Kazakstan in 1997 were developed by the Kazak armed forces together with the US defence ministry, and in September 1996 Uzbekistan was the host site for the Balance Ultra joint exercises with US army units.

Among the NATO states, the greatest assistance so far in establishing the national armed forces of the Central Asian states has been rendered by the United States, Germany and Turkey. From the first days of the establishment of diplomatic relations with the new states of Central Asia, they suggested various forms of bilateral military relations and began assistance with teaching in foreign languages, military education and the principles of construction of contemporary armed forces. According to a joint statement on the future of United States–Kazakstani defence and military relations signed in February 1996, regular meetings will be held between senior military officers of the two countries, and a schedule of military contracts has been established.[31]

In conclusion, it can be affirmed that the cooperation of the Central Asian states with NATO is not aimed at damaging collective security within the CIS framework. On the contrary, it acts to promote Central Asian security as a whole.

Notes

1. *Vestnik voennoy informatsii*, no. 11, November 1992, p. 7.
2. *Diplomaticheskiy vestnik*, no. 3, March 1995, p. 35.
3. *Nezavismaya gazeta*, 7 July 1994.
4. Ibid.
5. Ibid., 3 August 1994.
6. See interview of the then Kazak first deputy defence minister Alibek Kasymov on recently signed Russian–Kazak agreements, *Kazakhstanskaya pravda*, 7 February 1995. For the text of the Russian–Kazak declaration on expanding cooperation, which includes military provisions, see *Kazakhstanskaya pravda*, 21 January 1995.
7. *Kazakstan i mirovoe soobshchestvo*, no. 1, 1995, p. 107.
8. Ibid., p. 113.
9. Meeting of Nazarbayev with Kazak Defence Ministry Collegium, *Kazakhstanskaya pravda*, 22 December 1995.
10. Interview of Defence Minister of Kazakstan, Lieutenant-General Alibek Kasimov, *Nezavisimoe voennoe obozrenie*, no. 3. February 1996, p. 3.
11. Robert V. Barylski, 'Kazakstan: Military Dimensions of State Formation over Central Asia's Civilizational Fault Lines', in Constantine P. Danopoulos and Daniel Zirker, eds, *Civil-Military Relations in the Soviet and Yugoslav Successor States* (Oxford: Westview Press, 1996), pp. 123–51; Richard F. Staar, *The New Military in Russia* (Annapolis, MD: Naval Institute Press, 1996), pp. 14–24.
12. The last of the SS-18 missile silos were destroyed in September 1996. See S. Borisov, *Obshchaya gazeta*, no. 37, 19–25 September 1996.
13. Barylski, Kazakstan.
14. *Pravda vostoka*, 24 February 1995. For a document on the broad principles of Uzbekistan's military doctrine, see *Narodnoe slovo*, 7 June 1995, p. 1.
15. As claimed by Uzbekistan's defence minister, Lieutenant-General Rustam Akhmedov, *Narodnoe slovo*, 13 January 1996.
16. *Narodnoe slovo*, 10 March 1994.
17. Ibid.
18. Staar, *The New Military in Russia*, p. 144.
19. *Kazakstanskaya pravda*, 16 December 1995.
20. Document of 27 September 1996 signed by President Niyazov, *Neutral Turkmenistan*, 2 October 1996, in *FSU 15 Nations: Policy and Security*, October 1996. p. 93.
21. *Mezhdunarodnaya zhizn'*, no. 10, 1995.
22. For the text of this agreement see *Rossiyskaya gazeta*, 28 January 1995.
23. I. Shestakov, *Vecherni Bishkek*, 6 September 1996.
24. *Asia*, no. 4, February 1994, p. 2.
25. *International Affairs* (Moscow), no. 3, 1993, p. 41; A.V. Akimov, 'Russia and Central Asia: Perspectives of Economic Integration', *Oriens*, no. 4, 1994, pp. 120–30.
26. *National Doctrine of Russia: Problems and Priorities* (Moscow: Rau-Corporation, 1994), pp. 245–54.
27. *International Affairs* (Moscow), no. 1, 1993, p. 26.
28. *Asia*, no. 1, 1994, p. 2.
29. *Panorama*, no. 45, December 1994, p. 5.
30. *Diplomaticheskiy vestnik*, no. 7, July 1995, p. 44.
31. *OMRI Daily Digest* 1, no. 41, 27 February 1996.

Part III

Conflicts and CIS collective security efforts

11 Peacekeeping and conflict management in Eurasia

Pavel Baev

During the first half of the 1990s, the geopolitical space that at the beginning of the decade was occupied by the Soviet Union saw perhaps more violent conflicts than any other region of the world. It also saw an exponential growth of international involvement in managing these conflicts, channelled partly through various organizations (the UN, the OSCE and also, certainly, the CIS) but mostly improvised through ad hoc bilateral or multilateral arrangements. As a result of these activities, an unprecedented number of peacekeeping operations were launched with widely varying mandates, aims and participants.

This chapter will not attempt to give an overview of all the conflicts that have developed in the former USSR, nor will it seek to describe in detail all the peacekeeping operations. It will only touch on such key issues as the role of the CIS and military capabilities, since they are addressed in other chapters in this volume by Andrei Zagorski, Christoph Bluth and Roy Allison. What it will aim at is an assessment of how efficient the peacekeeping activities are in resolving conflicts and how instrumental they are in promoting Russia's national interests. Towards this end it will first compare the evolution of Russia's political and military goals in conflict management. Then it will take a closer look at the military pattern of peacekeeping. Finally, a brief assessment of the impact of the Chechen war on the sustainability of Russia's peacekeeping activities will lead to some conclusions on the involvement of 'external' international organizations.

Conflicts in the CIS area and Russia's post-imperial course

That Russia has assumed the main responsibility for conflict management in the former USSR and continues to carry this burden despite all internal hardships and external objections is a well-established political fact. What is less clear is whether Russia's course may be defined as neo-imperialist (aimed at restoring the Soviet empire in a new form) or rather as post-imperialist (pursuing primarily the goal of enhancing internal security by preventing spill-over from numerous conflicts in the neighbourhood). The key issue in making a judgment here is the level of integration between Russia's foreign and military policies.

What is immediately clear about Russia's current policy is that the desire to consolidate some 'great power' status and secure for itself a sphere of exclusive influence goes hand in hand with an aggravation of its economic situation. There is no space here to assess the gravity of the economic crisis, but it stands to reason that an inability to hold the depression in check could be the main source of, and the driving force behind, more active pursuit of the nationalistic agenda. It could be argued in this context that the economic situation in other newly independent states is even worse. Experts from the influential Council for Foreign and Defence Policy warned: 'As the neighbouring states are becoming weaker, in the Russian public opinion and political circles along with general growth of nationalism there is a growing feeling of Russia's imaginary omnipotence'.[1] But relative successes in economic reform could ill compensate for the absolute decline of the basic components of national power. So as a point of departure we can take it that the case for further analysis is definitely not a traditional imperialism arising from a position of strength, but a quasi-imperialism arising from a position of weakness.

The maximalist goal of rebuilding the former Soviet empire in its inviolable borders is obviously beyond the grasp of this quasi-imperialism. Even the communists who initiated the vote in the State Duma in March 1996 denouncing the Belovezhskaya Puscha Agreement of December 1991 hardly regard the issue as anything more than a campaigning tool.[2] The more moderate goals of building a hard core inside the CIS also show a certain logical inconsistency. The agreement on deeper integration signed in March 1996 by Russia, Belarus, Kazakstan and Kyrgyzstan in fact depends entirely upon the allocation of funds from the already overburdened Russian budget.[3] A focus on the issue of the Russians abroad would in principle dictate a concentration of efforts on Belarus, eastern Estonia, eastern Ukraine and Crimea, and northern Kazakstan. But none of the three latter cases provide a convincing example of an attempt by Russia to provoke internal dissension in order to absorb territory populated by Russians, though local reaction to Russian rhetoric has often been nervous and Moscow has been blamed for cherishing imperialistic ambitions.[4] In fact, it is conflict management primarily on the southern rim of the former Soviet Union that is the single most important activity of Russian quasi-imperialism. It could be called opportunistic in the sense that it often seeks to exploit the obvious lack of political organization across this space, where fledgling states are struggling with numerous challenges of transition and seeking to prove their viability. These challenges have no respect for the new international borders, which exist only on maps: various forms of spill-over (refugees, arms smuggling, training of combatants) are everyday facts of life. So the premise that Russia's internal security could best be achieved by controlling conflicts in this neighbourhood does indeed look convincing.[5] But only a thin line divides post-imperial security-building from neo-imperialist expansion.

The real 'litmus test' for the neo-quasi-imperialist policy is its military dimension: and not so much the scale of military activities as the question of how well they serve political purposes. Looking back to the year 1992, one can hardly avoid the conclusion that military operations were sharply at odds with declared political goals. The first half of that year saw an uneven escalation of four violent conflicts, of which three were attempted secessions (Nagorno-Karabakh from Azerbaijan, Transdniestria from Moldova, and South Ossetia from Georgia), while Tajikistan was a case of civil war. The Russian foreign ministry accepted a strict policy of non-interference, ignoring persistent appeals for support from Transdniestria and South Ossetia.

The military leadership saw the situation from a different perspective. In two of the four cases (Transdniestria and Tajikistan) Russian troops found themselves in the line of fire and quickly becoming parties to the conflict, despite orders to maintain neutrality. The most demanding pressure came from Moldova, where the 14th Army all but openly took sides with the ethnic Russians who initiated the secession and proclaimed the Transdniestrian Republic. The real possibility of losing either the 14th Army itself (which was on the brink of disintegration) or control over combat operations conducted by its units left only one option for the newly appointed Russian defence minister Grachev, namely to assume command. However, taking personal responsibility for giving combat orders was politically too risky, so Grachev sent in his trusted deputy General Lebed and then persuaded Yeltsin to appoint him commander of the 14th Army. In a matter of days Lebed worked a miracle: the troops became controllable and combat-ready; the clash around Bendery (20–25 June) proved his resolution; and since then the 14th Army has provided strong deterrence against any efforts on the part of the Moldovan government to restore territorial integrity by force.[6]

This military action was a crucial point in the emergence of the army's interventionist course. Moldova was immediately made a political issue by fledging Russian 'patriotic' forces, since this perfectly suited both the nationalists who emphasized the 'Russians-against-the-others' aspect of the problem and the statists who argued for 're-collecting lands' around Russia. Once Vice-President Rutskoi openly joined the latter cause, it became a matter of urgency for President Yeltsin to find some legal framework for the military initiative.[7] He proposed to make the 14th Army the guarantor of the ceasefire; the Moldovan government proposed instead to bring in a multinational force with Romanian participation. The compromise deal, which had no analogies in the annals of peacekeeping, was struck between Yeltsin and Moldova's President Snegur on 21 July. It envisaged the creation of a peacekeeping force comprising five Russian battalions and three each from Moldova and Transdniestria. The exclusion of the 14th Army from participation in this operation meant that one Russian army is keeping a peace that another has broken.

At the same time, a similar trilateral political framework was set for the South Ossetian conflict;[8] but during autumn 1992 new demands for Russian peacekeeping came from North Ossetia, Tajikistan and Abkhazia. The first of these conflicts was perhaps the most alarming, since it represented the first time that ethnic violence had erupted inside the Russian Federation: the response from Moscow was accordingly rapid, but it was also controversial. An airborne regiment plus some 2,000 interior troops were deployed to Prigorodny district, providing strong support to North Ossetian militia and suppressing Ingush resistance.[9] Order was restored in a matter of days, but the continuing presence of Russian troops was necessary to maintain stability, and this the Ingush side justly considered unacceptable.

Tajikistan represented a more complicated case. As traditional inter-clan controversies in this country escalated to fully-fledged civil war in summer and autumn 1992, the Russian military, while being highly reluctant to get involved, found it impossible to withdraw from its two key functions: protecting the 'external' border with Afghanistan and maintaining security in the capital, Dushanbe. While the former was justified by the Tashkent agreement on collective security (signed in May 1992), the latter was never formally recognized but performed in practice by the 201st Motorized Rifle Division, permanently based in Dushanbe. It is hardly possible to say that Moscow masterminded the return of the former communists to power, but the direct involvement of the 201st Division on the side of the Hissar and Kulyab clans, contributing to their victory by January 1993, is undeniable.[10]

As for Abkhazia, the official Russian position on the attempt by Georgia to restore control over this mutinous autonomous republic force was strict neutrality, but for the military commanders whose troops were stationed in the line of fire this idea was meaningless. There were several elements to the Russian military involvement in the fighting, some of which could perhaps qualify as peacekeeping. This refers first of all to the Russian troops in Eshera (reinforced with an airborne regiment) which prevented Georgian forces from launching a further offensive and stabilized the frontline along the River Gumista. Several operations aimed at the evacuation of refugees and the delivery of humanitarian aid were also conducted, some of them with casualties. But in a number of cases these activities provided a cover for military support to the Abkhazian side in various forms, for example the 'punishing' air strikes on Sukhumi.[11] Already in October 1992, Abkhazians (with hundreds of volunteers from the North Caucasus as well as Cossacks fighting on their side) defeated Georgians in Gagra, thus restoring control over the main line of communications with Russia. Afterwards, trench warfare became the pattern for nearly a year.

Even from this abridged description it is possible to establish that by the end of 1992 Russia was formally involved in three peacekeeping operations (Moldova/Transdniestria, Georgia/South Ossetia, North Ossetia/Ingushetia) and informally in another two (Abkhazia and Tajikistan), all of which looked rather open-ended. That this activity was scarcely compatible with 'non-interference' in foreign policy was one thing, but its shocking political expression was quite another: Russia backed three secessions (Abkhazia, Transdniestria and South Ossetia) and one case of ethnic cleansing (the Ingush minority from North Ossetia) and took sides with tribal communists in a civil war (Tajikistan). In fact, some of these interventions ran not only against declared political goals but also against Russia's perceived strategic interests. Georgia represented the most obvious example: while politicians claimed support for its territorial integrity and experts defined it as a key strategic ally for Russia,[12] the military had few qualms about dismembering this state.

From this moment both Russian foreign and military policies entered a phase of rapid evolution in remarkably different directions. As for the military, they had reasons to consider the operations relatively successful: the ceasefires were observed in all cases except Tajikistan. But the continuing presence of Russian troops was a prerequisite, so the key factor in the subsequent evolution of military policy appeared to be the deficit of battalions. In 1992, the military leadership operated on the assumption that they could use as many divisions (not to say battalions) as necessary in the 'hot spots', and the scheduled withdrawal from Germany would provide more combat-ready troops. But even in early 1993, trying to set the pattern of rotation for ten airborne battalions engaged in the operations listed above (plus another one contributed to UNPROFOR), the general staff discovered that their capabilities were stretched very thin. The status of the Mobile Forces is a separate topic,[13] but what is relevant here is the general change in the attitude of the Russian high command to military interventions in favour of a more cautious approach.[14]

This approach manifested itself in clear reluctance to get involved in Nagorno-Karabakh (and also in complete military withdrawal from Azerbaijan) and in keeping as low a profile as possible in Abkhazia, even though both conflicts looked rather inviting from a neo-imperialistic perspective. But the most symptomatic although often misinterpreted case is that of the three Baltic states, which during 1993 and most of 1994 were attracting considerable political attention. There are reasons to assume that in autumn 1992 the Russian defence ministry seriously considered options for preserving its military groupings in Latvia and Estonia and accordingly started to play on the most sensitive issue – the status of the Russian population.[15] Seeking to establish a direct link between the questions of troop withdrawals and alleged violations of the rights of Russian-speakers, the heads of the military in Moscow were actually preparing the ground for a Moldova-type 'peacekeeping' intervention. In early 1993, however, the need to concentrate military efforts dictated the decision on a rapid retreat from the Baltic area. As John Lough accurately pointed out, the military authorities 'have been negotiating with the governments of the Baltic states over the withdrawal of the North-Western Group of Forces without any political oversight'.[16] What he failed to notice was that this was not necessarily a bad thing, since the withdrawal continued according to schedule despite increasingly hostile political rhetoric.

This brings us to the phase of Russia's foreign policy which replaced the short-lived and naïve policy of 'good-neighbourliness'. Paradoxically, the starting point was Yeltsin's declaration in his 1993 new year message that 'the imperial period in Russia's history has ended'. On 28 February 1993, addressing the Civic Union conference, he made the first claim on Russia's 'vital interest in the cessation of all armed conflicts on the territory of the former USSR' and appealed to the UN 'to grant Russia special powers as guarantor of peace and stability in this region.[17] Initially, this looked like an attempt to borrow *post factum* some legitimacy for the continuing peacekeeping operations, but by summer 1993 the rhetoric went further and seemed likely to be preparing the ground for new interventions that should, as Kozyrev put it in an interview with *Izvestiya*, prevent Russia from 'losing geopolitical positions that took centuries to conquer'.[18]

The Baltic states were not exempted from this policy. Tensions with Estonia reached a critical level in June–July 1993 when a flurry of aggressive statements from Moscow accompanied the referendum on autonomy in Narva, a city east of Estonia populated almost exclusively by Russians. But the military authorities showed no interest in exploiting this issue with a possible aim of 'peace intervention'. By the end of August they had completed the withdrawal of troops from Lithuania, while the foreign ministry failed to prepare an agreement on this issue. During the rest of 1993 and spring–summer 1994, military forces continued to leave Estonia and Latvia according to schedule, despite sporadic heated political exchanges involving defence minister Grachev.[19] The swift implementation of the withdrawal allowed President Yeltsin to make a symbolic goodwill step: by 31 August 1994 the 'Russians' were gone. The long-predicted military pressure never materialized and without it the imperialist pose remained just a bluff.

But what made this bluff really dangerous was its instrumental role in introducing a new political discourse which was much more comprehensible for many in the political elite than the previous liberal one. Since early 1994 mainstream politicians, with very few exceptions, being close to panic that Zhirinovsky was hot on their heels, started to compete in their rhetoric on saving the empire. Foreign minister Kozyrev was quick to trim his sails to the new winds, and his address to Russian ambassadors in January 1994 set the tone for the campaign of that year.[20] Only after Kozyrev's dismissal in February 1996 was the rhetoric somewhat softened; his successor Yevgeny Primakov, while confirming the political priority attached to relations with the CIS states, abandoned even the term 'near abroad'. What was more surprising was that the military authorities except for Defence Minister Grachev, for whom it was perhaps more than just *noblesse oblige*, were not particularly eager to subscribe to the new proactive discourse. The generals no doubt started to suspect that the responsibility for implementing the 'can-do' approach would be placed on them, while no one would bother about the mobilization of the required resources.

What actually happened during 1993 and most of 1994 was the consolidation of the peacekeeping enterprises started in 1992.[21] Abkhazia remained perhaps the most unstable of all 'trouble spots', until the framework for another Russian peacekeeping operation to supplement rather than replace the one *de facto* in place since autumn 1992 was finalized in June 1994.[22] Tajikistan, on the other hand, gave an example of an operation which enjoyed plenty of political attention in the CIS, produced a legitimate mandate and even achieved some military burden-sharing, but still remained hopeless as all efforts to seal off the border with Afghanistan proved ineffective. From early 1994, Russia increased its activities around Nagorno-Karabakh; in May Grachev even negotiated a stable ceasefire; but the plans for a full-scale peacekeeping operation were frustrated by Azerbaijan's defiant insistence on an OSCE-sponsored action.[23]

In fact, the only 'quasi-imperialistic' initiative that could be attributed to the military leadership was the presidential directive on military bases in the near abroad issued in early April.[24] Notwithstanding its disproportionate resonance internationally, it merely provided some domestic legitimacy for what had been already settled bilaterally with a few neighbours, some of which (e.g. Armenia) were interested in keeping Russian soldiers on their soil, while others (e.g. Belarus) were not much concerned. More convincing evidence of the direction of policy was the agreement on withdrawal of the 14th Army from Moldova within a three-year period, which was finalized by August 1994 and signed by Russia's prime minister and defence minister in October. Certainly, this agreement was a declaration of intent rather than a firm commitment,[25] but the readiness of the Russian military leadership to suspend the operation that was supposed to serve as a model for conflict management was indeed symptomatic.

The Chechen war certainly supplies strong evidence for those who portray Russia as inherently neo-imperialist; this intervention follows too closely the blueprint of the 'Thrust to the South' declaimed by Vladimir Zhirinovsky. But it does not provide any proof of military interference in politics; on the contrary, it shows that the high command did not have a sufficiently strong voice to prevent the operation, which from their perspective seemed hopeless.[26] That conflict is analysed in Chapter 13 of this volume; what is relevant here is the dramatically altered context of the Russian military presence abroad, above all in the Caucasus. It is true that the Russian defence ministry succeeded in February 1995 in finalizing the agreement on military bases in Georgia, which was the only state unequivocally to support Moscow's action in Chechenia. But the perception of the Russian army as completely disorganized and demoralized by this dirty war is so widespread in the region that Russia's political ability to project force has been crucially undermined.

Military peacekeeping: doctrine and know-how

Russian military views on the conduct of peacekeeping operations are strikingly different from thinking in the West. Perhaps the fundamental difference concerns the concept of low-intensity conflicts. While Western theories suggest a rather ambivalent link, in Russia peacekeeping remains part and parcel of conflict-waging. The natural point of departure for Russian strategists was the war in Afghanistan: rather than agonizing over the lessons from this defeat they sought a new victory. This conceptual evolution quite naturally brought the army to Chechenia. But the experience accumulated during numerous Russian operations in 1991–5 is indeed unique, so that the operational and tactical principles developed on this basis are a valuable subject for analysis.

The initial requirement of the Russian military regarding 'peace inter-ventions' is that political arrangements should be clear, non-ideological and implementable. The Afghan experience is highly relevant here, since that military operation was completely at odds with vague political goals which failed to provide a comprehensible rationale except in terms of Soviet 'international duty'.[27] In a sense, the insistence of the Russian military on a clear political arrangement is similar to the basic peacekeeping requirement of a strict political mandate.[28] The main difference is the issue of political control over the military implementation of the mandate: a Russian general would consider as absurd a chain of command which included authorization of every air strike by a civilian 'commissioner'. Russian military authorities much prefer to take an active part in negotiating the political arrangement for every operation in order to secure their freedom in the field.[29]

While there is an understanding that all phases of a peacekeeping operation form a complex action in which the military is just one element, there is also a strong desire to subordinate other elements to the military goals. Therefore, the cessation of violence becomes the central issue of all Russian peacekeeping operations. A direct consequence is lack of political progress in settling the underlying conflicts. This makes nearly every deployment an open-ended one, in some cases perhaps against the best intentions of the Russian military. From this point of view, the only really successful peacekeeping operation in the former USSR has been securing the key lines of communications in western Georgia in autumn 1993 (one marine battalion from the Black Sea fleet and several units from the Transcaucasus group of forces were engaged): an outcome which lasted about a month.

The problem of political arrangements for peacekeeping operations includes three key interlinked issues: neutrality/impartiality, consent and credibility/minimal force. Russia could not even pretend to be neutral in any of the conflicts in the former USSR in respect of its own interests: to the contrary, many official declarations about the extent of Russia's vital interests make a commitment to provide leadership in the management of nearly every conflict. However, political leaders in Moscow still insist on their neutrality in the sense that Russia's interests are centred on the termination of conflicts as an end in itself and not on enforcing 'imperial' solutions. This claim, too, obviously comes into contradiction with many specific Russian interests in the near abroad: economic (especially oil), national (such as 'Russians abroad'), strategic (including forward military basing), etc.[30]

A way around these inconsistencies was found in making the parties to the conflict full partners and participants in the peacekeeping operation. Therefore, in this 'untraditional' approach the issue of consent became inseparably linked to the issue of Russia's impartiality. The hidden agenda here is that in secession-type conflicts, conferring equal status on the 'second' party comes quite close to recognizing secession, and thus the operation inevitably turns into securing the quasi-independence of a rebellious province. Accordingly, the main problem is to obtain the consent of the 'first' party, i.e. the state which is the victim of secession. It took serious political efforts from Russia to press Moldova into consent in summer 1992 (for the peacekeeping operation in Transdniestria) and Georgia in summer 1994 (for the operation in Abkhazia), but since the efforts were not particularly consistent in the case of Nagorno-Karabakh, Azerbaijan remained opposed to the operation. Part of the explanation is that one of the main Russian methods of arm-twisting was emphasizing the fact that no one else would contribute troops for the operation, while in Nagorno-Karabakh the option of the first-ever CSCE (now OSCE) intervention was kept open by the Minsk group.

The claim to impartiality becomes even less convincing if we take into consideration that in at least two cases Russia decided that giving recognition to the 'second' party was against its interests and launched peacekeeping or, rather, 'order-restoring' operations in support of the incumbent governments. One of these cases is Tajikistan, where Moscow pays a degree of lip-service to the ideas of 'national reconciliation' and 'dialogue with the opposition' while in fact the aims of the operation are to cut supplies from Afghanistan and to isolate the Gorno-Badakhshan area controlled by the opposition.[31] Another was the operation mentioned above aimed at securing lines of communications in western Georgia in autumn 1993, which gave strong backing to the government forces and helped to suppress the rebellion in a matter of weeks.

In both 'models' – pressing a government into consent or giving it support against opposition – the success of an operation depends crucially upon the credibility of Russia's military commitment. In fact, while inviting the parties to the conflict to participate in keeping the peace, Moscow never acknowledged them as equal partners in military terms, despite formal guarantees. In both Transdniestria and South Ossetia, Russian battalions were numerically and technically far stronger than other elements of the joint forces and the tripartite control commissions were dominated by Russian officers. Moscow's proposals for the organization of the peacekeeping force for Nagorno-Karabakh showed similar preferences.

Furthermore, even when dealing with 'frozen' conflicts Russia never limited its role to observing/monitoring the ceasefire; it insisted on securing it by providing a sort of 'deterrence by punishment'. Therefore, even if the agreement envisaged deployment of only a token peacekeeping force (with Russia contributing 30–50 per cent and the rest provided by the parties to the conflict), it was implicitly acknowledged that a powerful grouping of Russian forces based nearby would be ready to intervene in the event of a serious violation. The 14th Army played this role of a superior force 'in waiting' for Moldova, and the Mobile Forces' grouping in the North Caucasus military district was intended to do the same for Georgia. As far as Nagorno-Karabakh is concerned, it may be assumed that the Russian military grouping in Armenia (currently the 7th Army has only one division) could have been reinforced, in the first instance with a sufficient air component, in order to provide credible deterrence. And it was the lack of such capabilities in Tajikistan, which was all too obvious in comparison with the situation in the Afghan war, that from the very beginning made the operation vulnerable and even doomed to failure.

The need to maintain and uphold this deterrent effect for open-ended operations resulted in a steady increase in the numbers of Russian forces involved in them. Official information on the troops conducting 'peace' operations gave a figure in the range of 15,000–16,500, but the precise number remained unspecified and not particularly reliable.[32] My own estimates for the end of 1992 suggest a figure of 27,500.[33] By the end of 1993, this total had increased to 36,000, primarily as a result of reinforcing the 201st Division in Tajikistan and the deployment of new troops to Abkhazia and western Georgia. For summer 1994, my estimate is as high as 42,000, reflecting the new operation in Abkhazia, another battalion sent to UNPROFOR and more reinforcements for Tajikistan. This growth, while seemingly in contradiction to the restrictive approach taken by the Russian military leadership, was not accompanied by any corresponding increase in financing and therein lies the best explanation for the reluctance of the military chiefs to launch any new operations.[34]

More international attention was captured by the gradual increase of the military hardware concentrated in the North Caucasus. Indeed, this 'front-line' military district was assigned as the base for all continuing and expected 'peace' operations in the area. Defence minister Grachev made the assessment that 600 tanks, 2,200 ACVs and 1,000 artillery pieces would constitute a sufficient force.[35] It was fairly clear that no political manoeuvres (such as the redistribution of quotas settled with Georgia on a bilateral basis in May 1995) could bring this grouping under the CFE Treaty flank limits. Since President Yeltsin's formal letter in October 1993 there had been plenty of noise about the inevitable violation of this key treaty, but few efforts to find an acceptable solution.[36] The Western partners, perhaps extrapolating from arms control traditions of the Cold War era, expected that the simple existence of a firm deadline would result in some sort of solution. Accordingly, it was only in October 1995 that they finally realized that Moscow was determined to maintain its position, and the precedent of non-compliance was established. Since no one was interested in dismantling the treaty, the problem was downplayed until spring 1996 under the guise of a US–Russian confidential compromise which in May was reluctantly approved by all signatories of the treaty. It may be assumed that the lack of either firm pressure or constructive involvement from the Western side partly reflects an ambiguous attitude towards Russian conflict management in the Caucasus.

The strong emphasis on deterrence in Russia's conflict management policy had a direct impact on the operational principles of peacekeeping activities. The most striking difference here from the traditional UN peacekeeping 'code of conduct' is the basic approach to the use of force. While the main guideline for 'classical' UN operations was self-defence, in the peacekeeping now commonly described as 'second generation' a strong emphasis is placed on avoiding breaching consent, the absolutely central element of the operation. Thus Charles Dobbie, the author of the British Army field manual *Wider Peacekeeping*, proposes 'a helpful rule of thumb': the use of the minimum necessary force, specified as 'the measured application of violence or coercion, sufficient only to achieve a specific end, demonstrably reasonable, proportionate and appropriate; and confined in effect to the specific and legitimate target intended'.[37]

This school of thought remains absolutely foreign to Russian operational planning as related to peacekeeping. Notably, the term 'rules of engagement', certainly one of the key notions in the Western concept, is absent from the

Russian military vocabulary.[38] This is highly characteristic and testifies to the desire to preserve military freedom from any political interference in all high-risk situations of loosely controlled conflicts. Russian strategists, while agreeing that a peacekeeping force could in principle be kept at a minimal level, view it rather as a 'trip-wire' connected to the readily available prevailing force. As for those situations when an operation is launched before the ceasefire is established, the Russian planners certainly prefer to bring in as much force as possible, considering 'overkill' a much lesser danger than a 'position of weakness'.[39] The main constraint in such an approach is the shortage of peacekeeping forces, often taken by Russian officers to be a transitional phenomenon resulting from unsatisfactory funding for building the Mobile Forces.[40]

The Russian military doctrine approved in November 1993 gives few guidelines on conducting peacekeeping operations, though the local conflicts 'engendered by aggressive nationalism' are recognized as one of the main sources of military threat.[41] Two aims that are identified to localize the seat of tensions and stop hostilities at the earliest possible stage both point to a proactive strategy which employs maximum rather than minimum force. In reality, the pattern of peacekeeping that could be derived from a number of Russian operations is more cautious and reactive. In several cases (including South Ossetia, Transdniestria and Abkhazia), Russian military planners tended to wait until the conflict reached a 'natural' stalemate which would allow the establishment of a stable ceasefire. And it was the relative stability on the front lines around Nagorno-Karabakh from early 1994 that allowed the Russian general staff to give practical consideration to a possible peacekeeping operation.

Looking at these cases, it is possible to come to the conclusion that from a Russian military perspective, 'linear' peacekeeping (i.e. securing a ceasefire between two parties to the conflict along a specific dividing line) is a greatly preferable option to 'territorial' peacekeeping (i.e. securing order on a specific territory). The former could include full control over a specially defined demilitarized zone, but leaves the territories on both sides of it by and large in the hands of the parties to the conflict. Abkhazia represents the best example of such an operation, but even the 14th Army in Transdniestria refrained from taking any territorial control, and its commander General Lebed was actually involved in bitter controversies with the leadership of this self-proclaimed republic.

The 'territorial' option is recognized as unavoidable in conflicts inside the Russian Federation, or those affecting compact settlements of ethnic Russians in the near abroad (this remains to date a theoretical construction) or threatening regimes that are considered as important allies for Moscow. Two key principles for reducing risks involved in such operations are close cooperation with local authorities (and accordingly with local military/ paramilitary forces) and joint efforts with interior forces, border troops, etc.

The deployments in North Ossetia and Tajikistan (the latter actually combines linear and territorial options) illustrate that the Russian military leadership, while maintaining overall control, is trying to limit the tasks of the army units to those counter-insurgency operations which go beyond policing and do not require special anti-terrorist techniques.[42]

Among the few sources shedding light on the Russian military thinking related to such operations, the writings of General Ivan Vorobyev, head of the Tactics Department, Frunze Military Academy, are perhaps the most consistent. In several publications he made useful generalizations from recent experience, combining these with the lessons from Afghanistan.[43] His main point is that peacekeeping is always conducted in a highly uncertain environment where a fragile ceasefire could at any time be violated by actions of 'illegal armed groupings' leading to the resumption of high-intensity hostilities. The Russian troops, while conducting peacetime functions (observation, monitoring, etc.), should be prepared to act decisively against armed groups and to engage in various combat operations. Accordingly, the peacekeeping technique includes all sorts of counter-insurgency tactics (combing, blocking, ambush, etc.) and even elements of manoeuvre warfare (combined air and ground strikes). A counter-terrorist operation in Pervomayskaya (January 1996) demonstrated that the coordination between army units and various special forces remained notoriously poor.

From this perspective, the distinction between peacekeeping and peace enforcement which is one of the main issues in contemporary Western security studies looks utterly academic.[44] Russian strategists definitely place 'peace operations' within the continuum of low-intensity conflicts;[45] accordingly, the peacekeeping forces are taken as the first echelon, which provides operational intelligence and deals with small-scale threats but should be reinforced in a matter of days if not hours with more powerful second-echelon forces providing effective 'escalation dominance'.

Sustainability and Europeanization

Intervention in Chechenia seemed to mark an abrupt departure from the cautious and self-restrained course taken by the Russian military leadership since 1993. Some Russian liberals with few doubts levelled the accusation that 'the arm-twisting peace-keeping policy quite logically led to the first bloody war on Russia's territory in Chechnia'.[46] While quite understandable as an emotional reaction, such accusations are rather unfair. Perhaps the only factor that lends them verisimilitude is the Kremlin's attempt to disguise the war as just another 'peace' operation aimed at 'restoring constitutional order' and 'disarming illegal formations'.

A direct causal link between operations in Abkhazia, Tajikistan, etc. and the war in Chechenia is hard to establish. Certainly, the dynamics of conflicts in the geopolitical space of the former Soviet Union have been remarkably uneven. It is not sufficient to make a general calculation that the year 1992 saw seven serious conflicts (Nagorno-Karabakh, the attempted coup in Georgia, South Ossetia, Transdniestria, Tajikistan, Abkhazia, North Ossetia) and the year 1993 six (Nagorno-Karabakh, Tajikistan, Abkhazia, western Georgia, the coup in Azerbaijan and violent confrontation in Moscow). Some of these conflicts lasted for only a few days (the coups and also the conflict in North Ossetia) or a few weeks (the rebellion in western Georgia), while others had several periods of high intensity and intervening pauses (Abkhazia and Nagorno-Karabakh). But the trend towards de-escalation has become clear since November 1993 and it is undeniable that Russia's interference has substantially contributed to this. Since summer 1992 the deployment of Russian troops has resulted in the cessation of violence in five 'hot spots' (Transdniestria, South Ossetia, North Ossetia, Abkhazia and western Georgia), while the conflict in Tajikistan became controllable. After the Russian defence minister brokered a stable ceasefire in Nagorno-Karabakh in May 1994, for the first time since the break-up of the USSR a relative stability was found on its vast territory (except for some minor skirmishes in Tajikistan and periodic clashes between the forces of the Chechen leader, Dudayev, and the opposition in Chechenia). Russia's intervention in Chechenia in December 1994 not only added one more conflict to the list and raised the threshold of violence dramatically, but quite possibly broke the trend towards stabilization.

On the other hand, the question of the responsibility of the military leadership for the war in Chechenia is certainly linked to the question of responsibility for previous peacekeeping actions. It stands to reason that the initial military planning for the operation in Chechenia was done more according to the principles of peace enforcement operations (as, for example, in western Georgia) than those of manoeuvre warfare. Hence the slow advance of the armoured columns which tried to avoid direct clashes and to establish a kind of separation zone in the middle part of the republic between forces loyal to Dudayev in the south and various opposition groupings controlling the northern districts.[47] That the latter groupings ceased to exist and the former received thousands of volunteers as a direct consequence of the Russian invasion is a different story which is instructive about political ignorance on the use of military instruments. What is more, the scale of the war effort and the unpreparedness of the army for such an 'overload' are inevitably undermining the sustainability of other continuing operations and making any new military enterprises practically impossible. Even before Chechenia, the direct and indirect costs of maintaining several open-ended operations were becoming prohibitive. This was a result not so much of the financing of the 'forward deployment' itself, but rather of the expenses related to building combat-worthy mobile forces, manpower shortages, and the lack of training and logistics, which resulted in a 'peace-keeping overstretch'.[48] The only real solution for this could be a substantial reduction of military involvement in the near abroad, and the first symptom of this was, perhaps, the decision to reduce by half the Russian peacekeeping force in Transdniestria. This decision was taken unilaterally in mid-November 1994, despite valid objections from Moldova. Political pressure, however, prevented any further steps in this direction. While for many Western analysts the unsustainability of Russia's interventionist course was all too obvious,[49] little consideration was given to this possibility in Moscow.

While in Chechenia the Russian military leadership was compelled to abandon its more cautious approach to peacekeeping (based more on deterrence than on waging combat operations), it was hardly an attempt to solve the problem of overstretch with a small and successful war gamble. The army was pushed into a hopeless adventure; the failure in Chechenia was absolutely predictable and was indeed predicted by many in the military leadership, including General Gromov. The discredited defence minister Grachev was unable to secure even the minimal financing for prolonged counter-insurgency operations, thus leaving the composite military units to become marauder troops. The fact of a military defeat in Chechenia was recognized only in September 1996, after the failure of all attempts to win or negotiate anything that could pass for a victory. But Yeltsin's decree on the complete withdrawal of Russian troops, issued in late November 1996, did not restore the army's ability to project force; the damage is essentially beyond repair.

The sheer amount of military effort wasted in Chechenia inevitably undermines Russia's ability to maintain the peacekeeping operation in Abkhazia and indeed to continue its military presence in the Transcaucasus. While formally the basing arrangements for the Transcaucasus group of forces are quite stable, in fact the Russian divisions stationed in Armenia and Adzharia are becoming indigenized to such a degree that their control from Moscow is now only symbolic. Russia's extensive support for building the Georgian armed forces also hardly ensures sustainable Russian–Georgian military ties. Indeed, Moscow's decisive move against Chechenia (which coincided with Croatia's offensive in Krajina) made it tempting for Georgia to renew its attempt to re-establish control over Abkhazia by military means. Since Moscow had obviously lost any interest in supporting the Abkhazians and since none of the North Caucasian republics has been eager to become involved, Shevardnadze appeared to have quite a good chance of success in a new blitzkrieg of this kind. However, this option was renounced at a crucial meeting in Tbilisi in August 1997 between Shevardnadze and the Abkhazian leader Vladislav Ardzinba, during which the two sides agreed to confine themselves to negotiations in seeking to resolve the conflict over Abkhazia. Another Russian withdrawal that was conceivable at least from mid-1993 and now looks all but inevitable is from Tajikistan, and the consequences of this for stability in Central Asia, while not necessarily dramatic in the short term, could be quite serious in the next few years.

The military consequences of the Chechen war have had a complicated impact on Russia's foreign policy. While in public opinion and in the majority of the political elite the support for any neo-imperialistic schemes has all but evaporated, for Yeltsin and his entourage the idea of 'victory' has become an imperative. That Yeltsin was able to win the presidential elections without solving the Chechen problem (his peace plan of March 1996 was a shameless electoral bluff) means that the Russian leadership did not feel the need to draw lessons from the Chechenia conflict, even while acknowledging the humiliating defeat it represented. Consequently the scenario of a new, successful Russian intervention elsewhere that would overshadow the disaster in Chechenia is by no means inconceivable. At the same time, new opportunities could appear in the 'Europeanization' of Russia's peacekeeping activities. For quite a long time both sides in this process pursued remarkably unrealistic strategies. Moscow sought to obtain legitimation (and perhaps financial support) from international organizations without allowing them any real involvement in the Russian or Russian/CIS operations; the West wanted to bring Russia's peacekeeping closer to international standards without investing any substantial political or financial resources.

The all-European OSCE summit in Budapest in December 1994 opened a window of opportunity for closer cooperation in resolving the conflict in Nagorno-Karabakh. Certainly, Russia's consent to the first ever OSCE peacekeeping operation was less than wholehearted; it simply could not deny this organization the right to establish itself as a real security institution.[50] As further developments have proved, there is a large gap between political agreement and military deployment, but the legal precedent was established.[51] It was reinforced by the gradual increase of the OSCE role in Moldova, paralleling Russia's slow withdrawal from Transdniestria; and the OSCE's penetration into the combat area in Chechenia by establishing its mission there certainly marked a new extension of this organization's role in conflict management in the former USSR.

While these political developments are creating a new framework for peacekeeping, they still exert only a marginal influence on the military character of the operations. The key player in this crucial dimension is NATO, which has invested a great deal of effort in building military-to-military contacts. Cooperation in peacekeeping is exactly the issue that could prove the value of these investments, whose primary result so far has been an increase in 'military tourism'. Cooperation in the IFOR operation for the former Yugoslavia could make the difference here; the success of the new post-IFOR deployment is far from certain, but it is already clear that joint work in Bosnia has changed the attitude among the Russian military towards the NATO role in this conflict. That relations between Russia and NATO remain conflictual and that the issue of enlargement could bring new crises is a well-recognized fact of political life.[52] But Russia's decision to sign the Partnership for Peace programme, however hesitant and conditional, leaves the way open for new ties to be fostered. The Founding Act on Mutual Relations, Cooperation and Security between NATO and Russia, signed in May 1997, offers further cooperation on conflict prevention through diplomacy and joint peacekeeping missions. It is to be hoped that these new channels and links may contribute to the painful recovery of the Russian army from the 'Chechen syndrome', allowing it to rethink and reframe its role in conflict management. Ultimately, only the Russian army is capable of carrying the burden of peacekeeping in the CIS region; and it needs help rather than supervision, because its failure in this undertaking would be in nobody's interests.

Acknowledgments

The author's research in this field has been supported by the Norwegian ministry of defence and also by the NATO Democratic Institutions Fellowship, in addition to the Volkswagen Foundation. The author wishes to thank the commentators at the RIIA seminar in September 1995 and also the participants in the seminars at the Research Institute for International Policy and Security (Ebenhausen) in February 1996, the NATO Defence College in November 1996, and the Wilton Park Conference Centre in December 1996.

Notes

1. See 'Strategy for Russia 2: Theses of the Council on Foreign and Defence Policy', *Nezavisimaya gazeta*, 27 May 1994: the first report from this newly created council (established in 1992) that introduced the idea of an enlightened post-imperial course which should moderate the competition with the West and provide for conflict management in the near abroad. For a keen review see Suzanne Crow, 'Competing Blueprints for Russian Foreign Policy', Radio Free Europe/Radio Liberty *Research Report*, vol. 1, no. 50, 18 December 1992.
2. This essentially symbolic step received unusually sharp criticism from the United States. Secretary of State Warren Christopher, speaking in Kiev, said that the vote in the Duma had a certain quality of intimidation and was highly irresponsible. See Steven Erlanger, 'US Condemns Duma Vote Backing a Soviet Revival', *International Herald Tribune*, 20 March 1996.
3. The same can be said about the Union Treaty with Belarus, signed with great fanfare a few days later against the background of violent protest rallies in Minsk. These developments are analysed in greater detail in Pavel Baev, 'Russia's Departure from Empire: Self-Assertiveness and a New Retreat', in Ola Tunander, ed., *Geopolitics in Post-Wall Europe* (London: Sage, 1997).
4. Emil Pain, one of the sober voices in the Presidential Council, arguing against imperialistic aspirations, warned that expansion towards Abkhazia, Crimea or northern Kazakstan would create a peculiar hatred zone on the parts of the independent states remaining after annexation. See Emil Pain, 'Russia and Post-

Soviet Space', *Moscow News*, no. 8, 25 February–3 March 1994.

5. Former Russian foreign minister Kozyrev routinely exploited this premise: in regional conflicts, the intensity of which keeps mounting, there is simply no alternative to the use of force for the purposes of peacekeeping. For Russia this kind of isolationism would entail millions of refugees and chaos along the perimeter of the southern borders. See Andrei Kozyrev, 'Peace with a Sword', *Moscow News*, no. 36, 9–15 September 1994.

6. On Lebed's role see Sven G. Simonsen, 'Going His Own Way: A Profile of General Alexander Lebed', *Journal of Slavic Military Studies*, vol. 8, no. 3, 1995. The most outspoken and well-informed critic of the 14th Army's political performance is Vladimir Socor; see 'Russia's 14th Army and the Insurgency in Eastern Moldova', RFE/RL *Research Report*, vol. 1, no. 36, 11 September 1992, and 'Russia's Army in Moldova: There to Stay?', ibid., vol. 2, no. 25, 18 June 1993.

7. As Migranyan, who claims the laurels of reinventing the Monroe Doctrine for Russia, put it: 'Rutskoi giving full support to the actions of the 14th Army in Transdniestria and going tough towards the Moldovan leadership contributed substantially to the stabilization in Transdniestria.' See Andranik Migranyan, 'Russia and the Near Abroad', *Nezavisimaya gazeta*, 12 January 1994.

8. The agreement between the Russian government, Georgian State Council (an interim body created after the January 1992 coup against President Gamsakhurdia) and the South Ossetian Supreme Soviet (which Georgia refused to recognize as a legitimate body) was finalized at a meeting between Yeltsin and Shevardnadze during the CSCE summit in Helsinki on 9 June 1992. For a precise analysis see Suzanne Crow, 'The Theory and Practice of Peacekeeping in the Former USSR', RFE/RL *Research Report*, vol. 1, no. 37, 18 September 1992.

9. Felix Corley, 'The Ingush-Ossetian Conflict', *Jane's Intelligence Review*, vol. 6, no. 9, September 1994.

10. Lena Neumann and Sergei Solodovnik, 'The Case of Tajikistan', in Lena Jonson and Clive Archer, eds, *Peacekeeping and the Role of Russia in Eurasia* (Boulder: Westview Press, 1996), pp. 83–101.

11. For an accurate record see Catherine Dale, 'Turmoil in Abkhazia: Russian Responses', RFE/RL *Research Report*, vol. 2, no. 34, 27 August 1993.

12. See 'Strategy for Russia 2'; Victor Kuvaldin, 'Caucasian Options for Russia and Georgia', *Moscow News*, no. 43, 25 October–1 November 1992.

13. For a useful analysis see Roy Allison, *Peacekeeping in the Soviet Successor States*, Chaillot Paper 18 (Paris: Institute for Security Studies/WEU, November 1994).

14. Only by early 1995 did this trend begin to be recognized by some Western experts, despite the dark shadow of Chechenia. Benjamin Lambeth, for example, made the point that the military nonetheless remains a responsible and stabilizing force in Russian society, adding the observation that the high command genuinely seems to want Washington to perceive its near abroad peacekeeping activities as legitimate actions for the defence of Russian security and not as a pretext for rebuilding an empire. See Benjamin S. Lambeth, 'Russia's Wounded Military', *Foreign Affairs*, vol. 74, no. 2, March/April 1995, pp. 86–7, 95.

15. A mini-crisis erupted in late October when defence minister Grachev announced plans to suspend military withdrawals and one week later President Yeltsin issued a decree authorizing such a suspension and expressing profound concerns over numerous infringements of rights of the Russian-speaking population. Western comments draw a parallel with Gorbachev's bowing to military pressure in early 1991. See Jim Hoagland, 'With the Baltics, Yeltsin Heads Down that Same Unfortunate Path', *International Herald Tribune*, 5 November 1992.

16. John Lough, 'The Place of the Near Abroad in Russian Foreign Policy', RFE/RL *Research Report*, vol. 2, no. 11, 12 March 1993, p. 24.

17. Among the numerous attempts to trace these developments, Suzanne Crow's penetrating analysis deserves special mention; both the quotations in the text here are from Suzanne Crow, 'Russia Seeks Leadership in Regional Peacekeeping', RFE/RL *Research Report*, vol. 2, no. 15, 9 April 1993.

18. *Izvestiya*, 8 October 1993.

19. Thus, at a press conference marking the second anniversary of the Russian army, Grachev repeated the point that the withdrawal of Russian troops is closely linked to the guarantee of normal life for the Russian-speaking population, adding an explicit threat that it won't take long to send reinforcements. See Stephen Foye, 'Grachev Threatens Estonia with Reinforcements', RFE/RL *News Brief*, 9 May 1994.

20. Kozyrev declared that Russia's vital interests were concentrated in the CIS and the Baltic states and specified that raising the question of Russia's complete military withdrawal from the near abroad came as close to being an extremist approach as the idea of sending tanks into all republics for establishing some imperial order; see Alexei Pushkov, 'Kozyrev Started a Game on Alien Field', *Moskovskie novosti*,

no. 4, 23–30 January 1994. The prime ministers of Estonia, Latvia and Lithuania in a joint communiqué condemned Kozyrev's statement as directed against the sovereignty of the Baltic states. Dzintra Bungs, 'Baltic Premiers Say Kozyrev's Statement a Threat', RFE/RL *News Brief,* 20 January 1994.

21. One exception was the month-long deployment of Russian troops into Poti and along the key coastal railway, which helped to defeat the pro-Gamsakhurdia rebellion in western Georgia in November 1993. As Vladimir Baranovsky argued, it was a strange war, closer to farce than a large-scale tragedy: see Baranovsky, 'Conflict Developments on the Territory of the Former Soviet Union', in *SIPRI Yearbook 1994* (Oxford: Oxford University Press, 1994).

22. The CIS mandate for this operation was provided *post factum* in October 1994, but what really distinguished this operation was UN recognition and observation through UNOMIG, though it certainly stopped far short of Shevardnadze's appeal to the UN to take a real peacekeeping role. See Allison, *Peacekeeping in the Soviet Successor States*, pp. 46–7.

23. See Elizabeth Fuller, 'The Karabakh Mediation Process: Grachev versus the CSCE?', RFE/RL *Research Report*, vol. 3, no. 23, 10 June 1994.

24. The directive gave formal approval to the defence ministry's intention to establish some thirty military bases in the neighbouring countries, including Latvia. After a formal protest from the latter, a clarification was given that the radar station at Skrunda could not be defined as a military base; Russia's foreign ministry denied any responsibility for the directive or for the technical errors it contained. See Stephen Foye, 'Confusion in Moscow on Military Base Directive', RFE/RL *News Brief*, 8 April 1994.

25. General Lebed immediately responded with a statement that any withdrawal would upset the fragile balance of military-political forces and result in nationalization and privatization of the huge military stockpile in the region. Russia's deputy defence minister Kondratyev visited the 14th Army headquarters in late November and reassured the officers that no withdrawal mechanism or schedule had been finalized. See FBIS-SOV-94-231, 1 December 1994.

26. Mark Galeotti, 'Decline and Fall: Moscow's Chechen War', *Jane's Intelligence Review*, vol. 7, no. 2, February 1995.

27. It was former deputy defence minister Gromov who insisted most on the pre-eminence of the political side of peacekeeping over the military operations, and in this respect referred to his Afghan experience. See e.g. interview with Gromov in *Krasnaya zvezda*, 27 November 1993.

28. Brian Urquart defined most precisely the viable political context and the feasibility of the mandate as conditions for the success of peacekeeping; see Urquart, 'Beyond the Sheriff's Posse', *Survival*, vol. 32, no. 3, May/June 1990, pp. 196–205. This is not to say that these conditions are always met, and as Featherston has correctly pointed out, forced ambiguities, which reflect the lowest common denominator of agreement, leave peacekeepers caught in the middle of varying interpretations of equivocal documents: A. B. Featherston, *Towards a Theory of United Nations Peacekeeping* (New York: St Martin's Press, 1994), p. 37.

29. Deputy defence minister Kondratyev, who was in charge of several operations in 1992–4, made the point in a number of interviews that in certain situations the military could take on the essentially political task of negotiating the mandate for an operation; see Georgi Kondratyev, 'Russia's Blue Helmets', *Krasnaya zvezda*, 16 February 1993. This approach was taken particularly for the operation in Abkhazia launched in June 1994.

30. Suzanne Crow, pointing out that from late 1993 Russian officials openly described peacekeeping as a method of exerting influence, added: 'Russia's ceasing to hide its great power ambitions behind the rhetorically more palatable guise of humanitarian assistance is a direct result of the implicit acceptance of these ambitions by the West.' See Crow, 'Russia Asserts its Strategic Agenda', RFE/RL *Research Report*, vol. 2, no. 50, December 1993.

31. The incompatibility between the declared goal of national reconciliation and the real conduct of the operation became especially obvious in late 1994/early 1995 when Russian border troops refused to take into account the Tehran agreement between the Tajik government and the opposition that established a ceasefire from 20 October. It led to an escalation of clashes on the border, particularly after April 1995. See Vitaly Strugovets, 'Shots in the Back: Russian Border Guards are Under Fire', *Krasnaya zvezda*, 24 December 1994.

32. Deputy defence minister Kondratyev mentioned the figure of 16,000 in several interviews in early 1994, also specifying that 107 Russian soldiers were killed and 193 wounded in these operations. See e.g. *Segodnya*, 17 March 1993.

33. Besides the battalions that formally had peacekeeping status (in Transdniestria, South Ossetia and UNPROFOR), this includes also the 14th Army in Transdniestria, the 201st Division and border troops

in Tajikistan, army and interior troops units in North Ossetia and army units in Abkhazia. For more data see Baev, *The Russian Army in a Time of Troubles* (London: Sage, 1996), ch. 5.

34. As far as Nagorno-Karabakh was concerned, Grachev's apparent readiness to bring Russian peacekeepers in reflected partly plans to deploy primarily the units from the Transcaucasus group of forces and partly expectations of securing international financing, perhaps from the UN peacekeeping budget. Boutros Boutros Ghali, during his visit to Moscow in April 1994, indicated some flexibility on the latter issue. See Suzanne Crow, 'Results of Boutros Ghali Visit: Statement on Peacekeeping', RFE/RL *News Brief*, 6 April 1994.

35. See *Arms Control Reporter*, 1994, 407.B.509. This did not include the armaments of the 30,000-strong Transcaucasus group of forces (in 1995 it had some 310 tanks, 490 ACVs and 320 artillery items). The 14th Army in Transdniestria, with its 120 tanks, also comes under the CFE Treaty flank limits.

36. Richard Falkenrath provides a very detailed and precise diagnosis of this problem, and his prediction that it would not be solved before the CFE Treaty deadline because of insufficient political efforts was borne out by events. See Richard A. Falkenrath, 'The CFE Flank Dispute: Waiting in the Wings', *International Security*, vol. 19, no. 4, Spring 1995, pp. 118–44.

37. Charles Dobbie, 'A Concept for Post-Cold War Peacekeeping', *Survival*, vol. 36, no. 3, Autumn 1994. Giving a seminar at the Norwegian Defence College on 8 June 1994, Lt-Col. Dobbie provided details such as warning on the use of force and escape routes, the latter meaning that lethal force should not be used against belligerents who are in a position from which they cannot escape. From a Russian perspective, such requirements are simply incomprehensible.

38. I pointed out this symptomatic linguistic deficiency in Pavel Baev, 'Russia's Experiments and Experience in Conflict Management and Peacemaking', *International Peacekeeping*, vol. 1, no. 3, Autumn 1994. A Russian participant in the first US–Russian peacekeeping exercises in August 1994 became famous with the comment: 'They used the same tactics as we do, but I think they shot too late and they made too much noise.' *Newsweek*, 19 September 1994.

39. Useful analysis of the evolving operational principles can be found in James M. Green, 'The Peacekeeping Doctrines of the CIS', *Jane's Intelligence Review*, vol. 5, no. 4, April 1993. A discussion on the alternative models of coming symbolically versus coming in force among several officers involved in the training programme in the Volga MD in the pages of *Voennyy Vestnik* was keenly analysed by Roy Allison in *Peacekeeping in the Soviet Successor States*.

40. Aleksandr Lebed, 'Does Russia Need the Mobile Forces?', *Segodnya*, 7 February 1996.

41. A summary of the doctrine was published with substantial omissions. For an English translation see *Jane's Intelligence Review*, Special Report, January 1994. For a comprehensive analysis see Charles S. Dick, 'The Military Doctrine of the Russian Federation', *Journal of Slavic Military Studies*, vol. 7, no. 3, September 1994.

42. What makes this burden-sharing possible is the accelerated increase of combat capabilities of the interior troops and other special forces. See Mark Galeotti, 'Russia's Internal Security Forces: Does More Mean Better?', *Jane's Intelligence Review*, vol. 6, no. 6, June 1994. Quite typical in this respect is the largest ever counter-terrorist operation in Budennovsk in June 1995, where some 2,500 interior troops and such special units as Alfa confronted some 200 Chechen militants.

43. Ivan Vorobyev, 'White Spots in the Theory or What is Lacking for Peacekeeping', *Krasnaya zvezda*, 22 February 1994; A. Raevsky and I. N. Vorobev, *Russian Approaches to Peacekeeping Operations*, UNIDIR Research Papers no. 28, 1994 (New York and Geneva: United Nations).

44. According to Charles Dobbie ('A Concept for Post-Cold War Peacekeeping'), the British Army field manual *Wider Peacekeeping* postulates that there is no middle ground between peacekeeping and peace enforcement and that these two types of operations are guided by radically different principles.

45. Roy Allison (*Peacekeeping in the Soviet Successor States*) and Michael Orr ('Peacekeeping: A New Task for Russian Military Doctrine', *Jane's Intelligence Review*, vol. 6, no. 8, July 1994) arrived at similar conclusions, while Mark Galeotti ('Russia and Eurasia: Out-of-Area Operations and Peacekeeping', in *The World In Conflict 1994/95: Jane's Intelligence Review Yearbook*, pp. 30–35) insists on the distinction between peacekeeping and peace enforcement operations referring to two different Russian terms: *Operatsii po poderzhaniyu mira* (literally, operations in support of peace) and *Mirotvorcheskie operatsii* (literally, peacekeeping operations). In fact, the terms are often used interchangeably and, for example, the joint US–Russian exercises in August 1994 were called *mirotvorcheskie* although nothing other than traditional peacekeeping skills were involved in the training.

46. Yuri Afanasev and Len Karpinsky, 'Again at Russia's Crossroads', *Moskovskie novosti*, no. 32, 7–14 May 1995.

47. The operation plans which Grachev presented in February 1996, while most probably produced *post factum*, also confirm that the aim was to push the pro-Dudayev forces slowly southwards, giving them every opportunity to leave Grozny (Pavel Grachev, 'We Must Proceed from the Fact that this was a Special Operation', *Krasnaya zvezda*, 2 March 1995). I feel more confident about this assumption about a quasi-peacekeeping military plan for Chechenia after discussing it with Jacob Kipp at a seminar organized by the Swedish National Defence Research Establishment on 26 April 1996.

48. Michael Orr, 'Peacekeeping and Overstretch in the Russian Army', *Jane's Intelligence Review*, vol. 6, no. 9, July 1994.

49. Galeotti, 'Russia and Eurasia'.

50. Pavel Baev, 'Drifting Away from Europe', *Transition*, vol. 1, June 1995.

51. By late May 1996, at the time this chapter was completed, it remained by no means clear whether the operation will happen, but the OSCE High Level Planning Group has developed quite detailed deployment plans.

52. Alexei Arbatov, 'Nato and Russia', *Security Dialogue*, vol. 26, no. 2, June 1995.

12 The Tajikistan conflict as a regional security dilemma

Sergei Solodovnik

In the absence of tangible common external military threats, an important test of military and security policy coordination or, beyond that, integration among the CIS states lies in their response to regional conflicts within or on the borders of individual CIS states. The Russian response to such conflicts, and particularly the extent to which Moscow responds unilaterally or through collective CIS initiatives, is also telling. In this sense an analysis of the civil conflict in Tajikistan and associated efforts to seal the Tajik–Afghan border can contribute to an understanding of efforts towards integration and security policy dynamics in the broader CIS region. It also represents a case study of the specific interlocking (and to some extent diverging) security interests of a number of CIS states, most notably Tajikistan and Uzbekistan.

The following analysis shows the intractability of certain kinds of conflict and the unpredictable outcome of efforts to manipulate them. Such conflicts generate a continuing low level of instability in a number of the southern CIS states, and dependent client regimes may come to exercise a degree of 'reverse leverage' on Russia. Russia may become locked into conflicts for the lack of an alternative policy or as the 'lesser evil' relative to the security policy uncertainties of a military withdrawal. This raises questions about how far Russia is capable of assuming the burden of security policy manager in the CIS region and about the adverse effects of such attempts on less ambitious plans for military and security policy coordination among CIS states.

Tajikistan: problems of state cohesion

Geography does not favour the cohesion of Tajikistan. Half of the republic is situated in the Pamir foothills; the other half lies above 3,000 metres, mostly in the Gorno-Badakhshan region stretching up into the Pamir mountains and bordering on China and Afghanistan. That makes the majority of the country a grey zone, barely subject to effective control by the central authorities in times of turmoil. Only the valleys, perhaps some 15 per cent of the territory, are permanently inhabited.

Many Tajiks reside outside Tajikistan. The majority of the 3 million Persian-speakers in Afghanistan identify themselves as Tajiks, and according to official data from Uzbekistan there are some 700,000 Tajiks living in that country. Tajik ethnographers, on the other hand, maintain that this number may be as high as 3 million, depending on how Uzbeks are distinguished from Tajiks. Moreover, the historical Tajik cultural centres of Samarkand and Bukhara, which enjoyed the status of independent khanates for centuries, were absorbed by Uzbekistan when Central Asia was divided into republics in the first decade of Soviet power. This settlement produced uneasy feelings on the part of Tajiks and fears of separatism on the part of the ruling Uzbek authorities.

Trans-border and trans-ethnic factors play a decisive role in shaping regional security perceptions. In the Tajik lowlands and border areas there are large numbers of Uzbeks. In Kurgan-Tyube alone, more than a third of the population declare themselves to belong to that ethnic group. A recurrent theme in Uzbek nationalist rhetoric is that Tajiks are simply Persianized Uzbeks – that is, Turkic peoples who have succumbed to Persian cultural temptations or pressures and have taken on foreign ways. So far, such theories are not voiced at the top official level, but Tajiks living in the neighbourhood cannot take this general attitude lightly.

Tajikistan now seems, of all the countries of the former Soviet Central Asia, the one most vulnerable to Islamic extremism. Together with what later became Uzbekistan, it used to share the status of the most orthodox territory.[1] The Islamic upsurge in Tajikistan presents an immediate danger to the authoritarian regime of Karimov in Uzbekistan because of the possibility of spill-over effects. Kazakstan and Kyrgyzstan may subsequently also become vulnerable if Islamic groups gain the upper hand in Dushanbe. For this reason Russia found no difficulty in recruiting allies in the region at the start of its intervention in Tajikistan.

The majority of the arable lands in Tajikistan are located in the northern parts of the country, which geographically constitute part of the Fergana valley. This valley, which spans Tajikistan, Uzbekistan and Kyrgyzstan, is densely populated, and is vital to Uzbekistan, where the major part of it is situated, as well as to Kyrgyzstan. For purely economic reasons, therefore, Uzbekistan would have to intervene strongly if the northern part of Tajikistan became unstable and this instability threatened to spill over into adjacent Uzbek territory.

Today's Tajikistan can hardly claim to be a self-sustaining state. Declines in both GDP and industrial output are dramatic, having plummeted to less than 20 per cent of the levels attained before the civil war broke out. Its budget is almost totally supported by foreign, notably Russian, donations: massive external assistance enabled Dushanbe to produce a miracle in its budget statistics, with total income more than twice the level of expenditures.

During the period of civil war (summer 1992 to spring 1993) and the subsequent guerrilla campaign (which has continued at varying levels of intensity ever since), large portions of the population switched to military or military-related occupations as the major source of their normal income. Such activities included trafficking in guns and supplies, imposing taxes on those crossing the areas under the control of local warlords, or distributing and trading in humanitarian aid. As the normal economic network became disrupted, the paramilitary economy provided the only means of survival for the conflict-affected areas. The example of neighbouring Afghanistan demonstrates that such a pattern may become so entrenched that generations may come to know only the economy of the gun. Over 70 years of Soviet rule plus almost half a century of forced industrialization and accompanying urbanization had, moreover, only a limited impact on the traditional behavioural patterns and values of ethnic Tajiks. In the cities, traditional affiliations and clan-type relations were effectively conserved, and it was these that provided the means of mobilizing the combatant factions during the civil war.

Limits of Russian and CIS intervention in Tajikistan

Russia justifies its direct interference in Tajikistan by the principles of Chapter 51 of the UN Charter, and by the 1992 CIS Tashkent collective security agreement. For a number of months Russia was hesitant about whether to intervene or not, and in the first months of the civil war in spring 1992 the Russian 201st Motorized Rifle Division stayed on combat alert but neutral. The greatest concern of all the intervening parties in Tajikistan was to restore some semblance of order in the country, although the peacekeeping force claimed that its task was the protection of the country from external threat.

While the Tajik opposition entrenched itself on adjacent Afghan territory, forming refugee and training camps together with support bases, and establishing liaison arrangements with the local warlords, part of the peacekeeping function did become the task of protection against a threat (to the incumbent regime) from abroad. Russia maintains border guards on the Tajik–Afghan border almost solely at its own cost. Nevertheless, the strip of outposts proved unable to seal off the border effectively. The opposition can choose to cross the border whenever it wishes. If it prefers to harass Russian border troops, sizeable Russian casualties may be inflicted.

Russian garrisons inside Tajikistan have been reliable to a degree but only in maintaining peace in large cities and towns. The countryside has been mainly a grey zone, not effectively controlled by either the peacekeepers or the armed forces reporting to Dushanbe. The situation is much worse in Gorno-

Badakhshan, where local warlords exercise almost total control in the towns, villages and mountain passes. The general situation resembles some of the societal changes that occurred in Afghanistan during its protracted war. As noted above, a large part of the population has been removed from civilian sectors of the economy, especially from industry, services and commerce, and has entered paramilitary units. Since the population has become dislocated *en masse*, any peacekeeping force has to engage not merely mobilized guerrilla forces but large portions of the population. Thus, the Russian strategy to seal the Tajikistan border against guerrilla incursions from abroad has proved neither adequate as a peacekeeping effort nor effective as a deterrence strategy. The opposition units may easily penetrate Tajikistan and disperse in any particular location deep inside the territory.

Russian and CIS troops have been subject to various types of attack and harassment. Border posts have been repeatedly attacked by superior opposition forces both from across the border and from the rear. Some posts were held only with massive artillery and air assistance from regular army units, with border guards barely able to hold the ground. In order to discourage the opposition, which is based on Afghan territory, Russian troops engaged the adjacent Afghan areas either in the form of air and artillery barrage, or in attempted hot pursuit operations. Though there was an understanding that in extreme cases such cross-border operations could be conducted on a larger scale, this threat had limited effect. Afghan warlords have appeared to be little influenced by the civilian losses associated with such threats.

The initial appointment of Colonel-General Pyankov to lead Russian troops in Tajikistan was further evidence of interventionism by Moscow. Coming from the Leninabad (Khodjent) region, this general was supported by both the local clans and Uzbekistan's President Karimov. But interventionism without a supporting coalition appears beyond the means of the weakened Russia. Any officer stationed in Tajikistan may note the basic difference between the war in Afghanistan and his present situation. The Soviet troops during the Afghan war enjoyed reliable communication lines with their home territory. By contrast, present lines in Tajikistan may be impaired by any intense fighting between the 1st and the 11th Brigades of the government forces in Kurgan-Tyube.[2] According to some estimates, during the severe clashes of 17 September 1995 at least 200 men were killed and even more wounded, including a casualty in the UN observer mission.[3] It seems that control of the situation has been steadily eroded, whatever the numerical strength or technical capabilities of the government troops aided by the Russian expeditionary corps.

Sergei Solodovnik

The Russian involvement: a plausible rationale

Since 1992, a number of rationales for the Russian military involvement in Tajikistan have been advanced. The first stated objective was to secure the southern border of the CIS, which was proclaimed to be an extension of the Russian Federation frontier. Indeed, given the transparent borders between Russia and Kazakstan and non-existent controls within Central Asia, keeping the old Union border under direct control may seem a necessary expedient. This view may be contested, however, because when President Karimov opted to secure the border between Tajikistan and Uzbekistan in 1993, he did so quite effectively. Untrained Uzbek soldiers and a barely armed militia were quite sufficient for the task. It seems evident that the same approach, namely to confine turmoil to Tajikistan, could be a realistic option for Russia. Moscow, nevertheless, has chosen another strategy.

The second objective has been repeatedly cited by Russian top leaders since at least 1993: that all the territory of the former Soviet Union, or what is awkwardly termed the near abroad, is in the Russian sphere of vital national interest. As Tajikistan undoubtedly falls within this sphere, this view helps explain Russian interventionism and peacemaking on Russian terms. Such a strategy was reaffirmed by the September 1995 Guidelines on Russian policy towards the CIS signed by President Yeltsin.[4] Although there is some logic to such a strategy, it is overall far from rational. Russia's economic donations to Tajikistan in pursuit of this line are disproportionate to the likely benefits, if any.[5] Russia cannot conduct a policy based on a high degree of direct control over Tajikistan without the consent and assistance of the other Central Asian states, and they are becoming rather wary of Moscow's intentions and conduct here. Protection of ethnic Russians living in the conflict area is also part of this rationale; but the Russian community has declined dramatically since the civil war erupted, and Russian peacemaking efforts have not been able to discourage a further exodus. Soon there may be almost no Russians to protect in Tajikistan.

The third apparent objective is to curb a perceived radical Islamic threat. To be sure, the militant opposition, which is primarily of a radical Islamic form, has been checked for the time being. However, the more radical Islamic groups are engaged on the battlefield, the larger is the human resource pool they can count on in the future. This is suggested by events in various locations, including among others Iran, Afghanistan and Algeria.

Checking Islamic extremism is probably the only policy objective in its Tajikistan policy for which Moscow can hope to attract some foreign sympathy. Western states, China and India, as well as adjacent secular Central Asian states, may be expected to support this goal. Yet the West may feel discouraged from supporting Russia too far in an anti-Islamic drive in the area; China is very cautious about Islam in the region, though on guard against any extremist fundamentalist spill-over to Xinjiang; India has little influence in practical politics in Central Asia; and the local states understand that a stalemate cannot last for ever. Since in the future the present Tajik opposition may share power in Tajikistan, the leaders of Uzbekistan and Kazakstan are gradually withdrawing their support for Rakhmonov.

The last objective that Russia is pursuing in Tajikistan is related to the broader and more conspicuous task of forging a military alliance among the CIS member states. In September 1995 President Yeltsin declared that creating a new Warsaw Pact out of the former Union republics could serve as a counter-measure to NATO expansion eastward. Whether such a game plan is realistic, feasible or sufficient is arguable, but there are some indications that it will be attempted, at least in the short term. The conflict in Tajikistan may be perceived by Moscow as a means of increasing loyalty on the part of the states of Central Asia and their cohesion in a projected CIS alliance.

All in all, it seems that Russian attempts to play the role of arbiter in Tajikistan are the product of inertia and emotion, rather than the result of calculation and proactive planning.

Outcome scenarios

Four future contingencies are possible for Tajikistan: stalemate; a coalition government; a victory for the opposition; or fragmentation of the country. They promise significantly different impacts on regional stability.

A stalemate would mean a civil war held at the present, low-to-medium level of tension. Russian troops would be essential for peacemaking. However, if the Taliban capture of Kabul and its pressure on northern Afghanistan in 1996–7 lead eventually to the fall of northern Afghanistan to more extreme Islamic political forces, the numerical strength of the border guards on the Tajik side of the Tajik–Afghan border would need to be doubled or even tripled. In the scenario of stalemate some territories of Tajikistan would remain outside the control of the Dushanbe government, and more clashes within the armed forces of the republic could be expected. The traditional alliance between the Kulyabis and Khodjentis might break apart, and the economic crisis would deepen. Russian control of the interior might be limited to the Dushanbe area. Pressure on Russia from Iran, Turkey and other members of the Organization of Islamic Conference would increase. Uzbekistan might further distance itself from the Russian war effort in Tajikistan, and Kazakstan would be likely to follow suit, though on somewhat milder terms. International organizations would be more observant and critical of Russian operations, thus limiting their effectiveness in a military sense and destroying their political credibility. Under a stalemate scenario, however, the effects in respect of the spill-over of conflict and radical Islam into other CIS states seem rather limited. This scenario would be qualified if alarm over Taliban encroachments in Afghanistan leads to greater reliance by Uzbekistan on Russian military guarantees. Russian aid to the Tajik armed forces was increased by early 1997 in response to Taliban military successes and Russian defence minister Rodionov met Central Asian defence ministers in Tashkent to discuss the scenario of a Taliban breakthrough north to the Tajik (CIS) border and possible clashes with units of the armed forces of the Central Asian states, Russian border guards, and peacekeeping troops.[6]

The second scenario, of a coalition government, was brought closer by an agreement signed between President Imomali Rakhmonov and the leader of the united opposition, Abdullo Nuri, in December 1996 to establish a Commission of National Reconciliation in which the Tajik government and the opposition would be represented. A separate protocol was signed which prescribed a referendum on a new constitution, a new election law, reforms of the executive powers to include representatives of the opposition at all levels and suggestions for the date of new elections to take place under UN and OSCE monitoring.[7] This agreement resulted in a ceasefire which held in general until a peace agreement was signed in Moscow in June 1997 by Rakhmonov and Nuri, which indicated that Russia had finally accepted the need to find an accommodation with the opposition and to put corresponding pressure on Rakhmonov for concessions.

However, the prospects for a coalition government are not at all clear, since in some circumstances it could dramatically aggravate the domestic situation and create extra pressure on peacekeeping efforts. Two factors would determine the future of the country: namely, who held the key ministerial positions, especially in the army, police force and security units; and how power was shared regionally. If the present government manages to retain the key positions, while the opposition is granted ceremonial posts such as those of vice-president or parliamentary speaker, plus education, environment and health ministries, a new stage of the civil war could ensue. For a country with a poor commitment to legal principles and already great disrespect for the idea of democratic representation, disregard for any election results would lead to mass unrest and hostilities. Any distribution of power in that country should be based on a realistic assessment of the balance-of-power potentials of the two sides. If Russia tips this balance in favour of one single party, the other will avoid any cooperation with Russian troops and Russian or international observers and mediators.

Political stabilization at the provincial level seems crucial for the effective maintenance of peace. An ideal scenario would involve impartial governance at the centre coupled with regional governments recruited from the local people, who have refrained from joining sides during the conflict. However, such an arrangement seems far from realization.

The third scenario, a victory for the opposition, is an option possible only after a Russian withdrawal. It would require a drastic reappraisal of Russian strategy in both Tajikistan and in Central Asia as a whole. If this happened, Islamic influences in the region would greatly increase, Uzbekistan would feel still more insecure and overall regional stability would be gravely undermined.

The final scenario, the fragmentation of the country, could be the by-product of an unstable distribution of power between the present government and the opposition. If any of the parties felt unhappy with the accommodation reached, it could retreat to its regional support base and dissociate that area from the control of the central government. A fragmentation of Tajikistan could also result from massive intervention by either Uzbekistan or Afghanistan, in the event of the withdrawal of Russian troops.

If Uzbekistan were to enter the northern quarter of Tajikistan, and Afghan Tajiks were to hold the southern part, such a partition might prove quite stable in the short run, though a nationalist movement might undermine this arrangement in the longer term. Such an outcome would not necessarily need to be fixed *de jure*, and a nominal government and parliament could hold their sessions in Dushanbe, if only to satisfy international mediators.

It should be noted that the international community has few resources to influence the situation if regional actors opt for such a strategy. Indeed, this outcome could result from a perception by Russia that it had become overextended through its involvement in Tajikistan.

The role of Uzbekistan

Though Russia is currently the key foreign player in Tajikistan, the war is also greatly influenced by regional neighbours. Uzbekistan is the main CIS state involved besides Russia and wields considerable influence. The Uzbek minority in Tajikistan is a decisive factor in the Khodjent area. The energy supply from Tashkent is critical to Dushanbe, and access through the only reliable land route from Russia depends on the cooperation of Uzbekistan.

At the same time, Uzbekistan has much at stake in the Tajik civil war and Uzbek leaders perceive the main Islamic extremist threat as stemming from Tajikistan. Any unrest in the Tajik-populated areas of Uzbekistan is against the vital Uzbek interests of domestic stability. If an enlarged Tajikistan were to be formed from an amalgamation of Tajik areas of Afghanistan plus Tajikistan, that could produce a regional rival, a direct contender to Uzbekistan. If Tajikistan were to be absorbed by Iran in any form, either through the creation of a proxy regime or through Iranian direction of its foreign policy, the threat to Uzbekistan would be no less.

An ideal course for Tashkent would be a peaceful, non-aligned and semi-isolated Tajikistan, preferably united with Uzbekistan in some form of regional integration scheme. Yet it could be argued that Tajikistan is likely to achieve peace and stability only with the help of some foreign power other than Uzbekistan, and for this reason Uzbek interests may be satisfied in the medium term with a situation in which the current war and instability continue. This would help to preserve Uzbek leverage on Tajikistan. Naturally this is a costly approach, which involves direct support for the Uzbek diaspora in Tajikistan, plus the expense of maintaining extra troops on the borders, and low expectations about economic returns from the gas and energy supplies delivered to Rakhmonov. Judging by the actions of President Karimov, he believes that this approach is not an excessive price to pay for checking the influence and expansion of other powers in Tajikistan.

Tashkent is also aware of the way in which Moscow is using its influence in Tajikistan in order to contain Uzbekistan. While new treaties within the CIS were being negotiated and signed in the first half of 1996, President Karimov was wary about Russian appeals for CIS integration. All the Central Asian nations apart from Uzbekistan agreed with Russia on cooperation over defence of their outer (former Soviet) borders at a CIS summit in February 1996. Kazakstan and Kyrgyzstan have joined Russia and Belarus in the quadripartite treaty on cooperation, signed in Moscow in March 1996, which formed, at least on paper, a common customs area. Kazakstan, Tajikistan and Kyrgyzstan also joined Russia and China in April 1996 in an agreement on confidence-building measures within the border area of the five states. A formal treaty between these states on military force reductions along the former Soviet–Chinese border was signed in Moscow in April 1997. Uzbek officials apparently felt ignored by Moscow because of the lack of consultation before the important initial agreement of April 1996 between the five Asian nations was signed.[8] During recent years, Uzbek officials claim, Moscow has repeatedly used its direct political and military control over Tajikistan to apply extra pressure on Tashkent. In this sense Karimov may present Tajikistan's failure to join the March 1996 quadripartite treaty as a personal victory.

All in all, two factors appear to be particularly relevant for Tashkent after three years of civil war and intervention in Tajikistan. First, while there are risks attached to a continuation of war, making peace could prepare the ground for greater foreign influence in this area, vital to Uzbek security. Secondly, under no circumstances and under no scenario could Uzbekistan control the situation in Tajikistan unilaterally, although no allies seem available. Therefore Tashkent is not the champion of an effective national reconciliation for Tajikistan. Nor would stability in that country be viewed as in its interests if it is provided by a foreign intervention, even though Karimov has voiced support for the current Russian military presence in Tajikistan. Karimov has explicitly voiced his concern that Russian political instability may spill over to Uzbekistan, either directly or through Moscow's clients such as Tajikistan and Kyrgyzstan. He was also anxious in spring 1996, when the Russian Communist Party leader Gennady Zyuganov warned Yeltsin in the Russian presidential elections that Rakhmonov's regime could be susceptible to communist influences spreading from Moscow,[9] though this likelihood had declined by autumn 1996.

In the event of the fragmentation of Tajikistan, Tashkent could view as acceptable the *de facto* partitioning of Tajikistan, in a form that would bring part of the area under the control of Uzbekistan. Though this scenario could increase risks, from the viewpoint of Tashkent it would appear preferable to either the formation of a greater Tajikistan amalgamated with the Tajik areas of Afghanistan or an Iranian-controlled Tajikistan. Nevertheless, Uzbekistan remains very concerned about regional stability and maintaining a balance in the region, and would refrain from provoking any disturbances with potential spill-over effects, despite the possibility that continued low-intensity conflict in Tajikistan could promote Uzbekistan's own regional status and influence.

Conclusion: the Tajik conflict and the CIS

As a key test of conflict management in the CIS region and as a major regional security challenge, the civil conflict in Tajikistan and related foreign intervention in that country have a direct influence on integration processes in the CIS. Russia continues to maintain that peacekeeping efforts in Tajikistan are a joint CIS endeavour; but all the CIS military participants as well as other CIS states are aware that Russia is the real driving force and represents the real military capability behind 'collective' CIS peacekeeping in Tajikistan.

The case of Tajikistan has aroused much suspicion about Russia's self-proclaimed right to intervene in the post-Soviet territory when it deems this proper. While hypothetical foreign threats, including ones from Afghanistan if the Taliban extends its control further north, could result in more of a CIS consensus in joint defence operations and military planning, other contingencies for joint operations are viewed with considerable scepticism among most CIS states. The decision of Uzbekistan and Kazakstan to cut back their military, political and economic support for Rakhmonov failed in itself to influence Russian support for the official regime in Dushanbe, although by the end of 1996 the Russian position had evolved in a much more pragmatic direction. This reveals the unilateral decision-making of Russia towards Tajikistan. The impact of Russian intervention in Tajikistan on the future of multilateral CIS conflict management has been for the most part negative. The option of consulting jointly and acting unilaterally, which has clearly been preferred by Moscow, is not a means of creating better cohesion among CIS member states.

Notes

1. Shirin Akiner, 'Post-Soviet Central Asia: Past is Prologue', in Peter Ferdinand, ed., *The New Central Asia and its Neighbours* (London: RIIA/Pinter, 1994), p. 20.
2. *Segodnya*, 23 September 1995, p. 4.
3. Ibid.
4. *Rossiyskaya gazeta*, 22 September 1995.
5. Tajikistan had the lowest GDP per head when it was a Soviet republic, less than 39 per cent of the average, and this diminished to 14.3 per cent in 1993. See *Rossiya segodnya realnyy shans* (Russia Today Real Chance) (Moscow: Obozrevatel, 1994).
6. Y. Golotyuk, *Segodnya*, 22 February 1997, reporting on meeting of Rodionov with Central Asian defence ministers in late February 1997.
7. A. Dubnov, 'Tadzhikskiy Khasavyurt', *Novoe vremya 1997*, no. 12, 13 January 1997.
8. Interview with Uzbek officials concluded during author's visits to Tashkent in October and December 1995 and February 1996.
9. Interview with President Karimov on 17 February 1996, attended by the author.

13 The Chechenia conflict: military and security policy implications

Roy Allison

The conflict in Chechenia has had major repercussions for Russian security and military policies, and its destabilizing regional legacy overshadows most other security policy challenges for Russian leaders in the late 1990s. This chapter analyses the implications of this traumatic conflict in particular but not exclusively for Russia, and provides a case study for the examination of themes identified elsewhere in this volume.

The principal issues involved may be summarized as follows:

- Russian national security decision-making, as reflected in the original decision to use force in Chechenia; the failure to realize the divisiveness of a campaign against fellow Russian citizens, which was initially characterized as another peacekeeping operation;
- the critical problems in maintaining proper lines of Russian military command and control, as well as in ensuring coherent military policy decision-making throughout the conflict; divisions among the power ministries and their uncertain subordination to political authority;
- additional military operational weaknesses as revealed by the campaign; the impact of the conflict on the overall state of the Russian army and its effect as a stimulus for military reform;
- the regional effect of the conflict in the Caucasus, in the Russian Federation and for other CIS states; its impact on CIS integration trends and on the sustainability of Russian or CIS peacekeeping/peacemaking in other conflicts;
- the consequences of the Chechenia campaign on Russian security policy relations with non-CIS states, particularly Western states, and international organizations;
- the security policy consequences of efforts to ensure a peace settlement for Chechenia and future options for Russian relations with the breakaway republic.

Russian security policy decision-making: the decision to use force

The decision in autumn 1994 to use large-scale military force in Chechenia reflects core deficiencies in Russian security policy decision-making, which help explain apparent contradictions in the subsequent evolution of Russian policy towards the breakaway republic.[1] It followed an attempt by the Russian general staff and federal counter-intelligence service (the FSK) to depose the Chechen leader General Dzhokhar Dudayev through assisting Chechen opposition groups. A third attempt to do this in late November 1994 led to the capture of Russian soldiers and the exposure of these Russian special operations. Against this background Colonel-General Boris Gromov has stated that the decision to start the main military campaign was not discussed in advance at the defence ministry collegium (which had been sidelined over important defence issues during the previous two years), but agreed in secret and spontaneously by a few officials with particular support from the minister for nationality affairs and regional policy, Nikolai Yegorov.[2] Among defence officials it appears that this cabal included only defence minister Pavel Grachev and the chief of general staff Mikhail Kolesnikov, although a general staff operational team had been preparing scenarios for Chechenia, including military intervention, since October 1994.[3]

The fateful decision was taken at a Security Council meeting on 29 November 1994 involving only President Yeltsin's closest associates. But since the Security Council is only a consultative body for the president, and since a law defining its status and regulating its functions still had not been adopted by parliament, Yeltsin himself took the key decision.[4] Grachev has been portrayed as believing in a blitzkrieg solution, but after the initial disasters in Grozny he claimed that he had previously warned the Security Council that 'there will be a real war... lasting many years', a scenario which presumably was dismissed by others.[5]

This style of decision-making is reminiscent of the Soviet Politburo decision to invade Afghanistan.[6] Indeed, Gromov (the former commander of the 40th Army in Afghanistan) argued that the Afghan experience should have taught Moscow that in making a decision on military operations it is essential to take account of local historical, national, religious and geographical conditions. But nothing of the sort was done; the decision was adopted spontaneously. The upshot, he argued, was that troops dispatched to Chechenia were unprepared mentally, physically and professionally (see below).[7] Special preparation was required since, in Gromov's words, the army had never used 'against the people its entire arsenal of fighting means designed for waging a full-scale war'.

As with the decision to impose a military solution in Afghanistan, the timing of the decision to invade Chechenia was determined essentially by a political rather than a military cabal. There were Russian claims that the great majority of Russian defence ministry (MOD) and general staff officers viewed this decision quite negatively since they did not believe that the army (as opposed to the ministry of the interior) should be given the task of 'establishing constitutional order' with the help of tanks.[8] Formally, this should only have been possible after a declaration of a state of emergency in Chechenia, which was not done. The Russian State Duma therefore eventually declared the intervention unlawful and passed a law banning the use of the armed forces in the rebel republic, which Yeltsin chose to ignore.[9] The chairman of the Duma defence committee, Sergei Yushenkov, supported Russian generals who opposed the use of the regular army in resolving the crisis in Chechenia.

The decision to intervene with force overrode not only the prudence of the military leadership but also specialist advice on the North Caucasus. In early December 1994 experts from the presidential administration advised Yeltsin to impose a blockade on Chechenia and then to assemble and prepare several strong attack groups. If negotiations failed, then Russia could attack in spring 1995 and apply overwhelming military superiority from the outset. Instead, Russian politicians opted to send an unprepared army directly into battle to cover up the disastrous undercover operation against the Chechen leader Dudayev earlier in autumn 1994.[10] It was not surprising that fractures soon appeared in the command and control of Russian forces.

The challenge of internal war in Russia

For Russian officers the reimposition of an 'internal' role and mission for the regular army has been particularly controversial and unwelcome. This role (as applied to operations within the former USSR) had been virtually outlawed following the furore over repression by Soviet military forces (and those of the ministry of the interior or MVD) in Tbilisi in 1989, Vilnius in 1990 and Baku in 1991 – only to be restored and officially endorsed (despite opposition by military commanders) in the November 1993 Russian military doctrine (in relation to internal operations in the Russian Federation). As a result the demarcation of roles between the MVD, designated peacekeeping forces and regular military units became confused.

The Russian regular forces had no experience of combat in low-intensity operations against Russian Federation citizens in regions with large civilian populations, or (since the Second World War) of storming defended cities, and these proved to be critical weaknesses for combat capability and morale. The commander of Russian airborne troops, Colonel-General Yevgeny Podkolzin, reached the firm conclusion from the Chechenia campaign that 'the Army has, and will have, only an external function ... the defence of the Homeland and the Fatherland' since 'our units are not prepared to fight with our fellow countrymen – and hence these losses'. 'We are psychologically not prepared to fight on our own territory,' he concluded. Lieutenant-General Aleksandr Lebed, the controversial commander of the 14th Army, compared this Russian campaign with the 1940 campaign in Finland.[11] For the Chechens, he argued, it was a war of liberation, while the Russian soldiers did not know why they were fighting.

Podkolzin had been asked by the general staff in November 1994 to prepare regiments for a 'peacemaking operation' in Chechenia for what turned out, in his words, to be in fact 'a large-scale military conflict at the army-corps level'.[12] The idea that Russian forces could act as a 'forcible peacekeeper', by disarming warring sides in Chechenia through the introduction of a limited contingent of troops, was frustrated by the exposure and capture of Russian special forces in Chechenia before the December campaign commenced.

The mission area of military operations in Chechenia – an autonomous republic within the Russian Federation – also undermined the comparison with CIS peacekeeping. It is true that Russian officials have chosen to define as 'peacekeeping' Russia's operations around Ingushetia, even though these have involved Russian ministry of interior forces (with separate training and doctrine) rather than army units. But in fact such MVD actions should be defined as militia or policing operations, since Russian units on 'home' territory cannot be viewed as an impartial, external military agency. Such operations are clearly contrary to internationally accepted criteria for peace-keeping.

The joint operations of regular army forces, the MVD and others in Chechenia combined low- and high-intensity operations with the unambiguous goal of crushing the resistance of the principal military party in the republic. Therefore, the description of the operation as peacekeeping, as suggested by some Russian officials, is untenable. Nor does the Russian experience of military operations in Chechenia offer a body of knowledge applicable to peacekeeping efforts elsewhere in the CIS region, except in the rudimentary tactical sense of operating checkpoints and so forth. Instead, this experience has been counterproductive to peacekeeping endeavours in the CIS region through its splintering effect on the Russian military organization and by habituating the Russian MVD and regular forces (as well as the Russian public at large) to a high level of non-combatant, civilian casualties in conflict. In conflicts such as those in Tajikistan or Nagorno-Karabakh such casualties have tended to be a by-product of civil war and the actions of local military units rather than of Russian operations.

Problems of command and control

The decision to wage war against rebellious citizens of the Russian Federation under the guise of 'disarming bandit formations and establishing constitutional order', and the failure to clarify military objectives in Chechenia, help explain major breakdowns in Russian military command and control during the initial stage of the campaign, open criticism of the military campaign by senior officers, and growing cynicism among officers and personnel about their role as the war continued.

Fractures in the military establishment

During the conflict in Chechenia military authority was challenged on various levels. First, there were reports of units failing to obey orders. For example, officers from the Russian MVD Eastern District refused to be sent to Chechenia, as did some officers from the marines attached to the Pacific Fleet.[13] In the North Caucasus military district itself the ground forces, lacking training for internal or police operations, may have been loath to turn on North Caucasian peoples. This may help to explain why troops were brought to Chechenia from the centre of Russia, the Urals and Siberia. Even with such reinforcements, poor combat-readiness and morale were fully revealed in the disastrous initial Russian assault on Grozny. By the beginning of January 1995 senior military staff reportedly had 'partially lost control of their troops' and the Russian army was close to refusing to carry out orders.[14] This response was not exceptional. For example, in different circumstances, a year later interior ministry officers appeared to be on the verge of mutiny after several failed attacks on the Chechen-held village of Pervomayskaya, Dagestan. By April 1996 more than 500 staff officers had opted to leave the army 'without pension and gratuity on discharge' rather than fight in Chechenia; doubts about the competence of the Russian military high command and political leadership steadily grew among military personnel and officers.[15]

Secondly, the support of mid-level commanders for the campaign could not be taken for granted. Some Russian military commanders and units given responsibilities during the first weeks of intervention in the republic reacted with recalcitrance or defiance (notably Major-General Ivan Babichev, commander of a group of forces, who initially refused to advance his armoured column deeper into Chechenia in December 1994). The commander of the elite Kantemir tank division, Major-General Boris Polyakov, resigned in protest against the use of his subordinates in the Chechenia campaign.[16] The lack of combat-readiness of the North Caucasus military district was a key deficiency, and the refusal of its commander to organize and plan combat operations for

Chechenia (out of an awareness of this deficiency) resulted in his dismissal, together with his first deputy and his chief of staff, on 22 December.[17]

Thirdly, opposition to the Chechen campaign also surfaced at the Russian higher military command level. This reflected concerns over military operational weaknesses among the forces available as well as the choice of means to quell an 'internal' rebellion. Most prominently, on 10 December 1994 eleven generals from the military council of the ground forces led by Commander-in-Chief Colonel-General Vladimir Semenov bypassed Grachev (and therefore the official chain of command) by appealing to the State Duma and Federation Council and rejecting Grachev's view that the armed forces were combat-ready.[18]

A structural crisis in military command and control arose from the vocal opposition to the campaign by the key generals with special knowledge of low-intensity operations: Colonel-General Boris Gromov, First Deputy Defence Minister Colonel-General Georgy Kondratyev and Lieutenant-General Aleksandr Lebed (then commander of the 14th Army in Moldova). In January Kondratyev and Gromov, as well as Colonel-General Valery Mironov, were removed from their positions as deputy defence ministers (Gromov was transferred to the foreign ministry and became a deputy foreign minister).[19] Soon after this, the first deputy commander of Russian ground troops, Eduard Vorobyev, was also induced to resign for his criticism of the Chechenia campaign. These dismissals gravely weakened the military command expertise available for the conduct of operations in Chechenia and encouraged some of the dismissed generals to engage directly in political activity. The chairman of the State Duma defence committee, Sergei Yushenkov, supported the generals who opposed the use of the army in Chechenia.

The growing experience by key generals of peacekeeping efforts in the CIS region served to fuel their criticisms of the Chechenia operation. Kondratyev, for example, had developed since 1992 a concept for the employment of peacekeeping units in peacekeeping operations in the CIS. Colonel-General Eduard Vorobyev, first deputy commander of Russian land forces, also had extensive experience in conducting various peacekeeping operations on CIS territory, in particular in the Transdniester region. He was dismissed when he refused to take command of the operations in Chechenia on the grounds that the troops under his command were completely unprepared to take part in combat.[20] Lebed remained a figurehead of military criticism of the Chechen campaign and declared that servicemen of his 14th Army (which he continued to command until summer 1995) would not participate in the military operation under any circumstances. His trenchant critique of the Chechen campaign continued after he was ousted from command of the 14th Army and openly entered the political fray until he himself brokered the peace settlement (see below).

The specific frictions between Grachev and his deputy Gromov were acute enough even before military operations commenced in Chechenia for the liberal Russian press to view them as 'a sign of a most profound crisis within the army's upper echelons' and as 'evidence of the army's total ungovernability'.[21] In autumn 1994 Gromov had been openly critical of Grachev's failure to implement military reforms, and claimed that 'military excess' in Chechenia 'will lead only to prolonged hostility in the North Caucasus, and it will mutate into incessant terrorist actions'.

Divisions in the Russian military command may account for an otherwise baffling aspect of the initial military operations in Chechenia, namely the calibre of the troops initially used: in the main, chronically under-strength, poorly trained infantry and tank regiments together with MVD troops. Logistical problems, the severe undermanning of sub-units and the failures of military reform in the preceding period may not be sufficient to explain this.[22] According to one interpretation, the controversy attached to using military force against Russian Federation citizens, and Grachev's personal unpopularity, account for his apparent failure initially to persuade enough high-quality troops to join the operation. Therefore the operation commenced in the teeth of considerable resistance from some parts of the army and the initial deployments in Chechenia appeared to include few elite paratrooper and special forces units (which had been kept at higher manning levels). Grachev, although a paratrooper himself, it is argued, had become isolated from his fellow officers in the crack airborne divisions. Their commanders, especially in the case of the 76th Airborne Division, initially seem to have refused to put their weight behind the Chechen operation.[23] Elite naval infantry forces and parts of a special operations division were flown into the region only in mid-January.

The belated involvement of the airborne forces (VDV) and other elite formations may have reflected more than just the reluctance of their commanders to follow Grachev's plans. The choice of advance forces for the Chechen operation may also have reflected rivalry between the VDV and the ground forces for control over the new mobile forces command envisaged in military reform plans. Ground forces commanders, it has been argued, wished to prove that the VDV were unnecessary, so they were not part of the original campaign plan for Chechenia and were sent in only as a stopgap following the disastrous initial assault on Grozny.[24] Such service rivalries compounded larger failures in the political coordination of the military campaign.

Political coordination of military operations

Overall political control of and decision-making for the intervention in Chechenia was entrusted at the highest level to the Russian Security Council.

Initially Prime Minister Chernomyrdin was responsible for the operation; then, once Russian troops entered Chechenia in force, the operational leadership of the military–political operation was entrusted to First Vice-Premier Oleg Soskovets. Soon the Russian nationalities minister (and subsequently a deputy prime minister), Nikolai Yegorov, was tasked with coordinating the actions of the 'power' structures – the armed forces, the MVD and the federal counter-intelligence service (formerly the KGB, now the Federal Security Service). Later in August 1995 Oleg Lobov, the secretary of the Russian Security Council, was appointed Yeltsin's plenipotentiary representative in Chechenia. But Soskovets found it difficult to maintain political control over the operation and it appears that in reality, at least initially, Grachev had overall control of the operation as far as the Security Council was concerned (while the role of the general staff remained ambiguous) and merely informed Soskovets and Yegorov of its progress.

Despite the appointment of politicians with the task of controlling the Chechenia operation, the danger grew that the security ministries could assume the function of shaping immediate political tasks and that this could even be done by field commanders, who began to operate autonomously.[25] Such commanders appeared scornful of the efforts by politicians in Moscow to secure ceasefires in Chechenia before autumn 1996, paying only lip-service to them and showing determination to press home the advantage achieved by Russian troops when this was believed to exist.[26] Once committed to the conflict (unlike the commanders who initially had opposed the military operation and were dismissed), such commanders and the Russian general staff were determined that their military efforts and Russian military losses would not be in vain and that the army would not bear the blame for the mistakes made in the North Caucasus by the political leadership.[27] This was most evident in spring 1996 when Grachev stated that he was duty bound to fulfil the orders of the president on a ceasefire, but at the same time told the State Duma that he disagreed with Yeltsin's peace initiative since it gave Dudayev's forces the opportunity to regroup and recruit.[28]

This view from the top of the defence ministry, and the rift it represented between military and political approaches to Chechenia, changed only with Grachev's final replacement by Igor Rodionov as defence minister in autumn 1996. Rodionov may not have overcome his 'Tbilisi syndrome' (a response to the public outrage which followed the use of force 'internally' in the Soviet Union, in Tbilisi, in 1989 by troops in the Transcaucasus under Rodionov's command), but his commitment to the idea of a peaceful settlement of the conflict reflected not only his views on the regular army's non-participation in internal political showdowns but also his other priorities, such as reform of the Russian armed forces.[29]

These problems of political control of the military command were compounded by the lack of effective overall political coordination of the security ministries' activities in Chechenia. This helps explain the outbreak during 1994–6 of open rivalry between the different forces involved – the regular army, the interior ministry, the border guards and the Federal Security Service. This occurred despite the coordinating role given to the general staff operational team on Chechenia. The interior ministry and the MOD in particular had overlapping competences in the campaign. On 1 February 1995 the MVD commander-in-chief, Colonel-General Anatoly Kulikov, was appointed to head the joint command of Russian forces in Chechenia. This left unclear the delineation of responsibilities between the MVD and other forces in operations on Russian territory. In principle 'non-military forces' such as the MVD should have secured the 'rear' and assumed the main burden once key strongholds had been captured. But in practice effective coordination between regular army and MVD forces remained very poor throughout the campaign.[30] On another level, the GRU (Main Intelligence Directorate) military intelligence, a long-standing rival of the former KGB, opposed military intervention in Chechenia.

Rivalry between the MOD and MVD, as noted above, was particularly serious. The conflict between these institutions became acute in autumn 1996 when Aleksandr Lebed (during his brief tenure as secretary of the Security Council) sought to blame the MVD and Interior Minister Anatoly Kulikov personally for the débâcle in Grozny in August when Russian forces were overrun by the Chechen militia, and publicly called for Kulikov's dismissal.[31] This tension reflected a clash between two opposing viewpoints on how to settle the Chechen crisis.[32] As the new Russian defence minister, Rodionov, Lebed's protégé, stressed that problems of the Chechen settlement were not the military's business but that of special troops, particularly those of the MVD.[33] His emphasis was on a peaceful conflict settlement, although before the Grozny events in August he did not rule out the use of force. A Russian defence analyst argued that by this stage Rodionov and other senior officers wanted to effect a full or partial disengagement from Chechenia and to concentrate on reforming the army, whereas the MVD needed the Chechenia campaign to justify its own bloated forces.[34]

A critical struggle took place in August 1996 over the peace plan for Chechenia devised by Lebed. Senior military officers and Interior Minister Kulikov claimed that this plan would give Chechen militias the opportunity to regroup for a new offensive. They referred to a decree by Yeltsin on the need to restore control of the federal forces over Grozny, and Yeltsin's position indeed appeared ambiguous.[35] Lieutenant-General Konstantin Pulikovsky, acting commander of the united group of federal forces in Chechenia, issued an ultimatum demanding that the Chechen rebels withdraw from Grozny or else face the full firepower of the Russian army (at a time when some 150,000 people remained in the city).[36] Lebed claimed that this reflected the absence of a unified command in settling the Chechen conflict and countermanded the ultimatum. Rodionov also dissociated himself from Pulikovsky's ultimatum and the crisis was defused.[37]

Another axis of rivalry existed between Defence Minister Grachev and the chief of the border guards Colonel-General Andrei Nikolayev, and consequently between their respective force structures. This had already surfaced publicly in 1993 in a dispute over Russian forces in Tajikistan, and by autumn 1994 Grachev openly called for the resubordination of the border troops under MOD command, which would increase the size of the army. Some Russian general staff strategists were predicting that in the existing military-political situation in Russia and the near abroad, the focus of protecting the national security and strategic interests of the Russian Federation had increasingly been shifting towards state borders, and that consequently the Russian army might eventually come to resemble a border army. Such speculation boosted Nikolayev's standing. Grachev failed, however, to resubordinate the border troops directly under the MOD.

The character of military command of the Chechenia operation – riven vertically and fractured horizontally between the power ministries – has compounded military operational weaknesses and challenges the Russian capacity more generally to engage in significant military missions on its borders or in CIS conflicts. For example, the splintering of the Russian military command over the Chechenia operation could have longer-term adverse implications for planned Russian regional command structures. One such regional command may be formed in the North Caucasus military district; others have been earmarked since 1992 for the Transbaikal MD and the Far Eastern MD, although they remain blueprints.[38] A new Russian mobile force grouping is also being created for the Kaliningrad region. In the new, more politicized and divided military hierarchy the question arises whether Russian commanders could in future crises feel a greater allegiance to Russian regional political authorities than to the Moscow leadership.

Russian military operational capabilities and the implications for military reform

The campaign in Chechenia revealed major deficiencies in Russian military operational capabilities and performance which compounded command and control failures and which have wider significance for any assessment of the Russian military potential. The shifts in Russian operations reflected uncertainty among Russian commanders about which strategy to adopt to counteract the guerrilla warfare tactics chosen by irregular Chechen militias.

But such shifts also responded to weaknesses and inadequacies in the combat performance of the Russian forces, the steady erosion of their morale and consequent difficulties in implementing military tasks.[39]

Military operations

Detailed analysis by Russian and Western specialists of the disastrous initial Russian attack on Grozny in December 1994 has revealed a catalogue of military operational errors on strategic and tactical levels as well as logistical-technical problems on the part of the various Russian forces assembled for the assault.[40] This decisively punctured Russian military self-confidence, which had already been damaged by the succession of warnings from Russian commanders (noted above) about the lack of combat preparation and training of the Russian forces rapidly assembled in Chechenia.

From spring 1995 to summer 1996 the Russian campaign in Chechenia passed through various phases which brought federal forces no closer to achieving effective control over most of the republic, despite official rhetoric and wishful thinking. This impasse reflected the continuing reservoir of local support on which Chechen rebels could rely in such partisan warfare. Sporadic outbursts of fighting and a general policy of attrition favoured the resistance rather than the occupying forces.

In the second half of March 1995 Russian troops proceeded to take control of the towns of Argun, Gudermes and Shali after severe bombardment by air and heavy artillery, and effectively occupied lowland Chechenia. But by April 1995, after five months of intense fighting, Russian troops controlled only two-thirds of the overall territory of Chechenia and small, mobile Chechen armed groups were engaged in a guerrilla war in the south and southeast of the republic. Two months later the line of engagement lay across the foothill villages. Chechen military forces had divided into six so-called fronts, according to where they were stationed, and they still retained the combat initiative.[41] According to Russian military sources at least 8,000 men were involved, apparently capable of offering protracted resistance to Russian occupation.[42] By summer 1995 the Russian military goal was to eliminate those Chechen military bases that had exits through passes to neighbouring republics and subsequently to shift the emphasis largely to internal security.

However, a ceasefire was negotiated between Russian and Chechen forces in June 1995, following the Chechen terrorist attack on the Russian town of Budennovsk, although military skirmishes continued. In mid-December 1995 there was an upsurge in military activity by Chechen field forces, including an attempt to seize and hold Gudermes, the second largest city in Chechenia, which forced the Russian command to restore priority to military offensives in the field. In March 1996 Russian forces initiated a full-scale spring offensive; but their attempts to 'destroy fortified areas' led only to the pointless destruction of Chechen villages (notoriously the village of Samashki), and a group of Russian State Duma deputies visiting Chechenia argued that the number of Chechen rebels was increasing as 'a reaction by the population to actions on the part of the federal forces and the related civilian death toll'.[43] By July 1996, as large-scale Russian military operations continued near the village of Shatoi, the stated Russian objectives had reverted to those declared a year previously – to drive Chechen militias into uninhabited mountain regions and destroy them with attack aviation.[44] But this goal no longer appeared realistic with the Russian military resources available in Chechenia, once a lightning offensive by Chechen militias in August had wrested control of most of Grozny from Russian regular forces and local security forces. Chechen rebels also took control of Gudermes virtually without a fight.[45]

This turn of events proved conclusively the hollowness of Russian claims that the Chechen rebels had been demoralized and largely crushed and that they had no leadership and command structure left to mount coordinated operations.[46] It prompted some Russian analysts to recognize finally that the rebel fighters against whom their forces were struggling were the product of a whole system of resistance.[47] In fact, Chechen society had adapted its structures to protracted guerrilla warfare. A tightly knit society had been forged in Chechenia, specialists argued, which was willing to continue fighting for decades.[48] After meeting rebel leaders, including their commander Aslan Maskhadov, in August 1996, Lebed offered official Russian recognition for the first time that 'Chechens were and remain outstanding soldiers' and reminded his audience that 'Russia failed to defeat Chechens by force during the last century'. He concluded that it was time to withdraw the groups of federal forces from Chechenia 'and not use them as cannon fodder'.[49]

Military weaknesses

The campaign in Chechenia revealed Russian military weaknesses on various levels. These have acted as a stimulus for military reform of the Russian armed forces, although Russian military leaders have argued that the underlying need for military reform predates operations in Chechenia and that these specific operations (and their failures) should not be the driving forces of future efforts at reform of the organizational and personnel structures of the armed forces.

Military training deficiencies were paramount. These could have been anticipated by the fact that before winter 1994 training exercises against a notional enemy in the North Caucasus military district had been limited to command staff studies on maps.[50] In the days preceding the Chechen campaign Grachev had signed a top secret directive which outlined in detail the shortcomings of the forces of the North Caucasus.[51] Colonel-General Eduard Vorobyev, the first deputy commander-in-chief of the Russian ground forces, stated explicitly in January 1995 that the units mustered for combat in Chechenia were totally unprepared for action, especially in urban warfare, and needed at least two months' special training, which was not forthcoming.[52] The MVD troops were particularly poorly trained for combat operations.

For subsequent stages of the campaign the Russian armed forces had no special units trained for mountain warfare; the military schools that used to train such troops no longer existed.[53] This deficiency was clear despite the years of war in Afghanistan. In the words of one officer, the combat operations in Chechenia, 'planned and directed by generals who were in Afghanistan, have shown with absolute clarity that in fact there is no "Afghan experience" that anyone can be proud of'.[54] More generally, the ground forces had not been trained for guerrilla operations or for counter-guerrilla warfare. There were no such subjects and never had been in the training programmes and curricula of Russian military academies, schools and courses for advanced officer training, despite the historical experience of the civil war, 'Great Patriotic War' and Afghan war. Special training of this kind was particularly needed for border and airborne troops.[55] The preparation of officers for combat was also inadequate. Many staff officers in Chechenia had been called up from the reserve upon graduation from higher educational establishments. Former students with no military experience had been appointed platoon leaders and had to lead men into action.[56]

Secondly, severe logistical problems afflicted initial operations. The existence of general logistical problems for the Russian reinforcement of crisis zones was shown by the fact that for the initial assault on Grozny equipment and soldiers had to be brought in to the North Caucasus from the centre of Russia, the Urals, Siberia and the Far East.[57] The formation of units from other military districts to man the North Caucasus military district's units was completed between 9 and 23 December on the general staff's orders.

Thirdly, as a result of these logistical problems military coordination between units involved in the initial attack on Grozny and those involved in subsequent operations was notoriously poor. At first the troops were hastily knocked-together combined combat units and groups made up of various service branches. In Lebed's words, 'not a single regular regiment was brought into Chechenia – they are all patchy, put together from bits', and the soldiers concerned could not bond together. Most of the infantry came from MVD internal troops, newly formed mobile forces, light infantry brigades and airborne troops.[58] The formations which were at higher strength and were deployed as integral units, such as some of the airborne troops and naval infantry, the 74th Independent Motor Rifle Brigade and specialist peace-keeping units, performed better, but they were a minority of the forces deployed. The effect of uncoordinated units was exacerbated by rivalries between services and different forces structures, as noted above. This was highlighted by the Russian forces' siege of and attack on the Chechen-held village of Pervomayskaya in Dagestan in February 1996, which revealed a catalogue of military failures, particularly in the coordination of diverse units.

Finally, the demoralization of Russian forces in Chechenia was an important aspect of their lack of combat-readiness and was reflected in their willingness to surrender easily. Such demoralization was widespread before the Chechenia operation, but it was exacerbated by the material and psychological character of combat conditions in Chechenia, by the need to fire on fellow (Russian Federation) countrymen and by perceived defeats inflicted on Russian units by Chechen forces.[59] The role of Russian television and the liberal media generally was important in exposing the reality of the war and the realization throughout Russia that ethnic Russians as well as Russian citizens (*Rossiyane*) were being killed by Russian military forces. Cynicism spread among servicemen and officers in Chechenia about the competence of the Russian military high command and political leadership, accompanied by a belief that the war was serving as a cover for the enrichment of a certain circle of people. Morale eventually deteriorated to such a level over the prolonged occupation that a spirit of anarchism, violence and lack of discipline spread throughout the army units in the republic.[60] This was reflected in the 'commercialization' of military operations: officers of the Russian army and interior troops reportedly claimed that a 'price list' existed for a retreat from encirclement and the exclusion of certain towns from federal forces' mopping-up operations in Chechenia.[61] The unofficial sales of the weapons of Russian troops to their Chechen opponents was another stark reflection of the collapse of Russian military discipline.

The collapse in Russian military morale did not only affect operations in Chechenia but has had a more lasting traumatic effect on the Russian armed forces. If they (and MVD troops) had left Chechenia on the basis of earlier agreements which envisaged the withdrawal of Russian troops in coordination with the demilitarization of the territory controlled by Chechen militias, they could have left believing that they had assisted in the making of peace agreements advantageous to Russia. After the Russian military débâcle in Grozny in August 1996 and Moscow's subsequent decision to evacuate its troops from Chechenia, the army left 'only with a feeling of shame after an undisguised crushing defeat'. This sense of humiliation, which has been described by a Russian presidential council member as the 'Chechen syndrome', could further aggravate anti-Caucasian sentiments in Russia and complicate future Russian policy in the North Caucasus.[62]

These military operational weaknesses were reflected in relatively high Russian military casualties in the Chechenia campaign. As the war proceeded the Russian political capacity to accept continuing military casualties (quite apart from the high civilian casualties which outraged international opinion) in conditions of open media scrutiny was uncertain. Russian commanders were more concerned by these casualty rates than they were appreciative of any useful combat experience in low-intensity conflicts that the army and special forces may have gained from the campaign; by summer 1995 Russian soldiers and officers in Chechenia had already been rotated four times.

By January 1995, 1,160 Russian servicemen had already been killed. While only 178 MVD troops had been killed in the conflict by spring 1995, this compared to a total of only 69 men lost by the interior forces during the period 1988–94 in all their various theatres of operation.[63] By February 1996, out of 1,200 tanks involved in the operation 307 had been damaged beyond repair. This compared to the loss of 67 tanks in the storming of Warsaw and 113 tanks in the storming of Berlin during the Second World War.[64] In the short period of fighting during 6–22 August 1996 alone, when Chechen forces retook control of Grozny, 496 men of the federal forces were killed and 1,407 were injured.[65] By autumn 1996 a total of some 3,000 Russian soldiers had been killed. Once casualties suffered by interior ministry troops and special units are added, the total number of troops killed in twenty months of fighting was around 5,000, or about 30 per cent of the losses incurred by the Soviet army after nine years of fighting in Afghanistan. In addition, the civilian casualties were estimated variously at between 30,000 and 100,000.[66]

The financial burden of the war could not be managed within the Russian ministry of defence budget and required a separate budget item. Inadequate funding for the campaign reflected the overall financial crisis of the armed forces, which in turn was further aggravated by the diversion of funds for the unanticipated conflict. By autumn 1995 it was revealed that expenditures on the Chechen war had outstripped the military budget for that financial year by 1.9 trillion roubles. Some 1.7 trillion roubles ($400 million) was spent on fighting in Chechenia in the first six months of 1995, which left no money to pay officers and servicemen.[67] The commander of the group of federal troops in Chechenia complained that a practically bankrupt state could not finance the army in Chechenia, which owed large sums to its suppliers.[68] The interior ministry troops were generally better supplied and paid than the regular army forces, but in 1995 the state budget paid only 88 billion out of 670 billion roubles of budgeted expenditure for operations in Chechenia. As a result, the deputy commander of the MVD troops claimed that the war forced MVD troops 'to spend their inner reserves for these operations to the detriment of their combat-readiness'.[69] By early 1996, according to some Russian estimates, total Russian expenditure on the conduct of combat operations, including the costs of all the 'power ministries' in Chechenia, was in fact no less than 25 trillion roubles.[70] Large outlays from the state budget were also promised for the eventual socio-economic restoration of Chechenia.

The Russian army under Defence Minister Rodionov lobbied for increased funding to redress the failings revealed by the Chechenia campaign, and certainly the war was a further stimulus for military reform. As indicated below, however, Yeltsin has only contemplated such funding in the context of a radical reorganization of the armed forces, which in reality is too costly an option to be likely in the near term.

Military reform options

At a conference of the armed forces leadership to assess the results of the Chechenia campaign, held a few months into the course of operations, Defence Minister Grachev was reluctant to draw any searching conclusions for military reform. He explained that students at military academies would henceforth study contemporary local wars, taking into account the experience gained in Chechenia, but emphasized that reducing the armed forces to below 1.7 million would be impermissible.[71] In calling for an adjustment in military reform to enable assaults on cities and blaming military setbacks on military hardware problems, Grachev tried to divert attention from the real problems and mistakes exposed by the operation in Chechenia, which were, however, admitted by the chief of the general staff, Colonel-General Mikhail Kolesnikov.[72]

Grachev argued that the poor performance of contract servicemen in Chechenia demonstrated that 'the army should stake on the regular draft'.[73] This left unclear the status of Grachev's earlier commitment to create Russian mobile forces, which assumed an increasing reliance on contract soldiers. It also served to shift attention from the palpable failure to create effective mobile forces during 1992–4. Russian military analysts claimed that the priority should be not expanding the draft but concentrating resources to create two or three combat-ready divisions (in place of the composite battalions hastily thrown together for Chechenia), which would be fully manned.[74] The then foreign minister, Andrei Kozyrev, for his part, drew the lesson from Chechenia that Russia should create highly mobile forces capable of reacting to similar acute political crises speedily and with 'surgical precision'.[75]

In practice, Grachev's first priority in developing force structures was to manage and contain the Chechenia conflict. For this purpose he announced the formation of the new 58th Army in the North Caucasus military district (based on the Vladikavkaz army corps, headquartered in Vladikavkaz, the capital of North Ossetia), and persuaded Yeltsin to decree in July 1995 that a motorized infantry division (which was later downgraded to a brigade) and a number of auxiliary units and sub-units of internal troops would be permanently stationed in Chechenia.[76] However, this decision was reversed in autumn 1996 as Russian forces became increasingly beleaguered in Chechenia, and Russian units were fully withdrawn from the republic.

These shifts in military policy driven by short-term imperatives were a distraction from a type of military reform which would begin to internalize the Chechenia experience. Russian analysts have certainly begun to consider the implications of the conflict for the future training and reorganization of Russian forces. One specialist, for example, has analysed the future force requirements and forms of operational involvement for Russia in a new category of conflicts – which he terms limited military conflicts – that combine internal conflicts, specifically internationalized civil wars, together with local interstate conflicts.[77] But there is no evidence that such analyses have begun to influence Russian general staff thinking.

One problem in developing military reform has been the unclear effect of the Chechenia campaign on the Russian general staff, which maintained a low public profile during the operations (despite the key initial role of its operational team on Chechenia). Reports early in 1995 suggested that the general staff could be placed under the direct control of Yeltsin, through its chief Mikhail Kolesnikov, a move which would sideline the defence minister.[78] The general staff's main operations directorate could have been put in control of the whole Chechenia campaign. Since this body contains officers from all the services, it could have offered Yeltsin better and perhaps more balanced advice than the defence minister. But this did not occur and the future relationship between these key military bodies remains to be clarified.

Another uncertain institutional effect of the Chechenia conflict has been its reinforcement of the position of the ministry of the interior and its forces. This has happened at a time when the MVD's troop strength already exceeds that of the interior troops of the former Soviet Union and equals that of the Russian army taken as a whole.[79] Thus the role of the MVD in enforcing national security policy may now be compared to that of Russia's regular armed forces.

Regional military and security policy implications

The Chechenia conflict has had unsettling regional military and security implications and has influenced policy and integration dynamics between Russia and its CIS neighbours. In the first place, the conflict has reverberated through the North Caucasus region and other republics and regions of the Russian Federation, since the struggle for autonomy for Chechenia has represented a direct challenge to the integrity and military cohesion of the multinational and federal Russian state.

Implications for the North Caucasus region

From the Russian perspective the Chechenia campaign has significant implications for Russia's geostrategic interests in the south, or in the lexicon of the general staff the 'southern strategic axis'. Before the hostilities in Chechenia commenced this southern axis and specifically the North Caucasus region had already been defined as the main axis of military danger for Russia. The problems have been perceived on three levels.

The first level concerns problems associated with the disintegration of the Soviet Union, which left a narrow vulnerable strip of territory from the Sea of Azov to the Caspian Sea. Chechenia, which creates instability on the eastern flank of the North Caucasus border, occupies the southernmost end of this territorial 'tongue'. The western flank of this border is also not viewed as secure because of a weakening of Russian naval power in the Black Sea. In total this is seen to represent a serious problem for Russian strategic planning and long-term military structural development, which was only exacerbated by the original Conventional Forces in Europe (CFE) Treaty flank restrictions on arms. Secondly, fundamental security problems for Russia are viewed as arising from the role of the North Caucasus as a cultural barrier in preventing the spread of radical Islamic influences to the north. Thirdly, there is a perceived set of problems associated with the strategic need to defend ground, maritime and air borders. This raises the question of whether to bolster the southern border defences of the Transcaucasus CIS states or whether to develop the infrastructure for new Russian Federation southern borders, which would pass through the southern areas of the North Caucasus republics, including Chechenia, and along the northeast coast of the Black Sea. In addition to these military-strategic concerns in the Caucasus, the strategic and economic significance of oil and its transport routes remains a priority for Russia.[80]

Against the background of these strategic concerns, even before the onset of the Chechen campaign the North Caucasus military district was being transformed from its position in 1990 as a military backwater mainly concerned with training into a key 'front-line' border military district. It was here that the new Russian mobile forces with a rapid reaction core were being developed. However, the Chechenia campaign revealed that the rapid reaction forces that had been developed by 1994–5 represented only a limited and fragmented capability in the region. This conflict has ensured that the Russian military focus on the North Caucasian region will be further strengthened, within the limits of overall military resources available, since efforts to secure

Russian territorial integrity in Chechenia and adjacent regions are presented as front-line operations.

This is reflected in the creation of the new 58th Army (originally the 42nd Army Corps) based at Vladikavkaz in the North Caucasus military district. As a result the flank limits for this military district (and the Transcaucasus region) established by the CFE Treaty were breached and the other CFE Treaty parties agreed to treaty revisions to Article 5 at the May 1996 CFE review conference to accommodate the increased Russian military requirements in the region.[81]

The Chechenia campaign has stirred up immediate political challenges to Russian strategic control in the overall North Caucasian region and destabilized conditions in the south of Russia which compound longer-term Russian strategic vulnerabilities.[82] On the one hand, other republics and regions of the North Caucasus are not likely to be prepared to pay the 'Chechen price' in terms of war dead and devastation to promote further independence. Yet Russia's military weaknesses exposed by its Chechenia campaign and the example of continued Chechen defiance could embolden those forces in other republics and regions that support military or political separatism. At the least Russia faces the danger of a further weakening of central control, especially if a political agreement is eventually conceded to Chechenia that provides it with much of what it has been seeking.

This concern over the example of Chechen defiance was reflected in Yeltsin's prompt declaration of a state of emergency in North Ossetia and Ingushetia in January 1995.[83] It was also implied by some resistance which was offered to the passage of Russian forces in Ingushetia and Dagestan and the statement by the Ingush president Ruslan Aushev in December 1994 that Ingushetia would not permit Russian forces to move through Ingush territory to Chechenia. By February 1996 Aushev even demanded – to Russian indignation – that 'the territory of Ingushetia be freed from the presence of Russian troops'.[84] At the same time anti-Russian and anti-Moscow currents in Dagestan began to rise, especially after Russia's use of force in the Pervomayskaya operation, since Chechenia and neighbouring Dagestan are populated by peoples whose cultural traditions are very close to each other.[85] The danger that the war and its uncertain aftermath could destabilize the delicate ethnic balance of the republic increased. The Dagestani authorities fear that the potential for internal turmoil in Chechenia 'with blood feuds and a struggle for power forging alliances and enmities across the North Caucasus, could be more destabilising for Dagestan than the straightforward conflict between Chechenia and Russian federal power'.[86]

Tensions in the autonomous republics of Karachai-Cherkessia and Kabardino-Balkaria also have to be taken seriously. Kabardino-Balkaria, like North Ossetia, has broadly supported Moscow's policy in Chechenia and earlier divisions in the republic in 1991–2 were contained. But when a Balkar people's congress was convened in November 1996 and decided to name Balkaria a sovereign republic within Russia, some Russian analysts began to draw parallels with the earlier course of events in Chechenia.[87]

So far, however, none of the other North Caucasian republics has formally raised the idea of seceding from the Russian Federation. A meeting of the congress of the Confederation of Caucasian Peoples in January 1995 decided to create committees for support of the Chechen people and self-defence committees in all North Caucasian regions; but this decision remained largely rhetorical. A pledge by the Confederation to resist the Russian intervention by creating a regional alliance from the Caspian to the Black Sea was similarly only declaratory, since significant differences continued to divide the North Caucasian republics and regions.[88]

Even if incipient political efforts at secession within the other North Caucasian republics could be contained, the possibility of combat operations in Chechenia spreading to other North Caucasus republics was taken quite seriously by Russian leaders. In spring 1995 Grachev anticipated that small groups of 'bandit formations' would be operating in various regions of the Caucasus, not only in Chechenia, and proposed – unrealistically – that one combat-ready division should be introduced in each of them to isolate the fighters if necessary.[89] Russian leaders also attributed broad territorial designs to the Chechen rebels. Before the events of August 1996 Yeltsin used the spectre of Chechen fighters moving into and seizing Dagestan, Karachai-Cherkessia and other republics of the North Caucasus as an argument against the full withdrawal of Russian troops from Chechenia.[90] Even as Moscow was finally withdrawing these troops at the end of 1996, Russian officials speculated on the possibility of Chechenia launching a military invasion into neighbouring North Caucasus republics and acting to destabilize the region.[91]

Russian operations in the south of Chechenia in summer 1995 were aimed *inter alia* at destroying resistance bases which had exits through mountain passes to Dagestan, Georgia and Ingushetia and to prevent these regions being drawn into the conflict.[92] As border tensions increased, the Russian border guard units controlling Chechenia's borders with Ingushetia and Dagestan had to be reinforced with mobile groups from northern Russia and Kaliningrad.[93] A group of Duma deputies who visited Chechenia in spring 1996 emphasized that the attitude of North Caucasus republics, especially Ingushetia, to the Chechen resistance was one of latent sympathy, while in Dagestan military actions provoked hostility towards the federal forces.[94] As the advance of Russian forces from the central areas of Chechenia forced Chechen militias to the western and eastern borders of the republic, the threat of the transfer of military actions 'into the depths of the neighbouring territories' steadily grew.[95] This eventuality was made more likely by the existence of some 400,000 refugees from Chechenia in Ingushetia and Dagestan.

The end of combat actions in Chechenia did not eliminate cross-border frictions, which by autumn 1996 had led to a decision by Dagestan's Security Council to create self-defence units in the Chechenia–Dagestan border regions. Dagestan has also recruited additional ministry of interior troops to protect the border with Chechenia. But the Dagestani authorities are turning a blind eye to the increasing possession of firearms by the border population. They are seeking to establish direct relations with the Maskhadov government, including an agreement on mutual security guarantees, though they have doubts that the Chechen leadership is in full control of the territory and is able to implement agreements.[96] Russian analysts still refer to the threat of the export of the 'Chechen revolution' to Dagestan.[97] They consider Dagestan to be of exceptional geostrategic importance for Russia on account of the communications routes traversing it. One alarming scenario they raise begins with actions by Chechen and Dagestani nationalists on the territory of Dagestan triggering off violence against federal troops, which would compel Russia to introduce special units of its interior troops into the republic. This would offer such nationalists the pretext to accuse Russia of armed aggression on Dagestan. Chechen leaders could then call on the Caucasian peoples to rise against such aggression and to supply weapons to the Dagestani 'resistance'.[98]

An alternative scenario, however, suggests the danger of internecine rather than anti-Russian conflict. Dagestani Chechens and members of other ethnic groups in Dagestan may develop common anti-Russian sentiments, but historically they have clashed among themselves over the territory of the Khasavyurt district. This territory, between the Terek and Sulak rivers, is regarded by most Chechens as traditional Vainakh (i.e. Chechen) land, although it is now part of Dagestan. A purported official draft decree of the Chechen leadership published in June 1997 called for the restoration of Chechen jurisdiction over the disputed territory and ordered the deployment of units of the Chechen armed forces there.[99] Even if this decree was a forgery it suggested that there are efforts to use Chechen nationalism to incite ethnic conflict on the territory of Dagestan.

Instability in the North Caucasus republics impinges directly on the security of the core southern Russian regions of Stavropol, Rostov and Krasnodar. The spill-over of the conflict was dramatically clear from the terrorist attack in June 1995 on the city of Budennovsk in the Stavropol region by Chechen fighters led by Shamil Basayev.[100] This prompted the local Stavropol Duma to draft legislation to create local self-defence formations commanded by the local heads of administration.[101] The Chechen raid in Dagestan in January 1996 which resulted in Russian military humiliation at the village of Pervomayskaya,[102] and bomb blasts in Armavir and Pyatigorsk in April 1997, encouraged Yeltsin to sign a decree on a special status for the Stavropol region, which provided for a permanent operations group of military officers and security experts to be attached to the governor's office.[103] Such developments emphasized that internal security demands in southern Russia set this region apart from other Russian border areas and that in the pursuit of reliable security the Caucasus should be viewed as a regional security complex.[104]

New flashpoints could occur if calls for border revision by force in the North Caucasus are not controlled. A specific danger is posed by the demands of the Terek Cossacks for the return of the Shelkov and Naur districts from Chechenia (which only acquired these northern districts in 1957) to the Stravropol *krai*, while pressure is mounting for the partial breakup of Karachai-Cherkessia and its partial reintegration with Stavropol and Krasnodar *krai*.[105] The Chechens in turn could demand the Prigorodny district of North Ossetia and Aukhov in Dagestan. The Terek Cossacks have already tried to organize armed units to patrol the North Caucasus republics to protect the Russian population from 'Chechen banditry'. In January 1997 the Russian deputy Security Council secretary Boris Berezovsky expressed support for arming the Cossacks on a legal basis, although the Russian interior minister Anatoly Kulikov was only prepared for them to serve in regular Russian army units.[106]

If the Russian authorities eventually legalize the militarization of the Cossacks in the North Caucasus, it may reflect the view that the spontaneous arming of the local population seems unavoidable, and that armed Cossacks could defend Russia's southern borders, even if this poses significant dangers for future stability in this volatile region. At the same time, Russian leaders clearly wish to avoid becoming involved in a new Chechen conflict and must be aware that the leaders of the North Caucasian republics are fervently opposed to the creation of Cossack formations. Such a development could encourage each of the North Caucasian nations to seek to construct its own army, with obvious destabilizing consequences.[107]

Implications for other republics and regions of the Russian Federation

The example of Chechen defiance of Russian federal political and military authority and the ultimate failure of the Russian military response could also have major unsettling effects and reinforce centrifugal trends in republics and regions of the Russian Federation beyond the North Caucasus. This is possible even if the dangers of provoking Russian leaders too far were shown by the shocking readiness of Moscow to use brutal force in Chechenia.

This was indicated as early as January 1995 by the adoption of laws by legislative officials in Tatarstan, Karelia and the republic of Tuva preventing their servicemen and local officers being sent to the North Caucasus region.[108] Yeltsin clashed openly with the president of the Chuvash republic by declaring null and void a similar edict on military service issued by the latter.[109] Although a Russian government statement condemned 'attempts to sow the seeds of political strife and separatism under the guise of protecting servicemen',[110] a meeting of the leaders of seven republics in January condemned the Chechen invasion.

This simmering issue failed to erupt later in 1995 despite an early warning by Yegor Gaidar that the danger of the dissolution of the Russian Federation had become serious again as a result of the fighting in Chechenia.[111] Other parts of Russia may have been intimidated by the severity of Russian military efforts against Chechen separatism. At the outset of combat in Chechenia the Russian minister of the interior, Viktor Yerin, claimed that the success of the operation would provide an assurance to many other regions of Russia that 'we will not let them get into a state in which Chechenia has found itself'.[112] However, the exposure of Russian military weaknesses and Russia's reluctant decision in autumn 1996 finally to withdraw its forces from Chechenia have undermined this lesson for other republics and regions of the Russian Federation. The Russian use of force towards Chechenia has also aroused the mistrust of other parts of the Federation, which could be exploited by future nationalist politicians. In autumn 1996 many new regional governors were elected, so that these positions are no longer held by placemen of President Yeltsin. Against this background, the possibility of Moscow's ultimate readiness to sanction a Chechen autonomous state could result at least in the insistence of other parts of the Russian Federation on additional powers for themselves.

The issue of military autonomy is particularly sensitive and potentially catalytic. After the withdrawal of Russian forces from Chechenia, the decision by the new Chechen political leadership in early 1997 to establish separate armed forces, interior ministry detachments and power structures of the 'Republic of Ichkeria', which would control virtually the entire territory of that republic, has further undermined the authority of the Russian armed forces in the Russian Federation. It reinforces a growing perception in a whole series of Russian regions, especially in the Caucasus, that the Russian armed forces are something foreign and even hostile.[113]

In seeking to resist the idea of the withdrawal of Russian forces from Chechenia, Russian leaders had linked this scenario with the danger of demands for troop withdrawals from Tatarstan and other Russian regions.[114] By December 1996 Russian Duma officials claimed that pulling the final two Russian brigades out of Chechenia had set a dangerous precedent for new demands for Russian troop withdrawals from other Caucasus republics as well as from Bashkortostan, Tatarstan, Kalmykia and Yakutia, and their replacement by national military formations.[115] This scenario cannot be ruled out, and had indeed been evoked much earlier, after the break-up of the Soviet integrated armed forces in 1991–2.[116] But there have been no indications so far that in the medium term Russia will be faced by any insistent demands of this kind, as opposed to the broader economic or political demands currently being advanced by Russian republics and regions.

Implications for the CIS region and Russian–CIS state relations

The Chechenia campaign has had specific effects on Russian policy towards CIS states in the Caucasus, as might be expected from their proximity to the zone of conflict. But it has also had broader repercussions for Russian ambitions in the CIS region as a whole, particularly in efforts to sustain a military presence outside Russian borders.

The direct spill-over of the conflict to the Caucasus CIS states has been rather limited. There was no opportunity for Chechen partisan bases to operate on Georgian or Armenian territory with impunity since Russia itself had military bases in these countries. Nor was Azerbaijan prepared to risk an open conflict with Russia or incursions by the Russian army through harbouring Chechen resistance bases. This was true despite claims in the Russian media that arms were being transferred to Chechen fighters through Azerbaijan, and an overall deterioration of Russian–Azerbaijani relations during the war in Chechenia.[117] Russia has maintained a large border guard contingent, totalling some 31,000 men in early 1995, in the Caucasus Special Border District, responsible for sealing off the Chechenia conflict zone. This deployment was supported by a decision of the Russian Security Council in December 1994 to create a new inner border defence line along Russia's border with Georgia and Azerbaijan (which led to the border with Azerbaijan being sealed off on the Russian side for considerable periods of time), in addition to the outer CIS defence border with Turkey and Iran (which did not cover the Azerbaijani–Iranian border since Azerbaijan viewed this as its own responsibility, not that of Russia or the CIS).[118] This reflected the Russian view that transparent Azerbaijani frontiers meant that all kinds of undesirables could pass north from Azerbaijan.

In response to the crisis over Chechenia the Georgian president, Eduard Shevardnadze, supported the integrity of the Russian state, hoping for a reciprocal response from Russia in supporting Georgian claims on Abkhazia, or perhaps acceptance of the idea of a future 'military solution' of the Abkhaz secession issue (which Russia has failed to condone). He was also mindful of the fact that Chechen irregulars had helped the Abkhaz in their previous battle for secession from Georgia. Consequently Georgia had to exercise care to prevent Chechen militants from infiltrating Abkhazia, which Russian border guard commanders feared could be used as a base area for terrorist actions in southern Russian cities. This did not occur, although some hundreds of volunteers are rumoured to have crossed from Abkhazia to fight for Chechenia. Instead, Chechen leaders accused Georgia of permitting Russian bombers to launch attacks on Chechen targets from military bases located in Georgia.[119] From March 1995 Russian and Georgian border guards patrolled the Georgian–Chechen border by helicopter.[120]

However, since the May 1997 Russian–Chechen peace treaty, direct Georgian–Chechen relations have gathered momentum. The newly elected Chechen president, Aslan Maskhadov, has actively tried to develop friendly contacts with Georgia to bolster Chechenia's position in striving for complete independence from the Russian Federation, its only other direct neighbour. Friendly relations with Chechenia are also important for Tbilisi to counteract the plans of rogue Chechen fighters in Abkhazia. In June 1997, Shevardnadze obtained assurances from Maskhadov of Chechen military neutrality and political support for Tbilisi's position on Abkhazia, including a clear endorsement of Georgia's territorial integrity. A plan was even discussed to build a road between the capitals of Georgia and Chechenia that would give Chechenia access to the world outside Russia.[121]

These developments have occurred at a time when Russian strategic interests in Georgia, as well as Armenia, have been increasing in prominence because of competition over strategic access to Caspian oil resources, and Russia has sought to prevent the weakening of its overall position in the Caucasus region. Russian leaders regard continued challenges to the guaranteed transit of Caspian oil through Chechen territory as increasing the dynamic of competition with Georgia over oil export routes.[122]

Beyond the Caucasus region Russia's use of force in Chechenia has counteracted the fundamental Russian goal of fostering integration between Russia and other CIS states on both political and military levels. On the political level, despite the failure of Russia to impose its will on the defiant Chechen republic, the Russian preference for military force rather than negotiations in Chechenia in late 1994 increased suspicions of Russian intentions among a number of CIS states. For example, a significant proportion of Ukrainian deputies joined the international condemnation of the Russian military operation and initiated a campaign for withdrawal from the CIS (which has not succeeded).[123] A CIS summit on 10 February 1995 issued a joint memorandum urging CIS member states to refrain from putting military, political and economic pressure on one another, although formally the events around Chechenia were described as a Russian internal affair. Continued concern in CIS capitals about the readiness of Russia to use military force in Chechenia, and the nature of that force, has made the Russian concept of an exclusive 'near abroad' (which constrains non-CIS state relations with the CIS region) more difficult to sustain and has helped create a domestic audience more receptive to the claims of nationalists in a number of non-Russian CIS states.[124] This bolsters centrifugal tendencies, which limit Russian control mechanisms in the CIS state framework.

Secondly, Russian military influence on CIS states and the prospects for security policy integration with them have been further constrained by the clear evidence from operations in Chechenia of Russian military over-extension and deficiencies. As a result the implicit Russian threat to enforce its interests in the near abroad by military means if these interests are not fully acknowledged may no longer be taken so seriously by CIS leaders or by states south of CIS borders. In particular, this further reduces the likelihood of direct Russian military intervention in the Crimea dispute with Ukraine. The example of Russian military action in response to Chechen attempts at secession from the Russian Federation and the Russian denial of Chechen aspirations for independence also make it difficult for Russian leaders openly to favour the principle of secession in the case of Crimea, although Ukrainian military leaders must remain uneasy about the growing Russian military build-up in the North Caucasus military district. It also exposes a double standard in the sympathy or support from some Russian politicians for the separatists in Abkhazia and Nagorno-Karabakh. In principle, it could also encourage some political leaders in other CIS countries such as Georgia, Azerbaijan, Armenia and Moldova to carry out a forcible resolution of their territorial problems without fear of strong Russian protests (although of these states only Armenia may at present be capable of using force with any chance of success). On the other hand, the example of Russia's ultimate failure to impose its will on Chechenia and the emergence of a *de facto* independent Chechen state (Ichkeria) represent a challenge to a number of non-Russian CIS governments since they could further encourage separatist ambitions in Abkhazia, Trans-Dniester, Nagorno-Karabakh and other analagous regions in CIS states.

The Russian military over-extension and the military trauma of the Chechen campaign have had the specific effect of limiting Russian capabilities to engage in peacekeeping or peace enforcement in CIS conflicts. Pavel Baev argues in Chapter 11 of this volume that this will result in Russian military retrenchment and withdrawals from outposts such as in Tajikistan and that it offers new opportunities for OSCE involvement in conflict management in the former USSR.[125]

Indeed, a dynamic is likely to be reinforced between stability in the Russian Federation and the capacity of Russia to engage militarily outside its borders in the CIS, for example in Tajikistan, where resistance leaders took heart from Russian failures in Chechenia. This means that even though Russian forces have been withdrawn from the territory of Chechenia the increased demands on regular Russian forces to bolster the presence of interior ministry troops to protect 'internal' security (in the Russian Federation), for example in other

North Caucasus republics, siphons away units trained for more sophisticated non-combat roles which could otherwise be used for peacekeeping in CIS regions. It has also become even less likely, for example, that Moscow will revive its former plan to offer a dominant Russian peacekeeping force for Nagorno-Karabakh. Abkhazian support for the Chechen cause, possibly including the contribution of volunteers to fight in Chechenia, has also cooled relations between Abkhaz officials and the command of the Russian peacekeeping forces in the region. This could reduce Moscow's readiness to commit military assets to this peacekeeping mission.

Broader international implications

Beyond the CIS region, evident Russian military weakness in the Chechenia operation could eventually encourage geopolitical challenges to Russia from other quarters. Some Russian analysts, for example, have speculated that the Chechen operation may reduce Iranian and Chinese concerns about Russia's possible reaction to any efforts by them to expand into 'Russia's sphere of influence'.[126] However, there has been no evidence that either Iran or China has developed such expectations since December 1994, despite strong Iranian protests over the suffering of Muslims in Chechenia and an offer to mediate in the conflict. In fact, Russia's bilateral security policy relations with Iran and China have improved in this period, bolstered by Russian arms sales.

Turkey also has pointedly refrained from any open interference in the Chechenia crisis, despite a domestic lobby of support for the Chechen cause and the presence of many expatriate Chechens in the country, and ignored appeals from the former Chechen leader Dudayev to provide Chechen forces with anti-aircraft missiles or even long-range bombers. Turkey's view that a solution to the Chechen crisis should be found within the Russian Federation reflected its concern to avoid any developments that could further fuel secessionism in Turkish Kurdistan. Even so, many Russian politicians fear future Turkish encroachments in the Caucasus region.

In east-central Europe, the application of massed Russian armed force against the struggle for autonomy by a small republic has undoubtedly evoked painful memories. Soon after the initial Russian attack on Grozny, the chairman of the Russian State Duma's committee on international affairs, Vladimir Lukin, warned that the east European countries were gaining additional motivations to join NATO since 'our methods in Chechenia remind them of "something" historically recent'.[127] The spectacle of military mayhem in Chechenia did act as an additional inducement for east-central European states to seek early NATO membership, as well as for the Baltic states to press their claims for eventual NATO membership. In spring 1995, for example, the

Polish president Lech Walesa played up the Chechenia case of Russian 'neo-imperial ambitions' to accelerate the process of Polish accession to NATO.[128]

The crisis over Chechenia has called into question the Russian commitment to several international military security agreements. The forced revision of the CFE Treaty has already been mentioned. At the December 1994 Budapest OSCE summit, Russia was an enthusiastic supporter of the code of conduct on politico-military aspects of security; but subsequent action in Chechenia breached this code, which places conditions on the use of the state's army for internal security purposes. Under the 1994 Vienna document, OSCE states are also obliged to notify one another 42 days in advance of military activities involving at least 9,000 troops; but over 40,000 Russian troops were moved to Chechenia without notification.

The OSCE was strongly critical of human rights violations in Chechenia. To limit the damage to Russian relations with the international community, the then Foreign Minister Kozyrev eventually conceded that breaches of human rights in Chechenia could not be regarded as strictly the internal matter of one country, and he agreed to the creation of an OSCE mission of observers to examine conditions in Chechenia. This OSCE mission brokered the ceasefire reached in August 1996. Its head, Tim Guldimann, also took part in a key meeting between the Russian Security Council secretary Aleksandr Lebed and Chechen leaders which resulted in the Khasavyurt agreement. However, Moscow was always reluctant to accept an OSCE role on 'Russian Federation territory' and requested the closure of the mission in April 1997 on the grounds that the development of a direct dialogue between the 'central authorities' and the new leadership of Chechenia made OSCE mediation unnecessary.

In contrast to the OSCE, the United Nations has been unable to adopt any significant role in the Chechenia crisis. The former Secretary-General Boutros Boutros-Ghali viewed the Chechenia crisis as an internal Russian affair in which the UN was powerless to intervene unless both parties to the conflict gave their consent, although UN observers could be sent to new elections in Chechenia.[129] Russia has made clear that it would not accept a deeper UN role in such a conflict on Russian Federation territory. In July 1996 Moscow dismissed a Chechen proposal that UN representatives could be involved in Russian–Chechen negotiations and that UN peacekeepers could be used in Chechenia.[130]

The European Parliament, like the OSCE, condemned serious human rights violations by the Russian armed forces in Chechenia and called for a ceasefire. One result was the suspension for a year of the Russian bid for membership of the Council of Europe.[131] But the EU clearly did not believe that Russian conduct in Chechenia should destabilize EU–Russian relations.[132] Nevertheless, the scale of human rights violations by Russian military forces in Chechenia and the obscurity of Russian security policy decision-making around the conflict, set against the background of the controversies with Russia over NATO enlargement (and for a period also over the NATO/UN role in Bosnia), raised important questions for European states about Russia's reliability as a partner, which had to be considered by NATO.

These concerns could only be heightened by evidence from the Chechenia conflict of open divisions in the Russian military command, the unmanageability of the Russian army and uncertain political control over military leaders and security chiefs. This may have prompted doubts among other European states as to whether Russia could guarantee that it would fulfil various international obligations and agreements with west and central European states.[133] The Russian commitment to the Partnership for Peace programme, which has remained lukewarm at best, was called into question. As long as Russian combat operations in Chechenia continued, a shadow also remained over the prospect of forming special relations between Russia and NATO, and the expansion of NATO implied more serious negative consequences for Russia.[134]

Security policy options for Russian federal policy towards Chechenia

The conclusion of the August 1996 Khasavyurt agreement brought an end to the war in Chechenia but left Russian federal relations with the republic and the security policy dynamic between them shrouded in ambiguity.[135] The signing of a treaty on 'peace and the principles of relations between Russia and the Republic of Ichkeria' (Chechenia) in May 1997 failed to clarify the course ahead for Russian–Chechen relations.

In February 1996 a meeting of the Russian Presidential Council had already developed seven scenarios for resolving the Chechen conflict: military victory (involving wide-scale military action); capitulation (an unconditional withdrawal of Russian troops); blockade (placing troops around the perimeter of the border); partition of Chechenia (concentrating armed forces and resources in the northern regions of Chechenia and resettling the population); a split in the Chechen camp (leading to negotiations on a range of military issues); freezing the situation and an inter-Chechen dialogue (with Russia backing the pro-Moscow government of Doku Zavgayev); and a temporary special status for Chechenia (for three to four years, with trilateral political negotiations – a plan developed by the president of Tatarstan, Mintimer Shaymiev).[136] The Russian Security Council created a group headed by Prime Minister Viktor Chernomyrdin, to appraise these alternative approaches.

The security policy implications of these options varied greatly and divided Russian leaders. For example, the Russian interior minister Anatoly Kulikov appeared to favour partitioning Chechenia and positioning Russian troops to defend the northern lowland areas controlled by forces loyal to the pro-Moscow Chechen Doku Zavgayev. But the dynamic of conflict later in 1996, and the need for Yeltsin to avoid serious risks in the prelude to Russian presidential elections, narrowed down the options available and left the development of a strategy of containment as a central Russian objective in its policy towards Chechenia. This has been intended, first, to prevent the destabilization of neighbouring republics and regions and, second, to permit continued Russian leverage on Chechen leaders.

This strategy of containment was already expressed in Yeltsin's short-lived March 1996 plan for a settlement in Chechenia. The plan stipulated that Chechenia should remain an inseparable part of the Russian Federation (though a position of autonomy close to that of Tatarstan was envisaged) but proposed the gradual withdrawal of Russian troops from regions in Chechenia to its borders so that, in Yeltsin's words, 'a kind of belt of our armed forces can be organized around the border'.[137] However, the plan was not equivalent to Russian capitulation and would have left an interior ministry and an army brigade in the republic. These were believed to be sufficient, with support from combat aircraft and helicopters, to control all the strategically important points for Moscow on Chechen territory.[138]

Russian leaders remained adamant that for strategic reasons a full separation of Chechenia from Russia would have 'catastrophic consequences on all neighbouring republics and on Russia as a whole' because of Russian rail and road connections through Chechenia with the Transcaucasus, Dagestan and other republics.[139] The pipeline across Chechenia for oil supplies from Caspian fields (from Baku to Novorossiysk) is also part of this critical network for Moscow. The Khasavyurt agreement did not in itself change this Russian evaluation. Most people in the Russian government and the presidential administration still believed that the federal forces should maintain control over strategic objects in the republic (pipelines, factories, fuel depots, etc.). Loss of control over the Khankala and Severny airports was presented as particularly dangerous for Russia.[140]

The Khasavyurt agreement failed to clarify, however, the future of the two remaining Russian brigades in Chechenia (the 205th Mechanized Infantry and 101st Interior Forces Brigades with 6,000 troops). These units could be used in an attempt to maintain Russian control over such strategic installations, although Russian commanders claimed they were necessary to prevent revenge attacks in the territory not under the control of the Chechen leader Aslan Maskhadov, where internecine fighting would continue. However, their position as vulnerable outposts, even 'hostages', became untenable and on Yeltsin's decision they were finally withdrawn by the beginning of 1997. This brought Russian policy closest to the 'capitulation' scenario and a recognition that strategic access through and control of the rebellious republic had been lost.

One Russian policy response could be a fully-fledged effort to contain Chechenia, as advocated by the Duma defence committee chairman General Lev Rokhlin. This would require the construction of railways, oil and gas pipelines and other communications bypassing Chechenia; the fortification of the Russian–Chechen border; an increase in the Russian military presence in Dagestan and the other North Caucasus republics and the adoption of appropriate security measures there; the creation of a free economic zone in Dagestan; and the provision of economic assistance to Chechenia only under strict monitoring by federal power structures. The objective of these steps would be to ensure Chechenia's dependence on the Russian Federation and its eventual return to the fold.[141]

However, this strategy appears unworkable. Some strategic communications can and will be developed to bypass Chechenia. The authorities in Stavropol *krai* plan to dig a deep trench along the district's 114-km border with Chechenia, and the main roads linking Stavropol and Chechenia are guarded by checkpoints. But the Russian–Chechen border, which is over 400 km long overall, would be very difficult for Moscow to control effectively (and in any case, some 100,000 Chechens live to the east in Dagestan). Ingush President Ruslan Aushev has stated plainly also that there cannot be a closed border between Chechenia and Ingushetia. The resources required for even a partially effective blockade of Chechenia by Russian federal authorities have never been realistically calculated and are not likely to be made available from Russian state budgets at the end of the 1990s.[142] The strategy of full containment of Chechenia is driven more by Russian military anxieties than by a rational assessment of Russian capabilities. A shift away from commitment to such a strategy may be indicated by Yeltsin's decision in May 1997 to distance Interior Minister Anatoly Kulikov from decision-making on Chechenia. Russian policy on Chechenia would be made henceforth by the Security Council. Security Council Secretary Ivan Rybkin and his deputy, Boris Berezovsky, display a more flexible approach in developing Russian policy to Chechenia.

Russian federal authorities are worried and may find it difficult to accept that Chechenia has been left with substantial stocks of arms and ammunition and that Chechen leaders will not agree to the demilitarization or disbandment of Chechen forces, since the former Chechen rebels are likely to view Moscow as a potential aggressor for a long time despite the phrasing of the May 1997 peace treaty. Nor will Russian leaders reconcile themselves easily to the formation by Chechenia of its own regular military forces. On the other hand, Chechen security forces will be needed to guard strategic communications and installations in the republic (including pipelines and refineries).[143] Service in

Chechen armed forces, police or security agencies (if funded) will also have the benefit of establishing more manageable forces and absorbing the more militant Chechen fighters who might otherwise be difficult for the republic to control. The creation of formal Chechen security structures, whereby for example the Chechen commander Shamil Basayev and his units could be co-opted into a Chechen army or national guard, would also further reduce the likelihood of Chechenia repeating the scenario of Afghanistan after the withdrawal of Soviet forces – the division of the territory into the domains of irreconcilable commanders, fuelling protracted instability – which would certainly not be in Russian security interests.[144]

President Maskhadov has ordered the disbandment of all the armed formations in Chechenia that have not become part of its national guard. It will be difficult to ensure, however, that individual field commanders, such as Salman Raduyev, who have dominant influence in distinct zones of Chechenia, will lay down their arms and abandon their local authority. According to one report, by May 1997 Shamil Basayev (who temporarily held the position of first deputy premier) had managed to bring order and discipline to nearly all the Chechen armed formations, including those of Raduyev. The governmental troops at this time included detachments of the Chechen interior ministry, the National Security Service, the border guards, and the customs service and regular defence detachments. However, there remained several small but well-armed groups which defied Maskhadov's authority – for example, one which supports Chechen ex-President Zelimkhan Yandarbiev. It will be a challenge for Maskhadov to rein in these maverick formations.[145]

The key issue remains the status of Chechenia, a decision which the Khasavyurt agreement formally postponed to 31 December 2001, although the government in Grozny began to function as one of a *de facto* sovereign state. The Russian–Chechen peace treaty signed by Presidents Yeltsin and Maskhadov on 12 May 1997 built on the Khasavyurt ceasefire. It affirmed the agreement of the parties to reject for ever the use or threat of force to resolve any disputes and serves as a basis for future treaties and accords between the parties, but does not mention Chechenia's status. Chechenia has become *de facto* an 'unrecognized republic'. The Russian Presidential Council member Emil Pain has argued that by September 1996 the Chechen crisis had reached the phase which had earlier overtaken the armed conflicts in Nagorno-Karabakh, Transdniestria and Abkhazia – that of relatively peaceful equilibrium when the centre, after suffering a military defeat, is no longer able to renew hostilities, and the separatists, feeling triumphant, do not want to. He claims that the experience of these other unrecognized republics shows that over time they adapt, even in a very unfavourable environment, so that it should not be assumed that Chechenia cannot live without Russia. Despite this, he proposed that Moscow should pursue a policy of limited and calculated engagement with the republic, which would result in a forced but gradual resolution of Chechenia's status on the basis of 'economic aid for political compromises'.[146] In this way economic instruments would replace military ones in the continued attempt to restore federal political control over Grozny.

This is clearly a more sophisticated policy option for Moscow than the crude containment of Chechenia, although significant economic aid from Moscow for the republic may realistically not be available. But it is still directed at denying Chechenia independence and preventing the Chechen struggle from being transformed from an essentially domestic conflict (despite the international implications discussed above) into an international one, as happened for example in the dispute over Nagorno-Karabakh. Russian specialists argue, first, that Chechenia's independence would raise the stakes in a number of border delimitation issues, could lead to war with Georgia (perhaps precipitated by Chechen–Abkhaz relations), and could attract foreign financial and doctrinal support for an Islamic resurgence in the new state (in June 1997 Maskhadov announced measures to enhance the role of Islamic institutions in Chechenia). [147] Secondly, the further weakening of Russia's position in the Caucasus represented by the outcome of the Chechenia campaign is linked to the continuing struggle for access to the energy resources of the Caspian and control over the related regions.[148] The issue is not so much control over the Baku–Novorossiysk pipeline through Chechenia (through which oil continued to be transported even during the peak of combat operations in the republic), which could eventually be bypassed,[149] but Russian strategic influence more broadly over the Caucasus.

Ultimately, Russian leaders may realize that the promotion of regional economic development in Chechenia and neighbouring regions, assisted by revenues from Caspian energy resources, is a more effective means of counteracting destabilizing currents and security challenges issuing from the North Caucasus than efforts at containment, even if the former course provides no guarantee of restoring Chechenia to Russian federal authority. In particular, Moscow should not be tempted by a policy of divide and rule (as support for Cossack ambitions implies, for example), since this could have explosive consequences in the North Caucasus. Russian–Chechen negotiations in summer 1997 on the transit of early Azerbaijani oil through Chechen territory offered a means to develop joint Russian–Chechen economic interests. An agreement by Chechenia to supply oil to Stravropol *krai* in exchange for grain and help in repairing the existing pipeline similarly shows that economic interests may be able to displace military antagonisms in the region.[150]

Russian military priorities and expectations in the Caucasus should be downgraded in the aftermath of the Chechenia campaign and more consideration given to the broader context and dimensions of regional security in this volatile region, as well as its impact on other CIS regions and states. This approach was implied by Yeltsin in spring 1996 when he argued that Russia, the Caucasus countries and the North Caucasus republics should unite their efforts in search of means to resolve and prevent regional crises of any kind.[151] Such a reorientation of Russian policy can by no means be assured, but it would reflect the actual decline in the resources available for Moscow to exercise traditional forms of influence. It may be the only way for the Russian state to restore stability to its troubled southwestern flanks and to overcome the national trauma inflicted by the war in Chechenia.

Conclusion

The impact of the Chechenia conflict on Russian security and military policies has been profound, although it is not yet clear how far positive and necessary lessons have been assimilated by the Russian leadership from this disastrous episode for the new Russian state. The aftermath of the conflict will continue to afflict Russian security policy decision-making in the Caucasus and overall in the CIS region. The traumatic legacy of combat in Chechenia will also haunt the efforts of the Russian military command to reconfigure its forces for future military tasks and to restore their standing in Russian society at large. The effects of the 'Chechen syndrome' on Moscow's efforts to advance its diverse and often unrealistically defined interests towards other CIS states and on the choice of means to do this, as well as on its capacity to exercise authority over the republics and regions of the Russian Federation, are continuing to unfold. Moreover, the implications of the Chechen campaign on Caucasian and non-Russian CIS leaders' goals will influence future alignments, especially those that develop in the 'Eurasian corridor' between the Caspian Sea and Ukraine/Turkey.

Despite these elements of uncertainty some broad conclusions may be drawn. The Chechenia campaign demonstrated in stark fashion the tension between Russian security policy ambitions and means, even in relation to a crisis within the Russian Federation. It highlighted the confusion in Russian security policy decision-making and the uncertain line between military and political authority. It confirmed that brutal and large-scale conflict in one part of the CIS region has inevitable security policy repercussions not only regionally, but on larger designs for CIS integration and peacekeeping. It also confirmed that such military repression (despite its occurrence within recognized Russian Federation boundaries) is a European security concern. Finally, the search for a settlement of the conflict and the stabilization of the region has forced Russian leaders to challenge ingrained assumptions and priorities and may continue to act as an unpredictable catalyst for change in Russian security policy.

Acknowledgments

The author is grateful for comments on a draft text of this chapter from Edmund Herzig and Peter Roland. A first draft presented at a conference in Chatham House in September 1995 for the Volkswagen Project 'The Post-Soviet States and European Security' was comprehensively revised to take account of events to June 1997. The chapter also benefits from research undertaken in the framework of the Ford Foundation project 'Keeping the Peace in the CIS'.

Notes

1. The most complete analysis of Russian security policy decision-making over Chechenia, which applies different models of decision-making, is in Christer Pursiainen, 'Venäjän päätöksenteko ja Euroopan unionin vaikutusmahdollisuudet: Tshetshenian tapaus'('Russian decision-making and the possibilities of the European Union to exert influence: the case of Chechenia', in Finnish) (Helsinki: Finnish Institute, 1996).
2. Interview in article by A. Zhilin, *Moskovskie novosti*, no. 1, 8–15 January 1995, pp. 1, 5.
3. This operational team, headed by Lieutenant-General Anatoly Kvashnin, consisted of officers and generals of the general staff's 1st directorate of the main operational directorate. It was tasked with the function of coordinating the activities of the FSK, MVD, border troops and the ministry of defence on the territory of the North Caucasus MD during the course of planning and preparing for an invasion operation. *Nezavisimoe voennoe obozrenie* (supplement to *Nezavisimaya gazeta*), no. 1, February 1995, pp. 1–2. See also Colonel General Y. Podkolzin, in *Zavtra*, no. 50, December 1995.
4. See analysis by F. Burlatsky, *Nezavisimaya gazeta*, 31 January 1995. On the need to create a single centre under the auspices of the defence ministry and general staff to coordinate the activities of the Russian force structures, as well as a special structure for 'operational decisions on crisis situations emerging in Russia and in the areas of its vital interests', see G. Borzenkov, *Nezavisimoe voennoe obozrenie*, (Supplement to *Nezavisimaya gazeta*) no. 4, February 1996, p. 2.
5. *Krasnaya zvezda*, 12 January 1995.
6. Although, unlike the Politburo, the Russian Security Council is only an advisory body whose resolutions can only be put into action by presidential decree. The former Security Council secretary Oleg Lobov has claimed that Yeltsin asked the opinions of all the members of the Council at the 29 November 1994 meeting and that the decision to use force in Chechenia was unanimous. Interview with Lobov in *Berlingske Tidende*, 16 September 1995, as transcribed in *Foreign Broadcast Information Service, Central Eurasia* (FBIS-SOV) 95-183, 21 September 1995, p. 35.
7. Interview in *Moskovskie novosti*, no. 1, 8–15 January 1995, p. 5. This was the outcome despite the existence of the general staff operational team on Chechenia.
8. See article by S. Surozhtsev in *Novoe vremya*, no. 2–3, January 1995, pp. 14–15.
9. ITAR-TASS news agency, 12 April 1995, in FBIS-SOV-95-070, 12 April 1995, p. 24.
10. P. Fel'gengauer, 'A War Moscow Cannot Afford to Lose', *Transition*, vol. 2, no. 11, 31 May 1996, p. 30. The frustration of Russian specialists on nationality affairs about decision-making on Chechenia is well expressed by E. Pain and A. Popov in *Izvestiya*, 10 February 1995.
11. Interfax news agency, 28 December 1994, in FBIS-SOV-94-250, 29 December 1994; radio interview, in FBIS-SOV-95-005, 9 January 1995, p. 28.
12. Interview in *Zavtra*, December 1995, no. 50.
13. *Izvestiya*, 10 December 1994; ITAR-TASS report, 23 January 1995, in FBIS-SOV-95-014, 23 January 1995, p. 33. The commander of a Pacific Fleet marine assault battalion was dismissed for refusing to carry out an order to send his battalion to Chechenia: *Izvestiya*, 14 January 1995. Many officers of the Moscow military district to be sent with newly formed units to Chechenia flatly refused to go to the war; desertion among the rank and file also sharply increased; RIA news agency report 19 January 1995, in *BBC Summary of World Broadcasts; Former Soviet Union* (SU) 2207 B/4. By April 1995 557 Russian army officers who refused to fight in Chechenia had been dismissed from the armed forces and criminal cases brought against them; see NTV report 7 April 1995, in SU/2274 S1/1.
14. Report by P. Fel'gengauer, *Segodnya*, 5 January 1995. For an operational assessment of this assault at

the time exposing military failures see Y. Kalinina, *Moskovskiy komsomelets*, 6 January 1995, in FBIS-SOV-95-005, 9 January 1995, p. 34.

15. See article by V. Zolotykhin in *Nezavisimoe voennoe obozrenie*, no. 7, April 1996, p. 2.

16. *Rossiyskie vesti*, 13 January 1995, in FBIS-SOV-95-010, 17 January 1995, p. 26.

17. For this incident and for a detailed assessment of command, staff and operational weaknesses in the Chechenia operation, see the analysis by an unidentified senior officer in *Novaya yezhednevnaya gazeta*, 28 January 1995, in *Joint Publication Research Service Report: Central Eurasia Military Affairs* (henceforth JPRS-UMA) -95-007, 21 February 1995, pp. 6–9.

18. *Komsomolskaya pravda*, 10 December 1994.

19. For Gromov's new responsibilities see P. Fel'gengauer, *Segodnya*, 14 February 1995. For details on the views of the dissenting generals and the wider context of Russian civil–military relations, see L. Goldstein, 'Russian Civil–Military Relations in the Chechen war: December 1994 - February 1995', *Journal of Slavic Military Studies,* vol.10. no.1, March 1997.

20. Report in *Izvestiya*, 18 January 1995. Vorobyev was replaced by Colonel-General Anatoly Golomev.

21. V. Vyzhutovich, *Izvestiya*, 7 December 1994.

22. See *Novoe vremya*, no. 2–3, January 1995, pp. 14–15.

23. The commander-in-chief of the airborne troops (VDV), Colonel-General Yevgeny Podkolzin, argued in early January 1995 that Grozny should not be stormed, but surrounded and blockaded and then disarmed by specially trained units. Interfax, 6 January 1995, in FBIS-SOV-005, 9 January 1995, p. 23. Podkolzin escaped censure or dismissal for his criticisms of the Chechenia campaign.

24. M. Dementeva, *Segodnya*, 15 February 1995.

25. As claimed by Presidential Council member L. Smirnyagin, *Izvestiya*, 14 December 1994. For this political element of command and control see T. Thomas, 'The Russian Armed Forces Confront Chechenia: I. Military-political aspects 11–31 December 1994', *Journal of Slavic Military Studies*, vol. 8, no. 2, June 1995, pp. 242–5. See also the views of Alexei Tsaryov, adviser to the chairman of the State Duma, in *Rossiyskie vesti*, 13 January 1995.

26. Examples of autonomous military policy are the continued bombing of Grozny in January 1995 after Yeltsin's promise that this would cease and the notable failure of Lieutenant-General Vyacheslav Tikhomirov (the then commander of the group of federal forces in Chechenia) to halt all military operations on 1 April 1996 in line with Yeltsin's unilateral ceasefire to support his peace initiative (Tikhomirov and Grachev spoke of the need to continue 'special selective operations'; see Interfax, 3 April 1996, in SU/2578 B/4; 'Fighting Rages Across Chechenia', *International Herald Tribune*, 6–7 April 1996).

27. The possibility of an initiative to withdraw federal forces from Chechenia in February 1996 prompted a strong protest from general staff officers on these grounds. Report by I. Korotchenko, *Nezavisimaya gazeta*, 10 February 1996.

28. Report by G. Cherkasov, *Segodnya*, 20 April 1996.

29. Report by A. Kasayev, *Nezavisimaya gazeta*, 23 August 1996.

30. P. Baev, *The Russian Army in a Time of Troubles* (London: Sage, 1996), p. 147.

31. In July 1995 Kulikov had been promoted from commander of the joint grouping of the federal forces in Chechenia to Russian minister of the interior.

32. See M. Shevelyov, 'A Far from Personal Matter', *Moscow News*, no. 33, 28 August–3 September 1996.

33. Interview in *Krasnaya zvezda*, 7 August 1996; *Nezavisimaya gazeta*, 23 August 1996.

34. P. Felgenhauer, *The Observer*, 25 August 1996.

35. See *Segodnya*, 23 August 1996.

36. Statement in ITAR-TASS, 19 August 1996, in FBIS-SOV-96-162, 20 August 1996, p. 19; *Krasnaya zvezda*, 21 August 1996.

37. Moscow Russian Television, 21 August 1996, in FBIS-SOV-96-164, 22 August 1996, p. 23; Moscow NTV, 21 August 1996, in FBIS-SOV-96-164, 22 August 1996, p. 24.

38. See Roy Allison, 'The Russian Armed Forces: Structures, Roles and Policies', in Vladimir Baranovsky, ed., *Russia and Europe: The Emerging Security Agenda* (Oxford: Oxford University Press, 1997), pp. 188–90.

39. The most detailed analysis of the performance of the Russian armed forces in Chechenia is N. Novichkov, V. Shegovsky, A. Sokolov and V. Shvarev, *Rossiyskie vooruzhennye sily v chechenskom konflikte: Analiz. Itogi. Vyvody'* (Moscow/Paris: Kholveg-Infoglob, 1995).

40. See e.g. Colonel-General L. Shevtsov in *Krasnaya zvezda*, 8 June 1995. Russian claims about the strength of Chechen militias appear exaggerated, but still show that the numerical balance has been heavily in the Russian favour. Grachev claimed in spring 1995 that before the initial storming of Grozny in December

1994 38,000 Russian troops and 230 tanks faced 15,000 Chechen fighters with 50 tanks; *Nezavisimaya gazeta*, 1 March 1995. An excellent account of Russian and Chechen strategy and tactics during the initial battle for Grozny can be found in T. Thomas, 'The Russian Armed Forces Confront Chechenia: II. Military Activities 11–31 December 1994', *Journal of Slavic Military Studies*, vol. 8, no. 2, June 1995. Thomas extends this detailed analysis in 'The Caucasus Conflict and Russian Security: The Russian Armed Forces Confront Chechnya III. The Battle for Grozny, 1–26 January 1995', *The Journal of Slavic Military Studies*, vol.10. no.1, March 1997. See also A. Raevsky, 'Russian Military Performance in Chechenia: An Initial Evaluation', *Journal of Slavic Military Studies*, vol. 8, no. 4, December 1995; Baev, *The Russian Army in a Time of Troubles*, pp. 143–7; C. Von Dyke, 'Kabul to Grozny: A Critique of Soviet (Russian) Counter-insurgency Doctrine', *The Journal of Slavic Military Studies* vol. 9, no. 4, December 1996. pp. 696–702. Defence minister Grachev's proclaimed plans for the Grozny military operation, as outlined in a Security Council meeting on 21 December 1994, were published in *Nezavisimaya gazeta*, 29 December 1994.

41. See S. Grigorev, *Nezavisimaya gazeta*, 21 June 1995.
42. Y. Kalinina, *Moskovski komsomolets*, 10 June 1995.
43. *Moskovskie novosti*, no. 12, 24–31 March 1996.
44. As declared by Major-General V. Shimanov, *Segodnya*, 23 July 1996. See analysis by O. Blotsky in *Nezavisimaya gazeta*, 26 July 1996. The new defence minister Rodionov referred to a total of some 70 'bandit groups' totalling 3,000–3,500 men in Chechenia at this time, which should be dealt with by Russian MVD special troops; *Krasnaya zvezda*, 7 August 1996.
45. Report by I. Maksakov, *Nezavisimaya gazeta*, 7 August 1996.
46. See e.g. the claims of Tikhomirov in *Krasnaya zvezda*, 16 February 1996.
47. For an elaborate argument that Chechen militias benefit from the support of diverse sources outside as well as within Chechenia see A. Zhilin, 'Troops Will Not Crush the Chechen Resistance', *Moscow News*, no. 33, 28 August–3 September, 1996, p. 3.
48. See A. Iskandarian, 'The Unwinnable War', *War Report*, no. 45, September 1996, p. 26.
49. Moscow Interfax and ITAR-TASS World Service, 12 August 1996, in FBIS-SOV-96-157, 13 August 1996, p. 31.
50. Ostankino Channel 1 TV, Moscow, 8 January 1995, in SU/2197 B/5.
51. Y. Zaynashev, *Moskovskiy komsomolets*, 27 January 1995, cited in Raevsky, 'Russian Military Performance in Chechenia', p. 687.
52. *Izvestiya*, 18 January 1995.
53. P. Anokhin, *Rossiyskie vesti*, 30 December 1994.
54. Reserve Colonel Y. Deryugin, *Rossiyskie vesti*, 10 January 1995.
55. Colonel O. Namsarayev, in *Armeyskiy sbornik*, no. 5, May 1995, pp. 30–2. This also contains an analysis of the main features of guerrilla operations in Chechenia.
56. A. Zhilin, 'Army in Chechenia Ready to Explode', *Moscow News*, no. 1, 12–18 January 1996, p. 3.
57. These redeployments were reported in *Segodnya*, 29 December 1994; *Izvestiya*, 30 December 1994.
58. P. Felgengauer, *Segodnya*, 14 December 1994. A. Lebed on NTV interview, 14 February 1995, in SU/2229 B/9-10.
59. See Lieutenant-General Nikolai Tsymbal, *Rossiyskie vesti*, 10 January 1995. The main worries of servicemen in Chechenia in spring 1996 were listed by a group of State Duma deputies after a visit to the region; see *Moskovskie novosti*, no. 12, 24–31 March 1996, p. 6.
60. Zhilin, 'Army in Chechenia Ready to Explode', p. 3.
61. A. Zhilin, 'Army Hits Self-Destruct Button', *Moscow News*, no. 11, 21–27 March 1996.
62. Emil Pain, *Rossiyskie vesti*, 19 September 1996.
63. Reported by deputy interior forces commander, Lieutenant-General Stanislav Kavun, *Segodnya*, 4 May 1995.
64. V. Larionov, 'War in Chechenia: The View of a Russian Military Strategist', *FSU 15 Nations: Policy and Security*, February 1996. p. 4. On the technological failures of Russian tanks, armoured personnel carriers and other equipment used in Chechenia see *Ogonyok*, no. 21, May 1996, pp. 16–18.
65. As stated by Aleksandr Lebed at a State Duma hearing; report by O. Gerasimenko, *Komsomolskaya pravda*, 16 October 1996.
66. A. Kasaev, 'The War of Yeltsin's Succession', *War Report*, no. 45, September 1996, p. 25.
67. As stated by Major-General Vladimir Osadchiy and Vasily Vorobyov of the main directorate of the military budget and financing: ITAR-TASS World Service, 24 August 1995, in FBIS-SOV-95-156, 25 August 1995, p. 8, and 2 August 1995, in FBIS-SOV-95-148, 2 August 1995, p. 25.

68. Lieutenant-General Alexandr Naumov; Moscow ITAR-TASS, 19 October 1995, in FBIS-SOV-96-203, 20 October 1995, p. 45.
69. Lieutenant-Gen. Stanislav Katun, Moscow ITAR-TASS, 2 February 1996, in FBIS-SOV-96-023, 2 February 1996, p. 3.
70. Andrei Illarionov, *Moskovskie novosti*, no. 4, 28 January–4 February 1996, p. 19.
71. Conference during 28 February – 3 March 1995, *Nezavisimaya gazeta*, 1 March 1995.
72. *Obshchaya gazeta*, no. 13/89, 30 March–5 April 1995.
73. Meeting in the Russian defence ministry, ITAR-TASS 28 February 1995, in SU/2241 B/3.
74. For example, P. Fel'gengauer, *Segodnya*, 23 February 1995.
75. ITAR-TASS, 8 February 1995, in SU/22224 B/3.
76. ITAR-TASS, 4 July 1995, in FBIS-SOV-95-128, 5 July 1995, p. 15. For an interview with the commander of the 58th Army, Lieutenant-General G. Troshev, see *Krasnaya zvezda*, 2 March 1996.
77. D. Yestafev, *Nezavisimoe voennoe obozrenie*, January 1996, no. 1, p. 2.
78. P. Zhuralev, *Segodnya*, 13 January 1995; I. Bulavinov, *Kommersant-Daily*, 17 January 1995; A. Arbatov, *Moskovskie novosti*, no. 3, 15–22 January 1995, p. 7.
79. As claimed by Viktor Ilyukhin, chairman of the State Duma's Security Committee; Interfax, 18 February 1995, in FBIS-SOV-95-035, 22 February 1995, p. 28.
80. See the analysis by retired Major-General V. Larionov, in *Nezavisimoe voennoe obozrenie*, no. 1, January 1996, p. 4. For defence minister Grachev's view that Russia's enemies are dreaming that 'a part of the Northern Caucasus separated from Russia will block its access to the Black and Caspian seas', see Interfax, Moscow, 21 February 1996, in FBIS-SOV-96-036, 22 February 1996, p. 2.
81. For a breakdown of the Russian order of battle in the North Caucasus MD and the implications for it of the changes of the CFE review conference, see Andrew Duncan, 'Russian Force in Decline – Part 4', *Jane's Intelligence Review*, December 1996, pp. 540–54. The Article 5 limits on military equipment for the flank regions of the CFE Treaty were increased and the geographical scope of the flank zone was altered.
82. The legacy of such instability after the end of open hostilities in Chechenia has been emphasized by the federation council deputy chairman Valery Kokov; see *Rossiyskie vesti*, 4 December 1996.
83. Edict on 31 January 1995, in ITAR-TASS World Service 31 January 1995, FBIS-SOV-95-021 1 February 1995, pp. 25–6.
84. *Krasnaya zvezda*, 28 February 1996.
85. See *Izvestiya*, 17 January 1996; 26 January 1996. On the dangers of a popular rebellion in Dagestan see S. Cornell, 'A Chechen State?', *Central Asian Survey*, no. 2, vol. 16, 1997, pp. 206–7.
86. A. Matveeva, *Dagestan*, FSS Briefing, no. 13, May 1997 (London: Royal Institute of International Affairs), p. 5.
87. See S. Shermatova, *Moscow News*, no. 47, 4–10 December 1996, p. 2.
88. For the role of the Confederation in the Chechen conflict see D. Billingsley, 'Confederates of the Caucasus', *Jane's Intelligence Review*, February 1997, pp. 66–8.
89. Ostankino TV report, Moscow 28 February 1995, in SU/2241 B/4.
90. See his speech reported by ITAR-TASS World Service, 16 February 1996, in FBIS-SOV-96-033, 16 February 1996, p. 3. Defence minister Grachev went further to claim that 'Chechenia is a trial balloon of Russia's strategic enemies, whose major goal is to disintegrate and separate parts of Russian territory'; Interfax, Moscow, 21 February, FBIS-SOV-96-036, 22 February 1996, p. 2.
91. State Duma defence committee chairman, General Lev Rokhlin, *Krasnaya zvezda*, 4 December 1996.
92. Colonel-General L. Shevtsov, *Krasnaya zvezda*, 8 June 1995.
93. Moscow Interfax report, 21 June 1995, in FBIS-SOV-95-120, 22 June 1995, p. 42.
94. *Moskovskie novosti*, no. 12, 24–31 March 1996, p. 6.
95. See I. Rotar, *Izvestiya*, 14 March 1996; A. Zhelenin and I. Makhakov, *Nezavisimaya gazeta*, 19 November 1996.
96. Matveeva, *Dagestan*, p. 5.
97. See *Kommersant-Daily*, 17 December 1996.
98. See I. Peplov *Nezavisimoe voennoe obozrenie*, no. 11, March 1997, p. 2.
99. *Monitor*, vol. iii, no. 123, 24 June 1997.
100. See Scott Parrish, 'A Turning Point in the Chechen Conflict', *Transition*, vol. 1, no. 13, 28 July 1995. Yegor Gaidar predicted in December 1994 that the Russian use of force would result in 'an outburst of terror in the North Caucasus', which would require an extreme response and threaten the stability of democracy; Radio Russia report 10 December 1994, in SU/2177 B/4.

101. *Izvestiya*, 19 March 1996.
102. See *Nezavisimaya gazeta*, 23 January 1996.
103. L. Leontyeva, 'Armovir. Pyatigorsk – Where next?', *Moscow News*, no. 17–18, 15–21 May 1997, p. 3.
104. For the response of these Russian regions to the aftermath of the Budennovsk events see also Fiona Hill, *Russia's Tinderbox: Conflict in the North Caucasus and its Implications for the Future of the Russian Federation*, Strengthening Democratic Institutions Project, Harvard University, September 1995, pp. 90–2. This study is an excellent analysis of the relationship between the regional policy of the Russian Federation and conflict in the North Caucasus.
105. See Pavel Baev, *Russia's Policy in the North Caucasus and the War in Chechenia*, FSS Briefing, no. 2, March 1995 (London: Royal Institute of International Affairs). For an analysis of the Terek Cossacks see *Russia Briefing*, vol. 3, no. 5, 29 May 1995, pp. 7–12. See also L. Leontyeva, 'Redivision in Store for Chechenia?', *Moscow News*, no. 30, 4–10 August; G. Mashtakova, 'Cossacks Spell Trouble for Chechenia's Russians', *Moscow News*, no. 5, 13–19 February 1997.
106. 'Cossack's Last Stand', *Moscow News*, no. 3, 30 January–5 February 1997; interview with Berezovsky in *Nezavisimaya gazeta*, 18 January 1997; interview with Cossacks Union Senior Vice Chairman Vladimir Naumov, *Moscow News*, no. 2, 23–29 January 1997.
107. For the ambitions of the Terek Cossack Troops Ataman, Vladimir Shevtsov, see *Nezavisimaya gazeta*, 12 February 1997.
108. Reports in FBIS-SOV-95-012, 19 January 1995, pp. 24–5.
109. *Rossiyskie vesti*, 18 January 1995.
110. ITAR-TASS World Service, 17 January 1995, FBIS-SOV-95-012, 19 January 1995, p. 25.
111. *International Herald Tribune*, 10 January 1995.
112. Ostankino TV, 29 December 1994, in FBIS-SOV-94-251, 30 December 1994, pp. 11–12.
113. V. Zolotykhin, *Nezavisimoe voennoe obozrenie*, no. 7, April 1996, p. 2.
114. For example, Lieutenant-General Stanislav Kavun, deputy commander of the interior forces, in *Rossiyskie vesti*, 30 January 1996.
115. Viktor Ilyukhin, *Pravda*, 4 December 1996.
116. See Roy Allison, *Military Forces in the Soviet Successor States*, Adelphi Paper 280 (London: IISS, 1993), pp. 76–7.
117. Tbilisi Radio, 15 January 1996, in FBIS-SOV-96-010, 16 January 1996, p. 70.
118. Statement by Commander of the Russian federal border guards, Colonel-General Andrei Nikolayev, *Segodnya*, 4 February 1995.
119. Report by Iprinda news agency, 2 April 1996, in SU/2578 B/6.
120. Moscow Interfax, 1 March 1995, in FBIS-SOV-95-042, 3 March 1995, p. 24.
121. Interfax, 29 May–2 June; ITAR-TASS, 3 June, in *Monitor*, vol. iii, no. 109, 4 June 1997. However, Chechen former first deputy minister Shamil Basayev, who commanded a Chechen force in previous fighting in Abkhazia, still found it difficult to accept the new policy on Georgia.
122. See the analysis of visits to Chechenia and Georgia made by Russian Security Council deputy secretary Boris Berezovsky in autumn 1996, *Segodnya*, 11 November 1996.
123. The critical responses of various political parties and groups in CIS states to the Russian initial assault on Grozny are listed in *Izvestiya*, 24 December 1994.
124. For the initial responses to the Chechen campaign see Taras Kuzio, 'The Chechenia Crisis and the "Near Abroad"', *Central Asian Survey*, vol. 14, no. 4, 1995.
125. This argument is developed further by Pavel Baev in *Russia's Policies in the Caucasus*, Former Soviet South Project Paper (London: Royal Institute of International Affairs, 1997); 'Challenges and Options in the Caucasus and Central Asia', unpublished paper for conference at US Army War College, 22–24 April 1997.
126. For example, L. Shevtsova, *Komsomolskaya pravda*, 29 December 1994.
127. *Segodnya*, 11 January 1995.
128. See report by N. Kalashnikova, *Kommersant–Daily*, 22 February 1995.
129. Boutros Boutros-Ghali in report by ITAR-TASS World Service, 15 April 1995, in FBIS-SOV-95-074, 18 April 1995, p. 16.
130. Dismissal of proposal presented by Chechen leader Zelimkhan Yandarbiev by the Russian minister for nationalities Vyacheslav Mikhailov, Moscow ITAR-TASS, 24 July 1996, FBIS-SOV-96-144, 25 July 1996, p. 27.
131. For the overall Western reaction to the Chechen crisis see Taras Kuzio, 'International Reaction to the Chechen Crisis', *Central Asian Survey*, vol. 15, no. 1, 1996, pp. 97–106.

132. For EU responses to the Chechenia crisis and the options for EU influence on Russian policy in it, see Pursiainen, 'Venäjän päätöksenteko ja Euroopan unionin vaikutusmahdollisuudet: Tshetshenian tapaus', pp. 117–29.
133. See A. Kortunov in *Moscow News*, no. 2, 13–18 January 1995, p. 5.
134. This is argued strongly by the Russian security policy specialist Sergei Oznobishchev, e.g. in *Segodnya*, 3 February 1995.
135. For the text of the Khasavyurt agreement see *Izvestiya*, 3 September 1996; see also Peter Rutland, 'A Fragile Peace', *Transition*, vol. 3, no. 23, 15 November 1996.
136. See Valery Tishkov, 'Sem' variantov. Zametki o vykhode iz chechenskogo krizisa', *Svobodnaya mysl'*, no. 5, 1996; 'Seven Scenarios for the Sake of One', *Moscow News*, no. 13, 4–10 April 1996, p. 4.
137. Statement on 6 April 1996, broadcast by Russia TV, in SU/2580 B/4. For Yeltsin's assessment of the March 1996 plan on various Russian television and radio channels on 31 March 1996 see SU/2576 B/1-6. For the text of his decree on settling the Chechenia crisis see ITAR-TASS World Service, 1 April 1996, FBIS-SOV-96-063, 1 April 1996, pp. 5–6.
138. See assessment by P. Fel'gengauer, *Segodnya*, 1 August 1996.
139. Interview with Russian minister of nationalities, Vyacheslav Mikhailov, *Argumenty i fakty*, no. 31, 1995, p. 3.
140. Colonel. D. Stolbovoy, 'Will Lebed's Agreement with the Separatists Lead to Peace in Chechenia?', *FSU 15 Nations: Policy and Security*, August 1996, p. 24; Emil Pain, *Rossiyskie vesti*, 19 September 1996.
141. Speech at State Duma emergency meeting on the Chechen issue on 29 November 1996, *Krasnaya zvezda*, 4 December 1996.
142. For a critique of the idea of a Russian blockade of Chechenia see A. Sultygov, *Nezavisimaya gazeta*, 24 October 1996.
143. The Chechen side guaranteed the security of pipelines, oil extraction facilities and refineries to the federal centre; text of agreement in *Rossiyskie vesti*, 27 November 1996.
144. See *Izvestiya*, 30 January 1997.
145. *Obshchaya gazeta*, 8–14 May 1997, p. 3.
146. *Rossiyskie vesti*, 19 September 1996.
147. See V. Tishkov, 'Can Chechenia Survive without Russia?', *Moscow News*, no. 11, 27 March–1 April 1997, p. 5.
148. A. Pushkov, 'Shifts of Balance in the Caucasus', *Moscow News*, no. 40, 16–22 October 1996, p. 5.
149. On the initial guarantees by the Transneft company that Russia will ensure a stable supply of 'early' oil via the Baku–Grozny–Novorossiysk route, despite the outbreak of war in Chechenia, see *Izvestiya*, 21 December 1995. For the survival of the pipeline through the war and Chechenia's influence on the competition over future pipeline routes, see *Segodnya*, 11 November 1996.
150. ITAR-TASS, 11 June 1997; in *Monitor*, 17 June 1997. For a more pessimistic view that Russia and Chechenia were poised for an economic war, see *Segodnya*, 24 April 1997.
151. Interview with Yeltsin, *Izvestiya*, 24 May 1996. Yeltsin placed emphasis, however, on the capacities of CIS countries in resolving local conflicts in the region rather than international organizations and claimed that some international forces were 'interested in keeping a regional conflict on Russian territory smouldering'.

14 Regional structures of security policy within the CIS

Andrei Zagorski

The Commonwealth of Independent States was created in 1991 to preserve the complex economic ties between the various parts of the former Soviet Union and maintain a common security space in order to preserve the military power of the Soviet Union in some form. Such ambitions quickly proved incompatible with the process of state-building that began in the newly independent states. The preservation and consolidation of national independence *vis-à-vis* the old centre in Moscow was given precedence. Even Russia neglected relations with the 'near abroad' in the first two years of independence, concentrating on building a partnership with the West.

However, as has been explained in Chapter 1, after this initial period Russian foreign policy changed. Russia's strategy towards the CIS is now based on the concept of creating an integrated political and economic community of states. The pursuit of reintegration by Russia is taking place despite the potentially high economic and political costs, although how far it will go remains to be tested. It seems to be driven in part by a general reorientation of Russian foreign policy informed by the principles of Realist power politics and great-power ambitions.

The principal manifestations of this strategy are moves towards closer economic cooperation. As much of the decline in the economic output of the former Soviet states is due to the severing of economic and trade links, this is welcomed by the newly independent states (NIS). Security cooperation is more problematic, since the military resources of the non-Russian states are small. Closer military involvement with Russia, especially if it entails Russian access to military bases in other states, therefore gives Russia the means of exerting leverage on the other new Eurasian states. At the same time, security links with Russia are desirable for many of these states since they lack the resources to provide adequately for their own security.

Security cooperation in the CIS framework, defined in traditional military (defence) terms, involves various elements:

- a set of institutions and instruments of military-political cooperation;
- a collective security framework based on the Tashkent collective security agreement of 15 May 1992;

- maintenance of the infrastructure of strategic forces;
- keeping the peace in the CIS;
- border protection;
- intelligence;
- military-economic cooperation and procurement;
- social standards for military personnel and pensioners, and their family members.

This chapter does not deal with the whole set of security-related issues in the CIS. It seeks first to locate the CIS 'collective security' framework among other security-related instruments of the Commonwealth and to identify the kind of security cooperation which exists among the CIS states. Is it really a collective security framework, or a defence alliance, or neither? The chapter then examines the evolution of the collective security discourse in the CIS, from the attempts to retain single control of the armed forces of the former USSR to conceptualizing CIS security cooperation as a means of projecting the Russian military posture beyond Russia's national borders.

Security cooperation in the CIS does not involve all member states of the Commonwealth. After the extension of the 1992 Tashkent agreement to Azerbaijan, Belarus and Georgia in 1993, this multilateral framework has included nine states,[1] while three participating states[2] of the CIS (Ukraine, Moldova and Turkmenistan) have so far refrained from adopting any security instruments of the Commonwealth. Although Azerbaijan re-entered the CIS and acceded to the Tashkent agreement in September 1993, it remains one of the most uncooperative partners for Russia in the security field. Its position remains close to that of the three participating states mentioned above.[3] Especially since 1996 Uzbekistan has maintained a similar position in relation to CIS documents on military cooperation.

The 1992 Tashkent agreement on collective security: concepts and definitions

Military-political structures in the CIS: a space for the Tashkent agreement

For almost a year, from May 1992 until mid-1993, the institutional status of the Tashkent agreement remained rather unclear. On the one hand, there existed a set of CIS military-political bodies either provided for in the Charter of the CIS or established on the basis of special agreements. The Council of the Heads of State (CHS) was established as the supreme political body taking all decisions, including those on military-political issues; the Council of Heads of Government was to deal, as far as security issues are concerned, mainly with problems of military production, harmonization of social standards for military personnel and pensioners, etc. The specific military-political bodies reporting to the CHS have been the Council of Defence Ministers (CDM), the General Headquarters of the Joint Armed Forces of the CIS (GHJAF), headed by the commander-in-chief of JAF (for the whole period of the existence of GHJAF it was headed by the last defence minister of the Soviet Union, Marshal Yevgeny Shaposhnikov), and the Council of Commanders of Border Troops.

The Tashkent agreement on collective security of 15 May 1992 initially remained somewhat apart from other CIS structures, and not only because it then had only six members. The agreement explicitly provided for a parallel system of bodies. It envisaged the establishment of a separate political body, the Collective Security Council (CSC), consisting of the heads of the member states and including the commander-in-chief of JAF of the CIS. The agreement also envisaged other bodies to be established by the CSC for the purposes of coordinating and developing joint activities of the member states. The GHJAF was entitled to fulfil those tasks only provisionally, until the CSC and other bodies issuing from the Tashkent agreement were established.[4]

The Tashkent agreement entered into force on 20 April 1994 for five years; but it remained frozen even after this date until a visible *rapprochement* of the Tashkent framework and the reformed CIS bodies began. This resulted from both the gradual downgrading of the previous CIS bodies and the slow and incomplete institutionalization of the Tashkent agreement.

The CSC was inaugurated in December 1993 at a meeting of the CHS in Ashgabat, Turkmenistan. At the same meeting, the secretary-general of CSC was appointed. However, at this point the institutionalization of the Tashkent agreement came to a halt, and proceeded through absorption of the CIS structures; the CSC has never met separately, but only at the margins of CHS sessions.

This development was facilitated by the gradual enlargement of the membership of the Tashkent agreement. With its extension to Azerbaijan, Belarus and Georgia in 1993, membership has become identical to the composition of the CIS security bodies. This enabled the formerly purely CIS bodies to be used for the purposes of the collective security framework. Already in early 1993 the CIS Council of Defence Ministers began convening meetings of member states of the Tashkent agreement. Indeed, meetings of the ministers of those member states decided the fate of the GHJAF.

The fusion of the Tashkent agreement and CIS bodies was also made easier by developments in the Commonwealth. From 1993, the establishment of specific collective security mechanisms appeared unnecessary after the CIS bodies had lost any other rationale. The developments undermining the *raison d'être* of the common CIS military-political structures included:

- the failure, in 1992, to establish the common purpose forces (*Sily obshchego naznacheniya* or SON), which remained under GHJAF;
- the establishment of national armed forces by the newly independent states, including Russia;
- the transfer, in 1993, of the entire control over nuclear weapons from the GHJAF to Russia (informally, the 'CIS' nuclear forces always remained controlled by Russia even while formally incorporated into the GHJAF);
- the failure, in 1993, to develop a convincing CIS peacekeeping capability in the form of standby forces subordinated to the GHJAF during peacekeeping operations.

As a result of those developments, in 1993 the GHJAF had authority over only three dozen generals and 300 officers working for the CIS military headquarters in Moscow. This development resulted in the replacement of the GHJAF by the Staff for Coordination of Military Cooperation of the CIS countries (SCMC) under General Victor Samsonov in September 1993.[5] The key differences between the GHJAF and the SCMC were a downgrading from subordination under CHS to subordination under the CIS Council of Defence Ministers; and that the SCMC provides only coordination among the CIS states, whereas the GHJAF was an instrument for the management of armed forces.

With these developments, the only remaining purpose for the CIS military structures appeared to be that of taking over the collective security of the Tashkent agreement member states. Since 1994, the CDM and the SCMC have *de facto* become the relevant bodies of the Tashkent agreement, all defence and security cooperation within the CIS having been concentrated among the members of that agreement.

Collective security or collective defence? Or neither?

Collective security?

If one were to trust the official title of the Tashkent agreement one would have to assume that its purpose is to provide collective security among CIS members. The definitions of both collective security and collective defence in Russia and the CIS are rather broad.[6] 'Collective security' is usually defined as a framework which, prohibiting the use or threat of use of military force in interstate relations and providing for mechanisms of peaceful conflict resolution among its members, is directed inwards and seeks to prevent or to stop aggression among member states of the organization, whoever might turn out to become the aggressor. By contrast, 'collective defence' is a framework directed towards outside challenges and is aimed at containing or countering external threats. Examination of the provisions of the Tashkent agreement makes it clear that it has little to do with the concept of collective security, and much more with collective defence:[7]

- parties to the Tashkent agreement shall refrain from joining any military alliances nor will they participate in any groupings of countries or any actions directed against any other member state of the agreement (Article 1);
- they shall consult each other on all relevant issues of international security affecting their interests, and shall adjust their positions (Article 2);
- they shall start consultations immediately after a threat has arisen to the security, territorial integrity or sovereignty of any or of several member states, or to international peace and security (Article 2);
- aggression against one party to the agreement is regarded as aggression against all other parties, which shall provide the victim of aggression with necessary assistance including military assistance according to Article 51 of the UN Charter (Article 4).

Chapter III of the CIS Statute (on collective security and military-political cooperation) provides for similar obligations;[8] so do both 'military doctrines' of the CIS, approved respectively in November 1992 and February 1995. The 1992 Bishkek conception of military security of the member states of the CIS stipulates that 'the main purpose of the military policy is to ensure guaranteed protection of the member states of the Commonwealth of Independent States from external threats and a possible aggression'.[9] The 1995 Almaty concept of collective security of the member states of the agreement on collective security stipulates that the aim of the framework is to prevent wars and military conflicts and, in the event of their outbreak, to guarantee the protection of the interests, sovereignty and territorial integrity of the member states. The military forces of the collective security system shall be designed, according to the 1995 concept, to contain a possible aggressor, to uncover preparations for a possible aggression in a timely way and to counteract them, to ensure the protection of the borders of the member states, and to participate in peace-keeping operations.

The latter definitions are somewhat broader than those commonly understood by the concept of collective defence. The 1992 Bishkek concept also stipulates that member states shall assist one another in resolving and preventing conflicts on the territory of any CIS state. The former secretary of the CIS Council of Defence Ministers, General Ivashov, promotes the idea that the 'stabilization of relations within the Commonwealth, and the elimination of existing causes of tensions' should figure among the tasks of the collective security framework.[10] However, this task was explicitly delegated in Bishkek to separate CIS instruments providing for the modalities of establishing groups of military observers and collective peacekeeping forces.[11] Also, while the 1995 Almaty concept provides the CSC with the possibility of establishing peacekeeping forces, it is the practice of the CIS that the Tashkent collective security framework is kept clearly separate from the peacekeeping instruments. This was confirmed after Azerbaijan joined the Tashkent agreement and insisted, later in 1993, that the agreement should be activated not only in the event of an external threat but also in the event of a conflict among the parties to the agreement.[12] However, Moscow had no intention of allowing Baku to activate the agreement in the conflict over Nagorno-Karabakh and insisted that the framework was designed to deal only with challenges arising outside the CIS area, while the peacekeeping instruments of the CIS should be used for stopping and/or resolving the conflicts inside the Commonwealth.

A brief survey of the Tashkent agreement and other related provisions reveals that they are not directed inside the agreement area as a collective security mechanism would be; they are, rather, aimed at countering external security challenges, including military ones. References to peacekeeping operations should not be allowed to mislead in this context: the CIS peace-keeping instruments are no part of the Tashkent system.

Collective defence?

Judging from the Tashkent agreement and related documents, it would be correct to assume that they provide for the establishment of a collective defence system (or alliance). However, this conclusion can be questioned. In the first place, a collective defence framework is most likely to be based upon a community of values of its member states. This would be the case with the NIS only if they decided to re-establish the Soviet Union, though even in the Soviet period common values appeared only on the surface, while beneath the façade the traditional values largely prevailed. If the transformation of the NIS continues and deepens, it is most likely that they would represent different sets of values, with the basic divide occurring between the European and the Asian countries.

Linked to the question of common values is that of common interests. Not only are the interests of the NIS quite divergent, especially in the sphere of military security; in the case of the CIS another crucial prerequisite of a defence alliance is lacking as well, namely the existence of a serious common external threat which, in the eyes of the parties to the agreement, would make common defence necessary for all of them. If one speaks of common challenges for the CIS states, then this applies only at the regional level, not with respect to the entire Commonwealth. Interestingly, it was Marshal Shaposhnikov who came to the conclusion that the establishment of JAF was premature and that the re-establishment of these forces was hardly feasible, at least for as long as there was no explicit probable enemy.[13] The rationale which General Ivashov implies for the restoration of a single defence area appears insufficient to fill this gap.[14] This does not imply that there has been no rationale for the member states of the Tashkent agreement to join its framework, but it has had nothing to do with the recognition of a common threat to the member states.

For Armenia, Russia remains the basic strategic partner in a hostile environment, particularly against the background of the conflict over Nagorno-Karabakh. In this context, membership of the Tashkent agreement held a special value for Azerbaijan as well. Though attempts by Baku to activate the agreement in order to exert pressure on Armenia have predictably failed, membership of the agreement remains an important tool for Baku in neutralizing attempts by Armenia to activate the agreement against its neighbour.

For Georgia, accession to the Tashkent agreement was largely the price paid for the survival of the Shevardnadze regime. Later on, the bargaining with Russia over the military bases in Georgia, which form part of the military-political framework of the CIS, became an important element in Georgian efforts to activate Russian anti-Turkish sentiments in order to receive Russian support in the conflict with Abkhazia. The restoration of the territorial integrity of Georgia became a precondition of the deployment of Russian bases in Georgia.

Most of the Central Asian states (with the exception of Turkmenistan) sought, through participation in the alliance with Russia, to ensure support from the latter in developing and maintaining their national armies. After some hesitation, especially on the part of Kazakstan, most Central Asian states tended to regard Russia as the main guarantor of their security *vis-à-vis* a common challenge – China. For Uzbekistan, the Russian umbrella and the military involvement in Tajikistan gave it a useful means of asserting itself as a regional power and increasing its own regional role at the expense both of other Central Asian states and of Russia. For the current Tajik regime, no survival would be possible without economic and military support from Russia. For all the diversity of their particular interests, most of the Central Asian states see the Tashkent agreement as a means of preventing Russia from withdrawing from the region.

Specific interests in joining the Tashkent agreement were evident in Belarus even before summer 1994. The military-industrial complex sought to retain orders from Russia and to prolong Russian subsidies to military enterprises. Joining the Tashkent agreement was also largely regarded in Belarus as a part and condition of the overall *rapprochement* with Russia from which Minsk expected economic benefits.[15]

The members of the Tashkent agreement, then, appear to be bound together solely by their vertical relations with Russia; or, as Dmitri Trenin puts it, the CIS states have only one factor in common – they all are located in the Russian periphery, with Russia having interests in each of the regions of the FSU. The single strategic space – a buffer dividing Russia from the 'traditional abroad' – exists, therefore, only in Russian discourse and is nothing but a fiction for the rest of the NIS.[16] Indeed, the increasing differentiation of security challenges is admitted even by the current military bureaucracy of the CIS, which is obviously exaggerating the risks in order to strengthen the need for military input into the various CIS structures.

There is no or almost no readiness on the part of individual members to provide military assistance to one another under the Tashkent agreement. It appears obvious that neither Armenia nor Azerbaijan would assist each other against any enemy. For the 'failed' or almost 'failed' states (Tajikistan, Georgia) the question of providing assistance to other states is of no relevance at all – they need assistance themselves. The issue of eventually sending troops to Tajikistan played a role in the Belarusian debate in 1993 over the Tashkent agreement, and the precondition of the accession of Minsk to the agreement was that the Belarusian armed forces should not be sent to conflict areas, nor should foreign troops be deployed on Belarusian soil without the consent of the parliament.[17]

The constitutions of most of the Central Asian CIS states prevent their armed forces from being sent abroad without a special decision by their respective parliaments (actually, a legal provision to this effect also exists in the Russian Federation: sending troops abroad should be authorized by the Council of Federation, the upper chamber of the Federal Assembly). The reluctance of Kazakstan, Kyrgyzstan and Uzbekistan to participate to the agreed extent in guarding the Tajik border and in the 'peacekeeping' operation in Tajikistan reveals that they are neither in a position nor willing to contribute substantially to 'common defence', but rely instead on the Russian 'shield', including the nuclear one.

The reluctance of all CIS states, despite pressure from Russia, to send even symbolic contingents to join the 'CIS' peacekeeping force deployed since 1994 in Abkhazia (Georgia) shows that none of them takes the 'mutual' nature of assistance seriously.

Considering the lack of a common military threat as well as the reluctance of the members of the Tashkent agreement to provide assistance to one another, it would be reasonable to conclude that despite its formal designation the Tashkent agreement can hardly be characterized as a common defence alliance.

The evolution of CIS collective security debates

The initial stage: the attempt to maintain the integrity of the former Soviet army

The debates at the initial stage of the development of the CIS proceeded on the assumption that the integrity of the Soviet armed forces (unitary control over them, the maintenance of common infrastructure, military production and procurement, etc.) could be preserved despite the dissolution of the Soviet Union. The GHJAF, which became the manager of the former Soviet military assets, proposed a long transitional period during which the armed forces of the FSU would remain under the sole control of the GHJAF, and the member states of the CIS would refrain from establishing national armies. Later in 1991, Marshal Shaposhnikov, the last Soviet defence minister and the first commander-in-chief of the JAF, developed proposals to transform Soviet armed forces into the Joint Armed Forces of the CIS within five years.[18]

The essence of his concept can be boiled down to subordinating to the GHJAF almost all former Soviet defence structures and systems, while the armed forces would continue to be guided by the same objectives as before during at least the period of transition. In parallel, the NIS would be developing the relevant defence institutions and expertise, and would harmonize national approaches to military construction; jointly develop and implement a reform of the armed forces; and draft legislation on defence matters and on the social status of the military personnel, etc. During the period of transition, the NIS would have to refrain from establishing national armies and restrict themselves to forming only republican guards for domestic purposes. A single defence budget would be formed on the basis of financial contributions from all states. Military formations deployed on the territory of the CIS states, after full training, could later be administratively resubordinated to the defence ministries of the respective states while remaining under the operational control of the GHJAF. This would avoid the destruction of common defence assets – common air defence, ABM, command, control and communications, training of personnel, the development and production of armaments and military equipment.

The 'Shaposhnikov doctrine' provided the basis for the idea of establishing, for the transitional period, common purpose forces (SON) as laid down in the agreement of eight CIS countries endorsed in Minsk on 14 February 1992.[19] The concept of common purpose forces, while compromising the proclaimed intentions of a number of countries (primarily Ukraine, Moldova and Azerbaijan) to develop national armed forces, stipulated that all non-strategic forces should be divided into those directly subordinated to the GHJAF and those under national jurisdiction but subordinated to the GHJAF for operational purposes only. This concept dominated the agreement on the status of common purpose forces in the period of transition adopted by the CHS in Kiev on 20 March 1992. The Kiev agreement even provided for the establishment of common purpose forces headquarters within the GHJAF. However, even by the time of the summit in Kiev the concept of common purpose forces had lost its attraction, since four out of the eight initial signatories had decided to form national armed forces independent of the JAF and thus had abandoned the agreement.[20] The idea of common purpose forces was pursued merely out of inertia. Eventually, given that the NIS had decided to establish national armed forces and no conventional forces were any longer subordinated to the GHJAF, in July 1992 the CHS finally dissolved the common purpose forces headquarters.

The Tashkent agreement on collective security was signed on 15 May 1992 in the context of the failure to maintain the integrity of the former Soviet armed forces. According to General Leonid Ivashov, secretary of the CIS Council of Defence Ministers, the agreement offered the hope that, in a situation of almost uncontrolled disintegration of the conventional armed forces of the FSU, at least the core of the previous military system could be secured from total dissolution.[21] Thus the main task of the Tashkent agreement was to stop the progressive erosion of what remained of the former Soviet military infrastructure, and to maintain the integrity of the armed forces of the member states of the agreement to the greatest possible extent. However, the Tashkent agreement also failed to achieve this end. As General Ivashov admits, the treaty and other related instruments only slowed down military disintegration in the Commonwealth, which finally resulted in the dissolution of a single defence area, a low level of recruitment to the armed forces and a low combat capability.[22]

The failure to maintain the integrity of the armed forces of the FSU resulted in a crisis in the CIS military structures. This crisis broke openly in 1993 and was related to the discussion over the fate of the GHJAF. The general headquarters was finally dissolved, but the more substantial issue was how defence relations in the CIS could be conceptualized thereafter. According to Marshal Shaposhnikov, the following concepts had been under discussion in 1992 and 1993 after the failure of the common purpose forces concept:[23]

- Maintenance of the structures for military coordination which already existed in the CIS. This option implied a transformation of the GHJAF into a body for the pure coordination of military cooperation among CIS members, though the CIS faced increasing difficulties in securing funding for the maintenance of a military structure.
- A total bilateralization of security cooperation among members of the Commonwealth.

- The voluntary delegation of some areas of authority in the field of defence to one state which would have the capacity for leadership. This option implied the resubordination of the GHJAF to the Russian defence ministry.

While Russia went ahead with the bilateralization of defence cooperation without waiting for the outcome of the discussion over GHJAF, the debate concentrated in 1993 on the issue of subordination of the latter. While Russia and Uzbekistan favoured a Warsaw Pact-type alliance, with the commander of JAF being a deputy defence minister of Russia, the other four members of the Tashkent agreement and Shaposhnikov supported the NATO model, with the commander of JAF being subordinated to the CHS.[24]

While admitting that JAF might be the most promising form of military cooperation for the interested CIS states, the then Russian defence minister Pavel Grachev insisted during the 1993 debate that there were no political, legal, economic or military conditions for the creation of JAF. Emphasizing the need to develop national armed forces compatible in terms of their structure, training and equipment, Grachev only admitted the possibility of creating ad hoc coalition defence forces (*koalitsionnye sily oborony*: KSO). At the same time, he rejected the idea of establishing 'permanent' formations of coalition forces as militarily unnecessary and economically unjustifiable. In August 1993 the idea of ad hoc KSO as the main form of military cooperation of national armed forces was confirmed by CIS defence and foreign ministers, their support strengthened by the decision to start the first operation of ad hoc KSO in Tajikistan.[25]

This period was characterized by increasing scepticism on the part of Russia towards multilateral defence cooperation within the CIS. Without abandoning that framework, Russia started settling outstanding problems (providing a legal basis for the presence of Russian troops in the CIS countries, harmonizing the legal and social status of military personnel and pensioners, ensuring access to the strategic infrastructure of the FSU, providing joint border protection, etc.) and shifting most of its military links onto a bilateral or regional basis, taking the latter route with the Central Asian CIS states and also seeking to achieve some form of regional cooperation with the Transcaucasian states, though these efforts have been in vain so far because of the negative position of Azerbaijan.[26]

Andrei Zagorski

From a single defence area to differentiation? The grand design of the CIS staff

With the dismantling of the GHJAF, new aspects moved to the forefront of discussions over a CIS defence alliance. This debate has been affected by the following factors:

- While the GHJAF had been dissolved in 1993, the coordination staff at the CIS level had not been eliminated entirely. In this respect, Shaposh-nikov's option 1 (see above) has largely materialized.
- The debate superseded the previous concern over keeping the former Soviet military assets under one single control. With the disintegration of the Soviet army and Russia's policy of getting rid of supranational supervision within the Commonwealth, this was no longer a relevant question.
- At the same time, the idea of establishing a collective defence alliance was gaining momentum. The discussion over NATO enlargement eastwards and the introduction of the PfP programme led the proponents of a CIS military alliance to argue in favour of consolidating the CIS defence framework in order to counter the trend towards the development of bilateral relations between individual NATO states and NIS.[27]
- New discourses occurred, giving priority to regional cooperation within the CIS rather than multilateral cooperation across the whole grouping.

In the academic debate, the trend shifted from seeing the CIS as a single area towards perceiving greater differentiation among the member states, with the implication that different frameworks should be developed for each of them. Alexei Arbatov suggested that, instead of making unrealistic plans to bring all CIS states under the single umbrella of a Russian-led military alliance, Moscow should recognize the diversity both of its partners in the FSU and of Russia's interests with respect to them. While expecting Belarus to engage in closer integration with Russia, Arbatov regards Ukraine and Kazakstan as strategic partners of Moscow in the FSU, advocating that economic, political and defence cooperation with them should be promoted to whatever extent is possible without questioning their independent status.

The third group of potential partner states, according to Arbatov, includes Georgia, Armenia and Kyrgyzstan. Although they have neither the potential for, nor an interest in, political and economic reintegration with Russia, these states are deemed to need Russian security guarantees while, on the other hand, Russia's security interests are considered to be compatible with theirs.

Two other groups of states, according to Arbatov, comprise first Moldova and the Baltic states, which are not going to accede to any reintegration with Russia, and secondly three Central Asian states (Uzbekistan, Tajikistan, Turkmenistan) and Azerbaijan, from which Russia should withdraw even if those states would not wish it to do so entirely.[28]

Another view on the differentiation of the CIS states has been offered by Dmitri Trenin.[29] Instead of a single military alliance, he suggested a system of regional agreements with key partners whose long-term security interests largely coincide with those of Russia. In his view, the list of such regional partners would include Belarus in eastern Europe, Georgia in the Transcaucasus and Kazakstan in Central Asia. While developing defence cooperation with Armenia, Russia should avoid establishing an alliance with that country until the conflict over Nagorno-Karabakh is settled. Russia would also develop defence cooper-ation with Ukraine (integration of air defence and ABM systems, coordination of border protection, military-economic cooperation) and Azerbaijan (military production, border protection, early-warning systems).

The analysis of available options

The trend towards greater regionalization and differentiation of defence cooperation can be found not only in the academic debate but also in the policy of Russia and of the CIS institutions. After surviving the shock of GHJAF dismantlement, the remaining CIS structures had to adjust to that trend and also developed frameworks providing for greater regionalization of defence cooperation. General Ivashov, building upon designs by the SCMC, elaborated on the issue in a number of publications.[30] The 'grand design' developed and presented by the SCMC in 1994 comprised:

(1) a coalition of states (with non-institutionalized mutual assistance obligations);
(2) a military-political alliance (provided with permanent political and military bodies, common military structures, armed forces, and coordinated military planning and training);
(3) defence integration (including the establishment of common structures with supranational authorities administering a joint military budget, and of headquarters controlling JAF).

While acknowledging that currently the defence cooperation of the Tashkent agreement member states remains at the first level (a coalition of states), and envisaging option 3 (defence integration) as a long-term objective, the SCMC considers it realistic to pursue, for the time being, option 2 (a military-political alliance with limited supranational elements of authority).

At the same time, the concept implies the possibility of different kinds of defence cooperation among various CIS and non-CIS states. Fully-fledged cooperation would develop among member states of the Tashkent agreement alliance. Cooperation in selected areas (guarding the outer borders of the CIS, air defence, military production, infrastructure facilities, etc.) would be maintained with Moldova, Turkmenistan and Ukraine as well. The third (more remote) kind of cooperation would be developed with countries beyond the FSU borders.

Regional differentiation

Defence cooperation among member states of the Tashkent agreement would be differentiated. Basically, there would be four or five relatively independent subregional defence frameworks:

- in eastern Europe, including the west European part of the Russian Federation, Belarus and the Kaliningrad region;
- in the Caucasus, including the North Caucasian areas of the Russian Federation, Armenia, Azerbaijan, and Georgia;
- in Central Asia, divided into western and eastern parts, the western one including Tajikistan and Uzbekistan and the eastern one including the Urals and Siberia in the Russian Federation and the territory of Kazakstan and Kyrgyzstan;
- in eastern Asia, including eastern parts of the Russian Federation and of Kazakstan.

While each framework should involve the development of relatively independent regional 'theatre forces' in the form of KSO with their own command structures (*upravlenie*), provision should also be made for the development of JAF, including joint reserve forces, common military systems, operational navy units and other components.

Command structures

For the purposes of the Tashkent agreement the authorities would be divided into three levels: CIS, regional bodies and national authorities.

At the CIS level, the coordinating bodies would include the CSC and its secretary-general, the councils of defence and foreign ministers, the military-economic commission of the CIS, a committee of the heads of staffs and the SCMC. In war or during a period of danger a supreme general headquarters and its working bodies would be established and provided with supranational authority. The CSC should take general decisions on military policy, military construction, means of countering aggression and other significant issues on the basis of consensus.

At the regional level, a political and a military component of the structure were suggested. The political component would be the Defence Council (*sovet oborony*), concentrating in peacetime on the maintenance of peace and stability in the region, and the settlement of disputes and crises by exclusively political means and conciliation, while at the same time maintaining defence capability at the required level. The Council should take responsibility for countering any aggression and defeating the aggressor. The Council would consist of a chairman (the president of the country concerned) and members (vice-premier of the country supervising economic issues, its defence and foreign ministers, commander of border troops, chairman of the parliamentary commission on defence and security, the Russian ambassador in the country, heads of administration of the Russian regions included in the respective defence region and commanders of groups of Russian forces in the operational area).

The military component would be the Coalition Command of the Group of Armed Forces (CCGAF), consisting of KSO. The KSO in each region would include armed forces and other troops of the states participating in the regional system, and Russian forces operationally subordinated to the CCGAF. They may also include reserve forces consisting of national units of member states subordinated to regional headquarters at the start of hostilities or the strategic reserve forces of the CSC. The command structures of KSO are supposed to receive supranational authority (delegated by the CSC and fixed in the legislation of member states) in such areas as the maintenance of the required level of readiness, the training of forces and their command (*upravlenie*) in both peace and war. Decisions on the use of forces on several operational axes, on border protection, on the storage of material resources and on the development of infrastructure should be delegated to regional bodies.

At the national level, political and military authorities of individual member states would retain military units, command structures and training facilities not subordinated to the regional bodies. Particular tasks concerning the maintenance of combat readiness of the armed forces, their training, recruitment and procurement, and the maintenance of a stable situation along their borders would come under the authority of individual states.

The new 'CIS doctrine'

The first concept of military security of the CIS states was adopted by the CHS in Bishkek (Kyrgyzstan) on 9 October 1992. Elaborating on the issues affecting the military security of the member states and on the principles and tasks of collective security and collective defence, the document built upon the concept of maintaining JAF under joint command. However, with the progressive disintegration of the previous Soviet armed forces, the dissolution of the GHJAF in 1993 and the increased bilateralization of Russia's defence cooperation with individual CIS states, the Bishkek concept of 1992 became obsolete.

In April 1994 the CHS approved a working plan which commissioned the CIS Council of Defence Ministers to elaborate a new collective security concept. As a result, on 19 February 1995 the CHS approved the concept of collective security of the member states of the collective security agreement. This provided a tentative compromise between the approaches of the CIS staff and Russia to 'collective security'. While providing for the maintenance of the same CIS institutions as established later in 1993, it envisaged greater regionalization of defence cooperation among the Tashkent agreement member states. It stipulated, in particular, that the military resources of collective security would consist of:

- armed forces and other troops of individual member states;
- regional coalition (joint) groups of forces to be established in order to be capable of countering aggression;
- joint air defence and other facilities (presumably at the CIS level).

However, the grand design of the SCMC could not be approved in its entirety. The concept postpones its implementation while envisaging the establishment of a collective security system in three stages. At the current stage the task remains to complete the construction of national armed forces of individual states and to restore military-economic cooperation among them. The building up of CCGAF and of the common air defence system, and the beginning of discussions over the development of JAF, are scheduled for the second stage. The third stage would imply the final completion of a system of collective security. In May 1995 basic guidelines were approved for deepening the military cooperation of the member states of the collective security treaty. They included further staged measures for 1995–6 and beyond. However, by mid-1997 the CIS institutions had still failed to implement this schedule and disagreements remain between these states over the final objectives of this process.

Evaluation of the trend towards regionalization of CIS defence cooperation

While promoting the concept developed by the SCMC, General Ivashov drew attention to the incentives which might encourage Russia to proceed with the grand design. He argued that, in the end, Russia would benefit from a security zone in Central Asia and in the Caucasus while the main responsibility for maintaining security in each region would remain with the respective NIS. At the same time, if Russia were to remain outside this system, allegedly there would be no guarantees that the NIS would not be involved in other military blocs which might, to a lesser or greater extent, oppose Russia. In that case Moscow would have to deploy additional forces and develop a defence infrastructure along the entire length of its borders, which might turn out to be more expensive than the maintenance of CIS bodies.[31]

However, the essence of both the grand design and Russian measures aimed at developing bilateral or regional defence networks appears to aim at the same end while suggesting different means of achieving it. After the Soviet military assets had been largely nationalized by the NIS and a single control over them from Moscow had become impossible, both the Russian defence ministry and the SCMC developed options providing at least for the possibility of projecting the Russian military posture beyond Russian national borders while admitting greater flexibility over cooperation with individual NIS and their greater control over national armed forces. This was done without maintaining a single alliance. In this respect it is not horizontal defence cooperation among NIS which matters but the extent to which Russia can impose its posture on other NIS through bilateral or regional cooperation.

Even without any knowledge of the actual operational planning of the general staff of the Russian armed forces, an analysis of the division of regional defence frameworks provided in the SCMC grand design and in Russian policy leads to the conclusion that the 'theatres' or 'battlefields' implied in that division are nothing but a projection of Russian operational planning in various directions. The exception is those directions where Russia has no CIS military partners (the Pacific) or no cooperative CIS partners (the axis towards the Balkans).

In this respect both Russian bilateral or regional policy and the CIS project have the same aim: to restore not the integrity of the former Soviet army, which is impossible, but at least the capability of the Russian armed forces to project military power beyond Russia's borders in the directions which are considered militarily relevant for these or other purposes. The difference between the Russian and the SCMC policy, then, lies mainly in the means of achieving that end, whether through bilateral cooperation or within a multilateral framework.

It should also be admitted that this option, while in theory providing Russia with the capability to project power (it is still open to what extent this option would really materialize, or whether the project would fail as the previous one did), also imposes restrictions on Russia's policy. It provides Moscow with the possibility to operationalize the Tashkent agreement and other (bilateral and/or regional) defence cooperation schemes for the purposes of maintaining indirect control over political and military-political developments in the post-

Andrei Zagorski

Soviet space; providing a buffer security zone to the south of the Russian borders – in one of the most worrying directions according to Russian threat perceptions; and maintaining, if necessary, a 'forward defence' line beyond the national borders of the Russian Federation (a traditional approach of Russian defence policy). It is clear, however, that the framework will allow this only as long as the NIS remain unable to provide for their own defence, and is limited by the extent to which the NIS see Russia's involvement as a threat to their independence.

At the same time, such a framework scarcely provides Russia with the opportunity to project power beyond the borders of other NIS, which is implicit in the concept of maintaining the integrity of the former Soviet army: any decision on matters which extends beyond the borders of NIS would imply their consent. This can hardly be guaranteed unless those states once again become formally or informally dependent on Russia. The framework also provides the NIS with limited opportunities to activate it for the purposes of their own security policy: to ensure either Russian security (including nuclear) guarantees, or at least the formal neutrality of Russia in the event of a conflict with another member state of the collective security framework; to seek Russian concessions over other issues or with respect to other areas of cooperation in exchange for providing Russia with access to bases or facilities; and partially to ease financial (and even political) pressure from Russia through the leasing of strategically important facilities to Moscow.

Security cooperation in the CIS thus remains limited and uncertain. As the divergent responses to the issue of NATO expansion indicate, the NIS have widely differing perspectives on the international security environment and their own national interests. Thus the concept of deepening CIS integration on security in response to NATO expansion has been dismissed as unrealistic even in Russia. As a 'collective security' arrangement, the Tashkent agreement is virtually defunct. As a 'collective defence' arrangement, it has a very limited role in the absence of a major external threat. CIS reintegration is likely to proceed further in the economic sphere. In the sphere of national security the newly independent states, despite feeling for the most part that they need a Russian security guarantee, are wary of Russian dominance, and cooperation remains strictly linked to a narrow perception of the national security interests of each state.

Notes

1. Armenia, Azerbaijan, Belarus, Georgia, Kazakstan, Kyrgyzstan, Russia, Tajikistan, Uzbekistan.
2. In the CIS, there is a formal distinction between 'member states' and 'participating states'. The latter are those countries which have failed so far to ratify the CIS Charter of 1993 and thus cannot be legally

considered 'member states' of the Commonwealth under the Charter. For more on this see Andrei Zagorski, 'The Commonwealth of Independent States', in Alexander Lopukhin, Sergio Rossi and Andrei Zagorski, eds, *From Reform to Stability: Russian Foreign, Military and Economy Policy (Analysis and Forecast) 1993–1995* (Moscow: MGIMO; Industrial Herald, 1995), pp. 9–28.

3. Among the most recent publications on approaches of the new Eurasian states towards security cooperation in the CIS, see Heinrich Tiller, 'Die militärpolitische Entwicklung in den Nachfolgestaaten der ehemaligen Sowjetunion' (Teil I), *Berichte des BIOst*, 1995, no. 24. See also *Rossiyskaya gazeta*, 25 August 1993.

4. See Articles 3 and 5 of the Treaty in *Sodruzhestvo, Informatsionnyyi vestnik Soveta glav gosudarstv i Soveta glav pravitel'stv SNG* (Commonwealth, Informational Herald of the Council of the Heads of States and of the Council of the Heads of Governments), Minsk, 1992, no. 5, pp. 9, 10. A certain degree of confusion is apparent in discussions of the relationship between the Tashkent agreement and other CIS security bodies. The concept of military security of the member states of the CIS approved by the CHS in Bishkek on 9 October 1992, while addressing the issue of security of the CIS (and not only of the Tashkent agreement), stated that CHS held supreme authority in security matters. In the next paragraph, however, the concept stated that the coordination of collective security measures would be pursued by the permanent body established by CSC (see *Sodruzhestvo*, 1992, no. 7, p. 41). It is likely that, in the mindsets of the military staff of the CIS, the Tashkent agreement was never distinguished from a broader CIS framework. However, the distinction is explicit in the agreement; and the CSC does not figure in the Charter of CIS.

5. On 15 June 1993, the CDM recommended to the CHS that GHJAF should be replaced by the SCMC. After controversial discussions and an intervention by the secretary of the CDM, General Leonid Ivashov, the joint meeting of defence and foreign ministers on 24 August 1993 confirmed this recommendation. In September 1993 the CHS approved the recommendation, and in December 1993 it established the SCMC. See Tiller, 'Die militärpolitische Entwicklung in den Nachfolgestaaten der ehemaligen Sowjetunion' (Teil I), p. 8.

6. In Russia, 'collective security' and 'collective defence' are also seen as two distinct concepts. However, they are not seen as two different principles of developing security organizations. Collective security is used in Russia as a comprehensive concept embracing various dimensions of security policy: political instruments and institutions, including those regulating relations among states, the preservation of military security (which is then actually the task of 'collective defence' within a collective security system); economic security; and cooperation among a range of security relevant institutions. Thus collective defence is seen only as part of collective security. On this see Leonid Ivashov, 'Vozmozhen li voenno-politicheskii soyuz?' (Is a military-political alliance feasible?), *Nezavisimaya gazeta*, 18 October 1994.

7. *Sodruzhestvo*, 1992, no. 5, p. 9.

8. Article 12. See *Sodruzhestvo*, 1993, no. 1 (9), p. 21.

9. *Sodruzhestvo*, 1992, no. 7, p. 36.

10. *Nezavisimaya gazeta*, 17 May 1994.

11. *Sodruzhestvo*, 1992, no. 7, p. 38.

12. *Segodnya*, 18 February 1994.

13. Evgeny Shaposhnikov, 'Rossiya, armiya, politika i opyt kollektivnoy bezopasnosti v SNG' (Russia, army, policy and the experience with collective security in the CIS), *Nezavisimaya gazeta*, 6 July 1993.

14. (1) The groups of armed forces and all defence systems (air defence, ABM, command, control and communication, etc.), the system of military planning, procurement, training and infrastructure had been, for decades, based upon the security interests of a single country. Ivashov argued that the demise of this comprehensive mechanism had damaged the military security of all of the CIS states and the combat readiness of their national armies. (2) All NIS had been for decades involved in the deep integration of military production and had developed a single R&D potential. No single NIS except Russia was capable of providing the final assembly of weaponry and military equipment. (3) For centuries the peoples of NIS had been living in a single country and, according to Ivashov, cannot agree to the appearance of borders between them and to the break-up of ties of family and friendship. See *Nezavisimaya gazeta*, 17 May 1994.

15. See *Nezavisimaya gazeta*, 17 and 24 March, 13 April 1993; *Segodnya*, 13 April 1993.

16. *Nezavisimaya gazeta*, 4 November 1994.

17. Though the issue of parliamentary consent to deploying Russian troops in the country became controversial in 1995, the mood in Belarus with respect to being involved into the conflicts of other states was clearly negative in 1993, and the intervention in Chechenia has only strengthened that trend. In 1993, Pavel Kozlovsky promised: 'We can negotiate with the Russian Federation about joint activities

of the air defence, about forming a system of intelligence along the western border, and in the event of an aggression about joint defence measures. This does not imply, however, that we are going to send troops to Tajikistan. This will absolutely not be the case' (*Moskovskie novosti*, 22 August 1993).

18. Shaposhnikov, 'Rossiya, armiya, politika'.
19. Armenia, Belarus, Kazakstan, Kyrgyzstan, Russia, Tajikistan, Turkmenistan and Ukraine. For the text of the agreement of 14 February see: *Sodruzhestvo*, 1992, no. 2, p. 55.
20. Those that left the agreement were Belarus, Tajikistan, Turkmenistan and Ukraine.
21. Ivashov, 'Vozmozhen li voenno-politicheskii soyuz?'
22. Ibid.
23. Shaposhnikov, 'Rossiya, armiya, politika'.
24. See *Nezavisimaya gazeta*, 2 March 1993.
25. *Rossiyskaya gazeta*, 25 August 1993.
26. The process of bilateralization or regionalization of Russian defence cooperation with the CIS also had a negative impact on achieving some Russian objectives. This is indicated in the area of strategic infrastructure (air defence and early warning systems). According to a number of CIS accords of 1992, the respective facilities had been recognized as the property of the states where they were deployed. In return, those states provided those facilities for use by JAF. With the dismantlement of GHJAF the accords concerned lost their relevance and uneasy negotiations started with individual NIS concerning the terms of Russia's access to the respective facilities. Negotiations might have been simplest with Belarus, though even there hesitations have occurred at the parliamentary level. Many of the recent negotiations (e.g. with Kazakstan) or those still forthcoming (e.g. with Azerbaijan) have either been unsatisfactory for either side or been deadlocked in a controversy over the terms of the lease. Some difficult negotiations are yet to come (e.g. the issue of Mukhalatka in Ukraine). On this problem see Andrei Zagorski and Vladimir Egorov, 'Die militärisch-politische Zusammenarbeit der GUS-Staaten', *Berichte des BIOst*, 1993, no. 18.
27. General Ivashov argued, for instance, that without neglecting the participation of the CIS states in PfP, priority should be given to establishing an original Euro-Asian collective security framework. The head of the SCMC, General Victor Samsonov, proposed to NATO, during a visit to Brussels, that cooperation be developed between the two alliances in the '16 + 9' format. See *Nezavisimaya gazeta*, 17 May 1994.
28. See Alexei Arbatov, 'Rossiya: natsional'naya bezopasnost' v 90-e gody' (Russia: National security in the 90s), part 2, *Mirovaya ekonomika i mezhdunarodnye otnosheniya*, 1994, nos 8–9, pp. 5–9.
29. *Nezavisimaya gazeta*, 4 November 1994.
30. See a series of his publications in *Nezavisimaya gazeta*, 6 August and 22 September 1993; 6 July, 17 May, and 18 October 1994.
31. Ivashov, 'Vozmozhen li voenno-politicheskii soyuz?' See also *Nezavisimaya gazeta*, 6 August 1993.

Part IV

Multilateral security policy: Russia, Eurasia and the West

15 Arms control and proliferation

Christoph Bluth

The disappearance of the threat of a major war in Europe with the potential to escalate into a global nuclear conflict has without question enhanced the security of all European states immeasurably. However, the social and economic dislocation and the disintegration of political structures in the communist countries, especially the former Soviet Union, which accompanied the end of the Cold War have created new and unprecedented dangers. This chapter will focus primarily on the problems in Russia and their implications for arms control and proliferation, because even if its situation is mirrored in some of the other former Soviet republics, Russia is the principal source of these problems.

The primary role of arms control in the post-Cold War era is to eliminate the remaining elements of Cold War military postures and address the new threats. In this context the containment of proliferation – of weapons of mass destruction, of high-technology conventional weapons and even of small arms – has become the dominant objective of arms control. It is the purpose of the chapter to assess the security risks that arise from the remains of the Russian military arsenal and to discuss the conceptual basis for arms control both as a means of providing for a regime of international security and as an instrument of non-proliferation.

Nuclear weapons

Strategic nuclear weapons were fundamental to the US–Soviet relationship, and strategic arms control remains a central element of US–Russian relations despite the end of the Cold War. As long as the two countries retain the effective capability to destroy each other completely, nuclear weapons remain a factor in international security. However, other issues have now assumed greater prominence, especially the challenge of nuclear non-proliferation and the safety and security of nuclear weapons in Russia.

The impact of nuclear arms reductions

The START 1 agreement was signed by presidents Gorbachev and Bush in 1991. It envisaged a reduction in strategic nuclear delivery vehicles (SNDV) of about 35 per cent. For the Yeltsin government, strategic arms control was a central element of its cooperative relationship with the United States from the beginning. Thus the strategic arms reduction (START) process acquired an additional momentum. The dissolution of the Soviet Union, however, introduced the complication that strategic nuclear weapons were now located in more than one state: in Belarus, Ukraine and Kazakstan as well as in Russia. Thus strategic arms control ceased to be a purely bilateral matter. The United States and Russia adopted the position from the outset that there should be only one nuclear successor state to the Soviet Union, and that this had to be Russia. The legal mechanisms adopted to commit the Soviet successor states to assume the obligations of the START 1 Treaty were framed in such a way as to make START into an instrument of nuclear non-proliferation. In a protocol to the START Treaty originally concluded between the United States and the Soviet Union (the Lisbon protocol), Russia, Belarus, Kazakstan and Ukraine agreed to assume the obligations of the USSR under the treaty. Furthermore, Belarus, Kazakstan and Ukraine agreed to adhere to the nuclear non-proliferation treaty (NPT) as non-nuclear weapons states. For a time Ukraine was ambivalent about giving up the nuclear weapons on its territory, but this issue was eventually resolved after some financial aid was made available by the United States and Ukraine received certain security guarantees.[1] Thus the linkage between arms control and non-proliferation is apparent at an early stage.

Even before START 1 was finally ratified, Yeltsin pushed the strategic arms control process an important step further. Implementation of the START 2 Treaty signed at the end of 1992 will reduce the number of warheads deployed on SNDVs to less than a third of the pre-START level.[2] At the Helsinki summit in March 1997 Presidents Clinton and Yeltsin discussed the possibility of a START 3 agreement with reductions to levels of 2000–2500 warheads.[3] However, this does not fundamentally alter the strategic relationship, and the role of strategic nuclear weapons in military planning and the future direction of arms control after the Cold War still remains to be addressed.

Nuclear safety and arms control

In any consideration of Russia's nuclear weapons the country's ability to keep its weapons safe and secure is a major issue. Despite various disclaimers on the part of Russian and Western authorities, the administrative chaos in Russia affects all aspects of the nuclear weapons complex. The political and social disintegration of the former Soviet Union has indeed raised serious concerns about the fate of about 32,000 nuclear weapons accumulated by the Soviet military in the four decades of the Cold War.[4] Here it is useful to distinguish between the security of nuclear weapons and materials, and nuclear safety. Security refers to protection against terrorist attacks and the unauthorized use or illicit seizure of weapons or nuclear materials; safety refers to the safe storage and handling of radioactive or otherwise hazardous materials.

In response to the perceived dangers to the safety and security of nuclear weapons as a consequence of the Soviet collapse, the United States Congress passed the Cooperative Threat Reaction Act in 1991 (also known as the Nunn–Lugar Act).[5] This established a programme on nuclear weapons safety designed to be pursued in cooperation with the Soviet Union and its successor states. The principal objective was to aid the safe and secure dismantling (SSD) of nuclear weapons. This was intended to involve the safe and secure storage of tactical nuclear weapons and strategic nuclear warheads which were to be dismantled, safe and secure transportation of nuclear warheads to the dismantling facilities, and safe and secure storage of nuclear materials after the dismantling process had taken place. The objectives of the Nunn–Lugar Act also included the establishment of safeguards against the proliferation of weapons, the unauthorized diversion and export of nuclear materials, and the proliferation of nuclear expertise. The initial funding of $400 million has subsequently been annually renewed. The US Departments of Defense and Energy are principally responsible for SSD-related programmes. At the State Department there is a coordinator for SSD. Policy is coordinated by an interdepartmental group chaired by National Security Council (NSC) staff.[6]

Despite the initial sense of urgency over nuclear risks in the former Soviet Union, the SSD programme took a long time to make any progress. Thus over $300 million of funding was lost because it was not spent during the year when it was appropriated. By 1994 the following programmes had been established:[7]

- Measures to provide for more secure warhead transportation. The United States has modified Russian rail transport cars to improve their safety and provided 250 bullet-proof armoured blankets to protect Russian nuclear weapons containers. The United Kingdom has supplied 250 warhead containers and trucks to the former Soviet Union and is training drivers.[8] France has likewise supplied warhead containers. The United States is supplying a variety of equipment items, including clothing, for use in dealing with nuclear accidents. In 1995 a 'warhead technical exchange' agreement was signed with the aim of providing for the security of nuclear warheads along the entire military chain of custody.[9]
- Assistance for the dismantling of ballistic missiles and destruction of

silos. This includes the provision of housing for demobilized officers of the Strategic Rocket Forces.

- The establishment of an International Science and Technology Centre which distributes funding for civilian research projects to scientists hitherto employed in the nuclear weapons complex in order to provide them with incentives to remain in Russia and prevent the proliferation of nuclear weapons expertise.[10]

- Assistance with the provision of storage for nuclear materials equipped with modern materials protection, control and accounting (MPC&A) facilities. There are four facilities in Russia where nuclear warheads can be dismantled. It is reported that they have an aggregate capacity of 2,000 warheads per year.[11] This is a relatively slow rate given the large number of tactical nuclear warheads and strategic weapons that need to be dismantled. American experts have urged the US government to aid Russia in building additional dismantling facilities. Once the weapons have been dismantled, the fissile components need to be stored. There were plans for the establishment of a plutonium storage facility at Tomsk-7 (where a nuclear materials production facility is located) and another one at Mayak (also known as Chelyabinsk-65), to be financed by the United States. After much delay and political wrangling, work began at Chelyabinsk-65 in the autumn of 1994. The Tomsk facility may eventually be funded by Japan. In any event, the facility at Mayak, if it is ever completed, will not begin operations before 1998 and thus the immediate problems with the storage of weapons-grade fissile materials remain.[12]

The long-term disposal of nuclear materials represents an unresolved problem. The most obvious solution is the conversion of fissile materials to fuel for use in civil nuclear reactors. This is a commercially viable proposition with regard to highly enriched uranium (HEU). The United States has reached an agreement with Russia to purchase HEU for conversion into fuel.[13] In principle, weapons-grade plutonium could also be used as fuel if it were mixed with uranium to produce mixed oxide (MOX) fuel rods for use in light water reactors (LWR). However, the industrial capacity to convert plutonium to MOX on the scale required does not exist. MOX is also not an economic fuel to use in LWRs. Long-term secure storage facilities will therefore have to be constructed until an agreed method for disposing of the plutonium has been developed.[14]

Considerable evidence has now accumulated about 'leakage' of fissile materials from the former Soviet nuclear weapons complex. In mid-1992 1.68 kgs of HEU were stolen from the Luch Scientific Production Association at Podolsk, Russia, by an employee. The most prominent case was the discovery in Munich in August 1994 of 580g of MOX on an airliner from Moscow. This contained 300–350g of plutonium that was close to weapons-grade material. It is likely that the plutonium was produced in one of the three Russian reprocessing plants. In August 1994 in Tengen, near Konstanz, at the German/ Swiss border, 8g of plutonium were found which consisted of 99 per cent plutonium-239. This is more highly enriched plutonium than is normally found in nuclear weapons. It is believed by experts that it was produced for research purposes at Arzamas-16, the nuclear weapons research centre in Russia.[15] Naval nuclear reactor fuel under military custody was stolen in Murmansk in 1993, the thieves managing to overcome all the security precautions in this case. Russian security forces eventually recovered the fuel rods, which contained highly enriched uranium, and arrested the culprits.[16]

The security of nuclear weapons material in Russia has been put at risk as a result of several different factors. There are no acceptable MPC&A procedures, and consequently the various laboratories, research centres and weapons production facilities have no clear idea how much nuclear material they actually have. Military security guards have been removed from many research centres and weapons production facilities which now have to provide for their own security. It has been revealed that most facilities with nuclear materials even lack adequate fencing and security locks. The government has not been paying its debts to enterprises, and as a result many military–industrial facilities, including those engaged in the development and production of nuclear weapons, are starved of cash. Corruption and organized crime have penetrated every part of Russian life. The transportation of nuclear materials is often not secure and does not always conform even to Russian health and safety regulations.

In this environment, there is a real possibility that the theft of nuclear materials will occur, especially if sizeable sums of money are offered. One danger is that states which wish to acquire nuclear weapons will seek to purchase weapons-grade materials. Another is that materials illicitly transported across Europe will be used either deliberately or accidentally to cause environmental contamination. The contamination of water supplies or the release of radioactive materials in population centres are obviously especially potent dangers. The 'leakage' of nuclear materials constitutes a serious international security problem, and the safeguarding of nuclear materials must therefore be accorded the highest priority.[17]

Efforts to bring the ex-Soviet nuclear arsenal under control can boast a number of significant successes. All tactical nuclear weapons have been withdrawn from the non-Russian former Soviet republics, and all strategic nuclear forces outside Russia are being dismantled (or withdrawn) and the warheads returned to Russia. The principal failure of the programme so far is to make any significant progress with regard to MPC&A procedures for nuclear materials. As a result of disputes over financial aspects, projected storage facilities for plutonium have been delayed, and it remains to be seen whether they will be built. Today, five years into the Nunn–Lugar programme, the security of the Russian nuclear weapons complex has not increased, but indeed has significantly decreased. There is also greater political resistance in Russia to allowing the United States to gain access to Russian nuclear facilities or influence over the manner in which nuclear materials are treated and stored. The programme is also threatened in Congress, where aid to Russia generally is questioned by the Republican majority.

The danger posed by the nuclear weapons complex in Russia persists. All known facts point to the conclusion that substantial Western assistance and technology transfers will be required to provide adequate security for nuclear weapons and fissile materials. It is still conceivable that this could develop into technical cooperation with the Russian nuclear weapons industry to an extent that could itself contribute substantially to the development of a strategic partnership with significant political implications. Increasing contacts between top and medium-level military personnel on the two sides constitute a parallel track along which the development of strategic cooperation is taking place.[18]

Conclusion

This analysis shows that traditional issues in nuclear arms control and post-Cold War concerns over nuclear safety are closely linked. The fact that START 2 has currently stalled and that not much tangible progress has been made in preventing 'nuclear leakage' or in dealing with other safety matters is very alarming. This is perhaps the gravest threat to international security at the present time. It will require a major reorientation of policy priorities in Washington and Moscow to deal with this issue as seriously as it deserves.

Conventional weapons

Conventional arms control in Europe

During the Cold War period, the objectives of conventional arms control were defined by the military confrontation in central Europe. The Conventional Forces in Europe (CFE) Treaty which was signed on 10 November 1990 brought into being a pan-European conventional arms control regime that put ceilings on various categories of armaments for all signatory states. Although its initial assumptions, which were based on the confrontation between NATO and the Warsaw Pact, had already been overturned by the time the treaty was signed, it was universally accepted as an important international regime that would strengthen stability and security in Europe and prevent the re-emergence of arms races and major force disparities.[19]

The collapse of the USSR required a division of the limits on Soviet military equipment among the former Soviet republics. This was finalized at the Tashkent summit on 15 May 1992, when the eight former Soviet republics which were to become party to the CFE Treaty (Armenia, Azerbaijan, Belarus, Georgia, Kazakstan, Moldova, Russia and Ukraine) signed the Agreement on the Principles and Procedures of Implementation of the Treaty on Conventional Armed Forces in Europe, which codified the TLE allocations (see Table 15.1). On 10 July 1992 the agreement provisionally entered into force, subject to final ratification by all parties. One of the criticisms of the Tashkent agreement voiced by the military is that it was essentially reached by political bargaining and not on the basis of general principles related to military requirements.

Russia was allocated 48 per cent of the tanks, 48 per cent of the artillery systems, 67 per cent of combat aircraft and 59 per cent of attack helicopters in the European region of the FSU. The Russian military leadership is clearly dissatisfied with the CFE limits as it believes that they leave Russia with inadequate forces either for a large conventional war or for crisis intervention at its southern periphery. However, unless there is a complete breakdown in relations between Russia and the West, it is likely that the overall limits of the treaty at least will be respected.

In this context, the insistence by the Russian military leadership that the rules governing the 'flanks' in the CFE Treaty require revision is very

Table 15.1: Ceilings for treaty-limited equipment for the CIS states according to the Tashkent agreement

State	Tanks	ACV	Artillery	Aircraft	Helicopters
Armenia	220	220	285	100	50
Azerbaijan	220	220	285	100	50
Belarus	1,800	2,600	1,615	260	80
Georgia	220	220	285	100	50
Moldova	210	210	250	50	50
Russia	6,400	11,480	6,415	3,450	890
Ukraine	4,080	5,050	4,040	1,090	330

Source: *SIPRI Yearbook 1993* (Stockholm/Oxford: SIPRI/Oxford University Press, 1993), p. 597. Kazakstan ratified the CFE agreement. However, only a small portion of Kazak territory is in the territory covered by the CFE agreement. No military bases exist there. Therefore Kazakstan has no entitlements or obligations under CFE (i.e. no treaty limited equipment or obligations to destroy military hardware).

important. Article V of the CFE Treaty defines sub-limits for the so-called 'flank zones'. In the east, the flank zone originally consisted of Bulgaria and Romania, and the Leningrad, North Caucasus, Odessa and Transcaucasus military districts. After the break-up of the Soviet Union, six newly independent states had to share the sub-limits for the flank zone (see Table 15.2).[20]

The Russian military has argued strongly that these limits were devised for a situation which is no longer relevant, and that the conflicts at the southern periphery of the Russian Federation mean that they are no longer appropriate for Russia's security concerns. In this they are supported by the political leadership. Former defence minister Pavel Grachev has stated precisely how much additional equipment Russia requires in the flank zone: 400 tanks, 2,420 ACVs and 820 artillery pieces – enough for four fully equipped motor rifle divisions in the flank zone (where it can currently deploy only one). The request for the revision of the CFE sub-limits has been most strongly resisted by Turkey, which perceives security implications for itself. At the May 1995 summit President Clinton agreed that the flank issue should be considered, but without any concrete proposals. By 17 November 1995 the CFE regime seemed to be in jeopardy as Russia failed to meet the treaty obligations on the specified date. At the CFE review conference in May 1996 a compromise was reached. Russia has been given until 31 May 1999 to comply with the flank limits. Until then, Russian deployments in the flank zone will remain frozen at current levels: 1,897 tanks, 4,397 ACVs and 2,422 artillery pieces. Furthermore, the boundaries of the flank zones were redrawn, effectively shrinking them so that Russia will be able to deploy significantly greater concentrations of heavy weapons in the flank zone even after May 1999. Thus a complete breakdown of CFE has been avoided.[21]

Table 15.2: Flank zone entitlements according to the CFE Treaty

State	Tanks	ACVs	Artillery
Armenia	220	220	285
Azerbaijan	220	220	285
Bulgaria	1,75	200	1,750
Georgia	220	220	285
Moldova	210	210	250
Romania	1,375	2,100	1,475
Ukraine (active & stored)	680	350	890
Ukraine (stored in Odessa MD)	400	0	500
Russia (active & stored)	1,300	1,380	1,680
Russia (stored in S. Leningrad MD)	600	800	400

Source: Richard A. Falkenrath, 'The CFE Flank Dispute', International Security, vol. 19, no. 4 (Spring 1995), p. 138.

Despite the changed security environment, the CFE Treaty is still essential to reassure all states in the region that no country, including Russia, will engage in a massive military build-up. If Russia were to deploy large-scale forces against Ukraine, for example, this would constitute a breach of the treaty. The treaty is therefore essential to preserve military stability in eastern Europe.

The CFE Treaty is one of the few legal instruments giving the international community a role in regulating Russia's relations with its neighbours. It also provides complete transparency regarding military forces in the region, which in itself enhances security. The CFE Treaty thus remains one of the most significant and enduring achievements in international arms control.

Conventional arms proliferation

While in the nuclear sphere the main proliferation and security risks arise from unauthorized activities, the proliferation of high-technology conventional weapons is actively promoted by the Russian government. During the Cold War, arms exports were primarily an instrument used to secure political influence. Commercial considerations were subordinated to political requirements. Thus, for example, in 1989 Soviet arms exports amounted to $23 billion, of which $3 billion were given as aid and $14.5 billion under special financial conditions. During the entire Soviet period most of the debts incurred by Soviet client states for their imports of Soviet military hardware were not paid.[22]

The end of the Cold War accelerated a trend towards a reduction in the worldwide demand for weapons which began in the 1980s. In 1984 the total size of the global arms export market was about $42.2 billion (in constant 1990 dollars). Discounting brief surges associated with international conflicts, the market has been in secular decline since, reaching a level of $21.9 billion in 1993.[23] This trend was intensified by changes in the international security environment. The end of the Cold War and the resolution of various regional conflicts precipitated a sharp decline in military spending worldwide. At the same time the major arms producers, especially the United States and Russia, were faced with massive overcapacity that created an acute need in the arms industry for alternatives to government procurement.

After the dissolution of the Soviet Union, Russia faced a particularly difficult situation. Military industry constituted a substantial proportion (estimates range from 30 per cent to 70 per cent) of Russia's industrial base. During the Soviet period defence expenditure reached 35–50 per cent of GNP. The end of the Cold War, and especially the withdrawal from eastern Europe and the CFE Treaty, reduced the requirements for large amounts of military equipment. The deep economic crisis in Russia, in particular the inability of the government to pay its bills to industrial enterprises, combined with the changed international environment to produce a virtual collapse in military procurement. In 1991–2 state military orders were reduced by 68 per cent. In 1993, despite attempts by the Russian government to maintain military production at the level of the previous year, military procurement fell by 24–25 per cent. Furthermore, since tax revenues fall notoriously short of government projections, even the amounts allocated in the defence budget cannot be sustained, as a consequence of which the government often cannot pay for items it has procured. In 1994 there was a modest increase in procurement in real terms, but it must be borne in mind that the ministry of defence ordered items worth 28 trillion roubles, whereas the budgetary allocation was only 4 trillion roubles. This is likely to affect payment for all the items procured and reduce the level of future orders.

The consequences of this fall in procurement are considered to be very serious. The contraction of military industry has enormous social ramifications, given the sheer number of people previously employed in the sector, with whole towns and regions dependent on military production. Furthermore, the arms industry is one of the few areas in which Russians believe that they can manufacture products at a high level of technology comparable to that of other world leaders in the field. In this climate, arms exports are no longer considered to be a political instrument, given that Russia does not at present have the kind of ambitions for a global role harboured by the leaders of the Soviet Union. The purpose of arms exports now is rather to keep the beleaguered defence enterprises afloat and allow them to earn the hard currency required for retooling and defence conversion.[24]

The marked increase in the competitiveness of the shrinking international arms market has squeezed Russian exports particularly hard. From 1986 to 1992 the volume of Soviet/Russian arms exports fell from $17.745 billion to $3.265 billion, while the Soviet/Russian share of the global arms market declined from 39 per cent to 11 per cent. The official figure for the earnings from arms exports in 1993 was $2.117 billion. This rose slightly in 1995 to $3.1 billion.[25] Among the reasons for the decline in the Russian share of the market are the cessation of aid to client states in the form of arms and the perception that Russian weapons systems are less technologically advanced than Western systems. The international embargoes imposed on importers of Russian arms such as Iran, Iraq, Libya and the former Yugoslavia has exacerbated the effect of this shift. The reliability of weapons systems and service contracts became an important issue in view of the turmoil affecting the post-Soviet states, including Russia and its arms industries. The United States raised the stakes by promoting advanced weapons systems, especially virtually state-of-the-art fighter aircraft, on to the market. Weapons systems such as the US F-15E 'Strike Eagle' and F-16 fighter-bombers would not have been sold to non-NATO states in the past; now production lines for F-15 and F-16 aircraft, Apache attack helicopters and M-1A2 tanks remain open only for export. Even Stealth technology has not been excluded from technology transfers. The share of the arms market lost by Russia has thus been largely captured by the United States and Germany.

This is not to say that Russia does not produce weapons systems that are competitive and sought after. The increasing competitiveness of the international arms market led Russia, too, to relax its restrictions on military technology transfers, and it is now selling many weapons systems close to the state of the art, such as Su-27 and MiG-29 fighter aircraft, T-80 tanks and even the legendary S-300 air defence system. Most disconcerting to the West has been the proposed sale of missile technology to India, and of submarines to Iran and (civil) nuclear technology to Iran.

The regulation of conventional arms exports in Russia

The export of arms, especially high-technology weapons, is of course not simply a commercial question, but also involves considerations of national security. This is why states develop export controls, even though (as noted above) these have been relaxed considerably since the end of the Cold War. Russia faces the additional problem of controlling the illicit arms trade, which has begun to flourish. During the final years of the Soviet Union there was a substantial weakening of control over various aspects of society, including the armed forces. One of the more disconcerting aspects of this development was the increasing number of thefts from arms depots and the loss of control over the disposition and export of weapons systems. In September 1990 it was reported that the total number of weapons of various kinds that were missing came to 11,500. Regulations concerning the safe-keeping of weapons were being ignored, and many of the older arms and ammunition dumps were obsolete and insecure.[26] As military units throughout the Soviet Union and beyond found themselves short of housing, food and basic necessities, the practice of selling surplus military equipment to provide for their own needs became widespread. Even the bases responsible for the Strategic Rocket Forces did not receive enough food, as a result of which in at least one location SRF officers went on strike. Entire SAM complexes were abandoned without guard, so that anyone could have taken the missiles or any components.[27] The extent to which military hardware went missing is indicated by a number of anecdotal reports, for example of naval shells turning up in student accommodation.

Illicit arms exports are facilitated by the virtual collapse of border controls. The Soviet Union used to have very tightly controlled borders. Its disintegration has resulted in fifteen newly independent states with very porous borders. Both people and materials can easily move both within and beyond the area of the FSU, as custom controls do not operate over large stretches of the periphery. This has important consequences for security in the conflict regions of the FSU, as all parties to the conflicts are able to obtain weapons and ammunition in large quantities from various parts of the FSU.

Unofficial exports of high-technology weapons systems, such as combat aircraft, air defence complexes and missiles, are virtually impossible to arrange since they cannot be simply smuggled abroad; they require a continuous and stable contractual relationship with the supplier for spare parts and maintenance. They cannot be obtained without going through official channels. The transfer of low-technology weapons, and especially the export of small arms in large quantities, on the other hand, is one of the nightmares of the Western security services.

The export from Russia of arms and 'strategic materials' is regulated by a presidential decree of 22 February 1992 and a series of subsequent decrees. On 12 May 1995 a decree was issued on military-technical cooperation with foreign countries (i.e. arms exports). Every application for a licence to export weapons systems or related items is reviewed by an interministerial committee. The foreign ministry is represented on this committee in order to ensure that account is taken of the implications for Russia's foreign relations, including compliance with international arms control treaties. The operational and technical aspects of military-technical cooperation (arms exports) are handled by an agency called Rosvooruzhenie. Its creation by presidential decree on 11 November 1993 centralized the administration of arms exports and made them subject to presidential control. The main administration for military-technical cooperation, which was previously under the authority of the ministry of foreign economic relations, is now directly under presidential control. In July 1994 Boris Kozyk was appointed as a presidential assistant for military-technical cooperation to establish oversight of the arms trade.[28]

The uncertainty over Russia's regulatory framework stems both from the political struggle over its foreign policy, and its adherence to inter-national norms and arms control regimes, and from the conflict between civil and military authorities for control over arms exports. These conflicts are sharpened by the fact that despite the radical decline in arms sales the hard currency income they represent ($2–4 billion annually), while small compared with Russia's requirements, is still considered to be very significant – especially since optimistic Russian analysts believe that the potential exists for a very substantial increase in the volume of the arms trade.[29]

The competition between different Russian manufacturers for a single contract has in various cases resulted in a substantial reduction of the price, and the centralization of the arms trade through Rosvooruzhenie has been accom-panied by an effort to limit the volume of arms exports and achieve higher prices. This centralization is vigorously opposed by those representing the interests of military industry, such as Viktor Glukhikh, chairman of the State Committee for Military Industry, and Gennady Ianpolsly. They have argued that military enterprises should be able to produce and directly export military hardware on the basis of their own business strategy and independent of government procurement;[30] and, furthermore, that military enterprises should be authorized to transfer hard-currency earnings from their exports into their own accounts and maintain direct contacts with customers, in order to be able to serve them in a flexible manner. The military leadership appears to support a controlled expansion of military sales. While it supports maximizing foreign currency earnings, the general staff is aware of the strategic implications of selling high-technology hardware. The ministry of defence also seeks greater income for itself from arms sales especially of surplus equipment which is already in the possession of the armed forces, to alleviate the social problems in the armed forces.

The consequence of these various countervailing pressures is that while the Russian government has continued to cooperate with existing international conventional arms transfer control regimes (including the arms embargoes against the former Yugoslavia and Iran), the policy is constantly under siege and indeed is disintegrating at the margins. Depending on the balance of power in Moscow and the future course of Russia's relations with the West, many existing restraints could well be abandoned in future.

Proliferation concerns

There are some very specific proliferation concerns. The most frequently discussed relates to the proliferation of weapons of mass destruction and their delivery vehicles. The proliferation of ballistic missiles is of particular concern as far as the latter are concerned. At the Soviet–American summit on 31 May–2 June 1990, President Gorbachev committed the Soviet Union to abide by the terms of the missile technology control regime, of which Russia is not a member but whose guidelines it has adopted. Nevertheless, there have been efforts to sell Russian missile technology, the most prominent example being the negotiations for the sale of rocket engines to India.

The sale of civil nuclear technology also has proliferation implications in so far as civil nuclear programmes can be used as the base for developing a nuclear weapons capability. When Russia decided to sell civil nuclear reactors to Iran, this became an interesting test case which revealed some of the political forces at work. Early in 1995 it was revealed that Iran and Russia had finalized an agreement to cooperate in the development of civil nuclear power in Iran. Russia was to provide assistance for Iran to complete LWRs at Bushehr, as 1,000 MW units of the Russian VVER type. (The construction of

LWRs was started by the German firm Siemens but was abandoned after the Iran–Iraq war broke out.) Russia would also help with the construction of a further 1,000 MW reactor and two additional 440 MW units. The most disturbing element of the reports was that Russia intended to provide Iran with centrifuges to build a uranium enrichment facility. This would have provided Iran with the capability to produce weapons-grade material.

These reports drew a sharp response from the United States. The Clinton administration has adopted the view that any transfer of nuclear technology to Iran is dangerous and unacceptable. It believes that Iran is seeking to acquire a nuclear weapons capability, contrary to its undertakings as a signatory of the NPT, and will constitute a grave and unpredictable threat if it acquires such a capability. This stance put the United States in violation of its own obligations under the NPT to allow non-nuclear weapons states to have access to civil nuclear technology under IAEA safeguards; nevertheless, the United States mounted a vigorous diplomatic and public campaign against the Russian–Iranian deal. Not much progress was achieved during the Clinton–Yeltsin summit in May 1995. Russia declared it would not provide enrichment facilities and centrifuges to Iran, but asserted (correctly) that the LWRs would not provide Iran with technology or nuclear materials useful for a weapons programme. Russia's position on the deal appears to be based both on the substantial economic rewards to be gained from it and on its continuing interest in a cooperative relationship with Iran. It was also quite clear that Yeltsin was under very severe pressure to be seen to stand up to the United States in this instance and look after Russia's vital interests. Russian irritation about the manner in which the United States, in the name of global security and non-proliferation, has been constraining Russia's ability to export its high-technology products and expertise, was strongly focused on this particular deal and Yeltsin had no option but to reject US demands to cancel it.

This episode is very instructive because it shows up the tension between Yeltsin's commitment to being a responsible partner to the United States in international affairs in general and arms control in particular, and the pressure to pursue a policy that is based on Russian national interests as the principal objective. The deal with Iran does not aid an Iranian nuclear weapons programme. For this reason, Yeltsin may have felt safe in not bowing to US pressure. As Russia is determined to export its high technology, both civil and military, the emphasis may shift against international cooperation to prevent proliferation. This may mean inevitable failure for the US endeavour to construct a regime of controls on high-technology exports that would include Russia. The deal with Iran symbolizes Russian resistance to joining such a control regime. Russia may, then, become a more active proliferator of high technology with military applications in the future.

The second area of concern is the transfer of high-technology weapons to crisis regions or 'rogue states'. Again, it must be made clear that so far Russia has a reasonable record in adherence to international arms transfer regimes. The Soviet government took part in the London meeting of the five permanent members of the UN Security Council in October 1991, and signed the guidelines for conventional arms transfer of 18 October. The Russian government considers itself as having inherited the rights and obligations of the former USSR in such matters, and the ministry of foreign affairs has reaffirmed Russia's commitment to the guidelines. The problem for the Russian government in this area is that once again the United States is seen as driving Russia out of the market. Countries in crisis regions or 'rogue states' include former client states of the Soviet Union (such as Iran, Iraq and Libya) and therefore potential client states for Russia. The same applies to Serbia, which is currently subject to UN sanctions.

Again Iran, which is engaged in a steady military build-up, provides a useful example. To the United States, these developments are extremely alarming. The Clinton administration has imposed a complete embargo on Iran and expects Russia to comply with it. In September 1994 President Yeltsin agreed to halt arms sales to Iran, except for the fulfilment of contracts already signed, which include the delivery of one further Kilo submarine. This indicates that, until now, the need to preserve a good relationship with United States has overridden many other concerns and Yeltsin has been willing to risk domestic political capital to maintain it. In line with the general trends of Russian foreign policy, this may not last.

The attempt to develop a multilateral regime of export controls for conventional weapons and dual-use technologies resulted in the so-called 'Wassenaar arrangement'. However, the conference held in Vienna on 2–3 April 1996 to inaugurate the Wassenaar arrangement, involving representatives from 31 countries, ended in failure as the US and Russian delegations could not bridge their differences. These related in part to the Russian rejection of a ban on transfers to Iran, Iraq, Libya and North Korea. It remains an open question whether agreement on an export control regime like the Wassenaar arrangement can be reached.[31]

It is also noteworthy that the drive to increase sales of Russian arms is taking place without much concern about Russian strategic interests. This is indicated by the volume of advanced aircraft sales to China. Russian security analysts understand very well that China is the only power that could present a direct military threat to Russia in the long term. China's economy is rapidly expanding, its political system remains unreformed, and it is engaged in a sustained build-up of conventional and nuclear forces which is dependent on the import of Russian weapons and technologies on a massive scale. The apparent willingness of Russia to sell China large quantities of the Su-27, MiG-29, MiG-31 and Tu-22M, and to license production lines for the manufacture of Russian combat aircraft, seems to indicate that Russian national security concerns are being ignored.[32] It must nevertheless be pointed out that similar contradictions apply to Western arms export policies, and the United States in particular may likewise be storing up problems for the future in conducting a more indiscriminate arms export policy.

As noted above, in the area of high-technology conventional weapons systems, the concern does not lie with illicit smuggling of weapons because these systems require continuous support and servicing and therefore a stable relationship between supplier and purchaser. However, Russian government adherence to existing international arms transfer regimes may break down for political reasons. It is also conceivable that the internal export control regime may at some point fragment and companies may be able to export relatively freely. Until a proper international arms export and technology transfer control regime (such as the Wassenaar arrangement) is put in place, Russians may find that their incentive to conform to international expectations is declining as the market becomes even more competitive.

The third area of concern is the uncontrolled proliferation of small arms, especially from the former Soviet Union to central and even western Europe. Here the problem is both the illicit export of weapons stolen from the armed services or military arms dumps and commercial trading by weapons manufacturers. Russian manufacturers of light weapons face the same dilemmas as other parts of the military-industrial complex and are therefore producing aggressive sales strategies, with a wide range of new and innovative models designed to penetrate the international market. Alongside production of light arms known to and sanctioned by the Russian government, there is also illegal production of firearms using idle production facilities, while large quantities of weaponry have been stolen from the inventory of the Soviet mobilization reserves and sold, especially in Ukraine and Belarus.[33] The military itself is one of the major sources of illicit light arms, as weapons are sold to ameliorate living conditions. President Yeltsin himself admitted that military personnel had illegally taken possession of and sold the contents of entire ammunition depots. The Western Group of Russian forces in Germany was a notorious source of black market weaponry. It is quite clear that many weapons go to crisis regions, both inside the former Soviet Union and beyond (e.g. Serbia). The proliferation of light weapons therefore has immediate security implications for Russia and Europe. The other dimension of the proliferation of light weapons in large numbers is that they are used to support the activities of organized crime. There are no precise numbers available for the sales of light weapons, given that much of this trade is uncontrolled. A seizure of 10,000 Russian military pistols in Hamburg in spring 1994 is one of many indications that the numbers concerned are large – millions of weapons throughout the former Soviet Union and potentially beyond. The flood of illicit weapons designed for military purposes into central and western Europe is therefore becoming a major concern of internal security agencies in those countries.

Implications for European security

Russia does not pose a direct military threat to central and western Europe. However, the breakdown of social order in a state as highly militarized as Russia creates dangers which affect that country itself most of all, but which could spill over into central and western Europe. It is difficult to assess the urgency and scale of the risks faced by western Europe. As far as the nuclear weapons complex is concerned, there is very clear evidence that nuclear materials can be procured. What is yet unclear is to what extent there is a market for such materials. States seeking to develop nuclear weapons will most likely seek to develop their own capabilities to enrich uranium or produce plutonium in order to maintain a steady supply. Terrorists are unlikely to attempt to build a nuclear weapon, but might use nuclear materials to acquire a capability to cause serious nuclear contamination. Very urgent and determined action to enhance the security of the nuclear weapons complex in Russia is needed. The activities financed by the Nunn–Lugar Act are a step in the right direction, but their scale is not nearly adequate.

The proliferation of advanced conventional weapons is less of a threat to Europe. Indeed, this seems to be a more problematic issue for Russia's own security, given that it is selling weapons to potential future adversaries. Europe could of course be affected if, for example, arms transfers to the Serbs were resumed without the agreement of the United States or the west Europeans, or if European states once again became involved in a crisis out-of-area, such as the Gulf, into which large quantities of Russian weapons had been exported. Weapons transfers to crisis regions and 'rogue' governments are of course a major international security concern. If arms exports were to cause a major downturn in Russia's relations with the West (for example with the resumption of sales to Iran, Iraq and Libya and/or the sale of SS-25 missiles to India), then this would have important implications for European security.

Finally, the uncontrolled trade in light arms is a major security concern for central and western Europe, and may have far-reaching implications as law enforcement agencies find themselves dealing with gangs with a great deal of firepower.

It is unclear to what extent these dangers can be controlled, since they all originate essentially in the anarchic conditions in post-Soviet Russia and their management is ultimately dependent on the development of a legitimate but orderly government and the stabilization of the economy. Until this is achieved, international arms control regimes offer one instrument to contain the risks. This has been clearly illustrated by the Nunn–Lugar process, which despite its imperfect implementation constitutes a very good model for cooperative threat reduction. As long as the Russian government retains some commitment to partnership with the West, it can use international arms control regimes to enforce restraint on its arms manufacturers. However, this may become increasingly difficult in the future unless Western governments also restrain their arms exports and allow Russia a greater share of that section of the market to which arms can be sold without undermining international stability. The West also has to consider whether it is willing to share some of the financial burdens of bringing the rogue weapons depot that is the former Soviet Union under control.

Traditional arms control concerns have become less important after the Cold War, but they remain on the international agenda. Strategic arms control is still an integral component of US–Russian relations and needs to move forward in order to eliminate this last vestige of the Cold War. The CFE regime retains an important role as a framework for security and stability across Europe. These arms control agreements are crucial for the success of multilateral non-proliferation regimes, such as the NPT, the Comprehensive Test Ban and multilateral weapons technology export controls. Moreover, they are a crucial element in any strategy to enhance the safety and security of nuclear weapons and materials in the former Soviet Union. As Alexei Arbatov has said, it remains to be seen whether the world will survive the collapse of a nuclear superpower.[34]

Notes

1. See Christoph Bluth, 'Strategic Nuclear Weapons and US–Russian Relations: From Confrontation to Cooperative Denuclearization', *Contemporary Security Policy*, vol. 15, no.1, April 1994; 'Nuclear Weapons in Ukraine', *Bulletin of Arms Control*, no. 14, May 1994, pp. 17–21. For a more general analysis of the problem of nuclear weapons in the former non- Russian Soviet republics, see Alexei Arbatov, *Yadernoe Vooruzheniya i respublikanskiy suverenitet* (Moscow: Mezhdunarodnye otnosheniya, 1992).
2. For details on START, see Chapter 3.
3. A START 3 Treaty currently remains a hypothetical possibility until ratification of START 2 by the Duma takes place and implementation of START 2 begins. See 'Russia: Rodionov Voices "Concern" Over US Calls To Leave ABM Treaty', Moscow Interfax 1754 GMT, 14 May 97.
4. There is much debate about the actual size of the ex-Soviet nuclear stockpile According to Russia's atomic energy minister, Viktor Mikhailov, the stockpile peaked at 45,000 warheads in 1986 and declined to 32,000 warheads in May 1993. See *Rossiyskie vesti*, 19 May 1993, p. 7; Lawrence K. Gershwin, National Intelligence Officer for Strategic Programs, Central Intelligence Agency, Hearings before the House Committee on Appropriations, DOD Appropriations for 1993, Part 5, 6 May 1992, p. 499; also Thomas B. Cochran, Robert S. Norris and Oleg A. Bukharin, *Making the Russian Bomb* (Boulder, CO: Westview, 1995), pp. 31–2.
5. For more detail, see Theodor Galdi, *The Nunn–Lugar Cooperative Threat Reduction Program for Soviet Weapons Dismantlement*, CRS Report for Congress, Congressional Research Service, 6 December 1994. Recently, funds have been increasingly channelled through the Department of Energy.
6. Philip Zelikow, 'Current Organization of the International Community for Cooperative Denuclearization',

in Graham Allison, Ashton B. Carter, Steven E. Miller and Philip Zelikow, eds, *Cooperative Denuclearization*, CSIA Studies in International Security no. 2 (Cambridge, MA: Center for Science and International Affairs, 1993). President Clinton appointed Ashton Carter to a position at the Defence Department to oversee denuclearization.

7. For details of all the programmes and monies appropriated, see *Nuclear Successor States of the Soviet Union* (Moscow: Carnegie Endowment for International Peace/Monterey Institute for International Studies, Moscow, December 1994).

8. Information based on interviews with officials from the UK Foreign Office and the US Department of Energy.

9. Graham T. Allison, Owen R. Coté, Jr, Richard A. Falkenrath, and Steven E. Miller, *Avoiding Nuclear Anarchy*, CSIA Studies in International Security no. 12 (Cambridge, MA: MIT Press, 1996, p. 89).

10. The ISTC began work in Moscow after much delay on 3 March 1994. The present author had the opportunity to visit the institute and witness some of its activities in May 1995. A parallel centre was set up in Kiev on 16 July 1994. The effect on the 'brain drain' from the nuclear weapons complex, however, is likely to remain limited. See Dorothy S. Zinberg, *The Missing Link? Nuclear Proliferation and the International Mobility of Russian Nuclear Experts*, UNDIR Research Paper no. 35 (New York: United Nations, 1995).

11. Dismantling means dismantling the so-called 'pit level', when the 'pit' of primary fissile material is separated from the surrounding secondary thermonuclear fuels and the high explosives which are detonated to create a critical mass for nuclear fission. For more detail, see Ashton B. Carter and Owen Coté, 'Disposition of Fissile Materials', in Allison et al., eds, *Cooperative Denuclearization*, pp. 117–36.

12. For more detail, see Allison et al., *Avoiding Nuclear Anarchy*, pp.106–8.

13. This is a bold measure both to provide an incentive for Russia to continue dismantling warheads and to render fissile material secure. The HEU deal was jeopardized for some time by disagreements over the technical and financial arrangements but at the time of writing appears to be secure. For a detailed analysis, see Richard A. Falkenrath, 'The HEU Deal', in Allison et al., *Avoiding Nuclear Anarchy*, pp. 229–92. It is also worth mentioning 'Project Sapphire', which refers to an operation in November 1994 when 600 kg of HEU were flown out of Ust-Kamenogorsk in Kazakstan by US military aircraft. This material was discovered by the Kazak government stored in unsafe conditions.

14. For more detail on the various alternative methods of the disposal of fissile materials, with various cost estimates, see Carter and Coté, 'Disposition of Fissile Materials'.

15. Some embarrassment was caused by the revelation that this had been an unauthorized 'sting' operation by the German intelligence services. German intelligence officers actively procured the radioactive material, which was obtained in Russia. For more detail on this and other incidents, and on the status of nuclear export policies in the former Soviet Union, see *Nuclear Successor States of the Soviet Union*, no. 2, December 1994.

16. Joshua Handler, 'Radioactive Waste Situation in the Pacific Fleet', Greenpeace trip report, Washington DC, 27 October 1994.

17. For more detail on the institutional problems in Russia regarding the safeguarding of nuclear materials, see Oleg Bukharin, 'Nuclear Safeguards and Security in the Former Soviet Union', *Survival*, vol. 36, no. 4, Winter 1994–5, pp. 53–72.

18. For more detail on such contacts and recommendations for their intensification, see Graham Allison, 'Defense and Military Cooperation in Denuclearization', in Allison et al., eds, *Cooperative Denuclearization*, pp. 146–62.

19. Christoph Bluth, *The Collapse of Soviet Military Power* (Aldershot: Dartmouth, 1995), Ch. 7.

20. For a detailed analysis of these issues, see Richard A. Falkenrath, 'The CFE Flank Dispute', *International Security*, vol. 19, no. 4, Spring 1995, pp. 118–44.

21. OMRI *Daily Digest*, 1, no. 107, 3 June 1996.

22. INOBIS, *Russia's Arms Export Policies: Implications for International Security* (Kaliningrad, Moscow oblast: Institute for Defence Studies, 1995), a report commissioned for the Volkswagen RIIA/BIOst research programme on *The Former Soviet States and European Security*; see also Thomas Sachse, *Russische Rüstungsexportpolitik 1993/94*, Berichte des BIOst 25-95, Cologne, 1995.

23. Kevin P. O'Prey, *The Arms Export Challenge* (Washington, DC: Brookings Institution, 1995), p. 5.

24. These objectives were expounded by the former Russian head of the state committee on defence conversion, Mikhail Maley. See *Rossiyskaya gazeta*, 28 February 1992, pp. 1–2.

25. Sachse, *Russische Rüstungsexportpolitik*, pp. 7–8. These data are somewhat uncertain; the higher estimates put the value of arms exports at twice the cited figures.

26. Moscow television service in Russian, 1700 GMT, 27 September 1990, cited from FBIS-SOV-90-192, 3 October 1990, p. 58.
27. Yotzhak Klein, 'Russia and a Conventional Arms Non-proliferation Regime in the Middle East', *Contemporary Security Policy*, vol 16, no.1, April 1995, pp. 34–47.
28. Judith Perera, 'Russia's Arms Sales Increasing – Part I', *Jane's Intelligence Review*, No. 1, January 1997, p. 2.
29. Optimistic estimates indicate that Russia could expand the volume of its arms trade to $20 billion annually. See INOBIS, *Russia's Arms Export Policies*, p. 2.
30. Sachse, *Russische Rüstungsexportpolitik*, pp. 30–1.
31. Natalie J. Goldring, 'Wassenaar Arrangement in Limbo', *Basic Reports*, no. 52, 13 May 1996, pp. 1–3.
32. Alexei Arbatov, 'Editor's Comment: Economy and Security in Exports of Combat Aircraft', in Randall Forsberg, ed., *The Arms Production Dilemma* (Cambridge, MA: MIT Press, 1994), pp. 100–9.
33. Ksenia Gonchar and Peter Lock, 'Small Arms and Light Weapons: Russia and the Former Soviet Union', in Jeffrey Boutwell, Michael T. Klare and Laura W. Reed, ed., *Lethal Commerce: The Global Trade in Small Arms and Light Weapons* (Cambridge, MA: Committee on International Security Studies, 1995), pp. 116–26.
34. Alexei Arbatov, 'Russia's Foreign Policy Alternatives', *International Security*, vol. 18, no. 2, Fall 1993, pp. 5–43.

16 The post-Soviet space and Europe

Christoph Bluth

The end of the Cold War, which imposed a bipolar structure on the system of states in Europe, has removed the fundamental existential threat to their security that west European states faced for over forty years. A stable new order has not yet fully emerged in Europe and the political dynamics of the post-Soviet space in particular harbour potentially serious implications for European security. At the root of the problem is that the states which emerged from the dissolution of the Soviet Union are not stable. The collapse of the communist political order has resulted in a degree of anarchy as a functioning democratic political system has not yet emerged in any of the former Soviet republics. Although the old decision-making structures of the communist system have disintegrated, the transition to a liberal democratic state is far from complete. Indeed, with the loss of power of the CPSU and the disintegration of the union, the 'newly independent states', including the Russian Federation, have emerged as territories which lacked many fundamental institutions of state and the process of state-building is still continuing.[1] This chapter assesses Russia's relations with Europe, with a particular view to the implications for the European security environment, and the interaction of this relationship with the dynamics of integration and disintegration in the former Soviet space.

Russian foreign policy in transition

Russia's relations with Europe cannot be separated from its relations with the West as a whole and the broad features of its foreign policy in general. Russian foreign policy is still in a state of flux. Like the other former republics of the Soviet Union, the Russian Federation seeks to come to terms with being an independent state needing to define its national interests and foreign and security policy objectives.

The principal element in the new frame of reference for Moscow is the disintegration of the Warsaw Pact and the Soviet Union itself. The Russian Federation is now virtually surrounded by former Soviet republics, all of them with deep political, social and economic problems, some of them highly unstable and subject to violent civil conflicts. The territory of the Russian

Federation itself, about 75 per cent of the territory of the former USSR with about 60 per cent of its population, is still not properly defined, given that significant sections of the borders are purely notional, and the degree of control that Moscow can exercise over the entire Federation is uncertain.[2]

Both the external and the domestic environment faced by Moscow's policy-makers have been transformed. Russia has emerged from a tremendous global conflict with the highly industrialized countries of the West which endured for over forty years, and from an even longer period of totalitarianism and mismanagement of all aspects of government. In this context, Russia, as the largest and by any measure most powerful of the Soviet successor states, has to deal with the many issues arising from the loss of empire: relations with the former Soviet states and eastern Europe, policy towards the former adversaries of the Soviet Union, and the extent of any remaining global role that Russia might play. More fundamental and important is how the Russian people, having been defeated in the struggle with the West and betrayed by the totalitarian misrule of their own leaders, and having rejected the most basic values on which their society had supposedly been based, redefine their own national identity, and how this determines their relations with the rest of the world.

Russia and the world

There is at present a general consensus in Russia that it does not have the resources to play a global role. Accordingly, Russian involvement in Third World countries not contiguous to its own borders, including allies of the former Soviet Union, has virtually ceased. Nor is there any interest in resuming a hegemonic role in eastern Europe. More importantly, from the point of view of relations with the West, the confrontation with the West, and with the United States in particular, is considered to be over.[3]

The first two years of the Yeltsin government were characterized by a foreign policy in which the development of closer relations with the West dominated everything else. The continuing decline of Russia's economy and the bitter conflict between Yeltsin and the parliament which was resolved by the use of force have resulted in a political climate marked by disillusionment with economic and political reform. Since the events of October 1993, when President Yeltsin broke up the sit-in at the parliament, forcibly dissolved it and restructured the Russian political system by means of a new constitution, Russian democratic forces have been continuously losing influence. This trend has been accompanied by an increasingly assertive foreign policy which stresses Russia's role as a great power on the world stage and its special interests in 'the former Soviet space'. At the same time, relations with the West have cooled somewhat, and the concept of a partnership between Russia and the West has openly come into question.

There are a number of factors that account for these developments. The first is the emergence of new conceptions of Russia's national interest. While no single concept of national security exists, there are some distinct elements of the debate around which a certain consensus has formed. The first of these is that Russia is and remains a great power. This means that while Russia seeks a cooperative relationship with the West, it does so on equal terms and it will not toe the Western line in international organizations. The second is that Russia claims the right to a dominant position in the former Soviet space, which remains its special sphere of influence. This claim has a range of implications. For Russia, the external border of the Commonwealth of Independent States is perceived as the geopolitical boundary of the Russian Federation. Russia sees itself as the sole guarantor of security within that area, bearing the main responsibility for conflict resolution and peacekeeping in the CIS. This assumption has an economic dimension as Russia increasingly asserts a right to be involved in the disposition of major reservoirs of natural resources in the CIS, such as oil and gas. Another facet of this stance is the intention to exclude any external powers from major influence in the periphery of the former Soviet space. The perception that these are vital elements of a strategy designed to safeguard Russian national security, which is perceived to be under threat especially at its southern periphery, explains to some extent the shifts and changes in Russian policy towards the West.[4]

The second factor is the reassertion of the conservative institutions of the *ancien régime*. These include the armed forces, the military-industrial complex, the gas and oil industries, the agricultural sector and the security services (the successors to the KGB). These institutions do not have a common agenda, but they exercise a great deal of influence on policy outside the democratic process. This is exacerbated by the fact that the middle layer of the bureaucratic apparatus in all the ministries is dominated by people from the Soviet era who largely dislike the West and who share the objective of restoring both Russia's great power status and a new union of the former Soviet states. Given that the influence of the parliament is more restricted under the new constitution, it is now believed by many expert observers that democratic control over the policy process, in so far as it ever existed, has largely been lost. The extent to which power struggles in the Kremlin impact on policy was vividly demonstrated by the short period during which Aleksandr Lebed headed the Security Council after the presidential elections in 1996. Although Lebed's efforts to concentrate power in his own hands were ultimately defeated, this episode, which coincided with Yelstin's prolonged and severe illness, demonstrated the deficiencies of the political process.

The third factor is the sharp and prolonged downturn in the Russian economy. There was an expectation that market reform, Western economic aid and Western capital investment would transform Russia's economy. This has not happened, partly because of gross mismanagement, partly due to systemic factors. The entire industrial base of Russia, which is dominated by military production, needs to be fundamentally restructured in order to be able to produce goods capable of competing in the world market. The investment capital required to retool Russia's industry is enormous and the entire process will require decades. Although Russia has undertaken systematic reform of the economy and industry has been privatized on a huge scale, this is only the beginning. So far the principal outcome of the reform process has been a rapid fall in the level of production, government insolvency (which translates into insolvency for the major companies which relied on government orders), unemployment, a precipitous rise in the cost of living and a concomitant fall in the standard of living. Attempts by the Russian government to control inflationary pressures have been rather uneven, although this element of economic policy has been comparatively successful since mid-1995.[5] Another fundamental problem has been the absence of an effective legal system to regulate economic activity. These difficulties are exacerbated by the growth of organized crime and corruption, which pervade every aspect of economic activity in Russia today.

The consequence has been that Western investors have remained reluctant to become involved. Cumulative foreign investment in the Soviet Union and Russia from 1988 to 1994 amounted to a mere $2.7 billion. Of particular symbolic significance has been the Russian perception of the rather small scale of Western aid and credits. Germany has been the most substantial and reliable donor, providing DM81.2 billion to the former Soviet states between 1990 and 1993.[6] The United States has been hesitant to commit major sums, partly as a consequence of its own large deficit, partly from a lack of confidence that a larger financial commitment would benefit the Russian economy. The conclusion drawn by many in the Russian political elite is that the hope for Western aid is illusory and that Russia will have to rely on its own resources, while among the general population the failure of the Russian economy has resulted in a general disenchantment with reform.[7] Although economic constraints still provide a powerful motivation for good relations with the West, this is less strong now than it was in 1991 and 1992. In particular, what is remarkable about the more recent trends in Russian policy is that Russia is willing to pursue the reintegration of the CIS as a priority objective, despite the potentially high costs and despite the detrimental consequences on Russia's extended integration into the world economy.[8] The Russian government appears to be willing to take greater risks in pursuit of a more independent foreign policy.

One consequence of this shift is that Russian policy towards the West has become less predictable and cooperative. This does not mean that Russia will threaten the West directly, although it may act against Western interests in international organizations; certainly, the return to a more adversarial relationship with the West cannot be ruled out. Another danger lies in the outbreak of internal conflict in the Russian Federation that may get out of control altogether, or complete societal breakdown. Either situation would inevitably have repercussions for the whole of Europe.

Russia and Europe

Russia's policy towards Europe is subject to similar contradictions and internal political controversy as its policy towards the West in general. However, it is possible to identify certain principles that define Russian policy objectives in its relations with Europe.

First, Russia wishes to be acknowledged as a great power with its own specific interests and geopolitical role. In the perception of the political elite, Russia has a decisive influence on the security and stability of Europe and thus plays a leading role in the definition of the European security order. The problem is that both Russia's internal problems – its lack of socio-political cohesion and economic weakness – and the absence of a coherent philosophy guiding its relations with the outside world substantially inhibit the exercise of such a role. Furthermore, from the Western standpoint, a strategic partnership with Russia as a major player in world affairs requires a clear commitment on Russia's part to international norms and democratic principles, and the existence of a sense of common purpose. The perception in the West is that Russia's transition to such a state is far from complete and, indeed, appears to be faltering. In particular, it is unclear whether Russia's relations with its 'near abroad', most acutely in respect of its intervention in Chechenia, can be reconciled with the guiding principles and norms of international relations.[9]

Secondly, Russia at the same time seeks to be closely linked to Europe. Indeed, Russia's political and economic transformation may only be assured by a well thought-out strategy for its gradual integration with the rest of Europe. Acknowledgment of this necessity is currently evident in Russia's expressed wish to be and act as a full member of pan-European organizations, especially the OSCE and the Council of Europe. With regard to the EU and NATO, if Russia cannot become a member even in the long term, it would at least like to have the kind of relationship with these organizations that would give it a decisive voice in the development of the post-Cold War European order. The expansion of the EU has important implications for Russia. In preparation for membership, central European countries will adopt economic policies designed to enable them to fulfil the criteria for membership. They have already begun to form closer economic and political ties with western

Europe, further weakening links with the former Soviet space. There are also implications for the international security environment, as some central European countries will be invited to join NATO and prospective EU members will prepare to join the WEU, thereby acquiring Western security guarantees and effectively pushing the boundaries of Western security organizations further east. Once central and east European countries have fully integrated with western Europe, Russia will find itself outside a large integrated system of states with economies that have achieved a degree of harmonization and that are part of an integrated framework of security that involves the United States and Canada.[10]

Thirdly, the relationship with western Europe is of central importance to Russia's integration into the world economy. The Russia–EU partnership may be the main driving force of Russia's social and economic progress and the best guarantee against the revival of authoritarian rule and the return to adversarial Cold War-type international relations which would be dangerous both to Russia and to the rest of the world.[11]

The principal question for the future of Russia's relationship with the EU is whether full membership is a serious option in the future, and if not, what kind of relations can be envisaged. Not only are there problems associated with integrating Russia into the EU, the future shape of the Union itself remains uncertain. The many elements on the current agenda, such as the widening of membership and the deepening of European integration (including economic and monetary union, financial and structural reform and the implementation of a common foreign and security policy), all have profound implications for the future of Europe. Their implementation will require deep structural changes in the Union that will only be achieved if the opposition of powerful vested interests and political constituencies in many member states can be overcome.

The different elements of Russia's policy towards Europe therefore remain inconsistent, although the centrality of Russia–EU relations is clear. There are two opposite but related dangers. One is that the process of European integration and its extension to central Europe is not accompanied by a determined process of mutual engagement between Russia and the West and that this process therefore excludes Russia. On the other hand, Russia's insistence on being a great Eurasian power with its own sphere of influence in eastern Europe may hinder the development of a European partnership with Russia and also serve to isolate the former Soviet space from the West. It is a common concern for Russia and Europe that Russia should not be isolated but should be a close partner in Europe, whether or not fully integrated into the European Union.

There is a desire for close political cooperation on both sides. At the diplomatic level, two summit meetings between the president of Russia and the presidents of the European Council and the European Commission are envisaged by the partnership and cooperation agreement signed in June 1994. This agreement emphasizes the importance of common values, the rule of law, respect for human rights, the protection of minorities and the establishment in Russia of a multi-party system with free elections. Indeed, it makes economic cooperation conditional on adherence to fundamental political principles.[12]

This reflects the perception in western Europe that there is a need for a continued process of building a functioning democracy in Russia, based on the principle of the division of powers, the rule of law and the creation of a civil society, and that the transition from a totalitarian to a democratic political system is as yet incomplete. Engaging in partnership with Russia therefore requires instruments for the development of coherent responses to situations where Russia perceives its interests to be contrary to the interests of EU member states, or even to common Western perceptions of the interests of the international system (such as international peace and security). West European states have found it especially difficult to respond to violations of international norms, democratic principles or human rights in Russia, as exemplified by the continuing Chechen crisis. New policy instruments need to be developed which allow both for clear and determined responses and also for continuing engagement with Russia. One approach to this which has been attempted with limited success is to integrate Russia into a range of international institutions and agreements which both legitimize and constrain Russia's international actions. The partnership and cooperation agreement is one example of this; Russian membership of the European Council is another. They demonstrate that the European Union clearly has a significant role to play in conducting its bilateral relations with Russia. The critical question, which so far remains unanswered, is at what point and how the various institutional mechanisms, including the threat of suspending the partnership agreement and/or Russia's membership of the European Council, are to be used. This is one of the principal challenges for the common foreign and security policy.

Russia and the European security architecture

As the Cold War came to an end and the Warsaw Pact collapsed, the Soviet Union was one of the principal promoters of the CSCE as the framework for a new European security architecture. This enthusiasm was prompted by a number of considerations and objectives. First of all, it fitted in very well with Gorbachev's new [political] thinking and the concept of 'mutual security'. It was only logical that the Cold War system based on two opposing collective defence alliances should be replaced by a pan-European collective security system. Furthermore, with the collapse of the Warsaw Pact the Soviet Union was hoping that NATO, which continued in existence, would fade into irrelevance and be superseded by a cooperative structure like the CSCE. Finally, the Soviet Union did not want to be isolated in Europe and considered that it should be one of the principal architects of a new European security framework.[13] Much of this thinking was adopted by the Russian leadership after the Soviet Union collapsed. However, while the CSCE was formally made into such a pan-European collective security structure – the OSCE – the realization of these ideals turned out to be impossible. Over the years it became evident that no member state, not even Russia, was willing to invest the OSCE with the powers and instruments that it would require for effective peace keeping and crisis management.[14]

The situation is compounded by the problem of conflicts in the FSU and Russia's role in them. It is clear that only the military establishment of Russia has the means and the domestic political backing to engage in effective peacekeeping and peace-making operations in this region. The crucial issue here is the nature of Russian policy towards regional conflicts and its international legitimization. While the West must recognize that Russia has a legitimate interest in preventing or resolving such conflicts, the concept of Russian hegemony in the FSU should be resisted. Here collective security can come into play, given that Russia has asked to be mandated by the UN and/or the OSCE to provide security in the CIS. The Russian endeavour to obtain a UN mandate foundered on its insistence that only Russian/CIS forces should be involved in peacekeeping in the former Soviet Union and that the UN should only provide observers. This proposal raises a number of problems. Most obviously, it sets a question mark against the impartiality and neutrality of the forces. Moreover, UN-mandated peace keeping is traditionally carried out by fully multinational forces, under sole UN command. The formula put forward by Russia thus contradicts many of the essential requirements for UN-mandated peacekeeping operations. Furthermore, in several of the crises in which Russian forces have been engaged, the task has been one not of peacekeeping (after being invited to do so by all the sides involved in the conflict) but rather of peace-making. Thus Western policy-makers face a dilemma. On the one hand, Russia is asking for an international mandate, both to legitimize its actions and in order to obtain financial support. Such a mandate, if given, could be used to establish the framework and limits of Russian actions. Moreover, no Western state is willing to contemplate a substantial military engagement anywhere in the former Soviet Union. However, on the other hand, Russia remains unwilling to fulfil the conditions necessary to achieve a UN mandate and certainly would under no circumstances contemplate transforming the peacekeeping forces in the CIS into UN forces, evidencing continued unwillingness to permit international control over, or the involvement of foreign troops in, peacekeeping operations in the former Soviet space. Nor is Russia's impartiality in its involvement in regional conflicts in Eurasia beyond question. The concept of CIS peacekeeping and the notion of recognizing the CIS as a regional organization that could engage in peacekeeping under a UN mandate also remains dubious as long as no CIS states other than Russia are involved in more than a token form in terms both of troop presence and of decision-making.[15]

Russia's endeavour to obtain a CSCE mandate for peacekeeping and peacemaking operations in the former Soviet Union followed similar lines and encountered similar obstacles. In July 1992 the CSCE was declared to be a regional agency according to Chapter VIII of the UN Charter. This endowed it with the authority to carry out peacekeeping operations. The Rome Council meeting of the CSCE in December 1993 considered a Russian request for authorization to conduct peacekeeping missions in the CIS. This was not accepted. The meeting approved the concept of setting up a CSCE cooperative arrangement that would, *inter alia*, ensure that the role and functions of the third-party military force in a conflict area were consistent with CSCE principles and objectives.[16] In June 1994, however, Russia made it clear that it would not accept the monitoring of its forces by CSCE representatives.

It is ironic that the Budapest summit in autumn 1994, at which the CSCE was finally transformed into a security organization (the OSCE) and where a decision was made to prepare for its first major peacekeeping operation in Nagorno-Karabakh, took place shortly before the Russian military incursion into Chechenia. Discussions about an OSCE mandate for peacekeeping in the former Soviet Union were put on hold as a consequence of this crisis, in which international norms and humanitarian principles were violated on a large scale. Nevertheless, the OSCE did assume a role in the Chechen crisis when the Permanent Council decided to deploy the OSCE Assistance Group to Chechenia.

The part played by the OSCE in the former Soviet Union thus has been a very limited one, confined mainly to observer missions and involvement in the negotiation of political settlements (for example in the Transdniestria dispute).[17] The OSCE still lacks the instruments for effective peacekeeping and enforcement, and Russia is as yet unprepared to give up control over operations in the former Soviet Union. It nevertheless remains imperative to make collective security in Europe effective, precisely in order to place constraints on Russian military actions in the FSU.[18]

A related issue is that of the extension of NATO membership. One of the reasons why NATO members have been reluctant to extend membership to central European countries is that this is not perceived as enhancing the security of the alliance as currently constituted. Indeed, the opposite might be the case, in so far as western Europe might be drawn into conflicts from which it would otherwise remain isolated. Secondly, the extension of NATO membership to the central European countries and the Baltic states without including Russia itself would lend strength to those forces in Russia that seek to hinder the process of political reform and integration in the world community.[19] Nor would re-creation of a military confrontation at the Russian border enhance the security of east European countries; again, quite the reverse would be the case. However, to provide security guarantees without putting in place the means to support them would be irresponsible. There is currently in effect an extensive conventional arms control regime (the CFE Treaty) which is in principle capable of preventing local arms races in central and eastern Europe and particularly constrains Russian military deployments west of the Urals. It is in the security interest of all European countries that this regime remains in place and that Russia remains an adherent to it.[20]

For Russia, the issue of NATO extension has become an important symbol of relations with the West and the military and political elites are adamantly opposed to it. For this reason, NATO first created the North Atlantic Cooperation Council (NACC), which allowed for consultation with the former Warsaw Pact countries, and then the Partnership for Peace (PfP), which allowed for more concrete military cooperation. Even Russia eventually signed up to the Partnership for Peace, after first demanding to be treated, as a great power, differently from the other east European countries; but it has not signed the PfP framework document and its commitment remains ambiguous.

These steps fell far short of the demands of the central European states and in December 1994 NATO initiated a study of the conditions for extension of the alliance which has since been concluded. Although no definite decision to proceed with extension has been made, it is inconceivable that, at the very least, some central European countries will not be invited to join the alliance.

Russian opposition to the extension of NATO is almost ubiquitous throughout the political elite. At one end of the spectrum of opinion it is presented as an aggressive move that threatens Russia's security and therefore demands a response. A detailed exposition of this view was given by Pavel Fel'gengauer, allegedly representing the scenarios developed by the general staff. [21] According to this analysis, the risk of war between Russia and NATO is currently low because of the geographical distance separating them. After the inclusion of central and east European states in the alliance, NATO operational plans would be revised and the infrastructure for a rapid forward deployment of NATO forces in Poland would be put in place. NATO would create a unified operational space in a territory reaching right up to the Russian frontier. Integrated mobile air and ground forces could be moved across a distance of thousands of kilometres in a short period of time in order to inflict massive and decisive strikes against Russia. In the view of the general staff, as reported by Fel'gengauer, this transformation of the strategic environment of Europe harbours a real threat of war. In the event of a crisis NATO might begin forward deployment of substantial forces in order to be able to exert pressure on Moscow. Russia would then have no choice but to react with a pre-emptive strike. If Poland were to become part of the NATO integrated military structure, Russia might have to respond by deploying hundreds of tactical nuclear weapons in Kaliningrad in order to be able to target the infrastructure in Poland designed to support NATO mobile forces. The same factors would also affect Russia's attitude to the integration of the Baltic countries in western structures, in whatever form. The danger that the extension of NATO could provoke a new military confrontation and arms race in Europe has been emphasized by various military and civilian analysts. The danger that it might lead to actual war has been reiterated by General Lebed and on occasion even by President Yeltsin.[22]

A threat perception, of course, is not generated purely by military capabilities, but is also based on the interpretation and perception of the international political environment in which they exist. The view that the extension of NATO represents a threat to Russia presumes the existence of an adversarial relationship with the West to the extent that the West may indeed have reasons to plan military strikes against Russia. On the surface this appears to be completely absurd and is in contradiction with various assertions made by Yeltsin and Kozyrev about Russia's relations with the West. While the military scenarios posited are dubious enough, given the risks that the West would be running – not least because Russia is still a strategic nuclear power – none of the Russian statements that condemn the expansion of NATO suggest any political motives or even give a hint of how this could conceivably be in the Western interest. Indeed, any objective analysis would suggest that the effect of the extension of NATO, at least to the Visegrad countries (the Czech Republic, Hungary, Poland and Slovakia), would make very little difference to the European security environment. The threats that Russia faces to its security and stability derive not from the West but from its own internal problems and the conflicts at the southern periphery. The West is the principal source of stability and security even for Russia itself.

Western attitudes, however, exhibit similar contradictions. The principal argument in favour of NATO expansion has been that it would contribute to the stability of the former communist countries in central Europe. Some, however, have argued that the central European countries face a genuine security threat, especially given the prospect of a nationalist and/or communist leadership in Russia.[23] The strident manner in which Lech Walesa and Vaclav Havel demanded NATO membership with reference to developments in Russia have encouraged such views. Republican members of the US Congress have also treated Russia as if it were still the enemy, and are dealing with security issues such as the ABM Treaty, strategic arms control and cooperation on nuclear safety on the basis of an adversarial relationship with Russia. They look at the issue of NATO expansion similarly, as a means to deal with a potential Russian threat.

If NATO expansion is designed to enhance political stability, then it is a questionable instrument to achieve this objective because it is difficult to see how it will affect the internal sources of instability in the central and east European countries in a tangible manner. If, on the other hand, it is designed to address an external threat to the stability of that region, then the Russians are correct to interpret it as a move against them (albeit a defensive one) and put it into the framework of a (potentially) adversarial relationship between Russia and the West. The conceptual contradictions in Russia's response mirror the conceptual contradiction in the process of NATO expansion itself.

The strong Russian reaction to the prospect of NATO expansion is not based solely on considerations of military security, but also on its perceived political implications. The view of the ministry of foreign affairs has been articulated in a planning document which states that the expansion of NATO will create a new European security system which will ultimately embrace most central and east European states, but not Russia. This will impede Russia's participation in a pan-European security structure and a full security partnership with Western states. The document reaffirms that a strategic partnership with the West is in Russia's interest and evidences a discernible fear of isolation and the political consequences. The latter could include the strengthening of anti-Western forces in Russia and the weakening of the democratic, pro-Western elite, leading ultimately to the 'Weimarization' of Russia. A significant downturn in relations with the West could result, one manifestation of which would be the breakdown of arms control regimes and the renewal of efforts to restore Russia's military capabilities, with devastating political and economic consequences.

The problem of Russia's potential international isolation is exacerbated by the ambiguous nature of the NATO enlargement process. The pressure from central European states for admission to NATO derives primarily from their wish to be firmly integrated into the Western alliance and thereby enabled to deal with internal political elements that threaten the stability of the newly democratic regimes. The ideal solution for this problem would in fact be membership of the EU; but as a consequence of the difficulties associated with the transition to the modern market economy, full EU membership is likely to be more distant. NATO membership is therefore seen to some extent as a substitute. However, there are also concerns about Russia in some central European states, given the political instability of the Russian Federation and the rise of anti-Western and nationalist forces there. The need for a security guarantee against Russian hegemonic ambitions has been stated most explicitly by Poland. Although Western leaders deny it, the Russian view that NATO expansion is directed against Russia is not entirely without foundation. It is strengthened by the ambiguous position on Russia's potential NATO membership. While the United States has insisted on keeping this open as a possibility for the future, the European allies – Germany in particular – have insisted that Russia could never be a member of NATO. Although there are strongly conflicting views within Russia about the wisdom of Russian membership of NATO, these attitudes reinforce Russian perceptions of the hostile nature of NATO expansion.

On Russia's interpretation, the expansion of NATO would have a fundamental impact on the future European security architecture at odds with the terms under which the Cold War was ended. In this context, it must be remembered that there remains a widely held view in Moscow that Gorbachev's agreement that a united Germany could be a member of NATO was a historical mistake. Nevertheless it is believed that the extension of NATO violates the understanding that Gorbachev reached with Helmut Kohl at the time. Thus President Yeltsin wrote in 1994 to the heads of state of the United States, United Kingdom, France and Germany that the extension of NATO contravened the 'two-plus-four agreement' of 12 September 1990. From a purely technical point of view, this is clearly not the case. However, the 'two-plus-four agreement' prohibited the deployment of NATO tactical nuclear weapons and the stationing of non-German NATO troops in the territory of the former GDR. In this sense there was a commitment not to extend NATO eastwards beyond its Cold War borders, including the former inner-German border. It is quite undeniable that the Soviet Union was given assurances that NATO had no intention of extending eastwards. Gorbachev has stated that a 'gentlemen's agreement' was reached in the course of the negotiations of the 'two-plus-four agreement' not to extend NATO eastwards.[24] The Russian ministry of foreign affairs and various specialists have therefore argued and continue to maintain that the plans for the expansion of NATO violate the 'spirit' of the 'two-plus-four agreement' and constitute a fundamental breach of trust.

This interpretation is not without some merit, in view of the assurances the Soviet Union was given in order to obtain acceptance of full NATO membership for Germany after unification. However, it is questionable that the intention was to preclude NATO membership for central and east European countries indefinitely. The defining period was the first four years after unification, during which Soviet/Russian troops were withdrawn from Germany. Nevertheless, the Russian stance may be an indication that the transformation of the international system in Europe after the Cold War has not proceeded far enough to justify further moves on the basis that these assurances are now no longer relevant.

The Russian case is considerably weakened by the fact that the Soviet Union itself made a public declaration, in a final communiqué to the agreement of 25 February 1991 which dissolved the Warsaw Pact, that all states – including all former Warsaw Pact states – had the right to decide whether or not they wanted to be part of any alliance. All Russian protestations to the contrary, therefore, it would seem that the free choice of the central and east European countries to join NATO should be respected in the new international environment. However, it is quite clear that at present these arguments are not politically effective in Moscow. NATO enlargement has become a symbol of relations with the West more generally and a political instrument of those who support a more independent, less pro-Western – or even anti-Western – foreign and security policy. In other words, NATO enlargement has become a political wild card which serves to promote the interests of a range of political constituencies in the Russian political elite and therefore is not susceptible to rational counter-arguments based on an 'objective' assessment of Russian national security interests. The attitude taken by the Russian government is that the decision to accept new members in the NATO alliance is not final and therefore can be reversed. There is consequently no willingness to prepare fallback positions or develop political compromises at present.

On the other hand, ultimately Russia is not in a position to prevent NATO expansion. Among the possible Russian responses to any widening of the alliance, the following have been mooted:

- The creation of a military alliance in the CIS. This option was proposed by former Russian defence minister Grachev but is widely considered to be unrealistic.
- The strengthening of a special military relationship with Belarus. This appears to be already in progress.
- The deployment of tactical nuclear weapons in Belarus and Kaliningrad, and other forward-based areas.
- The renunciation of the INF Treaty, the redeployment of INF or/and the targeting of strategic nuclear forces at military targets in central and eastern Europe.
- The renunciation of the CFE Treaty and an all-round build-up of Russian conventional forces.
- The end of strategic arms control (i.e. non-ratification of START 2).
- Disregard of Western concerns about arms exports to 'rogue states', including Iran and Libya, and collaboration in missile production with India.
- The occupation of the Baltic states, if they are to be accepted into the NATO alliance.

Despite the generally uncompromising stance taken by all shades of opinion in Moscow, some possible avenues towards a solution were explored. From the Western side, there was the concept of a special partnership with Russia that recognizes Russia's special position as a great power and seeks to diminish the perceived threat posed by NATO enlargement by reassuring Russia through a variety of consultative mechanisms. Such gestures did not for some time appear to be sufficient to overcome Russian opposition. In the Russian foreign ministry, the suggestion has been made that Russia's principal concern is the deployment of nuclear weapons or nuclear infrastructure in the central and east European states, so that a commitment by NATO not to recreate a new theatre nuclear threat in central Europe could be an important element of a deal involving Russian acquiescence in the extension of NATO membership to some central and east European countries. At the NATO foreign ministers' meeting in Brussels in December 1996, the outgoing US Secretary of State Warren Christopher stated that the alliance had 'no intention, no plan and no need to station nuclear weapons on the territory of any new members'.[25] At the same time it was announced that NATO would agree on a timetable for enlargement by July 1997, with a view to completing the first phase by the time of NATO's fiftieth anniversary in 1999. This stage is to be accompanied by an 'Atlantic Partnership Council' designed to establish a special relationship with Russia. The Russian response to this proposal has so far been very negative.

The debate about NATO expansion is a dangerous distraction. It deals with symbols, rather than with the real and unprecedented security threats that confront Russia and, to a lesser extent, the rest of Europe. The post-Cold War environment requires a security architecture that provides collective security. NATO is a collective defence organization that despite the transformation of its military structure remains maladapted to the requirements of collective security.

Until the Helsinki summit in March 1997, despite the various hints of a possible resolution of this issue, a complete rejection of NATO expansion in all its forms remained at the core of the official Russian stance, as expressed by President Yeltsin himself:[26]

> I do not rule out the possibility that we [Yeltsin and Clinton] may disagree on something. The position of the Russian leadership is known: we do not intend to make concessions that would undermine the defence capability of the country. What the Americans are suggesting – the spread of conventional armaments to Eastern Europe – the effect of which would be to seal Russia off. We will not agree to that … Our other categoric condition is that Baltic and CIS states not be drawn into NATO in any form.

Clearly, the Russian leadership had become alarmed by NATO's contacts with the leaders of countries in the former Soviet Union, in particular the tour of several CIS nations by NATO Secretary-General Javier Solana. Yeltsin also dismissed any suggestion that Russia itself might join NATO.[27]

Yeltsin also made it clear that Russia did not fear a military attack by NATO, but was seeking to prevent isolation as a result of NATO enlargement. But already prior to the summit his language became somewhat more ambiguous. Instead of a complete retreat by the American president, he merely demanded some unspecified 'compromise'.

In the course of the Helsinki summit which took place on 20–21 March 1997, it became clear, if it had not been before, that NATO enlargement would proceed and Yeltsin was forced to acknowledge the fact that it could no longer be prevented. Indeed, to many in Russia the results of the Helsinki summit looked like a total surrender on the part of Yeltsin.[28] The principal objective of Russian policy became damage limitation. The most suitable device for saving face was an agreement between NATO and Russia that would in some form safeguard Russian interests and define the future relationship between Russia and the Alliance. For Russia, such an agreement had to have at least four basic elements:

- No nuclear weapons would be stationed on the territory of the new NATO members.
- There would be no substantial forward deployment of NATO conventional forces or NATO's military infrastructure.
- The CFE Treaty would have to be adapted to take account of the changed international security environment in which Russia would find itself after NATO enlargement.
- Russia would have a voice in NATO decisions, especially with regard to those affecting relations with the East, so that diplomatic means would exist to prevent actions inimical to Russia's national security.[29]

Intensive talks were held between Russian Foreign Minister Primakov and NATO Secretary-General Solana and also between Primakov and US Secretary of State Albright to finalize such an agreement. The principal point of disagreement right until the last moment was that Russia was seeking cast-iron guarantees on the four basic elements outlined above. This was obviously incompatible with the obligations under the NATO Treaty, and in the end NATO did not budge from a formulation that conceded that these demands could be met under present conditions, but that NATO reserved the right to deploy its forces in whatever way it deemed necessary in the event of an emerging risk to international security in the region.

The 'Founding Act on Mutual Relations, Cooperation and Security between NATO and the Russian Federation' was signed by NATO Heads of State and Russian President Boris Yeltsin in Paris on 27 May 1997. According to the document,

NATO and Russia will help to strengthen the Organization for Security and Cooperation in Europe (OSCE), including developing further its role as a primary instrument in preventive diplomacy, conflict prevention, crisis management, post-conflict rehabilitation and regional security cooperation, as well as in enhancing its operational capabilities to carry out these tasks.

NATO and Russia will base their relations on a shared commitment to the following principles:

The development, on the basis of transparency, of a strong, stable, enduring and equal partnership and of cooperation to strengthen security and stability in the Euro-Atlantic area; the acknowledgement of the vital role that democracy, political pluralism, the rule of law, and respect for human rights and civil liberties and the development of free market economies play in the development of common prosperity and comprehensive security; refraining from the threat or use of force against each other as well as against any other state, its sovereignty, territorial integrity or political independence in any manner inconsistent with the Charter of the United Nations and with the Declaration of Principles Guiding Relations Between Participating States contained in the Helsinki Final Act; respect for sovereignty, independence and territorial integrity of all states and their inherent right to choose the means to ensure their own security, the inviolability of borders and peoples' right of self-determination as enshrined in the Helsinki Final Act and other OSCE documents; mutual transparency in creating and implementing defence policy and military doctrines; the prevention of conflicts and settlement of disputes by peaceful means in accordance with UN and OSCE principles; support, on a case-by-case basis, of peacekeeping operations carried out under the authority of the United Nations Security Council or the responsibility of the OSCE.

The agreement partially satisfies Russia's requirements, but in a way which does not bind NATO in the event of a real crisis in relations with Russia. Thus NATO has said that the deployment of nuclear weapons on the territory of future NATO members is not anticipated in the foreseeable future, but has refused to give a definite guarantee that this will never happen. Moreover, the Alliance has stated that it does not intend to deploy any significant combat forces on a permanent basis in these countries. On the basis of Article 5 of the NATO Treaty, the Alliance reserves the right to deploy whatever forces are necessary on the territory of all its member states in a crisis situation.

The creation of a NATO–Russia Council has the purpose of providing a forum for consultation to reassure Russia of NATO's intentions at all times. It even provides Russia with a voice – but no vote – on internal issues of the NATO Alliance. Yeltsin and Primakov heralded the 'consensus rule' as a veto on all NATO actions, but in reality the rule of consensus will only be applied during the adoption of decisions concerning bilateral cooperation between Russia and NATO.[30] The resolution of the dispute over the enlargement of NATO at the time of writing appears to have had the effect of creating an agreed framework for Russia's relations with the West and thereby improving relations considerably. However, NATO enlargement has the potential of re-emerging as a political problem if countries of the former Soviet Union, such as the Baltic states or even Ukraine will demand membership at a later stage.

In this context the nonchalance with which the enlargement of the European Union to embrace central and east European countries is viewed in Moscow is remarkable, suggesting that the EU is a more promising institutional framework within which to promote pan-European collective security. The process of the widening of the EU, although it will take longer than NATO enlargement, has much greater significance than the latter. The effect on the European security environment will remain limited, especially given that NATO has neither the intention nor the capability to launch an attack on Russia, or get involved in any military conflicts on Russia's periphery. EU membership, on the other hand, will have a fundamental impact on the political system and the economies of post-communist states. This will result in deep integration of central and east European countries with western Europe, from which Russia will remain excluded. There is, of course, also a security dimension to EU membership. If the WEU does become the defence arm of the European Union, then EU membership will also mean WEU membership. The WEU involves a security guarantee which is even stronger than that provided by Article 5 of the Washington (NATO) Treaty. This creates a strong rationale for the German view that all members of the WEU should also be members of NATO. Even if this does not happen, an expansion of the WEU represents an indirect expansion of NATO as a consequence of the interlocking and overlapping security guarantees in the Paris and Washington Treaties. Thus it could be said that Finnish EU membership has brought an indirect NATO commitment right to the Russian border. The relationship between the WEU and NATO is particularly relevant in respect of the Baltic states. Although they will probably not be admitted into NATO during the initial phases of NATO expansion, they are high on the list for EU membership. As seen from Moscow, the European framework for Russian–Western cooperation in the field of foreign policy and security is more consonant with Russia's foreign and security policy priorities than the creation of a NATO-centred security system in Europe. This will strengthen the rationale for a common foreign and security policy in the EU.

The end of the Cold War seemed to promise a fundamental transformation of international relations in Europe from the Atlantic to the Urals as the massive military confrontation in central Europe was dismantled and the threat of global conflict receded. Since then, optimism has been replaced by a more pessimistic mood as parts of Eurasia have become embroiled in violent conflict to which no end seems to be in view and the depth of the economic problems in the region of the former Warsaw Pact has become apparent.

It is fundamental to west European security interests that the predictions of an unstable, conflict-prone Europe should not be fulfilled. There are three essential prerequisites for such an outcome:

- the recognition of international norms (as enshrined in the UN Charter) by all states in the region;
- the successful transition of the post-communist countries to functioning liberal democracy;
- the rebuilding of the shattered economies of central and eastern Europe and their integration with the other advanced industrial economies in the world.

The most important factor in all aspects of the process is Russia. Its political future remains uncertain, and relations with the West will remain difficult unless it moves decisively to fulfil these prerequisites.

We may, however, have to face the fact that neither economic nor political developments move in a positive direction. The Chechen crisis has given us a glimpse of the contents of the Pandora's box that is the former Soviet Union. The Western response to Chechenia, just like its response to the break-up of Yugoslavia, shows that we are ill-equipped to deal with the situation.

The call for collective security and new security architectures has so far foundered on the exigencies of realpolitik. Although the concepts of collective security seem abstract and the organizations founded to give them reality lack the necessary instruments to achieve it in practice, it is nevertheless a matter of great urgency that the nations of Europe develop the political will and commitment to construct an effective system of collective security based on an accepted system of norms and principles. This is a major challenge for academics and politicians alike in the years ahead.

Conclusion

The European system of states is undergoing a major transformation. The west European states are engaged in a fundamental process of integration. At the same time the former communist states have abandoned central planning of their economies and embarked on the attempt to transform them into market economies and integrate them into the world economy, while the EU is set on extending its membership towards central Europe.

These processes are of fundamental significance for our understanding of the nature of the international system, international cooperation and processes of integration. At the same time, these issues are of high policy relevance. The changes in Europe may produce outcomes which are very dangerous for all European states. If Russia were to become isolated as a result of European integration, this would strengthen the neo-authoritarian and anti-Western forces in Russia. It could destroy progress towards democracy and economic reform. It could encourage Russia to reassert hegemony over the former Soviet space, a dominance which could take very unpalatable forms. The net effect would be a fundamentally antagonistic relationship with the West, a form of non-ideological Cold War.

The opposite possibility would be the further disintegration of Russia and the balkanization of the former Soviet Union. The conflict in Chechenia has highlighted the sheer ungovernability of many regions of Russia. The destruction and 'occupation' of the Chechen capital Grozny has not brought the Chechen Republic under effective Russian control, and there is no prospect of this being achieved. Many current trends point in the direction of the destabilization of the Russian Federation. The same applies to several CIS states, especially in the former Soviet south. Indeed, the 'afghanization' of some parts of Central Asia cannot be excluded. The NATO alliance might come under very considerable pressure to provide security guarantees to the countries of central Europe and the Baltic states at least. Although such a development would threaten current NATO members directly only if control over Russian nuclear weapons were lost, the threat to the entire region would be on such a scale that the indirect effects on the West would be very substantial. Certainly neighbouring countries could be drawn in, resulting in the destabilization of much of southern central Europe. It is clear that the prevention of such an outcome must be the highest policy priority for western Europe.

It is therefore in the interests of the whole of Europe that the deepening and widening of the European Union is accompanied by the development of a framework of partnership and cooperation with Russia. The Founding Act on Mutual Relations between NATO and the Russian Federation is a small, but significant step in this direction. The EU has a vital role to play, both in aiding the development of democracy and economic reform in Russia and in integrating Russia into pan-European institutions.

Notes

1. Ole Diehl, 'Eastern Europe as a Challenge for Future European Security', in Mark Curtis, Ole Diehl, Jérôme Paolini, Alexis Seydoux and Reinhard Wolf, eds, *Challenges and Responses to Future European Security: British, French and German Perspectives* (London: European Strategy Group, 1993), pp. 15–68.
2. For a more detailed exploration of these factors, see Alexei G. Arbatov, 'Russia's Foreign Policy Alternatives', *International Security*, vol. 18, no. 2, Fall 1993, pp. 5–43.
3. This can be taken as a fundamental premise of Russian foreign policy, despite the prevalence of anti-Western sentiments in parts of the bureaucracy and political elite which have come to the fore in the debate over the expansion of NATO (see below). See Alexei G. Arbatov, 'Russian National Interests', in Robert D. Blackwill and Sergei Karaganov, eds, *Damage Limitation or Crisis?* (London: Brassey's, 1994), pp. 55–76; see also Chapter 1.
4. Alexander A. Pikayev, 'The Russian Domestic Debate on Policy Towards the "Near Abroad"', in Clive Archer and Lena Jonson, eds, *Peacekeeping and the Role of Russia in Eurasia* (Boulder, CO: Westview Press, 1996), pp. 33–50.
5. The extent of deindustrialization in Russia is documented and discussed in Roland Götz, 'Rußland auf

dem Weg zur Deindustrialisierung?', in BIOst, *Zwischen Krise und Konsolidierung* (Munich: Carl Hanser Verlag, 1995), pp. 247–56.

6. Hannes Adomeit, 'Russia as a "Great Power"', *International Affairs*, vol. 71, no. 1, January 1995, pp. 35–68.

7. The decline of the Russian economy may have bottomed out and GDP is expected to rise from 1997, but this does not affect this point.

8. Abraham S. Becker, 'Russia and Economic Integration in the CIS', *Survival*, vol. 38, no. 4, Winter 1996–7, pp. 117–36.

9. For a thorough analysis of this issue, see Christer Pursiainen, 'Russia and International Security Regimes: Chechnya as a Noncompliance Case', paper presented at the International Studies Association conference, San Diego, 1996; see also *Doklad lichnogo predstavitelya deystvuyushcego Predsedatelya OBSE o visite v Rossiyskuyu Federatsiyu, Chechenskuyu Respubliku*, 3 February 1995 (mimeograph); Pikayev, 'The Russian Domestic Debate on Policy toward the "Near Abroad"', in Archer and Jonson, eds, *Peacekeeping*, pp. 51–66; Piotr Switalski and Ingrid Tersman, 'The Organisation for Security and Co-operation in Europe', in Archer and Jonson, eds, *Peacekeeping*, pp. 173–87.

10. Heinz Timmermann, 'Die europäische Union and Rußland - Dimensionen und Perspektiven der Partnerschaft' *Integration*, vol. 19, no. 4, 1996, pp. 195–207.

11. Heinz Timmermann, *Rußland's Außenpolitik: Die europäische Dimension* (Berichte des BIOst no. 17, Cologne, 1995).

12. Heinz Timmermann, 'Rußlands Außenpolitik in Richtung Europa', in BIOst, *Zwischen Krise und Konsolidierung*, pp. 311–23.

13. Andrei Zagorski, A Kreikemeyer and H.-G. Erhart, *Strany byvshego SSSR i evropeyskaya bezopasnost'* (Moscow: Mezhdunarodnye otnosheniya, 1994).

14. Peter Schmidt, ed., *In the Midst of Change: On the Development of West European Security and Defence Cooperation* (Baden-Baden: Nomos, 1992); for a more cynical view, see Philip Zelikow, 'The Masque of Institutions', *Survival*, vol. 38, no.1, Spring 1996, pp. 6–18; see also Philip. H. Gordon, 'Recasting the Alliance', *Survival*, vol. 38, no. 1, Spring 1996, pp. 32–7.

15. For a detailed discussion of these issues, see Roy Allison, *Peacekeeping in the Soviet Successor States*, Chaillot Paper no. 18 (Paris: WEU), 1994, pp. 30–50.

16. 'CSCE and the New Europe – Our Security is Indivisible', *Decisions of the Rome Council Meeeting* (Rome, 1993), p. 7.

17. For more detail on the role of the CSCE/OSCE in the FSU, see Piotr Switalski and Ingrid Tersman, 'The Organisation for Security and Co-operation in Europe (OSCE)', in Jonson and Archer, eds, *Peacekeeping*, pp. 173–88.

18. Allison, *Peacekeeping in the Soviet Successor States*.

19. Suzanne Crow, 'Russian Views on an Eastward Expansion of NATO', RFE/RL *Research Report*, vol. 2, no. 41, 15 October 1993, pp. 21–54.

20. This does not preclude some adjustments to allow Russia to deploy forces in crisis regions, in particular the Caucasus. For an analysis of the current debate, see Jane M. O. Sharp, 'CFE Treaty under Threat as Russia Requests Revisions', *Bulletin of Arms Control*, no. 12, November 1993, pp. 2–4.

21. Pavel Fel'gengauer, *Segodnya*, 6 October 1995.

22. Press Conference given by Yeltsin, 8 September 1995.

23. This argument has been put forcefully by Zbigniew Brzezinski, 'A Plan for Europe', *Foreign Affairs*, vol. 74, no. 1, 1995, pp. 26–42.

24. *Frankfurter Allgemeine Zeitung*, 8 May 1995.

25. *Financial Times*, 11 December 1996.

26. 'Yeltsin Foresees "Most Difficult" Talks With Clinton', Moscow, Interfax in English, 14 March 1997.

27. 'Yeltsin: Talk About Russia Joining NATO "Completely Unreal"', Moscow NTV in Russian, 17 March 1997, cited from FBIS-SOV-97-076, 17 March 1997.

28. Sergey Maslov, *Komsomolskaya pravda*, 28 March–4 April 1997, p. 3.

29. Some of the elements were reported on the basis of statements by Yeltsin in Moscow, Interfax, 8 May 1997; see also the report on the talks between Foreign Minister Primakov and NATO Secretary-General Solana by Andrei Nizamutdinov and Andrei Shtorkh, Moscow, ITAR-TASS, 10 April 1997.

30. Vasily Safronchuk, *Sovetskaya Rossiya*, 17 May 1997.

Index

Index

Index

Biographical note about the Editors

Roy Allison is Head of the Russia and Eurasia Programme at the Royal Institute of International Affairs, London, and currently directs several major research projects. He has been Senior Lecturer in Russian International Security Policy at the Centre for Russian and East European Affairs, University of Birmingham, a Senior Associate Member and Research Fellow at St Antony's College, Oxford, and a Guest Scholar at the Brookings Institution. His recent publications include *Internal Factors in Russian Foreign Policy* (as co-author, 1996), *Peacekeeping in the Soviet Successor States* (1993), and, as editor, *Challenges for the Former Soviet South* (1996) and *Radical Reform in Soviet Defence Policy* (1992).

Christoph Bluth is Professor of Politics and Director of the Graduate School of European and International Studies at the University of Reading. He was previously a Lecturer at the Department of Government, University of Essex, and a Research Fellow at the Department of War Studies, King's College, London. He is the author of *The Collapse of Soviet Military Power* (1995), *Britain, Germany and Western Nuclear Strategy* (1995), *Soviet Strategic Arms Policy Before SALT* (1992) and *New Thinking in Soviet Military Policy* (1990).